Cutting the Wire

Cutting the Wire

The Story of the Landless Movement in Brazil

Sue Branford and Jan Rocha

Latin America Bureau

LONDON

Cutting the Wire was first published by
Latin America Bureau
1 Amwell Street
London EC1R 1UL
in 2002

Latin America Bureau is an independent research and publishing organisation. It works to broaden public understanding of issues of human rights and social and economic justice in Latin America and the Caribbean.

Editing: Marcela López Levy
Cover design: Andy Dark
Design and typesetting: Kate Kirkwood
Printed by JW Arrowsmith Ltd, Bristol

The authors of this book were supported by a Grant for Research and Writing from the John D. and Catherine T. MacArthur Foundation, Chicago.

A CIP catalogue record for this book is available from the British Library.

ISBN 1 899365 51 6

Contents

Testimonies

Illustrations and Tables

Glossary

CEB	*Comunidade Eclesial de Base*
	Catholic Grassroots Community
CIMI	*Conselho Indigenista Missionário*
	Indigenous Missionary Council
CONCRAB	*Confederação das Cooperativas da Reforma Agrária do Brasil*
	Confederation of the Agrarian Reform Cooperatives of Brazil
CONTAG	*Confederação Nacional dos Trabalhadores na Agricultura*
	National Confederation of Agricultural Workers
CPT	*Comissão Pastoral da Terra*
	Pastoral Land Commission
CUT	*Central Única dos Trabalhadores*
	Unified Workers' Central
EMBRAPA	*Empresa Brasileira de Pesquisa Agropecuária*
	Brazilian Agriculture and Livestock Research Company
FUNAI	*Fundação Nacional do Indio*
	National Indian Foundation
INCRA	*Instituto Nacional de Colonização e Reforma Agrária*
	National Institute for Colonisation and Land Reform
PMDB	*Partido do Movimento Democrático Brasileiro*
	Party of the Brazilian Democratic Movement
PNRA	*Plano Nacional de Reforma Agrária*
	National Plan for Agrarian Reform
PROCERA	*Programa de Crédito Especial para Reforma Agrária*
	Special Credit Programme for Agrarian Reform
PRONERA	*Programa Nacional de Educação na Reforma Agrária*
	National Programme of Land Reform Education
PT	*Partido dos Trabalhadores*
	Workers' Party
UDR	*União Democrática Ruralista*
	Ruralist Democratic Union

acampado	camp dweller
acampamento	camp
arrendatário	tenant farmer
assentado	settler
assentamento	settlement
bancada ruralista	the rural bloc
Banco da Terra	Land Bank
bóia fria	rural day-worker
brasilguaio	Brazilian who has settled in neighbouring Paraguay
camponês	peasant
cerrado	savannah region in central Brazil
chimarrão	drink made from *mate* tea
churrasco	barbecue
ciranda	popular children's dance
colono	settler in areas originally settled by European immigrants or settler on government schemes in the Amazon
com-terra	person who has won land
frente de massa	the vanguard of MST militants sent into a new region
granjeiro	big farmer
grilagem de terra	the falsification of land titles
grileiros	bogus landowners
latifúndio	large landed estate
lavrador	agricultural worker
meeiro	sharecropper
militante	full-time MST activist
minifúndio	smallholding
mística	MST collective theatre and mythmaking
mutirão	self-help scheme for collectively building houses or clearing land
posseiro	land squatter
quilombo	freed slave, or slave descendant, community
sem-terra	landless person
sertão	semi-arid zone
sítio	plot of land
terras devolutas	public lands

Acknowledgements

We would like to express our thanks to the MST who provided us with contacts, allowed us to sit in on meetings and discussions, but never tried to influence where we went, who we talked to, or what we wrote. Also to all the men and women we met in camps and settlements, who made us welcome, shared their food and told us their stories.

We would particularly like to thank Bernardo Fernandes Mançano, who generously allowed us to use his detailed research on the movement, and José de Souza Martins, whose publications on the land question in Brazil have been a source of information and inspiration over many years. Among the many who contributed to our book with their thoughts, experience or information are Gerson Teixeira, Osvaldo Russo, Pedro Casaldáliga, Paulo Schilling, Dan Baron Cohen, Darci Frigo, Marluce Melo and Thiago Thorlby.

We are grateful to the John D. and Catherine T. MacArthur Foundation for a grant for Research and Writing which enabled us to write this book.

Lastly we would like to thank our families – Ralph, Plauto, Camilo, Becky, Alexandra, Matthew and Bruna – for putting up with our frequent absences on field trips and for their encouragement and support during the long process of writing the book.

Introduction

We have written this book to tell one of the great untold stories of modern Brazil – the dramatic fight of thousands of men and women to escape from poverty and degradation to find a new life and to become active citizens, not second class people on the margins of society. For eighteen months we travelled around Brazil by plane, bus, canoe and ox cart to hear the stories of scores of landless peasants, known as *sem-terra*, who set up Brazil's Movement of Landless Rural Workers (*Movimento dos Trabalhadores Rurais Sem Terra*, MST). This is today one of the most powerful popular movements in the world. Almost without exception, the people we spoke to had extraordinary tales to tell.

Some of the older men and women had undertaken epic journeys across this huge country, making their way from the extreme south with its chilly winters up to the hot and humid Amazon basin, or facing the challenge of a new language and a new culture in neighbouring Paraguay. Others had moved down from the impoverished northeast to the giant metropolis of São Paulo and, after living for years in the city's violent, drug-ridden shanty-towns, had decided to go back to the countryside. Everyone shared a common aim: to find land to plant. It might seem an easy goal in a country like Brazil with its vast tracts of unoccupied land. Yet it was only after the creation of the MST in the early 1980s, and then only with great difficulty, that these men and women could realise their dream.

For a while we experienced some of the hardships routinely faced by the *sem-terra* in their struggle to conquer the land. One night we and 40 *sem-terra* were sleeping in makeshift huts, built out of branches and black polythene, when 30 gunmen arrived to evict us. Armed only with hoes, sticks and a few rusty rifles, the *sem-terra* forced the gunmen to back off. In the same camp we all had to drink and cook our food in water from a stream that the landowner had deliberately contaminated with dead animals.

The hardship in some of the camps is intense. Sleeping in damp, draughty huts, children get ill and occasionally die. The gunmen, sent in by the landowners, often manage to evict the families, set fire to their huts and destroy their crops. Some of the families lose heart, giving up the struggle. Yet the most determined are not deterred, reoccupying the land, even though each time they have to begin planting all over again. They usually receive the support of other *sem-terra* families who have won their land and remember well the hardships of the struggle. On many an occasion a camp has been saved from closure by supplies of food sent in from a neighbouring MST settlement.

The *sem-terra* know that the conflict is dangerous, as landowners will use every means available to stop them winning. Several hundred *sem-terra* have been killed since the movement was formed. Sebastião de Maia, one of our key interviewees in the particularly violent state of Paraná, was assassinated just a few weeks after we had interviewed him.

The MST has been remarkably successful in what it set out to do. Today it has about one million members and has won nearly five million hectares, or 50,000 square kilometres, equivalent to about three-quarters of the area of the Irish Republic or half the area of the US state of Ohio. Over 100,000 children now study in MST schools. Although its settlements account for only a fraction of Brazil's total farm land, it is an impressive achievement for a movement not 20 years old.

More important than the numbers, however, is the example that the MST offers. Brazil suffers from many of the problems characteristic of the developing world – sprawling mega-cities, huge income inequalities, widespread unemployment and underemployment, a large informal sector, pervasive drug trafficking and drug addiction. Throughout the developing world these conditions are fuelling crime and, in a few countries, they are inciting terrorism, as desperate people, faced with a hopeless future, cling to fanatical ideologies that give some meaning to their lives.

The MST shows that there is another way forward. As it has demonstrated time and again, it can recruit 'hopeless cases' – drug addicts, emotionally disturbed street kids and violent criminals – and turn them into productive, fulfilled citizens. The MST has no magic solution. Not infrequently, people with severe behavioural problems leave the movement after a few months, unable to make the difficult transition to citizenship. Even so, the MST's achievements are truly impressive, particularly as they have been made in the face of largely hostile government authorities, who are exasperated by the MST's disregard for the finer points of the law in its struggle to conquer land.

Our interest in the MST is no sudden whim. As reporters who have lived in Brazil for many years, stories about land issues – whether development schemes, road building, conflicts over indigenous reserves or debt bondage – have been our daily diet. We have followed the progress of the MST since its earliest days and seen it grow from a small regional uprising in the south to a national movement, internationally recognised and frequently in the headlines of the Brazilian press. Despite our delight at seeing the MST gain strength and experience, we have sought to portray honestly and accurately the problems, some of them self-inflicted, that the movement is currently facing.

What the MST can achieve by itself is clearly not enough. The movement needs to work with an enlightened government committed to far-reaching social and economic reforms. Then the MST could use its capacity to mobilise the poor as part of a much broader programme to show that there are solutions to the global problems of social exclusion and economic marginalisation.

This book is divided into four parts. In the first we trace the expansion of the MST from its origins in the early 1980s to today's national movement. In the second we look at the MST's strategy for conquering land and at its achievements, particularly in farming and in education, once it has conquered land. In the third we examine the formidable obstacles that the MST faces. These range from violent repression from gunmen sent in by landowners to the rapid globalisation of Brazilian agriculture, which leaves little space for the kind of sustainable peasant farming that the MST promotes. And in the fourth we look at the MST's response to these challenges, with its development of an economic alternative, based on organic farming, and its somewhat faltering attempt to develop a new cultural paradigm to defend its values in a hostile world. In this section, too, we place the MST within the historical context of similar social movements in other countries and assess its ability to survive where these have generally failed.

NORTH ATLANTIC OCEAN

COLOMBIA

VENEZUELA

GUYANA

SURINAM

FRENCH GUIANA

Boa Vista ⊙

RORAIMA

AMAPÁ

Macapá •

Equator

0°

Marajó Is.

Belém ⊙

Manaus •

Santarém •

São Luis •

Fortaleza ⊙

AMAZONAS

PARÁ

Marabá •

MARANHAO

Teresina •

CEARÁ

RIO G. DO NORTE

Natal ⊙

Solimões

Amazon

Xingu

Tapajós

ACRE

Pôrto Velho ⊙

Rio Branco ⊙

Corumbiara •

RONDÔNIA

PERU

BOLIVIA

Araguaia

Tocantins

PIAUÍ

PARAIBA

PERNAMBUCO

João Pessoa

Recife ⊙

Palmares

Lagoa Grande

Petrolina •

ALAGOAS

Palmas •

TOCANTINS

SERGIPE

Maceió

Aracaju

10

BAHÍA

São Francisco

Salvador ⊙

MATO GROSSO

Cuiabá ⊙

GOIÁS

D.F. Brasília

Goiânia •

MINAS GERAIS

MATO GROSSO DO SUL

Campo Grande ⊙

Paraná

SÃO PAULO

Belo Horizonte ⊙

ESPÍRITO SANTO

Vitória ⊙

20

PARAGUAY

Pontal do Paranapanema

Queréncia do Norte •

Teodoro Sampaio •

Maringa •

Cascavel •

PARANA

Medianeira •

Curitiba

São Paulo ☐

Rio de Janeiro

R. DE J.

SOUTH ATLANTIC OCEAN

SANTA CATARINA

Sarandi •

Florianópolis ⊙

ARGENTINA

RIO GRANDE DO SUL

Bagé •

Porto Alegre ⊙

URUGUAY

CHILE

0		400		800m
0	400	800	1200km	

30

60°

50°

40°

30°

Brazil

PART ONE

CHAPTER 1

The Founding of the MST

If humanity is to have a recognisable future, it cannot be by prolonging the past or the present. If we try to build the third millennium on that basis, we shall fail. And the price of failure, that is to say, the alternative to a changed society, is darkness.
Eric Hobsbawm, *The Age of Extremes*[1]

On Sunday 24 July 1982 an old VW van drove up to the ferry on the River Iguaçu about 40 kilometres upstream from the famous falls. Eleven men were crowded into the van, and they were eager to cross the river and get on with the long drive home to Rio Grande do Sul, Brazil's most southerly state. But the ferry operators were busy watching the World Cup final between Italy and Germany on television. If they bothered to glance at the van, they probably decided that the group of shabbily dressed countrymen who talked with the lilting accent of the far south were not important enough to interrupt their viewing. The driver was a young man with a beard, and the van was evidently falling to pieces. They could wait.

The ferrymen did not know it, but within a few years the bearded man, João Pedro Stédile, would become a household name in Brazil, and the organisation that was to develop from the semi-clandestine meeting they had been at would become Brazil's most famous social movement, known as the Movement of Landless Rural Workers (*Movimento dos Trabalhadores Rurais Sem Terra*, MST).

The men were travelling home from a meeting in Medianeira, a town situated not far from the confluence of the Iguaçu and Paraná rivers. A few years earlier 10,000 families had been dislodged from their plots beside the River Paraná to clear the way for the construction of the giant dam needed to drive the enormous hydroelectric power station of Itaipu that Brazil was constructing with Paraguay. Having lost their livelihoods, many of the families had sought refuge in Medianeira. Brazil was still run by the military, who had seized power in a coup in 1964, and protest meetings were frowned upon. Only the churches offered space and support for such gatherings, especially where the clergy were followers of liberation theology, the progressive doctrine that had spread through Latin America in the 1960s. Most of its practitioners were in the Catholic church, but in Medianeira the Lutheran church, which had reached Brazil with German immigrants a century earlier, was also strongly committed to social justice and consequently to the cause of the landless workers.

This was the first meeting to bring together men and women from the growing contingent of landless families in Brazil's three southernmost states – Rio Grande do Sul, Santa Catarina and Paraná. There were other forces, apart from the building of dams, which were creating an army of desperate people looking for land. Agriculture was going through 'the most rapid and most intense period of mechanisation in its history'.[2] Thousands of families were being forced off their *minifúndios*, the smallholdings set up in the nineteenth century by their European ancestors. Some were being expelled to make way for large, mechanised farms of soyabeans, the new wonder crop that was to earn Brazil millions of dollars in export earnings. Others had their debts foreclosed by the banks after a series of bad harvests. Yet others had become day workers on the big farms because their parents' plots were too small to divide yet further. It was all part of what José Graziano da Silva, one of the country's leading agricultural experts, has called the 'painful modernisation' of Brazilian agriculture.[3]

Land Concentration

Even before these changes Brazil had a heavily concentrated system of land tenure, a legacy from the Portuguese empire. In the 1950s it had seemed that the logic of capitalist development would force the government to carry out a radical programme of agrarian reform. The large unproductive estates were beginning to act as a brake on industrial development, which required an abundant supply of cheap food for urban workers. The 'historical impasse' – which the sociologist José de Souza Martins says has occurred in every country prior to it carrying out radical agrarian reform[4] – was finally emerging in Brazil. Rural workers began to mobilise. When in 1962 the left-of-centre president, João Goulart, himself a landowner, began to talk about dividing up the big estates, it seemed that the moment for agrarian reform had arrived.

But it was not to be. After first gaining the backing of the US government, powerful farming and industrial groups, alarmed by the social unrest, enlisted the armed forces to carry out a coup in March 1964. It was a huge setback for the rural workers but, even so, it seemed for a while that limited agrarian reform might still happen. The new military government repressed rural workers but also rapidly approved a Land Statute (Estatuto da Terra), which would have permitted some reform. Just a few months after the coup, Walt Rostow – the US economist and military strategist who had thought up the concept of 'economic take-off' – told a packed audience of leading businessmen in São Paulo that agrarian reform would 'integrate the huge rural population into the market and encourage industrial development'.[5] The United States, which in the post-war period had encouraged

Japan and South Korea to pave the way for rapid industrial growth by dividing up their big estates, appeared ready to do the same for Brazil.

But by then the international political climate was beginning to change. Fidel Castro had come to power in Cuba and, in the wake of the 1962 missile crisis, Havana was developing increasingly close relations with the USSR. The Brazilian military – and the United States – became frightened by the spectre of a communist take-over of Latin America. These fears were exacerbated by the discovery in the late 1960s of an incipient rural guerrilla movement near the Araguaia river in the Amazon basin. The military undertook a massive counter-insurgency operation. 'A wave of repression covered not only the small area in the south of the state of Pará, where the guerrillas were localised, but also large sections of the states of Goiás, Mato Grosso and even Maranhão, regions that could be as much as a 1,000 km away from the focus of activity'.[6] The rural guerrillas were defeated before they had even got started and most were summarily executed, but the anti-communist hysteria that had taken hold of the military made a far-reaching programme of agrarian reform inconceivable.

Instead, the military looked for another way of both defusing the social unrest caused by the problem of landlessness and of occupying Brazil's remote frontiers to make sure that the country would never again be vulnerable to insurgency. While continuing to repress dissent, it announced an ambitious project for occupying the Amazon basin. It created a system of tax breaks to encourage big industrial groups, including multinationals, from São Paulo and other cities to set up huge cattle ranches in the region. It also introduced a land settlement programme to take landless families from the semi-arid regions of the northeast to the Amazon basin, matching 'men without land' to 'a land without men', in the words of General Emílio Garastazzu Medici, president of Brazil from 1970 to 1974. (For the military, the large number of indians in the region did not count as people.) Although this was never made explicit, these colonisation projects – which in reality were no more than clearings hacked out along highways being driven through the jungle – were intended to guarantee a pool of labour for the ambitious mining, ranching, farming and logging projects that the military planned for the region. Predictably enough, the settlers did not flourish. Battling against a hostile climate, they found it difficult to survive with slash-and-burn subsistence farming. Once the settlers had cleared enough forest, big companies and commercial cooperatives moved in, buying up the land for a pittance or simply expelling the small farmers. Some of them ended up as day-labourers on land they had once owned. In 1976 Brazil's Catholic bishops stated in a report that the colonisation projects had done more to enrich large landowners in the south than to solve the problems of the landless families in the northeast.[7]

The families were angered by their treatment but the authoritarian military government did not tolerate opposition. It employed violence to suppress demand for agrarian reform and encouraged its use by others. 'Military repression in itself paved the way for the big landowners to deploy gunmen and bandits all over the country in the certainty that they would not be punished and would even be seen as allies in the use of violence to maintain order', commented José de Souza Martins. 'Never in the history of Brazil did the *latifúndio* make such unbridled use of private violence as during the military years'.[8] Together these initiatives had profound consequences for the 'agrarian question'. Turning industrialists into big landowners in the Amazon broke the emerging impasse between what Souza Martins called the 'rationality of capital' and the 'irrationality of Brazil's land structure'. Quite bizarrely and retrogressively, industrialists became 'rentiers', that is, they began to earn an income from land ownership and to have a vested interest in maintaining the concentrated land structure.[9] The potential alliance between the industrial bourgeoisie and the rural poor that in many other countries had paved the way for radical agrarian reform was precluded.

The only remaining problem for the military government was to disperse the groups of discontented landless families who, particularly in the south, were seen as potential troublemakers. So the government decided to extend the colonisation projects, originally devised for northeasterners, to include families from the rest of the country. But this policy did not take into account the courage and tenacity of some of the landless families in the south. Even before reports of the difficulties in the projects had filtered back, they were determined not to be bullied into travelling to an unknown, hostile region at the other end of the country nor to be forced to move to the cities. What they wanted was to continue working the land, as their parents and grandparents before them had done, ever since their forebears crossed the Atlantic in steerage, fleeing poverty to a promised land of plenty.

Historical Origins of the MST

By the late 1950s there were about 270,000 landless families eking out a living in the state of Rio Grande do Sul. In the early 1960s, the left-wing governor of the state, Leonel Brizola, began to expropriate some of the large estates and to divide them up among these families. The coup ended this incipient reform. The new military-backed state government handed out many of the expropriated areas to its friends and political allies and presented the landless families with bleak options: they could migrate to the Amazon; they could cross the border to neighbouring Paraguay, where land was cheap; or they could invade land in indigenous reserves. This was, of course, illegal but the government hinted that it would in the circumstances turn a blind eye to this inconvenient fact. By the mid-1970s over 8,000 families had moved into reserves in the three southern states.

About 2,000 families went into the reserve of the Kaingang indians at Nonoaí, some of them paying rent to the indians. Eighteen-year-old Vilmar Martins da Silva, who was later to become a national MST leader (*see* box 1.1), was among them. FUNAI, the federal government's indigenous agency, should have protected these indians, but local personnel found that they could make easy money by selling logging concessions to the families, so instead they encouraged the illegal invasion. The Kaingang, who rightfully claimed ownership of the whole 34,908-hectare reserve, protested to the authorities, but nothing was done. By 1976, 974 families had built homes on the reserve and were earning their living by logging and farming. They had even begun to be taxed by INCRA, the federal government's institute for land reform and colonisation, which they felt legitimised their right to be there.

On 4 May 1978 the Kaingang declared war: armed with rifles, bows and arrows, they set fire to the seven schools built for the settlers' children, seized crops and expelled the families. Many had time only to grab some clothes and tools, leaving everything else behind. The weather was cold and rainy and some families, with nowhere else to go, took refuge in cowsheds and stables. A local judge, who found three families living in part of a pigsty, which had been divided into five stalls, described what he had seen to a committee of the state Legislative Assembly: 'Some maize is stored in the first of the stalls; the families, each with five or six children, are in the next three; and the pigs are in the last one.'[10]

The state government once again insisted that the families should move to the Amazon and many accepted, believing they had no choice. In July 1978, 500 families climbed aboard a fleet of buses and travelled 3,500 km north to Terranova (literally 'Newland'), a colonisation project in Mato Grosso on the southwest fringe of the Amazon basin. It is a humid, tropical region, where the temperature regularly reaches 32 degrees Celsius, quite a change for families accustomed to the temperate climate in Rio Grande do Sul. Another 128 families were given land in the south of their own home state.

Some 350 families, however, had nowhere to go. Father Arnildo Fritzen, the parish priest at Ronda Alta, sympathised with their plight. Father Arnildo was a member of the CPT, the Pastoral Land Commission, set up in 1975 by the Roman Catholic bishops of the Amazon basin to draw attention to the violent land conflicts in the region. Attracted by the military government's tax breaks, Brazilian and multinational companies had hired gunmen to evict the thousands of peasant families who had earlier migrated to the region from the impoverished northeast. These gunmen had burned homes, terrorised communities and assassinated leaders. As social unrest had spread to the rest of the country, the CPT had extended its activities. Gradually the CPT was changing its perception of the role it should play: it was beginning to believe that the landless families should start deciding for themselves what action to take to defend their own interests and that the CPT should intervene only if it considered that the families were being manipulated by trade unions, political parties or even the church itself. It was a process of transformation that gained impetus from the creation of the landless movement.

'After the eviction at Nonoaí, Ronda Alta became an avenue of suffering', Father Arnildo recalled, sitting in a pew in his parish church. 'People began wandering up and down, asking for food and clothing. There were 78 families living in this church.

Box 1.1 *Vilmar Martins da Silva*

My parents were small farmers. I had four brothers and a sister. In the beginning, we brothers worked together on my father's plot of land. But then, in about 1975, we realised that the 30 hectares of land that my father owned wasn't enough for all of us. There was an Indian reserve in the district belonging to the Kaingang Indians, and my oldest brother began to rent land from them. I was unmarried, about 18 years old at the time, so I went with him. All went well until 1978. Then the Indian agency, FUNAI, went to court to evict the non-Indians from the reserve. They said the Indians needed all the land. Altogether, we were about 2,000 families in the reserve, renting about 16,000 hectares of land. We didn't take what FUNAI was saying very seriously. The other families told me that FUNAI had been saying the same thing for 17 years but had never done anything about it.

But this time, at the end of May 1978, FUNAI meant it. Its officials came back and told us 'you've got to get out in 24 hours'. Then they came back – the Indians, FUNAI officials and the police – and forced us out. There was real panic. People had to take everything out of their houses and pile it on to lorries, without knowing where they were going. The people who tried to resist were forcibly evicted. Then the police came and burnt their house or immediately put an Indian family in it. They took us to villages in the region, leaving us with relatives or dumping us on football pitches. My brother and I felt desperate. The government wanted us all to go to a colonisation project in Mato Grosso. Some families went, but we didn't want to. At that time, it seemed so far away. It was like sending us to Japan or France. So we stayed in the region, living with relatives or camping on the side of the road. We spent two years like that.

Then Father Arnildo called us all to a meeting. He asked us what we wanted to do. Were we prepared to struggle to get a plot of land? João Pedro Stédile was there. It was the first time I met him. He told us that there was unregistered land in the region and, if we organised ourselves, we could conquer it. So that's how we organised the first occupation – of Macali, on 7 September 1978. The following year we occupied Brilhante.

I didn't have any political awareness then. I realise now that I got involved in the struggle because it was fun. I was always a bit of a rebel. I liked doing risky things. At one stage the families at Brilhante were in a very bad way. They had no money and very little food. But the families in Macali, which was just over the river, were much better off. They'd already won their land and the government was sending them food baskets. They wanted to send food to the families in Brilhante but they'd been forbidden to do so. So my task was to go secretly at night and take food across the river. I remember it so well. When we got back to Brilhante, we used hats to divide up the food. The men all used those old country straw hats, so they'd take them off and we'd fill them with food. That was their ration.

We won land in Macali, but there still wasn't enough for everyone, so we set up the camp at Encruzilhada Natalino. That was a difficult struggle. And then we occupied Fazenda Annoni. I was married by then but I'd gone alone, leaving my wife and children at home. We had a small house in a village but we were heavily in debt, as I'd been spending so much time in the struggle. My family was suffering. I felt bad. So after about three months I went back home and told my wife I was going to come back and work on a farm to pay off the debts. But my wife said no. 'We'll sell the house to pay off the debts and we'll all come to the camp'. That's what she said, without any hesitation. So that's what we did. We burnt our boats. There was no going back then. We had to make it work.

It was then that I started to change. I went on MST courses. I talked a lot to Darci Maschio. He was younger than me, but he was my master. He'd had very little formal education, but he was very intelligent. I began to realise that people listened to what I said, that I could become a leader. We began to discuss what we'd do with the land once we'd conquered it. We decided to farm collectively. We worked it all out beforehand, so when we got our land, we knew what to do. That's why we got our cooperative to work, while others failed.

Even so, it was difficult. We wanted to do mixed farming. We wanted to produce a bit of everything – cattle, pigs, grain and soya. And we wanted to start processing some of our own products, to set up a dairy. But when we got the PROCERA funds from the government, the MST leadership didn't want us to do that. They wanted us to invest in big tractors, big machinery. We didn't agree. We had a long debate and we won. We got our dairy and we did things in the way we wanted. It's worked out but we've still got problems. People are so busy that they don't have time for political meetings. They're losing their militancy. I coordinate 65 MST groups in this region, but the people I find most difficult to organise are the people in my own cooperative. Perhaps that's always the case.

They had nowhere else to go'. He decided to bring the families together to talk about what they could do.

I remember very well the first meeting. It was a very wet and windy night. We met in my house and we began to discuss a biblical text, from Exodus: 'And the Lord said, I have surely seen the affliction of my people which are in Egypt, and have heard their cry by reason of their taskmasters; for I know their sorrows; And I am come down to deliver them out of the hand of the Egyptians, and to bring them up out of that land unto a good land and a large, unto a land flowing with milk and honey.' I read this text to them. And they said: 'That's us, searching for the Promised Land.' It was a shock for me. I'd been trained to believe that only educated people understood the Word of God. It was wonderful – the Word of God was among the people.

The eviction from Nonoaí was undoubtedly a turning point for the land question in the south. 'It forced the landless to abandon their confrontation with another marginalised segment of society – the indians – and to face the real enemy, the authorities who refused to change the land structure, who refused to implement land reform, and whose only answer to their predicament was to tell them to go to a colonisation project at the other end of the country', said Telmo Marcon in his thesis on the early history of the movement.[11] Yet, at the same time, the families did not feel confident in their ability to think and act by themselves; they needed the support of Catholic priests – and even, it seems, of the state governor himself – before they had the self-assurance to confront the established powers.

The families began meeting every week. At first, they merely bemoaned their fate, blaming their situation on the Indians, but gradually their attitude began to change. Vilmar Martins da Silva, who lived with his family in Nonoaí for 17 years before being evicted, recalls the contribution made by a young economist who worked for the state department of agriculture and started coming clandestinely to these meetings. On one occasion he had asked to speak. 'Forget the indians. It's their land', he said. 'We know there's plenty of other land here in the state. You can conquer it, but you'll have to organise.' The young man's name was João Pedro Stédile, later to become the MST's most important strategic thinker.

The Occupation

The families took Stédile's advice. They still petitioned the government for a solution but they began to get organised, making contact with groups of landless families in other parts of the state. Stédile, who had had a strong Catholic upbringing and had studied for several years in a college run by the Capuchins, began to work closely with the families, passing on information he obtained through his job. He and Father Arnildo developed a code for talking on the telephone, which they feared was bugged. They spoke of bringing 'boxes of candles' and 'statues' to a meeting when they were really referring to landless peasants and priests who would be attending.

Not far from Ronda Alta was the big Sarandí estate. In 1962 the state governor, Leonel Brizola, had expropriated the estate, but after the coup it had been divided into two farms, Macali and Brilhante, and leased to private landowners. Stédile discovered that the lease for Macali had expired, which meant that the land could, in theory, be allocated to the families. Slowly and cautiously, the families began talking about an occupation. Vilmar says that it was another landless worker – Darci Maschio – who arranged the details. 'Darci was the one who really got us organised', he said. 'He was 27 years old; he'd had very little formal education but he was very bright. He coordinated the meetings and organised the occupation. Stédile was there, but even then he was more interested in the overall strategy than in detailed planning.'

It was not easy for poor rural families, brought up to respect the law and to regard landowners as their superiors, to take the momentous step of invading private property. Brother Sérgio Gorgen, a Catholic friar who has provided the landless movement with great support at key moments in its history, says that in August 1979, just as the families were beginning to think about occupying an estate, their request for a meeting with the state governor was unexpectedly granted. At the end of the audience, one of the landless peasants suddenly asked the governor how he would react if they were to occupy an estate. The others were horrified at the question, but the governor just laughed, saying 'I'd probably join you!'[12] It was, in fact, a throwaway remark, indicative of just how unthinkable the idea was, but for many families it meant that the authorities were endorsing their action, and that was still very important for them.

Inês Maria Tchik, who had been expelled from Nonoaí with her parents and six brothers and sisters, still remembers the excitement she felt as the preparations for the occupation got under way. 'We didn't know the exact day and we didn't even know where we were going. We had agreed, for reasons of security, that very few of us would be involved in the detailed planning. All we'd been told was to have a bag of clothes ready, so that we could leave at very short notice.' When word came that it would be that very night, her husband was away. 'He'd gone to Santa Catarina with his father to bring back one of his sisters and her family, who were also landless. They wanted to take part too. But even without them, I decided to go with my daughter, who was 4 years old. We'd dreamed for so long of having our own bit of land. So I put my pots and pans, along with some rice and oil, into a cardboard box and went out on the road to wait for the cattle truck.'

While Inês was waiting, her husband and the rest of the family returned unexpectedly early. 'I was so pleased', she said. 'It was like a dream come true'. It was nearly midnight before the truck came. It was already so crammed full of people that it was difficult to find a place. 'We had to put all our belongings on top of us', she said. 'If anyone had got out, they wouldn't have been able to get back in again!' They travelled in total silence, hushing the children to stop them crying. It was a very cold night, at the end of winter.

Leading the convoy of 43 trucks was Father Arnildo in his familiar white VW Beetle. 'He was our guide', says Inês. Though she was crouched in the back of a lorry in the middle of the night, on the way to an unknown destination, she was elated. 'It was a strange feeling. I'd never done anything like it before, but I wasn't scared. I didn't want to go on living with my father-in-law, sharing a small piece of land with two other families'. The date, 7 September 1979, had been carefully chosen. It was Independence Day, when the police and the military would be getting ready for parades and ceremonies, and not on the lookout for lorry-loads of peasants on their way to occupy land.

One hundred and ten families took part in the occupation. They arrived at about two o'clock in the morning. Adelino, one of the settlers, remembers that the first thing they did was to plant a small cross in the ground, 'because the cross represents the suffering of the landless worker'. They put up tents and shared the food they had and, at 10 o'clock, Father Arnildo said mass under the trees. As it was Independence Day, they flew the Brazilian flag and sang the national anthem. The police came later in the day but made no attempt to evict them. Inês said that, in spite of the harsh conditions, everyone was happy. 'We were all poor. We'd brought what we could – rice, a few beans, a little piece of pork fat. Everything was divided out, even the food brought in by relatives'.

By chance, João Pedro Stédile, whose involvement with the families had been kept a complete secret from the authorities, was sent to Macali by the state secretary of agriculture to find out what was going on. 'I went there with three policemen, whose job it was to protect me from these dangerous people', Stédile recalls with a laugh. 'I was a bit worried that people would let on that they knew me, but they didn't.' Jandir Bueno, who, as a 12-year-old child, took part in the occupation with his family, remembers Stédile's visit. 'He had to hide his views when he was with the police, but then he came to visit us secretly afterwards and told us to stand firm. I was delighted by the furtiveness of it all. It seemed a real adventure to me.' Father Arnildo visited the camp every day. 'He used to say mass and play his mouth organ,' Jandir Bueno recalls. 'He kept us all cheerful'.

Nothing like it had happened in Brazil since the military coup in 1964. The occupation was followed closely by the national – and even part of the international – press. The military government, already under pressure from a pro-democracy movement, felt unable to send in the army to evict the families by brute force. Yet it was clearly unhappy with the situation and urged the state government to take action. After 78 days a group of heavily armed policemen from the state government's military police made a serious attempt to evict the families. Father Arnildo was there. 'The women, with their children, formed a barrier. They told the police commander that, if he wanted to get at their husbands, he'd have to deal with them first. And the commander, bewildered, didn't know what to do. In the end, he and his men left. It was one of the most beautiful things I've seen in my life. And it was a turning point. From then on, I knew they would win.'

They camped for just under a year in difficult conditions. As they had no farm machinery, they ploughed with oxen and planted by hand. 'We planted rice, beans, maize, potatoes and soya', said Inês. 'And we had a good harvest. It was as if we'd been blessed by God.' They worked collectively, for the first time in their lives. 'I changed a lot', said Inês. 'I came from a German family and we'd been brought up to look out for ourselves, not to help others. I learnt that you live better when you share things. And that lesson has stayed with me ever since.'

Unsuccessful in their use of force, the local authorities embarked on a war of attrition. The state government ordered the police to surround the camp and to create all kinds of bureaucratic obstacles both for visitors and for the families themselves when they wanted to travel to local towns. And once the families managed to get out, they found that people in the neighbouring towns, egged on by the local authorities, treated them as tramps or scroungers. Not surprisingly, some families got dispirited and left, but those who stayed were rewarded for their tenacity. At the beginning of September 1980, just a year after the occupation, the state governor told the families they could stay. He took his decision just after a publicity campaign organised by the CPT, apparently believing that a quick resolution to the conflict would get the case out of the press and limit the damage. It was a serious miscalculation. As Telmo Marcon has shown, Macali was an important psychological victory for the landless families: 'it boosted their confidence, showing them that, with organisation and struggle, they could win land in their own state.'[13] Instead of defusing the situation, it encouraged other families to join the struggle.

More Occupations

The land at Macali was not enough for all the Nonoaí refugees, so on 25 September 1980 170 families occupied the neighbouring farm, Brilhante, where the lease still had several months to run. Catiane Machado da Silva (*see* box 1.2), 4 years old at the time, took part in this occupation. Even so, there were another 70 families with nowhere to go. On 8 December 1980 a man called Natálio and his family set up their tent on the grass verge near a crossroads. (On the other side of the road was a bar belonging to another man called Natálio, from whom the crossroads had acquired its name: Encruzilhada Natalino – Natálio's Crossroads.) After a while, the camp, straggling along the edge of the road, began to act as a magnet for other landless families. By April 1981, when INCRA carried out a survey, there were 469 families living there. They had constructed shacks as best they could, using black polythene, wooden planks, wattle-and-daub and even grass, which they had used for the roofs. By then only 42 of the families were from Nonoaí. The others were sharecroppers, rural workers and tenant farmers, all poor and landless and seeing this as their one chance of obtaining land. The families had not yet organised themselves into a mass-based movement to campaign for agrarian reform, but events were gaining their own momentum.

A few families who had returned from the land settlement project in Mato Grosso joined the camp. Daví Alves de Moura, who had gone off to Terranova in November 1978, said life had been very difficult. He had not been given the subsidised farm credit that the government had promised and, after several bad harvests, he had got heavily indebted. His small daughter had died from typhoid, having had no proper treatment. In desperation, he had joined thousands of other men who had swarmed to the huge open-cast gold mine at Serra Pelada in the south of the Amazon, but he had not struck lucky. He had returned to Terranova to make one last attempt to pay off his debts by working as a labourer. In the end, he had given up and returned to Rio Grande do Sul to fight for a piece of land in his home state.

Box 1.2 *Catiane Machado da Silva*

I'm 24 years old. I was born in Ronda Alta in Rio Grande do Sul. My father worked as a lorry driver but he always wanted his own plot of land. Then he hurt his back, and couldn't drive any more. So he and his brothers decided to join the occupation of Brilhante in 1980. We all went with him. I was only 3 or 4 years old but I remember it. It was a very rainy day. As there were so many people, we had to share a tent with three other families. After three months, my father gave up. It was too hard.

My uncles stayed. They were in the camp at Encruzilhada Natalino. My father used to take me there to visit them. We'd bring food and do whatever we could to help. I was about 7 or 8 years old then. My father was always tempted to join them but he was afraid that his children would go hungry. My uncles won land and my father was envious. So when he discovered that a widow in Brilhante wanted to give up, he offered her his house in the town, with its fridge, television and vegetable garden, and said he'd take over her land along with her debt with the Banco do Brasil. She accepted and we moved in. Right from the beginning, my father loved having his own land to farm.

But he'd only brought in one harvest of wheat and another of soyabeans when he died. It was a stupid death. A footpath to the nearest community crossed his land. One day a young lad came back, a bit drunk I think, and trampled on my father's wheat. They had a row and the lad ambushed my father, knifing him in the back. He cut part of my father's liver. No one had a car and it took us two hours to get him to hospital, even though it was only 18 kilometres away. My father was only 36. He took two days to die. He kept on shouting that he didn't want to die, that he loved his wife and his children.

I was 10 years old. I had two brothers, one 8 and the other 5. My mother, who was 29, had always been submissive. She didn't even know how to sign a cheque. And she'd been brought up in a town. She wasn't used to country life. We had no electricity and no running water. She had to get all our water out of a well. She thought of selling up but then she said 'No. This land is my children's future' and battled on. And she won. She's still there today. She likes it now. She's begun to cultivate medicinal herbs.

I was part of the first group of children in Brilhante to complete the whole eight years of primary school. I always took part in events, but I didn't really get involved in the movement. The MST wasn't working with children as much as it does today. I wanted to leave the settlement and see the world. So I went to Porto Alegre in 1994. I was only 18 and within six months I'd got married, to a security guard. We were very happy. Then in 1996 he discovered he'd got AIDS. A doctor told him he was going to die and he gave up all hope. He even stopped eating. He came back with me to my mother's house in Brilhante. But he got worse. Two hospitals in Ronda Alta refused to see him, when they discovered he'd got AIDS. It was such a stigma then to have the illness. He died after just three weeks. The news exploded like a bomb in our community. He'd been ashamed and hadn't let me tell anyone. I knew I must be infected too and I was frightened of telling my mother. I used to lie awake at night, worrying. But my mother was really supportive. She's everything for me today, my source of life.

I stayed in the settlement and started working with young people. Everyone in the MST was supportive. There wasn't any prejudice. I started taking AZT and then a cocktail of drugs. But I got depressed. I got a lot of infections and I thought my life was over. So I tried to pack everything I could into a few months. I travelled. I behaved wildly. I hardly slept. I didn't take my medicine properly. But I just got more depressed and more ill. Things started to change in May 1998. I went to a meeting of the women's collective in Porto Alegre. They made me feel I had a lot to offer. I started to get really involved in the movement. I went on a march to Brasília. I spent three days in a conference there, talking about urban problems, how the mass media deals with the MST. I took part in *místicas*. It was all so good. I went to a young people's conference in Campinas, over 1,000 of us, all working in the MST. We talked about all kinds of things – feelings, sexuality, love, AIDS. People wanted to hear what I had to say.

Since then, I've been working in the health sector of the MST. I'm talking to people about sexually transmitted diseases, helping to prevent them from spreading. And I'm working in adult education. We want everyone in the settlement to finish their primary education within a few years. I don't get paid, just pocket money and food but that's fine. I love it. And I've been well, now I'm taking my medication properly. I suppose I would like another relationship one day, but it's difficult. People accept me completely but it's quite difficult for a man to want as his partner a woman who's HIV positive.

Everyone shared this dream of a better life and, inspired by the victory at Macali, was prepared to strive after it with dogged determination. This time success did not arrive quickly, as the authorities tried to wear down the families with endless petty harassment. For almost three years Davi and the others had to put up with hostility from the authorities, attacks from the government-dominated press, and intimidation from the police and security services. But again the government's strategy backfired, though for a very different reason. As time went on, the landless families became symbols of resistance. Their defiance inspired solidarity from all over Brazil, and the support they received from the public put the question of land reform back on the national agenda. When eventually they won their land, their victory showed the country that the military government was no longer invincible.

At first, however, the families were on their own. They had arrived during the summer when the heat and the dust from the traffic on the road made people constantly ill. Their main support came – once again – from Father Arnildo, who was a constant presence in the camp and, through the CPT, organised donations of food and clothing. The authorities did all they could to demoralise the families. The police set up their own camp across the road and kept a close watch on all that was going on. Plain-clothes agents mixed with the families, trying to get the men drunk so they would talk more freely, and distributing sweets to the children. Some families left, worn out by the harassment, but others pressed on, undeterred. A twelve-man delegation travelled to the state capital, Porto Alegre, which only one of them had ever visited before. They asked for an audience with the state governor, Amaral de Souza, but he refused to see them. There was no point, he said, as there was no land available for landless families in Rio Grande do Sul. The families felt under attack on all sides. Government officials accused them of being 'workshy'. Newspapers claimed that some of them had criminal records and that others were cheats who already owned property.

Surrounded by enemies, the families turned more and more to religion. They replaced the small cross, which already stood at the crossroads and bore the inscription 'save your soul', with a much bigger one. 'It was a much heavier cross', said one of the settlers. 'It took a lot of us to carry it. It seemed a better symbol of our suffering and our determination to work together to find a solution.' Along with spiritual succour, the Church also provided the public support of what was in effect a powerful political institution. Two bishops from the Amazon region – Dom Pedro Casaldáliga, who was receiving death threats because of his work with Indians and peasant farmers, and Dom Tomás Balduino, the president of the CPT – came to the camp to celebrate mass. The Lutheran church, although less influential, was also supportive.

As winter approached, the flimsy shelters could not keep out the wind and the rain. In an interview for a local newspaper in June 1981, one of the men in the camp, Nereu José dos Santos, said: 'nobody managed to sleep last night because of the cold, the damp and the crying of the children.' The families' only drinking water came from a nearby lake, which was also used for washing clothes and taking baths. At times there was even horse dung floating in the water. After five babies had died of malnutrition and bronchial pneumonia, the families hung five white banners on the cross, 'so that they would not be forgotten'. Despite the problems, the families clung on. Gradually the camp, named from the crossing of two roads, became a political crossroads, the focus of an expanding movement that was demanding that Brazil should take a new direction. In a climate of growing political freedom, the press covered the story in detail. People in Brazil and abroad heard about this new movement among landless peasants, whose stubborn refusal to be sent to the hostile and distant Amazon stirred solidarity.

So the months went by. After almost a year, on 25 July 1981, which is celebrated as the Day of the Rural Worker in Brazil, scores of buses drew up by the camp, bringing people from as far away as São Paulo to join a demonstration of solidarity with the landless families. Catholic bishops, leaders of the agricultural workers' union CONTAG, and representatives of many other organisations spoke to the crowd of over 10,000 people. Seeing that the camp was becoming a focus for social and political discontent the government decided to intervene, not with strong-arm tactics, which could backfire, but with guile. The government turned to Major Curió, a colourful army officer who had made a name for himself in the Amazon as a successful troubleshooter who could twist illiterate, naive rural labourers around his little finger.

He arrived on 30 July, at the head of a large group of army intelligence agents and policemen. Repeating the tactics he had used with great success among 100,000 gold-diggers at Serra Pelada, he immediately set about imposing military discipline on the ragged camp, making the families sing the national anthem and salute the flag at the beginning and end of every day. Police barriers were set up to stop new families joining the camp and to prevent donations of food and clothes from reaching those inside. Without their own supply of food, the families had to queue for hours to receive government handouts. It became impossible for the families to hold meetings, because agents were everywhere, recording, photographing, intimidating. The press began to describe Encruzilhada Natalino as a 'concentration camp'.

Brother Sérgio Gorgen, a Catholic friar, was living in the camp at the time. He remembers it clearly:

> The Encruzilhada Natalino camp was going through its most difficult moment … All I saw around me was despair, disillusion, insecurity. I walked through the whole camp, which was surrounded by federal police agents, without being able to speak to anyone. I tried to exchange hopeful glances with some of the leaders, but at that stage I, too, considered it a lost battle. My heart ached and I couldn't think clearly. Then I noticed a child, about 4 years old, sitting on a tree trunk in the middle of the camp. Apparently oblivious to everything around her, she was singing as loudly as she could the song that the families had adopted as their anthem. I stopped, overcome with emotion on hearing that child's voice. It was breaking the silence imposed by the military dictatorship and by the elite on those poor peasant families, who were daring, through that child's voice, to proclaim that 'peasants and workers were waiting, anxiously, for the dawn of agrarian reform'. This innocent voice, with its song, brought me back to life. Suddenly, I became convinced: these people are going to resist and they are going to win. For the simple reason that only then would there be a future for that child and for the multitude of other youngsters who were playing in that camp.[14]

Major Curió had also noticed the presence of numerous children. One day, in what appeared to be a simple act of kindness, he told the children over his loudspeaker to come and collect some sweets. In fact, he had planned for the distribution of the sweets to be photographed by journalists as a publicity stunt to improve his public image. However, unknown to the authorities, one of the men, while fiddling on his radio, had discovered how to intercept Major Curió's messages to army headquarters in Brasília. So the families already knew what was planned and they briefed their children. When they lined up in front of the major, they all said together: 'we don't want sweets! We want land!' As Roseli Salete Caldart observes in her book, this is the first recorded political action undertaken by children in the movement, a harbinger of their later role.[15]

Major Curió increased the pressure on the families. He had a land settlement project in Mato Grosso, called Lucas do Rio Verde, especially set up for the Encruzilhada Natalino families. For weeks his agents were active in the camp, buying the men drinks and worming out information. And then Major Curió began to use this knowledge against the families. Vilmar Martins da Silva says he began interviewing the men, one by one, so that he could intimidate them. 'I know your father's got land in such-a-such region', he would say. 'You're not landless and there's no need for you to be here. Now, you've got 24 hours. You either agree to go to Mato Grosso or you leave the camp.' After two weeks, 113 of the 436 families had succumbed to this pressure and had agreed to go. These families were then moved to a temporary camp nearby and their huts were burnt to the ground so that they could not be occupied by anyone else.

Just over 300 families remained in the roadside camp. A member of the camp's central committee, Saul Marchiori, said: 'They can tear us to pieces, but we're not leaving Rio Grande do Sul. ... They can set fire to our huts, apply the National Security Law against us, put us in prison, but we're staying here to the bitter end.' Major Curió increased the pressure. On 15 August 1981 the police stopped a delegation of 75 people, sent by the Catholic Church's Justice and Human Rights Movement in Porto Alegre, from going into the camp. Two days later, Major Curió banned all clergy from entering the camp, threatening priests and nuns with the National Security Law if they dared to disobey. This decision backfired. Even conservative bishops, who had joined in the official criticism of the landless families, were angered by these threats against the church. On the very next day, the bishops of Rio Grande do Sul met for an emergency assembly in the nearby town of Passo Fundo and approved a document in which they expressed their support for the families of Encruzilhada Natalino and recognised the need for agrarian reform.

After this, the groundswell of solidarity gained momentum. Two congressmen came from Brasília to investigate the allegations of repression. The World Council of Churches and other international organisations sent messages of support. Human rights movements argued that the families' constitutional right to come and go as they pleased was being violated, and they demanded that the police take action against Major Curió if he continued to act unconstitutionally. For the first time the families felt that they were gaining the upper hand. On 24 August, in defiance of Major Curió's ban, 137 priests from Rio Grande do Sul and Santa Catarina took part in an open air mass and demonstration at the camp. Six days later the mayors of 30 rural districts in the surrounding region demanded an end to army intervention. Finally, on 31 August, Major Curió and his men left the camp.

Before he left, Major Curió issued a 22-page communiqué in which he attacked what he called the *movimento dos sem terra* (the landless movement), by which he meant not the landless families themselves but the organisations that supported them, particularly the CPT. He reserved special venom for Father Arnildo, whom he accused of leading a 'red church', manipulating the families and distributing bulletins full of hatred and slander. The day after Major Curió departed, Father Arnildo was arrested and taken to the small town of Santo Angelo, where he was held for 12 days. He was beaten and a revolver was held to his head in a vain attempt to make him confess that he was a communist and had had links with Carlos Marighela, a well-known urban guerrilla fighter who in 1969 had been killed in an ambush in São Paulo.

The military's withdrawal from the camp was a major victory for the families, but Father Arnildo believes that something else happened in the camp that was far more important than the conquest of the land. 'Even at the end very few of the families knew what the term "land reform" meant, but they had learnt that they had to organise themselves to achieve their goals', he said. 'That was the important lesson. It was here that the MST was born.' Vilmar Martins da Silva confirms that it was while they were at Encruzilhada Natalino that the families had the idea of setting up their own movement.

Remarkably, Major Curió was not aware that a new kind of peasant movement was being formed, even though he had himself inadvertently named it. This was probably because it never occurred to him that uneducated, impoverished peasant farmers would set their sights so high. He believed that the Catholic Church was manipulating the families, so it was always the priests and CPT that he attacked.[16] Major Curió's thinking accorded with the dominant view within the military intelligence services to which he was closely linked. They believed that a 'communist cell' within the Catholic Church was mobilising the peasantry throughout the country for a revolutionary insurrection. About 5,000 km to the north of Encruzilhada Natalino, in the small Amazon town of São Geraldo, 13 peasant farmers had carried out an ambush in which a policeman had been injured. Just as in Encruzilhada Natalino, the Church was blamed. The peasants were arrested and tortured to make them incriminate two French priests, who were eventually convicted under the National Security Law and expelled from Brazil. It seemed beyond the comprehension of the authorities that peasants families in many different parts of the country were rebelling against the state not because they were part of a conspiracy orchestrated by left-wing priests but because their lives had been made unbearable by the dislocations caused by agricultural modernisation and the expropriation of the peasantry.[17]

On 4 November a first detachment of 32 families, out of the group that had given in to the government's bullying, left for the long trip to Lucas do Rio Verde in Mato

Grosso. Escorted by police cars, they took five lorry-loads of animals with them. Less than a month later, however, some of them were back, saying that, despite Major Curió's fine words, conditions were intolerable: the land was poor, the plots were far from the road, they had not been given building materials for their homes, and they had arrived too late into the rainy season to be able to plant crops.

Despite Major Curió's departure, the impasse at Encruzilhada Natalino continued. In December 1981, exactly a year after they had set up the camp, the families celebrated Christmas with a torchlit procession. They stopped at key locations to recall some of the most important moments in the life of the camp, and then, towards the end, they blew out all the candles to symbolise the darkness of Major Curió's intervention, and then lit twice as many to express their determination to overcome the forces of oppression. They were already displaying that flair for imaginative gestures that the movement was later to incorporate into the daily life of camps and settlements under the name of the *mística*. It is a moment in which the families, tapping deep into Catholic traditions among the Brazilian peasantry, recall their past, express their commitment to the struggle and proclaim their belief in ultimate victory. The families needed this inner source of strength, for outside the struggle was more difficult than ever. The government and the conservative press renewed their attacks on the 'red church'. The adversity began to wear people down. 'It was very difficult to keep hope alive', recalls Father Arnildo. 'People were suffering in all kinds of ways, and they were often ill.' Some families found it all too difficult and left.

Finally the remaining families decided to ask the bishops to buy a plot of land as a temporary solution to their problems. A campaign in the churches raised enough money to purchase an area of 108 hectares, just 30 km from the camp. On 12 March 1982, the families moved. They built a new camp, free from the constant harassment of the police, who even so continued to spy on them with binoculars. They set about cultivating the land in a completely communal way. 'We set up the camp just as the priests suggested. And they were idealists, seeing us as the early Christians,' said Vilmar Martins da Silva. 'It didn't really work out. The food was divided equally among all families, irrespective of how much each had worked. This caused resentment. It was too paternalistic. We began to realise that we needed to be in charge and to draw up our own rules.' Even so, the families reaped a good harvest and sent the Secretary for Agriculture some bunches of radishes to show that they were hardworking.

Finally, there were signs that the fortunes of the landless might be changing. After a series of setbacks, the military regime began to falter and was forced to make concessions to the opposition. In November 1982 Brazil held its first fully democratic congressional, state and municipal elections for 16 years. In Rio Grande do Sul the election for state governor was won by Jair Soares, who during his electoral campaign had promised to find land for the families at Encruzilhada Natalino. After some delay, he kept his word: at the end of September 1983, one thousand days after the camp at Encruzilhada Natalino had been established, the families who had held out finally won their land.

As João Pedro Stédile has pointed out, it is possible, with hindsight, to see Encruzilhada Natalino as the military government's last, somewhat desperate attempt to impose its policies through repression.[18] It had not worked and, partly because of this defeat, the whole political climate began to change. By 1983 there was a new feeling of optimism in the air. With CPT support, landless families began to hold meetings in many areas of southern Brazil. Men and women crowded into parish halls and each other's homes to talk about what had happened at Encruzilhada Natalino. A film recording key moments in the history of Encruzilhada Natalino was widely shown. In the last three months of 1983 mass meetings of several thousand landless peasants were held in the towns of Tres Passos and Frederico Westphalen, bringing together people from the entire northwest region of Rio Grande do Sul and from Paraná. Most of the families hoped that they would be able to negotiate with the state government, particularly as Jair Soares appeared more sympathetic to their predicament, but they were beginning tentatively to talk about land occupation. Their determination to conquer the land through their own efforts received an enormous boost in January 1984, when a group of landless peasants formally launched the MST.

The Cascavel Meeting

From 21 to 24 January 1984, a group of almost one hundred landless workers – or *sem-terra*, as they were now being called – held a historic meeting in the town of Cascavel in the western corner of the state of Paraná to set up the new organisation. Cascavel was just 30 km from Medianeira, where the very first meeting had taken place, and only 18 months had passed, but a great deal had happened. Encruzilhada Natalino had shown that, with the support of the church and civil society, a few hundred poor, homeless and hungry men and women, united by a cause, could take on the military regime and win. At the same time, in the Amazon basin at the other end of the country, the violence of the gunmen and the police, unleashed against peasant families and those who tried to defend them – priests, lawyers or activists – showed that the battle would be tough.

One of the main organisers of the three-day meeting, held at the diocesan centre, was João Pedro Stédile. Ringing in his head as he planned the meeting were the words of sociologist José de Souza Martins, author of several influential books on land issues, who was a key adviser to the Catholic Church. At an earlier meeting of the CPT, Martins had declared that the emerging movement for agrarian reform would become an important agent for change only if it managed to spread to all regions of the country, particularly the northeast. Stédile became convinced that Martins' analysis was correct and that they had to build up a national movement, reaching out beyond the proud regionalism of the southern states, where people often regarded the poorer and more backward north and northeast of Brazil as alien and inferior.

For this reason, the organisers decided to invite a broad range of people from 13 states. There were *sem-terra* from the three southern states – Rio Grande do Sul, Santa Catarina and Paraná – and from São Paulo and Rio de Janeiro, Brazil's most industrialised states, in the southeast. There were rural union representatives from Espírito Santo and Bahia, two coastal agricultural states north of Rio de Janeiro, and from Goiás, a cattle-rearing state in central Brazil. And there were Catholic lay workers and trade unionists from four Amazon states: Rondônia, Acre, Roraima and Pará. As well as this, bishops, priests and nuns from Catholic bodies – the Pastoral Land Commission (CPT), and the Indigenous Missionary Council (CIMI) – and ministers from the Lutheran church also attended. ABRA, an association set up to lobby for agrarian reform, and CUT, a new trade union federation that had emerged out of the labour mobilisation against the military regime, also sent representatives.

They all knew that they wanted a national movement but they were unclear as to what, exactly, this meant. Everyone in the hall welcomed the recent changes in the Catholic Church, which, under the inspiration of liberation theology, had, in the words of Stédile, 'stopped being messianic and telling peasants: "Wait and you will inherit the Kingdom of Heaven", and was saying instead: "You need to organise to fight and solve your problems here on Earth".'[19] But, despite this consensus, it was not clear what the church's role should be in the new organisation. Should the movement be closely linked to – and, in some ways, dependent on – the CPT, which had already played such a fundamental role by organising rural workers and peasant families? Some argued that the movement would be stronger if it remained under the protection of the Catholic Church. But, if they chose this route, what would happen to activists from other churches – people like the Lutheran minister Werner Fuchs, who had played a vital role in Paraná by helping to set up the Land and Justice Movement, which had encouraged the families left homeless by the Itaipu dam to stand firm against resettlement in the Amazon and to demand better compensation? Others, including some of the bishops in the CPT itself, believed that the new movement had to be autonomous for its own sake. In his deep, passionate voice, Bishop Pedro Casaldáliga, the tiny Catalan bishop of São Felix do Araguaia, said prophetically, 'If the movement learns to walk on its own feet, it will go much further'. It was this view that prevailed.

What should be the relationship with the growing movement of combative rural trade unions, which were also defending the rights of farm labourers and small farmers? 'There were many union presidents who believed the fight for agrarian reform should take place within the unions', said Stédile.[20] But Brazilian trade unions only accepted workers as members, and the *sem-terra* realised, from their experience so far in the camps, that much of the movement's strength came from the involvement of the whole family – men, women and children. It was decided, after a long discussion, that the movement should be independent of the trade union movement and open to everyone in the family.

It was remarkable, in a society in which *machismo* was still so strong, and at a meeting at which there were so few women, that the *sem-terra* gave equal rights to all members of the family – old and young, men and women. Today Stédile believes that this last decision was of great importance. 'We realise today that this is our greatest strength, because men, besides being sexist, are conservative. By including all members of the family, the movement acquires a remarkable potential force. Adolescents, for example, who are used to being oppressed by their fathers, realise that their votes in an assembly are as important as their fathers'.'[21] In the same way, he says, the movement also helped to liberate women from their age-old subjugation to men.

What about the new movement's relationship with political parties? In 1979 a group of trade unionists from the industrial suburbs of São Paulo, led by a charismatic former lathe operator, Luís Ignácio da Silva, known as Lula, had taken advantage of the new political freedom to set up the Workers' Party (PT), a left-wing party committed to far-reaching social change. 'It wasn't yet clear what our relationship with the PT should be. Everyone had their own experience, their own vision of the world,' recalls Stédile. The only consensus that emerged was, once again, that the new movement must jealously defend its independence from all political parties. And what about people who were not rural workers? Should they be allowed in? Speakers argued that everyone had a role – rural workers, peasant families, priests, agronomists, teachers and lawyers. 'We had already had six years of struggle and we realised that, if things had gone right, it was because so many people had got involved', said Stédile. 'We knew that we must create a mass movement'.

After three days of intense debate, they established the key characteristics of the new movement: it was to be run by the landless workers themselves, independent of the church, the trade unions and the political parties; it was to be open to the entire family; and it was to be a mass movement. The *sem-terra* then decided on the four aims of the new movement: to fight for agrarian reform; to fight for a just, fraternal society and for an end to capitalism; to include rural workers, tenant farmers, share-croppers, smallholders and so on, in the category of landless worker (*trabalhador sem terra*); and to ensure that the land be used for those who work it and live from it.

Taken together, the decisions reached at this meeting show that, even at this early stage, the *sem-terra* were consciously attempting to create an organisation that was different from anything that had previously existed in Brazil. Unlike earlier rural movements, such as the famous *Ligas Camponesas*, which in the 1950s had fought for the rights of poor rural workers in the northeast of Brazil to be recognised within the union movement, they wanted their organisation to be completely independent of all other bodies. They also believed that they were different from the land squatters (*posseiros*) in the Amazon, who were fighting exclusively for the right to remain on the land that they had occupied for years. The *sem-terra* saw themselves as a new

type of exploited worker – people who had been expelled from the land by
agricultural modernisation – and, as such, they needed their own movement that
could respond in an appropriate fashion. They believed that their struggle for land
was part of a broader revolutionary movement to end exploitation and to create a
more just society for everyone. Their vision was unashamedly utopian, and in that
lay much of its appeal to the poor and excluded.

   With hindsight today, it is evident that, if the participants had taken a different
decision on any one of the key questions – and, at the time, it was by no means clear
which was the better route to follow on all issues – the dynamic of the movement
would have been stalled. These original goals were remarkably far-sighted: all the
movement's subsequent development, as it expanded and redefined its strategy, was
contained, in embryonic form, in this first statement of its objectives. 'The decisions
taken at this meeting were absolutely fundamental for the future of the movement',
said Stédile.[22]

   After the nature of the new movement had been defined came the question of its
name. 'For some time the press had been referring to us as *o movimento sem-terra* –
the landless movement – but the leaders didn't like it', Stédile recalls. 'If it had been
put to the vote at the beginning of the meeting, I think we would have chosen "The
Movement for Agrarian Reform", because it suggested a broader struggle than just
the fight for land. But then we began to realise that we needed a more political
name: we are workers, we live in a society with different classes, and we belong to
one of them. That became the debate. It wasn't a question of choosing a name
because we thought it was more attractive, or just because it was different'.[23] So in
the end, they decided to keep the name by which they were already known, but
adding 'Rural Workers', so that it became the Movement of Landless Rural Workers,
or Movimento dos Trabalhadores Rurais Sem Terra (MST), taking its acronym from
the shorter, handier version.

   They chose the term rural worker in preference to *camponês*, or peasant, because
it was more accessible. The Spanish equivalent – *campesino* – is widely used in the
rest of Latin America, but in Brazil it is not very common. There are a number of
words to describe people who work the land: in the south, where thousands of
European settlers set up small farms, the most common term is *colono*, which means
a member of an immigrant colony; in the north most small farmers are known as
posseiros, because they physically possess the land, sometimes for generations, even
though most do not have land deeds; and there are also a host of other terms to
describe particular relationships with the land: *meeiro* (sharecropper), *arrendatário*
(tenant farmer), *lavrador* (agricultural worker), *agricultor* and others. As the new
movement wanted to be open to all those who worked on the land, who had no land,
or who had only a tiny plot of land, it opted for *trabalhador rural sem terra* (landless
rural worker) as the most inclusive term.

   The meeting also decided to issue a forceful indictment of the government's land
policy:

From the reports of the struggles of comrades from different states, from the north to the south of Brazil, we realise sadly that our problems are increasing: there are more conflicts and more hunger, poverty, unemployment and deaths, and the number of our comrades brutally assassinated has increased. In 1983 alone 116 rural workers in 15 states were killed, and their murderers have not been brought to justice. More families are migrating from the south to the north as the result of a publicity campaign by government agencies and private colonisation companies. These ill-informed migrants live today in great poverty, facing gunmen, malaria and other diseases, and putting up with a severe shortage of schools and roads. Those who want to return are unable to do so because they cannot afford the fares.

The document blamed the military regime's economic policies for this situation. All the government wanted, it said, was to increase exports so as to improve the balance of payments to the benefit of big capital, both Brazilian and foreign and, as a result, land was becoming concentrated in the hands of a few and the number of landless was increasing. 'In Paraná alone, over 2.5 million people left the country-side in the 1970s. In Rio Grande do Sul and in Santa Catarina, the figures were 1.5 million and 600,000, respectively.' The document ended with the slogan that was to become the MST's war cry for the next few years: 'Land for those who live and work on it'.

The seeds of the MST were sown at Encruzilhada Natalino but the form of the new movement was determined at Cascavel. Today Father Arnildo is amazed by the organisation he helped to create. 'The movement has gone so much further than we ever imagined. There was always creativity, solidarity, and the sharing of the few possessions people had. We, in the CPT, dreamed of achieving agrarian reform, but not of the development of a new man and a new woman. And this is what the MST is giving us today. I have been privileged to play a part in this process.'

CHAPTER 2

The Consolidation of the MST

Muitos vão à frente
de nossa Esperança.
E detrás da gente
todo um Povo avança.

(Many are before us
as we go forward in Hope,
while behind us
an entire people advances)

Dom Pedro Casaldáliga, bishop of São Felix[1]

The new movement launched at the Cascavel meeting in January 1984 made its appearance when Brazil was in upheaval. After 20 years in power, the military regime was demoralised, the country was bankrupt, and unemployment and inflation were soaring. After years of censorship and repression, civil society was flexing its muscles once again. Strikes proliferated in the cities and land conflicts were spreading in the countryside. Between January and April millions of Brazilians in Rio de Janeiro, São Paulo and every other state capital joined mass demonstrations for *Diretas Já!* – Direct Elections Now! They were demanding the right to choose their president after years of rule by a succession of hand-picked generals. The military, however, rejected these demands, and intimidated Congress to ensure that a bill to introduce free elections was not approved. The armed forces would hand over power only on their own terms, and that meant Congress, acting as an electoral college, rubber-stamping their choice for next president – a radical right-wing populist called Paulo Maluf.

Such was the groundswell of opinion against the military, however, that the government's strategy failed. The pressure for change was too great and too close – large crowds had gathered around the Congressional building – for even the cowed electoral college to ignore, and it unexpectedly voted in favour of the opposition candidate, Tancredo Neves, a wily veteran who persuaded both left and right that he was the only person who could guarantee a peaceful transition of power. To the right, he pledged collaboration with the outgoing regime, no investigation into human rights violations committed by the military, and economic conservatism. To the left, he promised political democracy and agrarian reform. As José de Souza Martins has pointed out, he felt that he had to respond to 'the pressure of the rural populations and their demand for land distribution repressed by the years of military rule'.[2] Tancredo Neves, President-elect of the so-called New Republic, assured the MST that he would attend their first congress, to be held in January 1985, just two weeks after the college had selected him as president.

Throughout 1984 dozens of meetings had been held in preparation for this congress. For the first time ever, all who were fighting for land in different parts of Brazil came together. By now the MST was receiving the active support not only of the progressive wing of the Catholic Church (particularly the CPT and the local network of CEBs, the grassroots church groups to which many of the *sem-terra* belonged) and of part of the Lutheran Church, but also of the country's most important independent trade union movement, the newly formed CUT. At Cascavel there had been fewer than 100 people. Now, a year later, there were more than 1,500 delegates from all over Brazil, coming together for the first time ever to talk about land. Through them the organisers hoped to extend the MST to the whole country and to turn it into a truly national organisation, rather than a regional one confined to the south.

The three-day meeting, which ran from 29 to 31 January, was held in Curitiba, the capital of Paraná state. There was a climate of great hope in the country. Parliamentarians, representatives of NGOs, indigenous leaders and delegates from Latin American peasant organisations shared the crowded platform with those more directly involved in the struggle: *sem-terra* from 23 different states, trade union leaders, Catholic bishops and Lutheran ministers. Álvaro Tucano was one of several indigenous leaders from the Amazon basin who had come to the congress to talk about the situation of Brazil's remaining 330,000 Indians. Just over a year before, in November 1983, the Guarani leader, Marçal Tupã de Souza, had been shot dead in Mato Grosso do Sul by gunmen working for a local landowner. Lula, the president of the new Workers' Party, made a stirring speech, expressing confidence that his party would soon win power and promising, when elected president, to abolish the *latifúndios*, to support family farmers and to wipe out poverty. It seemed as though a new Brazil was just around the corner.

However, even before the congress began, the rural workers themselves had been wary of the climate of euphoria. They had chosen a cautious slogan for the event – 'there is no democracy without agrarian reform' – which reflected their belief that the return to civilian rule alone, without a far-reaching programme of agrarian reform, would not bring real political change for the rural poor. On the first day of the congress, there was an ominous sign that their prudence was justified: Tancredo Neves failed to turn up. The organisers kept an empty chair on the podium for him:

it was a chill warning to the plenary that, like the chair, the lofty promises of the new government might also prove empty.

In an interview many years later, João Pedro Stédile said: 'we took the political decision not to allow ourselves to be deluded by the New Republic. The communist parties were supporting it, as was a good part of the church, and they all told us to stop our mobilisations. Yet we became more and more convinced that land reform would only advance if there were occupations and mass struggles. We knew that we couldn't just wait for the goodwill of the authorities. We had to exert pressure.'[3] Stédile said in this interview that he believed, with hindsight, that it would have been disastrous for the MST to have pledged support for the new government. 'The MST was weak. It was only just beginning. If we had joined a much bigger, reformist force, we would have been finished'.[4]

Before deciding on their strategy, the *sem-terra* decided to examine the land situation. So for the next three days the delegates, many of whom had travelled three or four days in bone-shaking buses from the far corners of Brazil to be there, listened, studied and debated. Hands gnarled and blistered by farm work clutched papers. Faces weather-beaten by years in the open air bent over documents. Brazilians from the north and northeast encountered for the first time the strange habits of the southerners, who went everywhere with thermos flasks of boiling water for their *chimarrão*, the bitter drink made from *mate* tea, which they sipped from gourds. An Indian habit, it had been widely adopted by the European immigrants.

Each report from the different regions of the country confirmed what in their bones the delegates already knew: that there was no place for peasants, small producers, tenant farmers or sharecroppers in the economic model imposed on the country by the military government. It had provided generous tax breaks and subsidised credits for agribusiness projects, for cattle ranchers who cleared rainforest in the Amazon and for feudal sugar-mill owners in the northeast who treated their workers like slaves, but it had given nothing to small farmers. Driven off the land, thousands of families had migrated to the cities where they ended up living in sub-human conditions in shanty-towns.

The MST congress also examined the organisations set up to oppose these policies. The largest and most successful was the Catholic Church's CPT, which had been founded ten years earlier to expose and combat the violence in the Amazon caused by government-funded development projects. By 1985 the CPT had set up offices all over the country and was providing vital support for rural workers. The *sem-terra* had also set up their own independent organisations in five southern states – Rio Grande do Sul, Santa Catarina, Paraná, São Paulo and Mato Grosso do Sul. The most important of these was MAB, the movement that brought together people displaced by dams. Then there were three other landless movements – MASTRO, MASTEN, and MASTEL – in different regions of Paraná, a state long renowned for the violence of its land conflicts and the combativeness of its rural families.

In many other areas of Brazil, however, the only body to offer any kind of organised resistance was the rural trade union movement. The local union branches had very limited resources: most had no vehicles and many did not even have a telephone, which made it extremely difficult to operate effectively across the vast areas they had to cover. As they compared notes, the congress delegates realised that the military government had used the same tactics time and again to weaken the movements. First, they had threatened activists, put pressure on families to migrate to distant land settlement projects, and tried to co-opt leaders. Then, if these tactics failed, the government had resorted directly to violence. Of the 300 women at the Congress, several were widows of murdered peasant leaders. Over the previous three years, 277 peasant leaders, union officials and rural workers had been killed. The CPT had produced a report with the names and details of each crime.[5] Among the murdered leaders was one of Brazil's first women rural union presidents, Margarida Alves. Gunmen had shot her down in August 1980 as she stood at the front door of her home in Lagoa Grande, in the northeastern state of Paraíba.

Speaker after speaker got up to talk about the violence they had seen or suffered. Manoel da Conceição, a rural union leader from the northeastern state of Maranhão, had lost a leg from a gunshot wound and had been savagely tortured by the police. Father Ricardo Resende, a young Roman Catholic priest who ran the CPT branch in Conceição do Araguaia in the state of Pará, was later forced to leave the Amazon after constant death threats. The region he worked in was known as the *Bico do Papagaio*, because, squeezed between two great rivers of the Amazon basin, the Araguaia and the Tocantins, it had the shape of a huge parrot's beak. This was the most violent region in the country: almost half the murders of rural workers between 1982 and 1984 occurred there. The delegates listened and drew conclusions. They realised that their struggle would be prolonged and violent, and that their only chance of victory would be by working closely together. They had to organise national mobilisations that would put pressure on the politically sensitive parts of the country, particularly the federal capital, Brasília. It was a strategy that was to serve them well.

After listening to emotionally exhausting reports for hours, the congress delegates relaxed in the evenings with impromptu concerts. From among their number appeared amateur musicians and singers, many of them very talented, who strummed guitars, pumped accordions and rattled tambourines to songs of struggle and resistance. They sang of the day that would surely come when agrarian reform would be a reality. Music and song had been a part of the movement from the very beginning, when progressive Catholic priests had encouraged the families in the camps to reshape Catholic rites to make them relevant to their own struggle and culture. The leaders were already aware of the importance of these activities (which they were beginning to call the *mística*) in motivating the *sem-terra* and helping them to forge a collective identity. 'The *mística* expresses the optimism and determination that spring from our indignation against injustice and from our belief in the very real possibility of building a new society. For this reason, it isn't simple entertainment to help us to escape from the disappointments and difficulties of everyday life. It is an injection of vitality, which gives us determination and daring so that we can overcome pessimism and push ahead with our project for including the excluded in the liberation of the Brazilian people.'[6]

After three days of debate, the participants drew up a list of the movement's principles, which expanded the four goals established in Cascavel. The first two commitments – that 'the land should be owned by those who work it' and that the movement is committed to creating 'a society without exploited or exploiters' – have a strongly socialist ring to them. The other principles were less utopian and spelt out decisions taken earlier: that the movement should be independent, that it should be open to everyone and that it should be run by the workers themselves.

With its principles established, the Congress tackled the fundamental task of this meeting, which was to start building a national organisation. The first step was to decide on its structure. The *sem-terra* were anxious not to let a clique of powerful leaders dominate the movement, so they decided not to create individual posts, such as president, treasurer or executive secretary, but to run the movement as far as possible in a collective way, with a decentralised administration. There was also a good practical reason for not having a national president: any prominent leader would become an easy target for an assassin's bullet. So they decided to set up elected collective bodies – *coletivos* (which still exist today) – to be in charge of specific functions, such as recruitment, training and financial management. Delegates stressed the need to build a strong internal democracy. Leaders and coordinators must be permanently linked to the rank and file, they said, and every member should participate in decision-making through meetings and small group discussions. Information should be circulated to everyone.

The participants set up a national coordinating committee with representatives from the twelve states where the movement was already organised or in the process of being organised. They decided that, while the committee would establish 'guiding principles' for the movement, it would not dictate specific policies. These would be decided by the people in the regions, who were directly engaged in the struggle for land. This decentralisation helped the organisation to survive very difficult moments and has become one of its lasting characteristics. The MST faced its worst crisis when it attempted, for a brief period, to impose a single policy – the collectivisation of agricultural production – on the whole movement.

The congress also decided that it did not want a static, formal movement but one that was continually expanding and developing – 'we call it a movement because it is always moving'. The *sem-terra* meant this in two ways. First, they wanted the movement to help them to develop as individuals. José de Souza Martins says that this is the secret of the MST's appeal. The MST 'only succeeds because the people in it don't just want a piece of land; they also have a way of life as a banner. They have a *mística* of how to live, of how to be a human being'.[7] The *sem-terra* knew that if they were to put an end to the way they were humiliated and exploited by the rich and powerful, they needed to overcome the ignorance imposed on them by a social system that excluded them from schools and universities. So from this very early meeting the MST encouraged its members – old, middle-aged and young – to study.

Second, they wanted the movement to increase its membership dramatically. The best way to do this, they said, was to organise mass actions and mass occupations. They coined as their slogan for the next five years: 'Occupation is the Only Solution'. It is a surprisingly tough slogan, given the general climate of euphoria at the time, expressing the *sem-terra*'s view that agrarian reform would happen only if they made it happen. The delegates decided to set up local committees to organise new occupations that would target *latifúndios* (large estates) and *terras devolutas* (public lands). They said they must all work together: the states where the MST was already organised would send *militantes* to the states where it was just beginning.

Despite their firm belief in self-reliance, the MST still hoped that the new civilian government, which was coming to power in a national mood of such optimism, would listen to them. So they drew up a list of demands: they asked for the abolition of all the land and development agencies set up by the military government, beginning with the ministry of land affairs; they requested the immediate distribution of all the land owned by state and federal governments, the expropriation of all estates owned by multinational companies, and from then on a ban on foreigners acquiring land in Brazil; they drew attention to the wave of rural violence, pointing out that not a single person had been arrested or charged for the crimes, and they called on the federal government to take over all land-related murder investigations, as these were normally carried out by the local police, which worked closely with the local landowners (and were at times actually paid by them), and to punish both the *mandantes*, the instigators of the crimes, and the gunmen who had actually pulled the trigger; they demanded the dismantling of all police and armed forces units, including paramilitary forces, that had been illegally deployed against rural workers; and they asked for the creation of an independent judiciary and a special court within the judicial system to hear cases involving land disputes.

These were ambitious demands, but the military regime had finally been forced out of power. Almost 21 years after the military coup had crushed the attempt by popular organisations to participate in government and to get power and wealth more fairly distributed, workers and peasants were once again organising with the same objectives. The MST delegates left the congress fired with enthusiasm and confident that the historic moment for agrarian reform had arrived: with organisation and the backing of an apparently sympathetic government, they would get what they wanted.

The New Republic

Nobody could have guessed just how dramatically the promise of a new dawn would be dashed. The 74-year-old president-elect fell ill on the eve of his inauguration. For seven weeks Tancredo Neves lay in hospital while Brazil stood still. Finally, on 21 April 1985, he died, and vice-president José Sarney, a political boss from Maranhão and an ally of the military who had switched sides in order to stay in power, was sworn in as president. While governor of Maranhão, Sarney (who had earlier been accused of using forged land titles to obtain a large estate) had distributed millions of hectares to large companies from the south. As a result, thousands of peasant families had been violently evicted from their land. Manoel da Conceição, who had been at the congress, was just one of many peasant farmers who had suffered for attempting to resist.

Whatever his personal views about agrarian reform, Sarney had to respond to the widespread expectation among the rural poor. As part of his complex plan for achieving real change while placating the military and the landowners, Tancredo Neves had chosen the highly respected agronomist José Gomes da Silva, a veteran campaigner for land reform, as head of INCRA (the National Institute of Colonisation and Agrarian Reform), and Nelson Ribeiro, a progressive lawyer from the state of Pará, to head a new Ministry for Land Reform and Agrarian Development, known as MIRAD. Sarney confirmed them in their positions and in May 1985 he appeared in Brasília at a congress of rural workers, organised by CONTAG, to announce the ambitious National Plan for Agrarian Reform (PNRA). He promised to distribute land to 1.4 million peasants over a four-year period. Working with an enthusiastic group of rural workers and land-reform experts, Gomes da Silva and Ribeiro started to draw up detailed plans.

The MST, however, did not wait for the government. Despite the uncertainty caused by the death of the president-elect, the MST carried out a great wave of occupations, just as it had planned at its congress. In the southern states, where the organisation was already well advanced, the upsurge in activity happened rapidly. Over the following months about 50,000 families took part in occupations, often with the help of sympathetic Catholic clergy. In a coordinated operation on 25 May 1985, 5,000 families occupied 18 estates in Santa Catarina. Egydio and Irma Brunetto (*see* box 2.1) – who are today national leaders of the MST but were then poor agricultural workers, two of the six children of a smallholder who had lost his land to the bank after paying heavy medical bills for his sick wife – joined 1,500 families who were all heading for the Rio Grande, which they had to cross to reach the estate. When gunmen saw the lorries arriving, they set fire to the bridge. 'We all rushed out of the lorry,' said Irma Brunetto. 'All of us, including small children, passed up buckets of water and we managed to put out the flames'. This story soon became famous throughout the movement, and the settlement that the families eventually won as the result of that night's occupation was christened 'Fire on the Bridge'.

While the families were fighting on the ground to turn agrarian reform into a reality, the political situation in the country was changing. The old political elite swung into action. In Brasília one member of Congress after another spoke out

Box 2.1 *Irma Brunetto*

I'm 40 years old. I was born in Rio Grande do Sul, where my father had a small plot of land, about six or seven hectares. I had five brothers and sisters. When I was 9 years old, my father went bankrupt. He had a bad harvest and the bank foreclosed. We had to move to Santa Catarina, where he worked as a sharecropper. He'd clear the land for the owner, plant a harvest, and then have to leave. We were always moving and my mother used to get very ill. Though we were landless, there was a certain respect for us in the community. People were always sorry when we left.

We were active in the Catholic Church. The whole family was influenced by the progressive ideas of liberation theology. And it was through the Church that we helped organise the first land occupation in the state. Dom José Gomes, the bishop of Chapecó, gave us a lot of support. That first occupation took place on 25 May 1985. We were 1,500 families, all moving on to the land together on the same night. None of us had any experience. The gunmen protecting the estate made the first lorry turn back. And then they waited for us, by the bridge, a wooden bridge. It was the only way into the estate. When they saw how many lorries there were, they panicked and set light to the bridge. But we weren't going to let them stop us! We all – men, women and youngsters – rushed there and put out the fire. That story's famous now in MST history. We called one of the first settlement Fogo na Ponte (Fire on the Bridge). Perhaps because it was the first occupation, it's always been special to me. It was so wonderful, getting on to that land!

The owner had a dozen estates and eventually we conquered all of them. There are 18 settlements on his land now, with 1,200 families. My family spent three years in camps before we got land. There was always a draw after we conquered land, and it took time for our name to come up. But it was a great experience. We learnt a lot. I got used to running the assembly and talking in public. Necessity is a great teacher! It helped me gain experience as a leader.

Today I'm greatly respected in my cooperative. Sometimes I face *machismo*. It's usually when we're talking about farming matters. Men don't like women to have opinions on that. But it's changing. Now I'm a member of the national leadership. We're nine women now, out of a total of 23 national leaders. We're a strong presence. And we've started to tackle the problem of young people leaving. I haven't married and I haven't children but I encounter the problem all the time on the settlements. Young people often have to leave the settlement to carry on with their education. And then they get fascinated by the world out there. It's a fantasy but they don't realise it. We were very mature when we were young. We constructed the movement. Young people in the settlements aren't like that any more. They want more money. Often they leave and then they find life is much harder than they thought. Our cooperative has a rule: they can leave once and come back, but they're not allowed to do it a second time. We've got to work with them and encourage to get them more involved from the beginning, to make it their movement too.

vehemently against the agrarian reform programme and the MST's wave of occupations, which they claimed was 'illegal' and 'irresponsible'. In the countryside, landowners, exasperated by the government's reluctance to use force to evict the families, set up their own organisation – the Ruralist Democratic Union (UDR) – to carry out expulsions. 'As the state couldn't unleash repression on a huge scale, the UDR arose as a way of organising the *latifúndio* to do it instead', said Stédile. 'There were two intentions behind it: to crush the MST directly and, above all, to put pressure on the government. That is, to force the Sarney government to crush us.'[8]

The UDR held cattle auctions, which enabled them to raise money for the organisation and provided them with a platform for whipping up landowners' fears about the future. On 24 July 1985 about 800 ranchers and farmers met in the headquarters of an ultra right-wing organisation, Tradition, Family and Property (TFP), in the town of Santa Maria in the state of Rio Grande do Sul. One speaker after another attacked the government's agrarian reform programme, saying that it would lead to the 'installation of a socialist regime'. Rio Grande do Sul was becoming increasingly polarised: just a few days later, in the same part of the state, 3,000 families queued for days in the rain and the cold to register for a land distribution programme.

Under pressure from the landowners, the government revised the agrarian reform plan on twelve occasions, watering it down each time. On 10 October President Sarney signed the final version, which was a travesty of the original plan. José Gomes da Silva and Nelson Ribeiro both resigned in protest, with the latter commenting bitterly that 'the PNRA has been so disfigured that it has become unworkable, a victory for the political forces that oppose it'. José de Souza Martins believes that what lay behind the collapse of the agrarian reform programme was not Sarney's bad faith, as many *sem-terra* believed, but the alliance forged between the landowners and industrialists during the military government, which was particularly strong in Congress because of the institutionalised over-representation of the landowning class. 'Pressure from the peasant movement hit the wall of the alliance between capital and land, which prevented any substantive alteration to the political and social order', he commented.[9] The coalition was so strong that advocates of agrarian reform had very few allies in Congress. Fernando Henrique Cardoso, then a Senator who supported agrarian reform, commented ruefully: 'Proposals in favour of agrarian reform don't fail just because a majority votes against them. These questions are not even at the heart of political debate: they don't divide people. They are not at the centre of political discussions.'[10]

The Occupation of Fazenda Annoni

Just over two weeks after the collapse of the agrarian reform programme, the MST undertook the largest occupation of all – one that was to become an icon in the MST *mística*. In the early hours of 29 October 1985, 2,500 families poured into the

9,500 hectares of Fazenda Annoni, located between the towns of Sarandí and Ronda Alta in Rio Grande do Sul. The federal government had expropriated the estate 14 years earlier to settle 303 families evicted from their lands to make way for the Passo Real hydroelectric dam, but the Annoni family was still fighting in the courts to get its land back. The care with which the occupation had been planned took the press by surprise. A local newspaper, *Zero Hora*, commented:

> The invasion of Annoni was the result of a very well-organised operation, which demonstrates the level of organisation that has been reached by the rural workers, coordinated by the MST and supported by the Pastoral Land Commission (CPT)…. About 100 cattle trucks, 30 buses, 15 motorbikes and dozens of cars set out simultaneously at midnight from different areas in the north of the state, all heading for Fazenda Annoni. The people in the trucks hid under canvas to avoid detection but even so the police stopped five trucks and prevented about 1,200 people from arriving at the estate.[11]

Darci Bonato, who at that time earned a pittance working on a poultry farm, was one of those taking part. For about a year he had been going to MST meetings every Friday night to prepare for the occupation.

> Finally the word came: 'it's tonight'. Nobody told us where we were going, and we knew that it was best for us not to know, because that would make it harder for the police to get wind of our plans. I went with my wife and three children, all boys. The youngest was 5. That's why I wanted land, so that they'd have a chance of a decent life. We waited by the road at midnight. It was very cold, and we knew it wasn't going to be easy. It wasn't as if we'd go in to the estate and pick sweets off the branches of trees. We knew we'd have to face the police. We'd talked it through beforehand and we were ready for it. Our lorry arrived and we scrambled in. Every 10 or 12 km along the road there were more people waiting to be picked up. There was a team in charge, making sure that the trucks all arrived together. There were about 40 trucks, full of people from my part of the state'.

Darci Maschio – who had played a key role in the very first occupation at Macali – was once again involved.

> I was in charge of eight rural districts. The local priest had lent me a little VW Beetle and I rushed around, getting things ready. We had a leader in each area. His job was to set up a scheme so that he could contact all the families in his patch very quickly. We had some families coming from Santo Ángelo, 300 kilometres away, so we had to organise carefully. We'd thought up several codes for communicating quickly. We arranged for people to leave a branch at a crossroad if all was well. We told people to flash their lights if they'd been forced back by a police block. But we didn't have any real problems. Right at the end a few policemen realised what was happening, but there were too few of them to stop us.

There were a few hitches. 'I was all ready to go with my two sons, one of them was only a few months old', said Cresi Gobbi Machado. 'But the truck didn't turn up. The driver had overheard people saying in a bar that the police were going to attack, and he'd got frightened. We were left waiting by the roadside.' It took Cresi and her family two weeks to reach the camp.

The lorries arrived and the people unpacked. 'We hadn't brought many things because there wasn't room', said Darci Bonato.

> We'd a hot plate that we could use over an open fire, saucepans, food and bedclothes. The children had fallen asleep by the time we arrived and we laid them on a mattress under a tree, covering them with a blanket. Then we went back to the road to help guard the camp. That first night none of the adults slept. There was a full moon, I remember, and it was quite bright. When dawn came, some policemen arrived. Strung out along the fence, we were ready to stop them coming in. There were rumours that we were armed but we weren't. The only weapons we had were our hoes and scythes. The movement had told us not to take any weapons like shotguns, so as not to cause problems. The police told us to leave, to do this and that, but we didn't pay any attention.

Some lorries arrived late, as they had lost their way. 'The police tried to stop them joining us, but we just formed a huge crowd and walked towards them. There were so many of us that they couldn't stop us.'

The families started organising the camp. 'People began putting up their tents, collecting water from the river and lighting a fire for the cooking', said Darci Bonato.

> We'd thought it all through beforehand, so we'd already arranged teams. The atmosphere was more worried than happy on that first day, because we didn't know what was going to happen. We were thinking: 'And if I get sick here, or one of the children gets sick, what will I do? And when we run out of food? Will anyone send us supplies?' We'd been told to bring enough food for 10 to 15 days but not everyone had. We were all so poor. So we were anxious. The time for emotion came later, much later.

Over the first few days stories emerged of the adventures that some had faced on their way to the camp. Darci's neighbour, the appropriately named Hilário, who had been with him at the Friday night meetings, had got hold of an old pick-up. 'He thought he'd take this old vehicle', said Darci. 'He could sleep inside it and wouldn't need a tent. So he packed his entire family into the pick-up and set off, but he got a puncture and had to stop. A police car came along and, suspicious that something was afoot, the police asked Hilário where he was off to in the middle of the night. He said he was going on a fishing trip. And then they asked him why he needed a spade and a hoe for fishing, and Hilário said he had to erect his tent beside the reservoir.' The police swallowed the fisherman's tale and even helped him to change his tyre.

Later that first day, the police arrived in force. 'They looked as if they'd come to kill a bunch of bandits', said Darci Bonato. 'Lorry-loads of them, with bayonets and rifles, weapons we'd never seen; the only arms we knew about were machetes, scythes and shotguns. They formed a barrier to stop us leaving and anyone else

1. Entering Fazenda Giacometti (*Sebastião Salgado*)

coming in. There was a long tussle with the police.' Vilmar Martins da Silva, now an MST leader, recalls it well. 'It was a hot afternoon. The police moved forward and we in a group pushed them back with our scythes. Forward and back we moved. It was dangerous but it was also fun. I remember, strange as it was, that we were telling jokes the whole time.' Darci Bonato carries on the story. 'We had a fat man with us – I can't remember his name – but he hit a policeman, knocking him off the top of a hillock. He went tumbling down about 10 metres, breaking his arm. At least that one didn't bother us again. And then there was a comrade who became known from then on as "Bayonet", because a policeman stuck a bayonet in him, cutting open his back. He lost a lot of blood. He was almost dead when he reached the hospital.'

The police surrounded the camp for a year. For the first three months there was a large police presence – about 2,000 – and once again, fearful of using violence, they tried to wear down the *sem-terra* through attrition. They made it very difficult for people to go into the camp, even if they were taking in food, and to leave it, unless they were moving out. Sometimes they would keep people under arrest for two or three days. 'They were trying to intimidate us', said Darci. 'Some people did give up, those who hadn't been as well prepared as us. They arrived there, saw all that conflict, and after a few days they jacked it in and left. But only about ten per cent did this. The rest of us stuck it out. From the beginning there was a team working with us, telling us they didn't know how long we'd have to be there to win, but that we would win if we were well organised.' Even committed activists like Vilmar wavered. 'After about two months we went back for the weekend to my parents' house', said Maria, Vilmar's wife. 'Vilmar was ready to give up. "We're never going to win", he said. "It's too difficult." But I wasn't having any of that. "We've sold up everything", I said. "We haven't got anything to come back to. We're going back to the camp, and we're going to win".' Others, like Cresi Gobbi Machado, had health problems. 'My elder son got conjunctivitis so badly that we had to leave. His eyes have never recovered properly. But once he'd been treated we went back.'

Elza Pioletta joined her husband after a month. 'I didn't want to go. I thought it madness. I had two children, one 7 years old and the other 8. I kept on crying, terrified at the idea of it, but I didn't try to stop my husband from going. He was a rural labourer and life was so difficult. Once the camp got established, I knew I had to join him'. 'The children found it difficult in the beginning', she remembers. 'But soon the school got started. It was a very good school.' Elza Pioletta said that, in spite of her misgivings, she soon settled in. 'We shared a wood fire with two other families. I'd never done anything like that before.' Father Arnildo was once again a frequent visitor. 'Sometimes I'd be in my tent, feeling a bit depressed. Then I'd hear his voice or the sound of his mouth organ. I'd suddenly feel happy again. He was a real father to us.' Elza got pregnant in the camp and had a miscarriage. Later she had a baby boy, born in the black polythene tent. 'He's proud of it today', said Elza. 'He feels he's a real *sem-terrinha*.'

It turned out to be a long struggle in which people, true to the spirit of the movement, began to change. One turning point came in March 1987. 'The authorities kept on dragging their heels, so we decided we'd put a bit of pressure on them', said Darci Bonato. 'Some of us stayed behind to look after the camp and the rest of us went on foot the whole 400 km to the state capital, Porto Alegre. Sometimes people jeered, calling us tramps, layabouts, land invaders and so on, but in most places people were very supportive.' Darci Maschio said they held a long debate, 'not of one day or two but of weeks', on what they called 'the nature of their arrival'.[12] One group, linked to the CPT, believed they should present themselves as devout Catholics, who had carried out a long pilgrimage on foot and 'were appealing to the compassion of the population'. This faction said they should lie down in the central square and entreat the authorities to help them. But another group, made up of tougher *sem-terra* leaders, argued that they had rights and were carrying out not a pilgrimage but a march. They said they should occupy the INCRA building and present the government with a list of their demands. 'It was a choice between the cross and the sickle', says Darci Maschio. On this occasion the movement tried to reconcile both approaches, for one group lay down in the square while another camped in front of the INCRA building.

Darci Bonato believes that the divisions within the movement made it difficult for them to present a clear message to the population. 'Almost no one in Porto

Alegre supported us because they didn't know what we wanted.' The families also disagreed on how they should respond to the authorities.

> The government told us to go home, assuring us that, as they'd put us on a register, we'd be top of the list when they carried out land reform. They told us that we didn't have to stay there suffering. Some families went along with them, saying that it wasn't any use our quarrelling with the government, for it would do whatever it wanted to do. They said: 'How can we ask the government for land and at the same time fight it?' They even said: 'Would you fight with your father and then ask him for help?' They considered the government as a father! But our leaders weren't having any of that. They knew we would only get land if we put pressure on the authorities.

After the families had spent three months in the camp outside the INCRA building, the government finally offered them 16 scattered pieces of land. The families accepted, returned to Fazenda Annoni and drew lots to decide which family would go where. But even then the struggle was not over: they discovered that INCRA had offered them areas that it had not yet expropriated. By then, the families were at the end of their tether. They decided not to wait any longer but to travel directly to the plots, even though that entailed a long journey on foot. They had gone about half a kilometre when some 2,000 policemen appeared and started to drive them back towards the camp. Some of the *sem-terra* tried to resist and several were being beaten by the police when – in one of those incidents that has become part of MST folklore – a group of children went up to the police and handed them flowers. 'They were telling the police that we weren't fighting them, that our struggle was against the government that wouldn't expropriate the land.'[13] The police, shamefaced, stopped the violence but, even so, the families were forced back into the camp. 'We couldn't get out and they wouldn't let anything in, not even food or medicines. They wanted us to die of hunger', said Darci Bonato. 'Everyone shared what they had: someone who had a cup of oil would divide it between 20 people. We were under siege for three months.'

Eventually, under pressure from civil society, the government lifted the blockade, and in 1987 finally agreed to allow the families to stay on Fazenda Annoni. But it was not until 1993 that every family was officially allocated a plot of land. It was evident that, while the state government did not feel that it had the political strength to evict the families, it was equally reluctant to hand the MST a propaganda coup by admitting defeat, and delayed as long as possible the formal recognition of what had become a fait accompli.

The struggle had lasted far longer than Darci Bonato had ever imagined, but it was worth it, he says. 'I spent nine years in the camp, nine years living under black polythene. But I don't regret it. If I hadn't done that, I would have worked for 30 years as a farm labourer and ended up without a single hectare. So for me it was a huge victory. Today my sons are living on the settlement with me, each with his plot of land. They lived through it all with me, and now they're ten times better off than they would have been if I'd gone on working as a hired hand.'

The Struggle Expands

The occupation of Fazenda Annoni was not an isolated case. The defeat of agrarian reform in Congress did not check the growth of the MST. It simply strengthened the belief among its members that they could not rely on politicians and would have to conquer land through mobilisation and occupation. 'As the New Republic was a government that claimed to be democratic, it could not openly repress us', said João Pedro Stédile. 'It was the time when we occupied most INCRA buildings and one of the most fertile periods in terms of concrete achievements.'[14] Just as it had planned at its congress, the MST became a national movement with a rudimentary bureaucratic structure that spread across most of the country. During this period the movement also began to break free from the tutelage of the Catholic Church. Zander Navarro, a sociologist who has studied the MST, says that the movement entered a new phase. 'Until the end of 1985, the MST contained a large number of Catholic mediators, even within the leadership itself, and in general they opted for less confrontational tactics, arguing for dialogue with the state authorities. But after the collapse of the Sarney government's agrarian reform programme, the MST entered a new, more confrontational phase, in which it rejected the mediation of the Catholic Church.'

To a large extent, the change within the MST was a response to the new climate of repression in the later years of the Sarney government, which in turn was fuelled by the movement's growing momentum. Without support from the authorities, the MST had become ever more reliant on occupations for its growth. Occupation was clearly a highly effective tactic, for it inspired the landless families, providing them with a strategy for conquering land that relied exclusively on their own courage, tenacity and intelligence, but it provoked a backlash, particularly from the UDR. Small groups, in particular, were vulnerable to the UDR's violence. So, as it prepared to conquer land all over Brazil, the MST changed tactics: it decided that the 'guiding principle' would be to undertake big, well-planned 'mass occupations', for large groups of families would be more resilient. Such a strategem was not always possible, for in many states the MST did not have the capacity to mobilise large numbers of families and, as always, it was left it in the end to the local leadership to decide.

This period of rapid growth during the Sarney government was an intoxicating experience for the MST. As the movement began to grow beyond the confines of the southern states, the *sem-terra* were excited to discover that, just as they had expected, their movement tapped into the frustrations and dashed hopes of hundreds of thousands of rural workers, whose livelihoods had been damaged – or destroyed – by Brazil's process of 'painful modernisation'. But expansion brought its own problems. The MST was to learn through setbacks and disappointments to adapt its strategy to local conditions and to limit its rate of growth to its capacity to integrate new members.

CHAPTER 3

The MST Moves Northwards

American farmers developed new methods that enabled them to try to regain a measure of control over their own lives. Their efforts, halting and disjointed at first, gathered form and force until they grew into a coordinated mass movement that stretched across the American continent from the Atlantic coast to the Pacific. Millions of people came to believe fervently that a wholesale overhauling of their society was going to happen in their lifetimes. A democratic 'new day' was coming to America.

Lawrence Goodwin, writing about the Agrarian Revolt in the United States in the late nineteenth century.[1]

In the second half of the 1980s, the MST began to spread beyond the south into the rest of Brazil. The *sem-terra* encountered numerous problems. Some states had almost no tradition of peasant resistance and landowners reacted with unbridled fury at the very idea that the established order could be challenged. It was in these states that the MST faced the fiercest repression. But the movement also faced difficulties of another kind in states that had a long history of land struggle. Although the MST owes an enormous debt of gratitude to the Catholic Church's Pastoral Land Commission (CPT) and to the rural trade unions, the *sem-terra* did not always behave with deference and respect when they arrived in regions where these organisations were well established. Not surprisingly, the older organisations were resentful when the newcomer moved in and brashly demanded control, refusing to accept the other bodies as equal partners. At times, the *sem-terra* committed serious mistakes through their arrogant refusal to listen to the advice of local activists.

One of the first states the MST reached was Espírito Santo, a region with a history of violent conflict. A founder member was José Rainha, today a well-known MST leader. 'My parents worked as sharecroppers in São Gabriel da Palha in the north of the state', he recalled. 'I started to work with them when I was 7 years old. Like my brothers and sisters, I couldn't go to school. I only learnt to read and write when I was 15, as the result of a literacy programme run by the Catholic Church.' Rainha joined the Church's youth group. 'In February 1978, Frei Beto (a Dominican friar called Carlos Alberto Libânio Christo) came to talk to us. For the first time, I heard someone talking about agrarian reform and the need for peasant families to organise. It made so much sense. I never forgot what he said.'

Rainha went to the First Congress as the CPT representative. With him was a young woman, Maria da Fátima Ribeiro, who came from a very poor family of landless workers and was to become one of the movement's first woman leaders. She was one of 20 children, three of whom died as babies. 'We were very enthusiastic when we came back', said Fátima. 'I had been angry for so long about the exploitation I saw around me. For the first time I saw a way of changing it.' Rainha took up the story. 'We carried out our first occupation in Espírito Santo on 22 October 1985. We were about 400 families. I met Diolinda on this first occupation. She was only 13 years old at the time. Little did I imagine it then, but I ended up marrying her five years later. We were lucky. There were still a lot of people in government who supported agrarian reform, many of them members of the Communist Party. They helped us, and we won the land just four months later. It gave the MST a real boost.'

The MST started to expand into the northeast of Brazil too, as José de Souza Martins had so strongly recommended. By the time of the First Congress, the MST already existed in Bahia, the largest state in the northeast, but it was very weak. José Rainha was sent by the movement to get it properly established. 'It was difficult in the beginning', he said. 'When we first started talking of occupying land, other popular organisations accused us of imposing a "southern" solution. They said that people would refuse to live in black polythene tents in the hot climate.' After a while, however, the MST carried out two successful occupations. This brought its own problems, because the landowners, alarmed by the growing strength of the *sem-terra*, set up a local branch of the UDR. In early 1988 gunmen carried out a violent eviction, which almost destroyed the MST. The 600 families were saved by Capuchin monks, who offered four hectares of land next to their monastery as a refuge. It became a vital space for resistance.

Bahia's northern border is with Sergipe, one of Brazil's smallest states. With the support of the progressive Catholic Church, nine rural workers had made the long journey south to take part in the First Congress, but even so it was to prove a real struggle to set up the movement. Just as in Bahia, José Rainha was sent to help. 'At first, we didn't know how we were going to manage it', he said. 'There was so much violence and repression, particularly in the *sertão* (the semi-arid hinterland). The old political bosses were used to doing exactly as they wanted. We had to develop new tactics for the region and to get the families to understand that we didn't have all the answers. We told them that they were the MST as much as us.' As in Bahia, the local landowners responded to the MST by setting up a branch of the UDR. They orchestrated a forceful campaign against the MST, getting the local press to brand them as 'invaders and guerrillas'. In May 1989 the state governor himself gave orders to the police to evict 250 families from a farm that the federal government was already in the process of expropriating. The *sem-terra* reacted by occupying the INCRA building in the state capital.

In the 1980s Alagoas, a small state to the north of Sergipe, was run on almost feudal lines by the handful of wealthy families who owned the sugar mills. Two rural workers from Inhapi in the *sertão* had gone to the congress in Curitiba and returned full of enthusiasm, but it took them two years to organise the first occupation. Finally, on 26 January 1987, 66 tenant farmers occupied Fazenda Peba. The families had been angered by a cunning ruse that a local landowner had thought up, when in 1985 it had seemed that the Sarney government might really be about to implement agrarian reform. Because he claimed ownership over a large area of unproductive land for which he had no land titles – just the kind of property that the *sem-terra* said should be expropriated – the landowner had quickly rented out the land to peasant families, so that he could avoid expropriation by claiming that his estate was being used productively. However, when the programme of agrarian reform failed to materialise, the families lost their usefulness. In 1986 the landowner, who had by then set up a local office of UDR, deliberately let loose his cattle over the families' crops in an attempt to drive them out. The families responded with an occupation of his land.

The MST had to proceed slowly, working within the cultural traditions of the people. In December 1988 the MST, the Catholic Church and the local trade union jointly organised the first *Romaria da Terra*, or Land Pilgrimage. This was not a militant march, as was beginning to happen in the south, but a religious procession with a strong mystical component. About 2,000 families climbed to the top of the hills in the interior of Alagoas where, 300 years before, the African slave leader Zumbi had defied the slave owners and led thousands of runaway slaves to set up a free community, known as the Quilombo de Palmares. From 1630 to 1695 about 30,000 people had lived as free men and women in villages scattered over a wide area. Eventually soldiers and mercenaries had overrun the settlements but Zumbi had by then become a national symbol of resistance. The families paid homage to Zumbi, promising to carry on his struggle. Zumbi later became one of the MST's folk heroes.

In 1989 the MST set up a regional office for the northeast region in Maceió, the capital of Alagoas. The police, confident that they could continue to act as a law unto themselves, arrested the MST office staff and had them beaten. Times, however, were changing. The MST mobilised the national network of support that it had been carefully organising since the First Congress. A startled police chief found himself fielding protest telephone calls from members of Congress and Catholic priests from all over Brazil and was forced to free the prisoners.

One of the biggest delegations to the First Congress had come from Pernambuco, another state in the northeast, where thousands of children still worked alongside their parents, cutting sugarcane in semi-feudal conditions. But this state too was beginning to go through profound changes. In response to the world oil crisis in the mid-1970s, the government had set up the Pro-Alcool programme, which subsidised the planting of sugarcane for the production of alcohol fuel. Sugarcane spread into areas occupied by peasant families, who were unceremoniously evicted. A series of giant hydroelectric dams on the huge São Francisco river, which flows north from Minas Gerais to Pernambuco, also displaced thousands of peasant families. The delegates left the congress committed to the idea of setting up the MST in their state.

On the face of it, it might have seemed easy for the MST to get established in Pernambuco. The state had a strong tradition of labour resistance. In the 1950s Francisco Julião, a progressive lawyer, had set up the combative Peasant Leagues among sugarcane workers. Though these Leagues were viciously exterminated by the military, their memory lingered among rural labourers. Despite repression, the sugarcane workers held frequent strikes to demand improvements in their deplorable working conditions. And, under the leadership of Dom Helder Câmara, the archbishop of Recife (who once famously said 'when I give food to the poor, you call me a saint, but when I ask why the poor are hungry, you call me a communist'), the progressive wing of the Catholic Church became an outspoken critic of the repressive policies of the military regime. In 1973 Dom Helder and the other Catholic bishops of the northeast had signed a bluntly worded document, 'I heard the clamours of my people', in which they castigated the authorities for the hunger and poverty of the local population. When the MST arrived, Pernambuco was being governed by Miguel Arraes, a historic left-wing figure who had spent many years in exile. Arraes was promising radical agrarian reform.

Despite this, the MST took time to get established. In practice, the circumstances were not as favourable as they seemed. While Governor Arraes sympathised with the goal of land reform, he wanted to carry it out in his own way, with his own supporters, and did not welcome the arrival of the MST, with its militant strategy of land occupation. The CPT and the local trade unionists were also mistrustful of a new organisation that, with little knowledge of local conditions, seemed brashly to suggest that it had all the answers. After some initial problems, the national leadership of the MST once again sent in José Rainha to sort out the situation.

After just a few weeks, in July 1989, Rainha led 500 families on the MST's first occupation. Without bothering to find out all the facts, they chose a reserve owned by the state government and used by the armed forces for military training. Marluce Melo, who was working for the CPT at the time, says that it was scarcely surprising that the venture ended in disaster. 'The area was extremely remote', she said. 'I went as part of a CPT delegation to offer support, and even the MST leader who was acting as our guide got lost! It was also stupid to choose land used by the military. Of course, they were going to be evicted. The occupation only lasted three days. In the end, some of the families had to be taken out by helicopter, as access was so difficult.' Despite the problems, not all the new recruits were put off. Paulo Venâncio, today a leading MST *militante* and then on his first occupation, says that, despite all the difficulties, he knew straight away that the MST was the movement for him (*see* box 3.1).

Marluce Melo was not impressed by Rainha's efforts. 'He knew nothing of the history – or even of the geography – of the state. He negotiated deals with the authorities without knowing what he was doing.' She says that it was fortunate for the movement that Rainha was soon transferred to another region. 'After José Rainha left, two women took over – Vera, a black woman from Sergipe, and Birlé, a white woman from Rio Grande do Sul. They had a very difficult time. They had no resources and they had to face a lot of sexism. Even the trade unions were hostile in the beginning. But these young women listened and learnt. Although they are not given much credit for it today, they were the true founders of the MST in Pernambuco.' Within two years the MST set up its first settlement, which it called *Liberdade* (Freedom). Today Pernambuco is one of the states where the MST is growing most rapidly, with numerous occupations.

In Paraíba state, north of Pernambuco, the congress delegates returned eager to establish the MST but found that the CPT and CONTAG, which were already well established, wanted the MST to support their campaigns for better wages for rural workers rather than attempt to organise occupations. The church and union leaders argued that the MST *militantes*, who as usual had been drafted in from other regions, had to realise that it was impossible to organise occupations in this state because of the widespread violence. At first the MST leaders listened, but after a few years they decided to challenge the accepted wisdom and in April 1989 some 200 MST families carried out the first occupation. With considerable care, they chose as their target an estate that INCRA had already classified as 'unproductive'. Even so, the landowner hit back: gunmen, with their guns blazing, raided the camp in the middle of the night, burning down tents and beating up several MST leaders. An 18-month-old child was trampled to death. But what made the newspaper headlines on the following day was the landowner's claim to have found a machine gun among the *sem-terras'* belongings. The allegation was never proved, but several reliable witnesses have said that a few MST leaders carried weapons.

By the late 1980s, the MST began to feel confident that it was managing, despite all the difficulties, to get established in the northeast. In 1989, MST members from five northeastern states – Pernambuco, Paraíba, Sergipe, Alagoas and Bahia – and from Espírito Santo, set up a regional office in Palmares, a town in the heart of the canefields in the south of Pernambuco. Even so, there were still four states in the northeast where the MST was not yet established.

One of the states where the struggle was proving most difficult was Ceará, which lies to the north of Pernambuco. Periodically affected by severe droughts, it is one of the poorest states in Brazil. At the First Congress the activists concluded that it was not worth even trying to set up the movement there: not only were the drought victims so poor that they had little energy for anything except the struggle for survival, they were also deeply suspicious of outsiders, after decades of unfulfilled promises by politicians and government officials. However, at the beginning of 1989, the MST decided it was time to tackle Ceará. They sent in Fátima Ribeiro, the young woman from Espírito Santo. 'By then, I had gained a lot of experience in occupations', said Fátima. 'Even so, it was difficult. I was all alone in the beginning and I faced a lot of hostility.' Many rural workers, bitterly disappointed by the failure of the government's agrarian reform programme, did not believe that they would be able to construct the strong peasant movement that Fátima was proposing.[2] But with the help of Catholic Church activists and some sympathetic trade unionists, Fátima began to make progress. Together they cautiously built an organisation around the local practice of *mutirão*, a system of collective work in which peasant families help each other to clear and plant the land. In May 1989, 300 families carried out the first occupation, which they timed to coincide with the occupation of an INCRA building in the state capital. Partly because the government was already in the process of expropriating the estate, the *sem-terra* won this land in just nine days. It was an enormous boost to the movement.

On 1 September 1989, the MST undertook a more ambitious initiative: an occupation involving about 800 families.

> We knew it would be difficult', said Fátima, because the local UDR branch was furious about the publicity we were getting and wanted to teach us a lesson. I was travelling with another woman on a motorbike. The police stopped us. They had obviously been tipped off about the occupation but we pretended we didn't know anything about it. Perhaps because we were women, they let us go, but they took the precaution of puncturing our tyres. But we had to warn the others. So we hurried back along the road, with the metal rims of the wheels thumping on the ground. It ruined the bike, but we got there. We tipped off some of the lorries, so they immediately changed their target, going to another estate, as we'd planned to do if we had any problems. But we couldn't contact all the families, so we finished up carrying out two occupations!

Remarkably, in less than a year the MST won land in both areas and its presence in the state was guaranteed.

The rural workers from Maranhão state who took part in the First Congress were seasoned activists. Maranhão is a large state of semi-tropical forest and big farms, a buffer between the semi-arid northeast and the tropical rainforest of the Amazon basin. For many years this isolated state had been ignored by the authorities, so it had been heavily settled by fugitives – first runaway slaves and then the descendants of freed slaves. The origin of many villages is revealed by their suffix, *dos Pretos* (of the blacks). In the 1970s the isolation of the state began to be broken, as big companies from the south, encouraged by the military government's system of tax breaks, moved into the region. Many of the villagers who did not have titles for their plots were driven from their homes.

In scenes reminiscent of the Scottish highland clearances 200 years earlier, the new owners destroyed the villagers' crops, slaughtered their animals and burnt their homes. Among the many companies that installed cattle ranches or eucalyptus plantations were some of Brazil's household names: the airline company Varig, the consumer goods manufacturer Sharp, the high street supermarket Pão de Açúcar and the department store Mesbla. The state governor who welcomed the companies and turned a blind eye to the tactics they used was José Sarney, who was to become president of the new, democratic Brazil in 1985.

Box 3.1 *Paulo Venâncio de Mattos*

I was born in the *agreste*, the drylands, in the interior of Pernambuco. During the dreadful drought of 1970–71, when I was only 2 years old, things were so bad that my parents had to move to the Zona da Mata, where they started working on a sugar plantation. When I was 6, I started working with them. But just a year later my father died. And just a few days after that my mother married again. She had to, really. I don't blame her. It's very difficult for a woman with children to survive on her own. My stepfather was an ignorant, rough man. He beat me a lot. My mother wasn't strong enough to stop him. I knew that, if it went on, he'd finish up killing me. He was so violent. Even though I was only 7, I thought of killing him. I think I could have done it. But I realised it wouldn't solve anything. At my age, I couldn't support the family. So I decided to leave.

I was a child and all alone. I went north. I met a lot of criminals and drug addicts. But I never let myself be influenced by them. I don't really know why but all my life I've worked for my living. I've never been attracted to crime. I started working on sugar plantations. It's not so uncommon, to find 7- or 8-year-old children working all day to earn their keep. I used to sleep in a shed on the plantation. I had to start work in the mornings without breakfast because I didn't have the money to pay for it. It was only in the evenings, after I'd worked all day, that I could afford to buy food.

When I was 17 years old, I went south to Mato Grosso do Sul, to see if life was any better. I came back after two years or so. I was pretty disillusioned. I already wanted land. I saw it as the only way forward. But it was so difficult to get. So when the MST sent a group from Paraíba to set up the MST in Pernambuco, I leapt at the chance. I took part in the first occupation in July 1989. We made lots of mistakes. We just saw this empty land that looked fertile, and occupied it. We were 525 families. It was only afterwards that we discovered that it was a large reserve belonging to the army, navy and air force! Just imagine it! We stung the monster three times in the belly! Just two days later there were 2,000 soldiers there! I'd never seen so many soldiers! And we hadn't set up proper security, so we were taken by surprise. A lot of people were hurt. We were all evicted and we set up camp by a main road. In the end, the state government negotiated, giving us land in another area. Despite all our mistakes, it was a kind of victory.

I knew straightway that the MST was for me. I'd always thought you had to fight to get anything from the authorities. So two months after my first meeting with the MST, I decided to become a *militante*. It was the best decision I ever took. I started doing courses. I was always a rebel but it was only then that I started to realise what was wrong with society. I began to become politically aware. After just a single two-day course, I was sent to lead an occupation in the district of Escada, where the MST hadn't worked before. I was in charge of about 200 families. I didn't know how to talk to them. I kept getting tongue-tied. But I've learnt since then. Today I can talk in front of 5,000 people and I'm fine.

So I've been in the movement 11 years. I've done a lot of courses. I've learnt so much about how society works. I'm still studying a lot. And I must have taken part in about 300 occupations. Some were very violent. Sometimes the police arrived with cavalry, tear gas, riot shields, the lot. And they can be very savage, brutal. People aren't ready for this. When they first see a lorry-load of policemen arriving, they want to run. But you can work with them, prepare them, and then they can resist.

I've spent a lot of time in the camps. You get all kinds of people in them. Drug addicts, thieves, depressed people. It's the people from the shanty-towns who have the worst problems. The movement encourages them to join. It wants them to have a chance to rebuild their lives. You have to talk to people, help people understand why they're so poor, have such difficult lives. And once people understand that the reason why they haven't got a decent home and can't feed their children is because their boss takes all the money, then they start to feel angry, to hate the boss. And this helps to motivate them, helps to change them.

Many of the men who lost their livelihood went to join the gold rush in the Amazon. Others moved to shacks on the outskirts of Imperatriz and other towns in that part of the state. Violence followed them there. On 10 May 1985 a popular young black Catholic priest called Josimo Moraes Tavares, coordinator of the CPT, was shot dead as he climbed the steps to his office in Imperatriz. On the day of his funeral 150 landowners met in the town to found the local branch of the UDR and to warn the migrant families not to demand land. But the families were not intimidated. In June over 800 rural workers, desperate for land, went to a meeting called by INCRA. The institute promised to settle 110,000 families in the region within four years, but failed to do so. The violence carried on. On average one rural worker a fortnight was murdered in the state in 1985. It took a long struggle, with occupations, evictions, arrests, demonstrations and marches, for the MST to get established. But after five years it had conquered five settlements, one of which became a regional training centre.

The struggle was even more difficult in the remaining two states of the northeast – Piauí and Rio Grande do Norte. In Piauí the MST began cautiously. It collaborated with trade union activists, as they wrested control of the union body away from pro-government officials, and the CPT, which was helping peasant families to resist eviction. After four years the MST finally organised its first occupation. In the small state of Rio Grande do Norte the MST took even longer to get going. In 1998 the leadership once again sent in Fátima Ribeiro, who is still there today. 'It's proving even harder than in Ceará', she said. 'The police, the judiciary and the authorities all work together very closely. And they are very violent. They will arrest you on any pretext, however flimsy.' Rio Grande do Norte is being rapidly integrated into the world market. Big companies are irrigating the fertile soils of the *sertão*, producing tropical fruit for export. 'We are advancing', said Fátima. 'We have our camps and our settlements. But it is still difficult.'

The movement also reached central Brazil. Minas Gerais, a large state inland from Rio de Janeiro, was one of the first regions to be settled by the Portuguese. After gold had been discovered, hundreds of adventurers swarmed to the state, believing they had stumbled upon Eldorado, the mythical land of untold riches. A small group of noblemen and traders became extremely wealthy, building themselves elegant houses and endowing hundreds of churches with fine gold and silver carvings, statues and paintings. Old towns of cobbled streets and picturesque colonial architecture still nestle amongst the hills and valleys of this highland state. More recently, vast mineral deposits were discovered, which attracted modern mining companies and heavy industry. Despite this veneer of modernity, violence remained common in the rural areas, especially in the more impoverished north. In the 1970s the CPT and the Catholic Church's grassroots communities (CEBs) became strong in the countryside. They worked with many different kinds of rural workers – day workers, peasant farmers, squatters (*posseiros*), sharecroppers, tenant farmers and seasonal workers (*bóias frias*).

The people in these communities became curious about the MST, and they sent two delegates to the First Congress. The families began to talk about their experiences and became aware that, despite the different relationships they had with the landowners, they had something in common: they were all *sem-terra*. This became the identity that brought them together.[3] Even so, progress was slow. After three years of preparations, they finally organised their first occupation: on 12 February 1988 about 400 families occupied Fazenda Aruega, a farm of 638 hectares, of which less than half was properly registered. As happened so frequently elsewhere, the landowners responded by setting up a branch of the UDR. Although the authorities themselves had classified the farm as 'unproductive' and therefore eligible for expropriation, the state government sent 600 policemen to surround the camp and to stop supplies from reaching the families. The blockade lasted for four months and many families, worn down by hunger and isolation, gave up. In September rural workers occupied the INCRA offices in the state capital, Belo Horizonte, and that very same month the federal government expropriated the farm.

Further west, in the state of Rondônia in the Amazon basin, there was also interest in the new movement. In the 1970s the military had broken the age-old isolation of the Amazon by undertaking a massive road-building programme to open up the region to mineral companies, big cattle ranchers and settlers. One of the main access routes was a new highway, BR-364 (partly funded by the World Bank), which ran northwest from Mato Grosso into the newly created state of Rondônia. The military government decided that, while the east of the Amazon basin should be largely reserved for mining companies and big cattle rearers, Mato Grosso and Rondônia should receive the small farmers from the south of Brazil who had lost their land.

In 1970 only 100,000 people were living in Rondônia, many of them members of 'uncontacted' indigenous groups. By 1990 almost a million migrants had arrived, entire families with their possessions packed into buses and lorries and travelling for days along earth roads to reach their new homes in the rainforest. Dozens of land settlement projects were installed along the BR-364. Some of the migrants prospered, but many did not. The land was cheap, but the isolation, the lack of technical assistance, marketing difficulties and the sweltering heat created huge problems for the families. Hundreds of thousands succumbed to malaria, a disease unknown in the south.

Once the settlers had cleared the forest, the big landowners moved in. They offered paltry sums in compensation or even, waving fake documents and threatening violence, bullied them into leaving without paying them anything at all. Some found work on local ranches, where on numerous occasions the CPT found them held in debt bondage. Others went back south, joining MST occupations there. And yet others stayed to fight for another plot of land in Rondônia itself. Because the network of roads had made the region more accessible, loggers invaded the indigenous reserves, creating yet more conflict. Violence grew, involving Indians as well as landless families.

Desperate to publicise their struggle, some families decided to send a delegation to the MST's founding Congress in Curitiba in January 1985. On their return, the delegates worked with the CPT, the Catholic CEBs and the Lutheran Church to set up the MST. The situation was very tense. Six months after the MST Congress, gunmen from Catuva ranch in the district of Aripuanã, just north of the BR-364, ambushed and murdered a priest, Ezequiel Ramin, who had helped the small farmers. In revenge, over 100 farmers ambushed and killed the ranch owner and one of his hired guns.

The MST was not deterred by this violence. Experienced activists from other states introduced the MST way of fighting for land. They began to investigate carefully the legal status and level of productivity in a target estate, not rashly invading any area on the basis of rumours. They encouraged the men to take their families with them on the occupation and they trained the whole family in how to stand up to gunmen. But progress was slow. Some families went on invading land in a spontaneous and disorganised fashion. Others proved unreliable: they would attend preparatory meetings, but then fail to turn up for the occupation. On several occasions, the MST had to abandon occupations, simply because not enough families had shown up.

It was three years before the MST organised its first successful occupation. On 26 June 1989, 300 families occupied an estate of 8,000 hectares in Espigão do Oeste, in the east of the state. The families faced considerable violence – evictions, reoccupations, conflicts, gunfights and the arrest and torture of their leaders – but finally, after two years, they won the land and the MST was established in Rondônia.

Yet even this achievement brought problems. While the MST had been cautiously finding its way, relations with the Catholic Church and the local trade unions had been very good. Once they got established, however, conflicts emerged. The MST demanded both complete autonomy in the way it organised occupations and total dedication from its activists, many of whom were also members of the other organisations. Not surprisingly, the Catholic Church and the trade unions felt resentful, particularly as they had provided the MST with so much support. It took time to sort out these disagreements.

The New Constitution

While the MST was spreading across the country and the UDR was organising its own violent response, Brazil was beginning cautiously to dismantle the authoritarian legislation left by the military government and to construct a more democratic and equitable society. In 1988 Congress started to draw up a new constitution. Mass-based movements called for a whole series of reforms to be introduced. Despite the failure of Sarney's programme of agrarian reform, activists began to believe that there would be a second chance. Progressive organisations, including the MST and the CPT, collected over a million signatures for a petition calling for agrarian reform. Campaigners made important advances in many areas – personal freedom, labour legislation, rights of minorities, human rights, rights of children and others – but the hopes of the landless were once again dashed. Few Congress members supported the proposal and the petition was ignored. João Pedro Stédile commented ruefully: 'Practically the only social defeat that occurred in the new constitution concerned the agrarian question. Everywhere else there were advances.'[4]

The 1988 Constitution, still in force today, does not rule out agrarian reform. In Article 184, it gives the federal government the power to expropriate a large rural property, provided that it is not 'carrying out its social function' and that 'just compensation' is paid to the landowner. Remarkably, however, this article is less advanced than the provisions under the military regime's old Land Statute, which had permitted the government to expropriate *latifúndios*, defined either by size or by land use, without any reference to 'social function'. The introduction of this ambiguous concept created a loophole that, in a legal system notoriously biased in favour of property, greatly benefited estate owners. Under pressure from the landowners, INCRA defined 'social function' in a very lax way, so that almost entirely unproductive estates were saved from expropriation.

Stédile believes that the setback in the Constituent Assembly was largely due to the influence of the UDR over the state governments and the delegates in the assembly. This may certainly have played a part, but the mass-based movements also faced a more profound structural impediment. In the 1970s and 1980s the agricultural sector had continued to lose importance in the economy, as Brazil industrialised and urbanised. Brazil required an ever larger supply of food for its expanding cities, and export crops to earn the dollars needed to service the foreign debt, but the higher yields brought about by the 'green revolution' meant that a fairly small number of highly mechanised large farms could do most of the job (although peasant farmers remained an important, if neglected, supplier of some staple crops, such as cassava). The 'historical impasse' identified by Souza Martins as necessary for agrarian reform, which had already been weakened by the alliance between landowners and industrialists, was being further eroded by agricultural modernisation.[5] This may not have banished forever the possibility of agrarian reform but it has meant that a new alliance of political forces, constructed on a radically different foundation, will have to be developed.

At the time, however, the full implications of the reverse in the Constituent Assembly were not evident. Shrugging off the defeat, the MST pushed ahead with what it was best at: territorial expansion. It set its sights on the richest prize of all – the state of São Paulo. As well as being the country's industrial and financial heartland, the state capital – São Paulo – is also the largest city in South America, with a population of 17 million. It was the birthplace of both the trade union movement (CUT) and the new Workers' Party (PT), which had emerged from strikes in the late 1970s in the industrial belt around the city. São Paulo was also the centre of the progressive Catholic Church, under the leadership of the archbishop, Cardinal Paulo Evaristo Arns. The MST realised that they would only become a major player in the national political scene and gain visibility in the national media when they had conquered land in São Paulo state.

Among the rolling hills of the state's interior, agriculture had brought prosperity to scores of medium and large towns, which had benefited from the boom first in coffee, then cattle-rearing and oranges, and more recently sugarcane alcohol. Yet most rural families – small farmers, tenant farmers, sharecroppers, day workers and seasonal labourers – had remained excluded from the wealth they had helped to generate. As elsewhere in Brazil, landlessness had emerged as a serious problem. Rural workers had lost their jobs as farms became more mechanised. Family farmers had been forced off the land as banks foreclosed on their debts. Thousands of small farmers had also been left landless in the 1970s when several giant hydroelectric dams were built to meet the state's growing energy needs.

Gradually, from these localised struggles, rural workers began to forge a movement.[6] In February 1983 more than 1,200 rural workers from 34 rural districts squeezed into the parish hall of the church of Our Lady of the Graces in Andradina in the extreme west of the state of São Paulo for a meeting organised by the CPT. Everyone seemed to be talking about agrarian reform. All over the region rural workers had been holding semi-secret meetings in which they had excitedly discussed it. At gatherings of the CEBs, which always began with bible readings, people had quickly moved on to the subject that they really wanted to talk about: agrarian reform. What did it mean? Who would benefit? Whose land would be divided up? What would they do with the land? Would having land solve their problems?

Two hundred years earlier, tradesmen had met in secret in England to debate what had at the time seemed an equally outlandish idea: parliamentary reform, under the slogan 'one man, one vote'. Many were subsequently arrested, and even hanged for high treason, for these activities. In Brazil in the early 1980s the authorities regarded it as just as subversive for the poor to be demanding agrarian reform. If they reacted less repressively, it was because, at this stage, they did not see the landless movement as a serious threat. When in March 1983 4,000 people sent a petition to the minister for land affairs, General Danilo Venturini, in which they respectfully asked him for agrarian reform, he ignored it, apparently feeling that he was under no obligation to justify his position to the population. In other areas of the state (which is about the size of the United Kingdom) the CPT helped the rural workers to set up regional movements. Landless workers carried out their first occupations in São Paulo in 1983, occupying public land.

After the MST's First Congress, these movements, supported by a variety of different organisations, came together to form a state-wide body. Yet collaboration was not easy. From the beginning the CPT and the incipient MST supported the line established at the congress that 'occupation is the solution'. But the rural workers' union did not share their enthusiasm, preferring to negotiate with the government rather than join a mass movement that threatened a dangerous confrontation with the authorities, whom they still saw as all-powerful.[7] The collaboration between the organisations fizzled out and the MST began to develop independently. In 1987 it carried out its first occupation, invading a privately owned property of 17,000 hectares in the district of Promissão in the centre of the state. Three years later it struck lucky, discovering the vast region of Pontal do Paranapanema in the far west. More than 700 km from the capital, it contained scores of irregularly registered estates covering almost one million hectares. In July 1990 the MST carried out its first occupation in this area, initiating a period of rapid expansion.

It is remarkable that the MST was able to grow so quickly in São Paulo during the early 1990s because by then the political situation in the country had become very difficult for the movement. The Sarney government had ended in March 1990. During his administration the relentless pressure of the rural lobby had taken its toll on the ministry of agrarian reform. Ministers had come and gone and on 15 January 1989 the demoralised and debilitated ministry was finally abolished. Agrarian reform was entrusted to a mere department of the ministry of agriculture, a ministry increasingly geared to the interests of big landowners. During his five-year term of office, Sarney settled 84,852 families – just 6 per cent of the 1.4 million he had promised would benefit from his agrarian reform programme. His vacillating policy had meant that rural families conquered land only through confrontational tactics. Many of the families that got land were members of the MST and had won their plots by putting pressure on the government through occupations. By the end of 1989 the MST had set up a total of 730 settlements, covering 3.6 million hectares and home to over 80,000 families.

Rural violence had increased in many regions of the country: 585 people were murdered in land conflicts during the Sarney government. Only a handful of gunmen were arrested for these murders, and the death rate was actually higher than during the military regime, when 884 people had been killed over the 21-year period. The victims during the Sarney administration included the Amazon activist Chico Mendes, who, after successfully mobilising the rubber tappers to fight for their rights, was gunned down in December 1988.

In March 1990 Sarney handed over the presidency to Fernando Collor de Mello, who had defeated Lula in the 1989 presidential elections. Lula had held his most successful electoral rally outside the cities in the MST settlement at Encruzilhada Natalino in Rio Grande do Sul. About 40,000 people had attended, confident that Lula would win and that the new government would carry out a radical programme of agrarian reform. Lula's defeat crushed their hopes. 'We were badly hurt', said João Pedro Stédile. 'We were in our adolescence. We were still a weak movement and we felt as if we had been orphaned. We didn't have enough maturity to understand the historical moment we were living through.'[8]

That moment was to be extremely arduous for the MST. Collor had been governor of Alagoas, the small northeastern state where the MST was beginning gradually to make inroads into the *latifúndios*. He had presented himself during the campaign as the candidate of the *descamisados* (the shirtless), the poorest of the poor, but his commitment was really to the landowners and to the foreign investors who were demanding that Brazil open up its protected economy. Collor was aware that the market reforms he was advocating would create widespread economic hardship and he did not want the MST and other social movements feeding on this discontent. He cracked down with a vengeance on organised non-parliamentary opposition. It was the most difficult period the MST had yet encountered in its short history. 'Lula's defeat was a political defeat for mass movements in Brazil, after a ten-year period of growth', said Stédile.[9] The government treated the MST as a pariah, arresting its members and bugging its telephones. The new minister of agriculture, Antônio Cabrera, who was a São Paulo cattle rancher, refused even to talk to the *sem-terra*, although his ministry was supposedly in charge of the government's land policy. The federal police invaded MST offices.

Hounded by the authorities, the MST reacted aggressively. At the second National Congress in May 1990, it adopted two slogans: Agrarian Reform: By Law or By Force (Reforma Agrária: Na Lei ou Na Marra) and Occupy, Resist, Produce (Ocupar, Resistir, Produzir). Both reflected the movement's determination to push ahead, despite all the obstacles, and to achieve reform through its own efforts, even if it meant breaking the law. At the same time, the movement decided that it could no longer rely on financial assistance from the authorities for its settlements. Hoping to set up a system by which the movement could generate its own 'primitive accumulation', the leaders told the settlements to set up large Cuban-style collective farms. As will be discussed in more detail in chapter 5, this policy ended in disaster.

Pontal de Paranapanema

It was precisely at this difficult moment that the MST began to win large tracts of land in São Paulo and to gain a national profile. On 14 July 1990 some 400 families occupied Fazenda Nova Pontal in the Pontal de Paranapanema region. This area, which lies in the extreme west of the state of São Paulo, had once been home to the Kaingang and Guarani-Kaiowa Indians. When the Portuguese arrived in the sixteenth century, it was covered in dense vegetation, part of the Atlantic Forest that stretched from the coast right across southern Brazil. This land belonged to the state but during the early decades of the twentieth century bogus landowners, presenting fraudulent land titles, had laid claim to large chunks of it. This crime was known as *grilagem*, as the forgers used to shut the documents in drawers with *grilos* (crickets): once the insects had died, they gave out a toxic substance that stained the papers, making them look old.[10] It has been widely practised all over Brazil, but nowhere so extensively as in the Pontal, where it became the rule.

The historian P. Monbeig, who has carried out a detailed study of the occupation of the Pontal, was taken aback by the meticulous care the forgers took:

> The fakers had diabolical imagination and skill: they obtained crested paper with the Imperial arms, imitated old handwriting, affixed old stamps, deliberately yellowed their document, tore out pages from registry office books. They transplanted 20- or 30-year-old coffee trees to the forest clearings they were claiming. They transferred parts of old buildings to their houses, filling them with antique furniture to create the right atmosphere and make it seem as if the land had been occupied for many years.[11]

From the 1940s onwards, new landowners arrived, buying up estates from *grileiros* and clearing the land for cattle rearing. Some MST activists came to the region with their parents, hired to clear the land. Miriam Farias de Oliveira (*see box 3.2*) remembers what it was like. 'My mother used to cook for over a hundred men, all employed by the landowner to clear the forest. When we first arrived, it was slow work because there were no electric saws. It took several hours for two or three men with axes to fell a big tree.' Even so, the landowners devastated huge areas, with no regard for the environment. Perhaps the worst damage of all occurred in August 1973, when the owner of Fazenda Alcidia sent planes to spray a powerful defoliant, containing agent orange left over from the Vietnam War, on 5,000 hectares of forest. 'Witnesses say the effect was terrible. As well as destroying all the vegetation, which it did in about five hours, it caused the death of dozens of birds, grasshoppers, wild ducks, and even deer, tapirs, small jaguars, capybaras and monkeys. Carried by the wind, the herbicide affected fields of rice, groundnuts, cotton, sugar-cane and beans.'[12]

Zander Navarro, lecturer in sociology at the Federal University of Rio Grande do Sul, says that the Pontal de Paranapanema was a godsend for the MST. 'Everyone knew that the land there had been illegally occupied', he said. 'The MST knew it could organise occupations and conquer land without being accused of invading private property.' In 1990 and 1991 the MST organised scores of occupations. Hundreds of hastily recruited families were involved, in line with the movement's recommendation at the time to carry out 'mass occupations'. The *sem-terra* had the support of individual priests, nuns and lay workers, but not of the Catholic Church as an institution because the local bishop – Dom Antônio Agostinho Marochi, bishop of Presidente Prudente – was hostile to the movement; he even went as far as forbidding priests to say mass at MST camps and settlement. Zelitro Luz da Silva, a 38-year-old MST activist recruited into the movement at this time, commented: 'The MST fitted me, and hundreds like me, as snugly as a glove. Most of us had become politically aware through the Church and then felt frustrated at its caution. We joined the movement in our hordes. And we wanted to occupy land right away. "Let's go. Let's go", we said.'

Zander Navarro said the MST's success in organising occupations was crucially important. 'The occupations were happening within the state, so the powerful São Paulo press had to pay attention', he said. 'This meant that Brasília also had to take notice. João Pedro Stédile and José Rainha became national figures. Globo television even created a soap opera with a *sem-terra* woman as a central character.' Navarro believes that, if it had not been for this publicity, the movement might have run aground, for elsewhere in the country it was reeling from the problems created by the collectivisation of production. 'The MST was lucky', he said. 'The actions in the Pontal gave the movement enormous visibility, which helped it expand into the rest of Brazil.'

However, the rapid expansion also created problems. Because the movement had few experienced leaders, it started to take short cuts, sending keen but unprepared youngsters – *militantes*, as it called them – to organise the 'mass occupations', which often involved hundreds of people. Some families began to feel alienated, as if they were not full members of the movement. 'The *militante* became the commander, who was loved by some and hated by others', wrote Bernardo Mançano Fernandes. 'This paradoxical status, which contradicted the egalitarian aims of the movement, meant that many rural workers did not gain the political awareness that full participation in the movement required.'[13]

Several of the occupations in the Pontal suffered problems. In 1991 a group of families left an occupation, saying that their views had not been taken into consideration. The national leadership became concerned and in 1991 sent José Rainha down to São Paulo from the northeast. 'I was only supposed to go for a short period but I soon realised that the inexperienced leaders were making mistakes', he said. 'It was clear that we had to build the movement more slowly, giving the people time to participate properly. I contacted the national leadership and asked to be allowed to stay longer.' Rainha adopted a different approach from the early leaders. 'He was much less confrontational', said Alcides Gomes da Silva, a veteran activist. 'He made much more of an attempt to win people over to our side. He even got some mayors supporting us.' Rainha also trained new members. 'It was the easiest place in

Box 3.2 *Miriam Farias de Oliveira*

I'm 47 years old. I was born in Paraíba, but my parents migrated to São Paulo when I was a tiny baby. I had nine brothers and sisters. My parents thought we'd all have a chance of a better life down south. We went to Pontal de Paranapanema, because the whole region was being opened up at the time. A lot of land was being cleared and there was a lot of work. Sometimes my parents worked as day labourers, picking cotton. Sometimes they worked as sharecroppers, clearing land and planting it with pasture for the cattle-owner. Sometimes he'd move them off the land before they'd even had time to reap their first crop! For a while my parents worked for a ranch that was clearing a huge area of forest for cattle. My father worked with a hundred other men, cutting down giant trees with axes.

Then we moved to the town of Teodoro Sampaio. At that time it was still very small, with wooden shacks, only a few brick houses. My father worked on a coffee plantation. And we kids would help him pick the coffee. But by then my father was losing his sight. Eventually he went completely blind with glaucoma and had to go to the city of São Paulo to be treated. So my mother was left by herself with all those children. She took in washing, and my sister, who was 12, and me, who was 10, we worked as maids. Money was very short. I remember it was such a treat when my mother bought us sweets.

When I was 18 years old, I and a younger sister, who was 16, decided to move to São Paulo to work as maids. It was a big adventure. We travelled by train, arriving on Christmas Day. But it wasn't as we expected. The family I lived with treated me like a slave. I had to cook and look after the children, as well as doing the cleaning. I'd hoped to study but there wasn't time. I'd often still be washing up at midnight. They didn't even let me have weekends off. Just Sundays now and again. I'd wanted to send money to my mother but they paid me so little that I hardly ever had any left. I used to cry a lot, by myself in my room. And pray a lot. I stuck it out for 14 years, from 1970 to 1984. It got better when my parents arrived. They helped me. I got involved in the Catholic Church. I was active in the young people's group. We put on plays and worked in the shanty-towns. I enjoyed that.

Then I got married. Straightaway, we went off to Acre in the Amazon. My husband's two brothers already had land there. It was a hard life but I loved it! Our settlement was surrounded by virgin forest. We had monkeys running around in the trees behind our house. There were turtles in the river. We were 23 kilometres from the nearest town. I got a little school built and started teaching the children in the region. Some came from the families of settlers, like us. They were mainly of European descent. Others were dark-eyed and brown-skinned, Indian looking, the children of rubber-tappers. I didn't get paid but I loved it. My daughter was born in the hospital in the nearest town. She was only a few days old when I was back in the classroom, with her sleeping in a basket.

My husband didn't like it there. He'd been brought up in the city and wasn't used to working the land. He started to drink a lot so we went back to Teodoro Sampaio, in 1986. I had my son there. But my husband went on drinking. He wasn't violent but he became a pitiful figure. I had to leave him. I got odd jobs and then, when my son got hepatitis, I had to stay at home to look after him. So I started cooking food – lasagne, crisps, pies and so on – and selling them in the town. I still do that today, as much as I can.

I joined the MST in 1991. José Rainha and other *militantes* came to Teodoro Sampaio. I was still involved in the Catholic Church, particularly the CPT. And they were helping the MST. I supported the movement from the beginning, but I didn't take part in the occupations at first. My children were so small. I was afraid they'd be hurt. But in 1995 I started to participate. I was there when a thousand families occupied Santa Rita, but I didn't live in the camp. I kept my house in Teodoro Sampaio because my children were at school there. The climate was getting tense. The landowners had set up a UDR branch. It employed gunmen and they were very violent.

In 1997 we all decided to take a look at another estate, São Domingos. We'd occupied it once and then withdrawn. We'd planted crops while we were there and we wanted to go in a big group to harvest them. But we weren't planning to do it that time. Just take a look. See if there were gunmen there. We were about a thousand people. I was near the front, with three girl friends. We were talking and laughing. No idea of any risk. Then we heard shots. I thought it was fireworks. I stayed standing up. Then someone shouted for me to lie down. I heard a 'zoom' and then suddenly I realised that I'd been shot. I kept thinking, 'I can't die, my children are so young, there are so many things I want to do'. My left side was paralysed. Some men carried me to the road. Eight of us had been hit.

They took me first to the hospital in Teodoro Sampaio and then moved me to Presidente Prudente, as the doctors said I needed better equipment. I could only speak with one side of my mouth but I kept saying in interviews that I wasn't going to be intimidated, that I was going to stay in the movement. A few days later the MST organised 70 buses from São Paulo. About 3,500 people came. They occupied São Domingos and harvested the crop. The police were there but they couldn't do anything to stop them.

I was in hospital for 30 days. The first night I was there, the doctor came and asked me if I was strong enough to see someone. It was Senator Eduardo Suplicy. I'd always adored him. I was so excited! And then two days later, Lula [the president of the Workers' Party] visited me. I joked with him. 'So, Lula, I had to get shot to meet you'. A nurse secretly brought in a mobile phone from a journalist who wanted to interview me. It rang but I didn't know what to do with it. I'd never seen one before!

I slowly got better, though I'll never fully recover. I'm more involved in the movement than ever before. It's an organisation that I can identify with. It's got my face, as we say. It's a way of not being beaten down, of doing something to end the poverty and exploitation. If I'd met the movement sooner, before I was married, I'd have worked for it night and day. I don't think I even would have had children! I know it's not perfect. There's *machismo*, though that's often the fault of the women too, who don't let their daughters have the same freedom as their sons. I know it's difficult to change your culture. My father was very severe, authoritarian. My children say that I'm the same, that I shout at them too much. But I'm learning to be different. My children are helping me.

---

the world to organise occupations', Rainha said. 'Everyone knew that the *grileiros* didn't own the land. But first we had to make sure that the families understood the aims of the movement and supported them.'

Instead of tackling the authorities head on, Rainha preferred to wear them down through attrition, using against the government a tactic that it often employed against the movement. It worked particularly well with Fazenda São Bento, an estate claimed by one of the famous *grileiros* in the region, Antônio Sandoval Neto, who was also the mayor of the largest town, Presidente Prudente. 'We didn't resist eviction', said Zelitro. 'We let the police evict us from Fazenda São Bento 23 times. And each time we reoccupied, after the police had left and the eviction order had expired. It was a way of putting on pressure, without involving the families in a dangerous confrontation. On one occasion, on 28 February 1993, we brought 1,700 families together and organised a giant occupation of Fazenda São Bento. We called the action União da Vitória (Victory Union). We all went on to the estate to farm but we stayed living in tents outside, along an abandoned railway line.' The *sem-terra* brought in 12 tractors and planted 200 hectares with maize, cassava and beans. The landowner was angry but he didn't really know what to do. Each time he sent in gunmen to evict the families they found them living quite legally on the railway track, beyond his reach. In February 1994, the government expropriated the estate, paying a large sum in compensation to the landowner. 'Because Fazenda São Bento was owned by a famous *grileiro*, it was a particularly important victory', said Zelitro. 'It encouraged other families to join the movement, creating a kind of domino effect, which was what we'd planned from the beginning.' Rainha established himself as the main MST leader in the region, a position he still enjoys today.

In December 1992, after only two and a half years in power, Collor resigned, just a few minutes before Congress would have impeached him for corruption. Collor was succeeded by his vice-president, Itamar Franco, who proved to be a surprisingly tolerant and progressive president. By the time Franco left office in December 1994, the MST was well established in the Pontal and about 6,000 families had been settled on the land. Yet the MST's victory was not a defeat for the *grileiros*. The government could have expropriated the land for free, for the alleged landowners did not have valid land titles – indeed, many *sem-terra* believed that the *grileiros* should have paid the government compensation for the damage they had done to the environment – but instead the authorities went through the courts and ended up paying hefty compensation. It was yet another demonstration of the continuing political power of the landowning class, despite the decline of agriculture in the national economy. One landowner confessed to a local newspaper that he had been given even more than he had asked for. 'It was enough money for me to buy a good estate in Mato Grosso, far better than the one I had in São Paulo', he said.[14]

In this way, the MST spread throughout Brazil, organising, occupying and marching. It was building on the foundations laid by the CPT and other local popular organisations, especially the rural unions, but it was also creating something new – a movement led by the rural workers themselves. It was making mistakes, but also had the humility to learn from these mistakes. In the wake of the MST, like a spectre at the feast, came the UDR, and with it repression, arrests, murders, evictions and torture – the same tactics that had been used against generations of Brazilians who had defied the powerful land barons of their days.

As the MST spread it began to put down roots and win friends – a process that has been called 'territorialisation'[15] by Bernardo Mançano. We realised what this 'territorialisation' meant when we went by car to the Pontal de Tigre settlement, which is about an hour's drive from Querência do Norte in the north of the state of Paraná. The settlers there have built themselves some of the finest houses we saw on an MST settlement. As we sat drinking coffee in the sitting room of a very pleasant, open plan bungalow, the owner, Agostinho Anghinoni, told us that they had occupied the land in June 1988, choosing the farm, owned by Grupo Atlas, because it was poorly managed and provided few jobs, with just five families looking after the 3,500 head of cattle that roamed over 10,500 hectares. The first years, he said, were very difficult. 'We wanted to get the public on our side in our campaign to get the land expropriated', he said 'so we held our first march to Querência do Norte in, I think, November 1988. The tradesmen were so scared they closed their shops. They really were frightened that this "bunch of troublemakers", as they called us, would ransack their shops.'

The 336 families camped on the farm for eight years before finally winning the land in 1996. 'Once or twice I almost gave up', said Agostinho. 'We had so few resources. INCRA sent us a food parcel once every three months, and MST settlements sent us what they could, but it was tough.' Since conquering the land, the families have made remarkable progress. Agostinho has formed a small collective with two of his brothers. They produce almost all of their own food, cultivating rice, beans, manioc, lettuce and tomatoes, and rearing pigs and chicken. Their cash comes from two products: irrigated rice ('we use this money to develop the farm') and a herd of 90 dairy cattle ('it gives us enough income, just, for our day-to-day expenses').

Agostinho said that people gradually changed their attitude towards the MST. 'People in the shops and the bars became happy to see our caps and our t-shirts. A lot of people didn't agree with our politics, but they realised that we were bringing economic development to the region. Today the taxes we pay each year are worth about R$150 [about US$100] for every one of the 10,000 inhabitants. And that's not counting the benefits we bring to tradesmen. And this is happening wherever there are MST settlements.' But the attitude of the landowners did not change. 'They have remained as hostile as ever, and they have their allies. There are still some supermarkets which refuse to buy any of our produce.'

Agostinho's family has suffered more than most from the animosity of the landowners. On 29 March 1999, another of the Anghinoni brothers – 31-year-old Eduardo, who has no links with the MST – was paying a visit to Pontal do Tigre. He was in the house of his brother, Celso, who at that time was the MST's coordinator for the region. Eduardo was sitting on the sofa, watching television with Celso's two children, 12-year-old Fernando and 7-year-old Tassiane. Suddenly the glass in the sitting room window shattered and five shots were fired, at point blank range, at Eduardo. The MST had known for some time that Celso's name was on a UDR death list, and the gunmen must have mistaken Eduardo for his brother. Eduardo died on his way to hospital. The murder caused outrage in the region, and the police arrested three known gunmen who had been seen in the neighbourhood that evening. But Ricardo Baggio, a lawyer who often works for the UDR, took on the men's defence, and on 4 May 1999 the police released them. Stricken with remorse at his brother's death, Celso resigned from his leadership post. At the time of our visit, almost a year later, Agostinho said that Celso was still profoundly depressed.

A small incident confirmed the prejudice harboured by the landowners against the MST. As we were chatting to Agostinho, the third brother in the collective suddenly arrived in the house. He had cut off the index finger of his right hand while working with one of the farm machines. We were the only people with a car so we offered to take him to hospital in Querência do Norte, but we were driving a 12-year-old VW Beetle, which travelled slowly over the rough road. We saw a powerful pick-up van, parked by the side of the road, and we stopped to ask them to take the brother to hospital. The driver, evidently a landowner, took one look at the MST cap on the injured man's head, and drove off hurriedly, without a word.

The MST faced particularly fierce opposition in two states – Paraná, the soya-growing state south of São Paulo, where Agostinho and his brother live, and Pará in the east of the Amazon basin. In both states the reactionary and violent landowners have committed fearful human rights abuses, yet, because of their political power within the state and federal governments, their crimes have gone unpunished. Because of the importance of these states in the MST's history, we will devote a chapter to each of them in Part 3, but first we shall look in some detail at the MST's way of working.

PART TWO

The MST's aim is not just to conquer land for the landless but to create communities where the formerly excluded rural workers become active, socially engaged citizens who, instead of being marginalised, enjoy decent levels of education, health care and leisure. No other peasant movement in Brazil has ever viewed the struggle for land in quite such terms, which means that the *sem-terra* are often stepping, figuratively as well as literally, on to land where no one has trod before. In this journey of exploration the *sem-terra* have often stumbled, at times heavily, but they have also made great progress, developing exciting, innovative solutions to their problems. The three chapters in this section look in some detail at this voyage.

Chapter 4 deals with the first stage – the initial occupation of the land. Over the years the MST has accumulated a vast experience in this area, carrying out tens of thousands of occupations. It is scarcely surprising perhaps that it has developed a distinct methodology, with a clear MST identity. While it may be true, as MST leaders repeatedly say, that there is no blueprint for an occupation, as regional leaders have to adapt their tactics to the local conditions, it is also the case that many of the elements we describe in our first-hand account would be found in any occupation organised by the MST in any part of the country.

Chapter 5 looks at the final stage of the journey, when the families conquer the land and establish their own settlements. Paradoxically, it is here at the end of their journey that the MST has encountered its most serious problems. While MST leaders always knew that they faced fearsome odds in their struggle to win the land, many believed ingenuously that the battle was won once the land was conquered. Nothing could have been further from the truth. This chapter traces their painful experience as they discovered that they could not successfully copy the methods of the big farmers, reliant on costly and environmentally harmful inputs, but had to create their own way of farming, far more closely linked to older, more environmentally friendly, peasant practices.

Chapter 6 looks at MST schools. Education has always played a key role in MST ideology, as it is seen as the key to the mental liberation of those who have lived for so many years in subjugation to the rich and powerful. From the earliest days of the movement, *sem-terra* families were clear that they wanted to set up independent, free-thinking schools, far different from the mediocre schools found in most of rural Brazil, where pupils are taught to be subservient to the authorities and to the landowners. The MST does not wait until the families have conquered the land but sets up schools straightaway in the camps, sometimes building an improvised hut for the school on the day after the occupation.

2. MST flag is raised at Pasmado occupation (*Jaqueline Maia*)

CHAPTER 4

The Occupation

However much one cursed at the time, one realised afterwards that one had been in contact with something strange and valuable, one had been in a community where hope was more normal than apathy or cynicism, where the word 'comrade' stood for comradeship and not, as in most countries, for humbug, one had breathed the air of equality.

> George Orwell, writing about his time with workers' militias during the Spanish Civil War, *Homage to Catalonia*[1]

For the MST the act of occupying land – which they call 'cutting the wire' – is the cornerstone of their movement. It is the baptism of fire for the militant, an essential part of their identity. It plays a key role in the *mística*, the moment of collective theatre and mythmaking that kicks off all MST events. MST leader João Pedro Stédile recognises that it is a huge step for a poor rural family to take part in an occupation. 'The vehemence of this action means that no one can sit on the fence', he says. 'You have to have a position, either in favour or against'.[2] Another MST leader, Jaime Amorim, says it is the decision to risk all in a dangerous and arduous land occupation that sparks off a process of change in the individual: 'rural workers learn more on the day of the occupation than during a whole lifetime'.[3]

'When the pliers cut the wire and it snaps like the string in a violin and the fence tumbles down, the *sem-terra* lose their innocence', says Pedro Tierra, the MST poet.[4] Until that moment, explains Roseli Salete Caldart in her book on MST pedagogy, 'they have been trained always to obey, to obey the landowner, the priest, the political boss. They learnt this from their families and from the short period they spent in school'.[5] Taking their life in their own hands, she says, they gain political awareness. They realise that they will never achieve what they want, if they restrict their demands to what the establishment sees as acceptable. And they learn to impose their own agenda. 'We have always been told that agrarian reform is a good idea in principle, but the *conjuntura*, or present moment, isn't right', said Mônica, a woman leader from the northeast. 'Well, we make the *conjuntura* right.' In other words, they become subjects of their own history. And, in taking this step, they turn their world upside down. They start to realise that the established values are not immutable. As the historian Christopher Hill has pointed out: 'Upside down is after all a relative concept. The assumption that it means the wrong way up is itself an expression of the view from the top.'[6] The act of occupation becomes the fuse for a profound process of personal and political transformation.

The method that the MST has found for sparking off change recalls a phenomenon observed by Frantz Fanon in his book *The Wretched of the Earth*. Published in 1962, Fanon's book describes how the wars of liberation in Africa set in motion a process of self-liberation among the colonised population. Fanon believed, controversially, that involvement in violence acted as a catalyst for change. 'At the level of individuals, violence is a cleansing force', he wrote. 'It frees the native from his inferiority complex and from his despair and inaction; it makes him fearless and restores his self-respect.'[7] The MST activists see it rather differently. 'Land that we conquer through struggle is land that we win without the help of anyone', says Darci Maschio. 'We don't have to go down on our knees to give thanks to anyone. This allows us to go on to fight for other things.'[8] He says that government authorities tried hard to stop the families believing that they had rights. 'In the beginning', he said, 'the authorities made a point of saying to us "you're here to beg for land, aren't you, because no-one here is going to demand anything. You don't have that right". But we do have the right, a right constructed through struggle.'[9] So the MST does not believe it is violence that initiates the process of change, but rather the development of the collective capacity to stand up to their exploiters. 'Our unity is our strength', the activists say.

The MST says it has never won a single hectare of land without first carrying out an occupation. This has had a profound impact. 'I tell everyone who hasn't got land to do what we did, join the MST', said Zezilda Casamir, a settler from Rio Grande do Sul. 'But the MST won't give you land. You'll have to win it for yourself'. 'We know we will get nowhere without organisation and mobilisation', said Vilmar Martins da Silva, now a member of the MST's national executive. Stédile says that the act of occupation is 'the organisational matrix of the movement, in that it was around this concept that the organisation was built'.[10] In other words, he believes that the MST has to conquer every right that it demands at every stage of the struggle; nothing is bequeathed.

In 1996, shortly before his death, the educationalist Paulo Freire, who was a fervent supporter of the MST, recalled a visit he had made to an MST settlement. 'I shall never forget a beautiful speech from a literacy worker, a former landless worker, who was living in an enormous settlement in Rio Grande do Sul. "We managed through our work and our struggle to cut the barbed wire of the *latifúndio*, the big estate, and we entered it", he said. "But when we got there we discovered that there was more barbed wire, like the barbed wire of our ignorance. I realised that the more ignorant we were, the more innocent we were of the ways of the world, the better it was for the landowners, and the more knowledgeable we got, the more frightened the landowners became." As he was speaking, I realised what real agrarian reform was about'.[11] 'We have three fences to cut down', says Stédile. 'They are the fence of the big estate, the fence of ignorance and the fence of capital'.[12]

Frente de Massa

Because of the key importance of the occupation in the MST's methodology, the movement has always attributed enormous importance to the work carried out by the *frente de massa*, the vanguard of militants sent into a new region to contact landless families and to recruit them for an occupation. Local people, who know the geography of the region and its customs, do this work best. So, as the MST moves into a new region, it is common to find that this dangerous and demanding work is being largely carried out by recent recruits. It is their initiation rite, which helps them identify with the movement and be assimilated into it.

At times, the movement expands with lightning speed, with rural workers deciding to join after the very first meeting. 'My father was a migrant worker', said 27-year-old Maria José Bezerra from a settlement at Promissão in São Paulo state.

> He was always talking about agrarian reform. He spent his life travelling the country, working on different farms and always on the lookout for a plot of land. He picked oranges. He cut sugarcane. He looked after cattle. Always looking for land, but without money to buy a plot. We all travelled around with him, even when we were very young. We became a real family of migrants! But once he didn't take us with him. He went all the way up north to Rondônia in the Amazon basin, with three brothers and a brother-in-law. It was 1985, and the Sarney government was promising land. But they all came back after 15 days. They realised that the colonisation projects were not going to succeed. The families up there were starved of funds and very isolated, with no proper roads, schools or health posts. They couldn't even sell the crops they'd managed to produce. My father became very depressed. But just at that time the MST arrived in our region, in the interior of São Paulo state. My father didn't hesitate. He joined the movement straightaway and even helped to organise the first occupation.

Many members of Maria José's extended family won land through the MST. 'My father finally got what he wanted. But he still jokes with his brother from time to time: "We've been here for so long. Isn't it time we moved on?" '

On other occasions, the families hear about the MST through television. Even though coverage of the MST in the media is often hostile, people are able to extract the information they need. Edson Ferreira da Silva, 22 years old, chatted about his life, as he cleaned the red motorbike he uses to travel around the state of Pernambuco in the northeast.

> I spent two years in São Paulo, but I hated the noise and the violence. I decided to come back to Pernambuco after I'd seen a man killed in a robbery. I'd only been back in Caruaru for eight days when I saw a report on television about the MST. I didn't say anything to my family but borrowed a bike and cycled 130 km to visit their camp. It

took me 12 hours. The MST asked me if I drank or used drugs, and when I said I didn't, they let me stay. But after a day I left, as I knew my family would be worried. But soon afterwards I went to another camp and this time I stayed. Now I know I'm going to stay in the movement until I die. I like the way the MST works with people. And I like seeing people get out of poverty. It gives me a real kick.

Maria Sebastião da Silva, 53 years old, from Pernambuco, also first heard about the MST through television. She had had a hard life, with eight of her 14 children dying from diarrhoea in the *sertão*.

We moved to the town of Marajá. But everything was difficult. My husband started drinking more and the children missed the countryside, particularly the food. I was interested in the MST from the very first time I heard about them on TV. Then they set up a camp not far from where we were living. I decided to have a look. My daughter was the only one of my children who would go with me. She was always more courageous than the boys. People were talking about the MST at the bus stop, some in favour and some against. I kept quiet. When we passed the camp, I didn't dare get off, for what people would think. So we went on to the next stop and walked back. As soon as I saw the little tents, my heart leapt. I knew I was going to like it and I did. Several of my sons joined us later. And they got land too.

Very often the families agree to go on an occupation without even knowing where they are going. Clarinda Ernestina da Santa, 55 years old, now settled on land in São Paulo state, talked as she stirred milk in a giant cauldron, preparing *doce de leite*, a delicious kind of fudge, to sell in the MST shop.

I was born in the countryside, but I spent 17 years in the city of São Paulo, with my husband. We had five children. My husband worked as a gardener and I got cleaning jobs, but we never had enough money. I decided to move with my children to the town of Campinas, where life was a bit cheaper. The MST came to my neighbourhood. I liked what they were saying, so I decided to go on the occupation, with the children. I left at 8 o'clock one morning in a bus the MST had hired. We travelled all day. Very few of us on the bus knew where we were going, but we didn't care. We laughed a lot and sang. And the following night we occupied this land.'

The Story of an Occupation

We decided that it was time we experienced an occupation. We made contact with the MST office for the Zona da Mata, a region of large, semi-feudal sugar plantations in Pernambuco. For several years this region has been in crisis. Many of the sugar mills have gone bankrupt, unable to compete with the more mechanised and productive sugar plantations in São Paulo. In the past the federal government, which needed the political support of the plantation owners, bailed out their mills. But today the government has ended the subsidies and is encouraging the owners either to mechanise their sugar production or to move into new economic activities, such as tropical fruit cultivation or tourism. This modernisation has spelt disaster for the former workers on the sugar plantations. They have been sacked from the mills and turned off the plantations where their families have lived for decades. They have lost their *sítios*, the plots of land where they used to cultivate their food. The social discontent makes the Zona da Mata fertile ground for MST recruitment.

We decided to go to an area of the Zona da Mata where the MST had not been active before. It would be interesting, we thought, to see how they were received by the local population. So in December 1999 we arrived in the small town of Igarassu, part of the disorderly periphery around the city of Recife. MST activists had arrived only a couple of weeks earlier. In what was clearly an ambitious undertaking, they had decided to recruit both in the rural areas, visiting isolated hamlets scattered among the sugar plantations, and in the bustling, crime-ridden shanty-towns around Recife. We discovered that with great daring they were planning on the following Sunday, as part of a wave of occupations throughout the northeast, to occupy an estate belonging to the most powerful landowner in the region – Jorge Petribu. 'They won't be expecting us to take them on so soon', explained one activist.

The activists were finding it easier to recruit in the rural areas, where there is less crime, violence and alcoholism, so for the last few days before the occupation, the activists concentrated their activities there. We travelled around with them, often on the back of a motorbike. It was the beginning of the sugar harvest, which lasts from December to March. As we sped along the rough roads between the villages, we watched the rural labourers as they set fire to the sugarcane fields to burn the young vegetation and then, wielding sharp machetes, cut down the thick, charred stems that contain the juice. After a day's work, men, women and children came out of the fields, blackened all over from the soot. It was a scene that had changed little over the last 400 years. Cutting cane is dangerous work, with people regularly injuring themselves and being bitten by snakes. But the talk in the villages was not about this age-old problem, but about the growing unemployment and the loss of the *sítios*. There was real hunger in the hot dusty villages of wattle-and-daub huts.

Our first stop was Alto do Céu (Top of the Sky), a village of huts located, predictably enough, on the top of a steep hill. The single asphalted road up to the village led into the central square, overlooked by the Catholic church, the largest building in the village, where the meeting was to be held. About 30 villagers, several of them women holding babies, were waiting. There were fewer people than the MST leaders had been expecting and we soon found out that armed security guards from the Petribu sugar plantation had been in the village earlier that day, threatening reprisals if people listened to the MST's 'agitation'. It was hot and we borrowed red MST caps, printed with the MST flag, to keep off the sun. MST leaders are trained in communication skills and the most experienced of the activists, 30-year-old Cícero Onório Alves, could weave magic with words. 'I was once a *sem-terra*, a landless worker, like you', he told the group. 'But we occupied a plantation. We were evicted four or five times, violently, by gunmen. But we reoccupied, and in the end we won. Today we're producing rice, beans, cassava, pumpkin, passion fruit and other crops on the land we won. The agrarian reform train is passing by your village this week. It only comes once. If you miss it, you're robbing your children of a future, of a life where you can be people, not slaves.'

Cícero's rhetorical skills held the people enthralled, and more villagers crossed the square to listen to him. It was not just his words but the passion he put into them. He was offering them not just an end to starvation, but a new world, Utopia. Listening to him, we recalled the tradition of messianic movements in the northeast, with its powerful leaders, like the 'prophet' Antônio Conselheiro, an itinerant religious preacher who set up a free community in the interior of Bahia in the late nineteenth century, and our companion's namesake, Padre Cícero, a mystical priest, eventually excommunicated by the Catholic Church, who had a huge following in the northeast in the early decades of the twentieth century. The difference was that, unlike the messianic leaders, this Cícero was not telling the people that they would reach the promised land by blindly following him or any other MST leader; instead, they would have to conquer it themselves, by overcoming their fear, working together, and standing on their own feet.

'When we occupied the land', said Cícero, 'we were afraid, just like you are today. But we found that, compared with us, the enemy is just an ant. Let me tell you a story. There was a man who decided to hunt in the forest. But, even before he left, he was frightened. On the way he saw something move among the trees. It was only a guinea pig, but he was afraid. In his mind it was a wolf, and he didn't dare go on. As he made his way back home, it turned in his imagination into a werewolf, and he became even more frightened. He decided never to go hunting again. So because of a guinea pig, his family went hungry.'

After cheers, Cícero continued. 'But there's no need to be frightened. We're going with people from many other villages – from Botafogo, Treinadeira, Cruz de Rebouças, Ilha do Rato. Courageous, fighting people, like you. The MST is one, big united family and we work together. And there won't just be the occupation here. There's going to be 26 other occupations in the Zona da Mata. All happening early Sunday morning. We'll be setting up 26 camps.' (applause). 'Each camp will have 300 families. They won't be able to defeat all of us. We're a multitude of mice, putting the elephant to flight.'

Elena Monteiros de Barros, a pretty 32-year-old woman, with long, black hair, had been clapping Cícero enthusiastically. 'I used to cut cane with my mother', she said.

> But there's been no work for several years now. One of my brothers used to work in the sugar-mill, but he's been sacked too. I left my husband, because he drank too much. So there's six of us at home – my mother, my two brothers, me and my two daughters, one 9 years old and the other 11. None of us has a job. I cook a bit of food and try and sell it on the street. The only regular income we have is my mother's pension, which is just one minimum wage a month [about £50]. So I'm going on the occupation. I've got to get on with my life, have something to hand on to my daughters. They'll come to the camp later, when it's all sorted out, and then they can help me cultivate the land. I like working on the land.

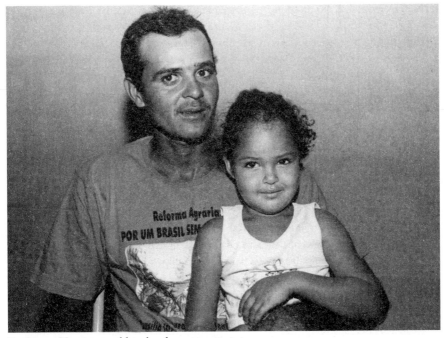

3. Cícero Honôrio and his daughter (*João Zinclar*)

The MST leaders took the names of the villagers who wanted to take part in the occupation. Then we got back on our motorbikes.

The next port of call was the hot, dusty village of Tres Ladeiras, which consisted of little more than a single main street, flanked by wattle-and-daub houses, with an open sewer running down one side. The activists held their meeting under a large, shady mango tree, behind the Catholic church, one of the few brick buildings in the village. To one side, a dozen boys were playing football on a makeshift pitch. Edson Ferreira da Silva, a 22-year-old activist, talked to the 30 or so people who had come to the meeting. 'Those of you who can, should bring some food', he said. 'Just for the first couple of days. Until we get the local government to send in supplies. Or find other ways.' Laughter. 'In a shop in Igarassu we bought up the last few rolls of black polythene for the tents. We won't have enough though. If you can, bring some plastic from home. But don't worry if you can't. If we run out, we'll share what we've got. That's what life will be like with the MST. And I want to make one thing clear – it won't be easy. The camp is our way of putting pressure on the government to expropriate the land. If we can, we stay on the land. But if we end up being evicted, we don't go back home. We rebuild our camp somewhere else and then we reoccupy. We don't give up.' Applause.

Ivaldo Martins da Silva, another militant (*see* box 4.1), took over from Edson. 'In the camp, we will sing MST songs and we will shout slogans. We haven't got time for much today, but I'd like to teach you a few, some of the ones we use when we're facing our enemies. The first one begins with the name of the movement – MST. I say that and you all reply "This struggle is for real! (Essa luta é para valer!)" So here we go. MST!' And the crowd replied 'This struggle is for real!' A dozen times the cry went out and a dozen times the crowd replied, with evident enjoyment. And then on to other slogans. 'Agrarian Reform! When do you want it?' 'Now!' shouted the crowd. 'When do you want it?' 'Now!' Everyone was laughing and shouting loudly. It was these people's first taste of the MST's *mística*. After a while a man dressed in an ironed shirt, smart trousers and leather shoes drew close. He would have passed unnoticed in a city, but here, among this ragged bunch, he immediately stuck out. Ivaldo paused, looked at him and then carried on. The villagers clearly recognised him, and their shouting faltered for a moment. Later he introduced himself as a municipal councillor. He politely asked Ivaldo a few questions and left.

Antônio José de Santos, 50 years old, with a lined face and dark, troubled eyes, sat on the church wall, a young child on his knee. He listened carefully and asked several apposite questions, showing quick intelligence and proud independence of spirit. Afterwards, he spoke to us, his voice tinged with sadness:

> I've been living here in Tres Ladeiras for 30 years. We moved here because we were turned off the sugar plantation we used to work on. When we lived on the plantation, we worked for six months, cutting cane. We were paid very little and we were badly treated. But during the *paradeira*, the dead season, we had our *sítios*, our plots of land. They were big. We could grow all the food we needed – cassava, beans, rice, pumpkin, breadfruit, oranges, lemons and so on. We even had food left over that we could sell in the towns. Since we've been here in Tres Ladeiras, we've only had tiny plots, and it's getting worse. So many of the plantations have closed down. There's really just this Petribu left. And there's not much work with them. The harvest today only lasts three months, four months, at times just two and a half months. I can't get any work there. I'm too old. And those that do are treated badly. I sometimes think we're worse off than slaves, for we don't even get enough to eat. We do our best. We go fishing. We get odd jobs when we can. Those of us who can get over our feeling of shame go begging in the streets. But there's a lot of hunger. There are 600 or 700 children living here. Their lives are a calamity.
>
> The only way out for us is through land invasions, with the MST. It's only together, through union, that we'll be able to get land and feed our children. No-one else is going to help us so we've got to help each other. Some families are in a desperate situation, overwhelmed with debts. And there are a lot of landowners who aren't planting any more. It's our right, I think, to invade this land, so that we can plant crops and feed our children. I don't think we can go back to the time of plenty, but we can't continue as we are. I've got 11 children. Some are adults – one's 22, another 18 and another 17. Fathers should be able to help their children, get them started in life. But I haven't been able to do anything for mine. We're all going on the occupation. It makes a better front, if the whole family's there.

A young woman, Lucinete da Silva, holding a young baby, was listening to the conversation. 'My husband's going to take part. We've got four children – a 6-year-old, he's playing football over there, a 4-year-old, a 3-year-old, and this one, just three months. My husband gets odd jobs now and again. We go hungry. We need a piece of land. You've got to have something in this world, or you don't live. I'd like to go, too, but I'm too frightened.' She laughs. 'I'll go later.'

The next day the activists spent the morning buying more rolls of black polythene, renting buses for the night of the occupation, and getting a couple of the motorbikes repaired. Money was running short and we went to the cheapest bar in town for a lunch of rice, beans and cassava flour. And then, in the middle of the afternoon, we set off, in a car now as well as on the bikes, for a meeting in Cruz de Rebouças, a large shanty-town on the outskirts of Igarassu. It was the MST's third visit to this overcrowded district which, like so many of Brazil's shanty-towns, had just sprung up without any planning. Most of the houses were simple brick constructions, built by the families themselves. We stopped on the outskirts to look for our guide, a veteran labour activist who had taken part in the land struggles of the 1950s and 1960s and who knew the shanty-town like the back of his hand. But he was not at home. There were no street signs, and many of the streets did not even have proper names, being known simply as 'the street of Zeca's bar' or 'the street of Maria Paula, the hairdresser'. We tried to find the way by ourselves but soon got lost – 'not again', moaned Cícero – in the maze of narrow streets, bars packed with drunks, small stores blaring pop music, and groups of men arguing noisily on corners.

We could not find anyone who knew the particular Pentecostal church we were looking for and had to go back to the entrance of the shanty-town, luckily finding that by then our guide had returned home. Getting into the car, he took us directly to the arranged meeting place, following a zigzag course. About a dozen people were waiting, with a few drunks listening on the fringes. The activists were disappointed at the low turn-out, as over half of the people in the shanty-town had no regular work. 'It's always more difficult in the cities', said Edson. 'People have lost hope.' Cícero, as usual, was captivating, and passers-by stopped to listen. He made no false promises, pointing out that there were strict rules in the camp. 'All of you are welcome to take part in the occupation', he said. 'But once we've set up camp, we don't allow alcohol.' Cheers, particularly from the women. 'If we find bottles of cachaça, we pour the contents on to the ground.' More applause. 'We can't build a new world if we're sozzled.'

On the way out of Igarassu, we stopped for a quick glass of water – we were gasping after the time we had spent standing in the hot sun – and then out to the cane fields. Our next stop was the sprawling village of Botafogo. None of the houses had running water, and there was an open sewer running down the road. Unemployment was very high and groups of men hung about the street corners. But compared to the noise, overcrowding and quarrelling of Cruz de Rebouças it seemed a haven of tranquillity. Most of the wattle-and-daub houses had vegetable gardens, and there were pigs and chickens rooting around in the roads. It was restful, with a strong sense of community.

Box 4.1   *Ivaldo Martins da Silva*

I was brought up on a sugar plantation, called Engenho Progresso, near the town of Ribeirão, here in the Zona da Mata. We weren't as poor as some of the others. My father worked for the plantation as a labour contractor. But when I was 11, my father lost his job and, with the compensation he got, he and my mother decided to buy a house in Ribeirão. My parents had 11 children and, as one of the youngest, I went with them.

My older brothers and sisters stayed, working on the plantation as cane-cutters. My father tried to get work in Ribeirão, but it was difficult for him as he had no qualifications for work in a town. I never actually went hungry, for we always had watered-down black beans and rice to eat, because my father, though he'd had little schooling, was an intelligent man, and he always found some way or other of getting enough food. But we went without a lot of other things. We had the electricity cut off four or five times, as we couldn't pay the bill. I only managed to study because my brothers sent a bit of money.

My brother Jonas and I trained to be agricultural technicians. We started to work for the sugar plantations. After a while, I got the sack. The plantations often do that – they sack you before you've had time to acquire labour rights, so that they don't have to pay compensation later on. I finished up stacking shelves in a supermarket and then working as a security guard for the Banco do Brasil.

I wanted to get back on the land, so I accepted an invitation from the MST to work with them. That was in February 1998. I was a bit apprehensive, because the MST has this image of being radical and violent. I went to one of their settlements and, after about three months, I started to like the work. I realised that people in these settlements still suffer a lot. Everything's a struggle – to get loans from the bank, to get help from INCRA, to get grants for building your home.

I got rather distracted from the technical assistance I was supposed to be providing. I started to get involved in the movement itself, helping the settlers to lobby the government. And, after nine months, the MST asked me if I wanted to become a *militante* and join the MST team that runs Pernambuco. I accepted and I find it really satisfying work. Of course, we have problems, particularly reprisals from the plantations. But it strengthens us, helps us grow as a movement. And the MST is expanding very quickly. Every two or three months we have another round of occupations and another load of new people join.

It's hard in the beginning to get people to change their way of thinking. They've been used to being under the boot of the plantation owner. But we go in with concrete proposals. And once they're in the camps, they change much faster. They learn to weld together and to become a community. We give them courses. We put them in school. We get them discussing political issues. They begin to feel strong. Of course, it takes a bit of time. People in this region are completely unprepared politically.

My views about agriculture are changing too. In college we learnt what the government wanted us to learn. And that means learning about farming with chemicals, because that's what the multinationals want to sell to us. But chemical farming is doomed in the long term. It poisons the soil. We've got to go back to organic farming, and let nature show us the way. It's hard, if you've been trained in a very different system, and I've still got a lot to learn. But I've taken that first step, which is more than our agriculture minister, Pratini de Moraes, has done. He's still hooked on chemicals and won't even listen to anyone putting forward an alternative.

We got lost again, but this time it was easy to get directions as everyone knew the large wooden Assembly of God church. While we waited for the villagers to arrive, darkness fell quickly. We amused ourselves as people came into sight down the road by guessing who was coming to the MST meeting and who to the Assembly of God's religious service, also due to start shortly. But the game proved too easy: those coming to the MST meeting wore ragged shorts, t-shirts, and flip-flops, while those on their way to Church were decked out in their Sunday best, men with ironed shirts and neat trousers, and the women invariably in prim-and-proper dresses. Cícero had told us that, before the MST arrived in this crisis-ridden region, the people had only two outlets for their anguish: to drink themselves silly with *cachaça* or seek personal salvation in the Pentecostal churches. Though the MST was growing fast, it could not yet compete with the far less demanding option of the Pentecostal churches: by our calculations, at least four times as many made their way into the church as stopped outside to listen to the MST. The two events started almost simultaneously. Cícero spoke and then Ivaldo taught the villagers a few slogans, moving the group away from the church so as not to disturb the service. Even so, it was a bizarre experience, hearing the villagers shout out in unison 'Agrarian reform! It's everyone's struggle! Agrarian reform! It's everyone's struggle!' against the cacophony from the church, where individuals stood up and cried out, possessed with divine inspiration.

Botafogo is situated near the main road to Recife. Just a few miles down the highway stands an old whitewashed church, Nossa Senhora de Boa Viagem (Our Lady of the Good Journey), built in the seventeenth century and now closed to the public. None of the villagers was supposed to know the area chosen for the occupation but a few of the cannier rural workers had already guessed. 'I bet we'll be going to the Terra da Santa (the Saint's Land)', said 64-year-old Maria Lúcia Gonçalves da Silva, known as Alice (*see* box 4.2), at the end of the meeting. 'That's land that the people need to win back.' Cícero smiled and said nothing, and everyone cheered.

The MST has drawn up guidelines for choosing the area for the first occupation in a new region: talk to local people and select an area that has water, is potentially fertile and over which there is some controversy as to its legal ownership. In the past, the MST had always chosen areas that were unproductive – that is, were not being farmed by the landowner. This allowed them to justify the apparently illegal occupation of private property by pointing to Article 184 of the 1988 Constitution, which states that land not being used productively should be expropriated and distributed in an agrarian reform programme. But at the time of this occupation the MST was tentatively adopting a new strategy: in rural areas of great poverty and hunger, it was beginning to occupy land that was being used to produce commercial crops such as sugarcane for the production of fuel alcohol, not food for the local population. 'We want to create a debate over the use of land', Cícero told us. 'We think that the government's first priority should be to end starvation, and that means giving the land to poor families so that they can grow their own food.'

The sugar plantation beside the church, known as Engenho Pasmado, fitted the MST's new criteria. Until the mid-1950s there had been a thriving community around the church. All the families had worked on the plantation, and during the *paradeira*, the dead season, they had cultivated large *sítios*. The old labourers looked back nostalgically to life during this period. Alice, who as a child lived nearby in another village, remembered visiting the community. 'There was one festival after another in January, to commemorate the day of the church's patron saint, Nossa Senhora de Boa Viagem', she said. 'There was no road then, and we would walk in a long procession along a rough track to the plantation owner's house, holding up the image of Our Lady from the church, singing and chanting. We ate so well during these festivities – there were wonderful harvests of cassava, beans, maize, bananas, mango, breadfruit and coconuts. People were poor but no one ever went hungry. It's so different today.'

The old inhabitants said that a large stretch of land round the community was known as Terra da Santa and belonged to the Catholic Church. 'I remember the posts in the land that marked the boundaries of the Saint's land', said Alice. But in 1956 the plantation owner, Alfredo Bandeira de Melo, an old-style patriarch who always wore a smart white suit and carried a stick, sold the plantation to another old northeastern family, Moraes, which by then was expanding south and had set up a large engineering firm, Votorantim, in the city of São Paulo. The new owners arrived with a new mentality, claiming it was wasteful to allow the workers to have so much land for their own use. They transferred the families to the village of Botafogo, planting sugarcane on the land around the church. The action had caused great resentment. Alice said that the Catholic Church should not have allowed it. 'People cried when their houses were knocked down and their crops destroyed,' she said. 'They were paid compensation but it was just peanuts'. Maurício Henrique de Nascimento, the old plantation administrator who now lives in Igarassu, said it still pained his heart when he drove past the church and saw sugarcane fields where so much food had once been harvested.

More recently, Votorantim, which had once been a large plantation owner, sold its remaining sugarcane interests in the northeast to Petribu. It was widely assumed that Engenho Pasmado had been included in the sale, for guards from Petribu had taken over responsibility for patrolling the whole area. Indeed, when we later telephoned Votorantim's office in Recife, we were told that the company no longer owned any plantations. But shortly before the occupation took place, Petribu said that the area still belonged to Votorantim, which was eventually confirmed to us by Votorantim's lawyer. This contradictory information led Jessimar Pessoa Boracho, the lawyer working with the MST, to suspect that Votorantim did not have proper land titles for the plantation, possibly because of the conflict with the Catholic Church, and for this reason had been unable to sell to it to Petribu. So there was a jumble of information over the legal ownership – which was all grist to MST's mill.

Though only a few people had guessed correctly where the occupation would take place, all the villagers were certain that it had to be Petribu land, as it was the only big plantation owner in the region. In their chats with the villagers, the MST militants did little to hide this, or the likelihood that Petribu would illegally send its security guards/gunmen to prevent the occupation. This clashed with the image the company presented to the world. We visited one of its mills – high productivity, modern machinery, polite employees and smart green and white Toyotas with the company logo. We spoke by phone to the owner, Jorge Petribu. 'We are one of the most efficient sugar mills in the northeast', he said. 'And we are environmentally aware. We have 30 biologists working on forestry regeneration. And we've signed up to the campaign to eliminate child labour on the sugar plantations'. They played everything by the book, it seemed. But, behind this appearance of civilised modernity, the company had a hidden persona of extreme violence. Everywhere we went we heard stories of Petribu's brutality. Jessimar Pessoa Boracho, one of the few lawyers in the region to defend the rights of rural labourers, told us that most of his cases involved Petribu. 'The Petribu family is part of that old established elite of plantation owners who have ruled the northeast since it was colonised by the Portuguese in the sixteenth century. They have that in-built arrogance that comes from centuries of domination. They're really members of the most famous family of all – the Cavalcanti. But some time ago they quarrelled with the rest of the family and adopted a new name – Petribu – which they took from an Indian tribe that used to live on the land where they had their first plantation. The old man, Paulo Petribu, is still the owner, but it's his son, Jorge Petribu, who's really in charge today.'

Jessimar introduced us to one of his clients, 31-year-old Edilson Vicente, whose father had worked all his life on sugar plantations. 'He didn't have a childhood', he said. 'My grandfather died when my father was only 2 years old, so he had to start work when he was 7. It was hard work, getting up at 3 o'clock and only getting home at 3 or 4 in the afternoon. My father suffers from chronic malnutrition, and he's never weighed more than 50 kilos.' In the early years the plantation had been owned by Votorantim, which, said Edilson, had not treated its workers well, but had at least respected their basic legal rights. But in 1996 the plantation got taken over by

Petribu. 'Petribu is a malicious, brutal company', said Edilson. 'It has its own militia of private gunmen, who go around beating up workers'. It was not long before Edilson's father, who was by then 52 years old and not in good health after an accident with a lorry, became a target. Petribu told him that he had been moved to another plantation 20 km away and that he would have to travel there and back, by bicycle, every day. 'They wanted him to leave of his own accord', said Edilson, 'so that they could get rid of him and get back the *sítio* without having to pay him for the rights that he had acquired under Brazilian law after 36 years of uninterrupted work for a single company.' Edilson's father turned for help to Jessimar, who took Petribu to court. He won compensation and the right for Edilson's father to stay on his *sítio*. It should have been the end of the story, but it wasn't.

Petribu appealed against the court's decision and began to send its gunmen to threaten Edilson's father. 'He has a lovely *sítio*', said Edilson. 'It's three hectares in size and my father used to grow a lot on it – yams, cassava, potatoes, sugarcane, pineapple, coconut.' Once there had been 30 rural workers living in that region, each with the right to stay on their *sítio*, but after persistent intimidation they had left one by one. Only Edilson's father was prepared to face a lengthy legal battle, with frequent threats of violence from the plantation's gunmen. Edilson, who by then was living in the town of Igarassu, 7 km away, became worried. He bought a mobile phone for his parents so that they could make contact if the gunmen started to use violence. On 20 September 1999, 20 gunmen appeared, with three electric saws and two caterpillar tractors. Edilson's 13-year-old brother and 18-year-old sister were the only people at home. They phoned Jessimar and in two hours he had been to the courts and obtained a judicial order to stop the gunmen. But by the time he arrived there, with a police escort, the gunmen had done a great deal of damage. 'They had cut down 100-year-old trees. They had trampled over 1,200 pineapple plants. They had dug up cassava crops', he said. 'If we had arrived later, nothing at all would have been left.' Jessimar took 86 photographs of the damage. At the time of our visit, the court case was still dragging on, but Jessimar was confident of an outcome in the near future. 'We will win', he said. 'The evidence is overwhelming. The only doubt is how much compensation the judge will settle for. I'm asking for R$50,000 which would allow him to buy another plot of land and live the rest of his life in relative comfort.' The authorities had taken no action to punish Petribu.

Soon it became evident that Petribu was prepared to use the same kind of tactics to prevent the occupation that we were hoping to join. We met Daniel Quirino da Silva, a 32-year-old unemployed cane cutter, who, after showing us deep, festering wounds on his legs, told us his story. Ten days earlier, he had been cycling home from mangrove swamps where he caught shellfish to sell in the villages to support his wife and four young children. He had stopped 'for an urgent necessity', as he put it, going into the cane fields. Gunmen employed by Petribu happened to be driving past in one of their pick-ups. For no good reason, they stopped, seized him as he was squatting down, hauled him out of the cane fields and kicked and beat him. Bleeding from the head, chest and legs, he was dragged off to the local police station, and thrown into a cell.

The only possible reason for the attack was a desire by Petribu to show the villagers what they could expect if they dared to take part in the occupation. But, if this was their motivation, they had made a mistake in the man they had chosen as their victim. A week later Daniel was still unable to walk without help, because of the wounds he had suffered from the iron tips of the gunmen's boots, but what had left him incandescent with rage was the humiliation he had suffered. 'I hadn't done anything but I still got treated like vermin and beaten up', he told us. 'The wounds still haven't healed so I can't work even now. I've decided to join the MST. I want to show Petribu that it doesn't own the world. My problem was that I was alone. Now we're in it all together. And I'll go to the bitter end.'

As the day of the occupation drew nearer, the pace of activity became more frenzied. On Saturday morning, Jaime Amorim, the MST coordinator for the state of Pernambuco, paid a lightning visit for a final strategy meeting, held in a small hall in Igarassu, which the MST had made its temporary headquarters. The hall was owned by the local branch of the Communist Party of Brazil, a tiny but active political party still loyal to Maoist-line communism, which, while not getting involved in the detailed arrangements for the occupation, had supplied much indirect support. We had all slept in the hall, us in hammocks and the five activists on thin mattresses on the ground.

As we waited for all the activists to arrive, we chatted to Jaime. He had been born in the southern state of Santa Catarina. Of European descent, he had a stockier physique than the northeastern activists, who were of mixed African, Amerindian and European blood and were darker and wirier. From the moment Jaime opened his mouth, it was clear that he had had more formal education. He had been one of a key group of four seminarists, all in the same year, who had decided simultaneously to leave the priesthood and help to set up the MST. 'So why did you leave the Church?' we asked. 'Because it cannot provide the people with what they need', he replied, somewhat tersely. Twelve years earlier Jaime had been sent from the south to help José Rainha set up the movement in the northeast. 'Over a third of the population of Brazil lives in the northeast', he said.

> It was clear that we couldn't become a national movement without expanding there. But it wasn't easy. Not only is the northeast as a whole distinct from the rest of the country, there are a lot of differences within the region itself. In Pernambuco alone, we have, on the one hand, the *sertão*, the hinterland which is subject to periodic droughts and has bred tough, fiercely independent peasant farmers, and, on the other hand, this Zona da Mata, where workers have been subjected for hundreds of years to the domination of plantation owners. We've had to develop different strategies for the different areas.
>
> Today in Pernambuco we have managed to establish 92 land settlements, with 8,000 families living on them. And we've got another 18,000 families in camps. That

means that one way or another about 25,000 families have joined the MST. But there are 340,000 landless families in Pernambuco, which means that so far we've recruited less than 10 per cent of the families that need land. Our challenge is to get people into the camps. We can talk and talk to them in the villages, but it's only when they live a different life in the camps that people really change. It's the organic structure in the camps that brings that about. People set up commissions and run the camps themselves. They discover that they can organise, that they can take responsibility for their own lives. And there they also have to face up to the gunmen. And that in itself is a liberating experience, to discover that together you have strength.

But for us that lay in the future. For the moment, the MST was organising that first difficult step – the initial occupation. The meeting with Jaime began, and Cícero outlined their plans – where the occupation would take place, the dispute over land titles, the involvement of the Catholic Church, the three buses they were organising, the villages where they would pick up families. Jaime listened and then commented: 'I think your strategy is good, but there's one point I'd like to make. Petribu is well run. It has good legal advice and tough security. If you manage to set up the camp, I think they'll choose the legal route for getting you out. They won't want the bad publicity around a massacre. And, once there are enough people in the camp, you can re-occupy, if you're evicted. The most difficult part is tonight. Make sure the "base" [he meant the people they had recruited] isn't intimidated by threats. Spread yourselves out. Go to the villages tonight and keep the people's spirits up.'

After a quick lunch, Jaime left in his battered car. Only a few years old, it was already giving signs of wearing out through heavy use. He was off to help in another occupation that seemed likely to be more violent. In Igarassu the activists rushed around sorting out last-minute hitches. The most serious problem came with the discovery that no one had confirmed the booking for the buses and one was no longer available. They phoned several companies, asking for buses for a fishing trip, but drew a blank. In the end, the situation sorted itself out, or seemed to. Someone from the village of Tres Ladeiras phoned to say that he had arranged a bus for the families there. In the confusion, the activists ignored Jaime's last piece of advice. Only one militant went off to one of the villages, Alto do Céu. It was taken for granted that the villagers would of their own accord be ready at 4 a.m. at the other pick-up points. It was to prove a costly assumption.

Everyone was excited and optimistic, but we felt apprehensive. Despite the warm reception the MST activists had received in the villages, we were not convinced that many people would actually take that first step and join in what was widely known to be a dangerous undertaking. But it was too late to be having second thoughts. At 3.30 a.m. a bus pulled up outside the MST headquarters in Igarassu. We got in and, after Cícero had explained to a somewhat startled bus driver that he was not going to take people on a fishing trip but on a land invasion, we left.

At first, all went well. We picked up about 25 people carrying farm implements, clothing and a little food, in the village of Botafogo. They included a young woman, whose 2-year-old daughter was shivering with cold and had to be wrapped up in a blanket, and an old man, wearing a trilby hat and a mackintosh, who seemed in his element, laughing and joking with the others. Then on to Alto do Céu. We found the main road into the village blocked by four white and green Toyotas. So we drove round to the back entrance, a rough dirt track leading to the village up an exceptionally steep hill. The driver said that his bus could not take the gradient, so a couple of activists and one of us climbed up the hill in the dark to tell the villagers to come down on foot, while the rest stayed in the bus. After about a quarter of an hour, three Toyotas appeared. Their lights flashing, they drove up and down. Eventually, one of them stopped by the bus and four men, one with his revolver clearly visible, came up. 'Where are you going?' demanded the leader of the gunmen. 'To do a job on a sugarcane plantation', replied Cícero, unconvincingly. 'Well, this job better not be on Petribu land. If it is, we'll be waiting for you.' And with that the Toyotas drove off up the hill.

Quick as a flash, Cícero pulled out his mobile phone (using modern technology in what in so many aspects seemed a medieval conflict). 'Look out', he shouted down the phone to the activists who had reached the group of villagers at the top of the long hill. 'The police are on their way up.' (The gunmen actually belonged to Petribu's security force, not to the police, but, for reasons that were becoming clear to us, local people do not distinguish between the two.) He rang off and, in a climate of growing tension, the people in the bus waited. After a few minutes another bus drew up, provoking exclamations of delight from the labourers. But this bus had come on a different mission: to pick up a few villagers for a day trip to the seaside. As the darkness began to lift, a couple of girls tripped down the hill, with sunhats and baskets of food. To relieve the tension one of the men in our bus cried out: 'You can take either bus, you know, lasses.' So the girls began to climb into the landless peasants' bus, to be greeted with guffaws of laughter.

Up at the top of the hill, the group of villagers ran to hide at the back of a bar on the edge of the square. One was holding a rifle, while the old man clutched a rolled up MST flag. The mothers hugged their children, telling them to keep very quiet. The Toyotas drove around the square, stopped, conferred, and then drove away. After waiting a while, the group emerged from behind the church and began walking down the road. The mobile phone rang again. 'Look out, the police are coming back!' This time the only place to hide was in a rather prickly hedge. We crouched down while a Toyota drove past the end of the road. Then we picked our way over the stones down a steep gully, a short cut to the road below. It was a difficult scramble in the half-light. Suddenly it felt as though we had travelled back 200 years, and this was a group of runaway slaves, fleeing the plantation to set up a *quilombo*, or free community. At last, we reached the bus at the bottom of the hill.

The Toyotas, too, had returned and parked about 100 yards away. Taking care not to be seen, the villagers clambered aboard. The bus departed hastily and, rather to everyone's astonishment, the Toyotas did not follow. It gradually dawned on the

Box 4.2 Alice

My proper name is Maria Lúcia Gonçalves da Silva, but everyone calls me Alice. I'm 64 years old. I was born near here on a sugar plantation in Tres Ladeiras. My mother was very religious and said the rosary a lot. When I was a child, we used to come here to the church at Nossa Senhora de Boa Viagem for religious festivities. My father had started cutting cane when he was 8 years old, and he expected us to do the same. When I was 13 years old, I got married. When I was 18, I already had four children. And I moved with my husband here to Nossa Senhora de Boa Viagem. The land here was called the Saint's land, as it belonged to the Catholic Church. It was a lot of land, the Saint's land. Like everyone else here, we worked for the São José plantation.

We had good *sítios* then, and we planted banana, breadfruit, mango, oranges. Sometimes we got 2,000 bananas a week from our land. We could go to town and sell them. It's so different today, now that the workers can't plant anything, and even have to pay one real for a dozen bananas. We could catch fish too in the Botafogo river. Some things were difficult, though. I had 16 children, and six died when they were small. They got diarrhoea, and there were no doctors, no medical care at all. And there were no real roads, just tracks, so you couldn't get them to hospital.

Everything started to change in the late 1950s. First the old owner, Bandeira de Mello, sold the land and the mill to Votorantim. And Antônio Ermírio de Moraes, the owner of Votorantim, came and told us we all had to leave. They knocked down our houses and planted sugarcane where we had our *sítios*. We got compensation but it was very little. People cried when they had to leave.

We had to move to the village of Botafogo. And then there was this terrible problem of pollution from the Botafogo river. It gave off a kind of mist that was like poison. It was the waste from the sugar-mill at Araripe. Children died from it, sometimes as many as three children a day. Thirteen of my grandchildren died. Altogether, 455 children died. Others were born deformed, with a kind of tail instead of legs. I started a campaign and eventually there was a big fuss about it. It got on television because Antônio Ermírio de Moraes was standing as governor in the elections in São Paulo state. I was interviewed by *Veja* news magazine. They cleaned up the river for a while, but it's polluted again today, though not as bad as in the past.

I've come on the occupation to help my children. Not one of them has a job. My youngest son is worst off. He's just got married. They have a baby and they haven't even got a house to live in. When I get a plot of land, I'm going to put it in his name.

families that the security guards had drawn the wrong conclusion. They certainly knew about a planned land invasion, and all day Saturday they had cruised around Alto do Céu in their Toyotas, distributing leaflets with warnings about 'evil elements' and 'agitators' who were deceiving the population with false promises of land. During the night they had been back in the village, speaking through loudspeakers and threatening the villagers with violent reprisals if they took part in the occupation. But – and this proved decisive – the gunmen believed that the MST was planning to launch the land invasion from Alto do Céu itself into an area of the plantation that bordered the village. They thought that the bus was trying to take people into the village, rather than out of it, so when the bus drove off they thought they had won.

Almost miraculously, the occupation went ahead as planned. After a ten-minute drive, the bus reached the church of Nossa Senhora de Boa Viagem. With dawn breaking, the families hurried out of the bus, carrying their farm implements, bags of food, pots and pans. Within an hour or two, they had cleared away the tangled scrub and bushes and put up their polythene tents. The camp held its first assembly. The red flag was hoisted and, in a climate of exultation, the people commemorated their first victory, singing and laughing. Many of the activities organised by the militants followed a planned routine, taught to members on training courses. This first assembly consisted almost entirely of *mística*, with marching and the shouting of slogans. It was designed to boost morale and to make people feel involved. The slogans both rooted the MST in the worldwide struggle for justice and equality and tapped into the northeastern tradition for resistance. One proclaimed:

'Che, Zumbi, Antônio Conselheiro,
na luta pela terra, somos todos companheiros'.

It referred to Che Guevara, who has become an icon of the movement, and to two northeastern revolutionaries: Zumbi, the Brazilian slave who headed a revolt in the sixteenth century, and Antônio Conselheiro, the nineteenth century mystic peasant leader. 'In the struggle for land we are all comrades', affirms the slogan. Oral traditions are still powerful in the northeast and in street markets roaming minstrels still sing about both Zumbi and Antônio Conselheiro.

One enterprising man climbed up a big stone cross in front of the church and tied a red flag on the top of it. Another climbed even higher, to the top of a billboard on the main road that passed the camp, and tied a red MST flag above an advertisement for insurance. The crowd below cheered enthusiastically and started to sing and dance. It seemed like Carnival. Yet the celebrations were premature. We were by then just 40 people, for the other two buses had failed to turn up. (It later emerged that the telephone call from the labourer in Tres Ladeiras to say that he had arranged a bus had been an act of sabotage. Along with the municipal councillor who had appeared at the MST meeting, the man had really been working for Petribu. The other bus had picked up some people in a couple of villages and then stopped in Cruz de Rebouças, only to find no one waiting. As it made its way half empty towards Engenho Pasmado, two Toyotas had swung across the road, blocking its way. Wielding a revolver, one of the gunmen then threatened to set fire to the bus with everyone inside it, and understandably the driver, who had arrived expecting to take people on a fishing trip, had refused to go any further.)

At about midday several jeeps and cars drew up near the church, and some 30 men marched in a phalanx towards the camp. About half wore the smart beige uniforms of official Petribu security guards, while the rest, wearing jeans, old t-shirts, and cowboy boots, were our old acquaintances from the previous night. At the sight of them marching towards the camp, men and women seized their hoes and ran to block their path, shouting slogans they had learnt just a few hours earlier. It was clear that the guards and gunmen would have to use violence to evict the families and, just as Jaime Amorim had predicted, they hesitated. They admitted, when we questioned them, that the land around the church did not belong to Petribu. In threatening language, they warned the villagers not to move into the adjacent cane fields, turned around, and strode back to their Toyotas. More celebrations.

Why had the gunmen backed off? The answer is complex. For all its imperfections, Brazil's political system today is basically democratic and there is considerable freedom of expression. As we had found out in our research, landowners frequently evict *sem-terra* families illegally but they like to do it discreetly, without press coverage. Even without the presence of foreign journalists, a violent eviction with deaths would have been picked up by the local press. There was also another factor, one that is never mentioned publicly by MST leaders. Many peasants have firearms, even if they are only rusty shotguns. The peasants use them for hunting animals but, if fired at close range, they can also kill a man. At the back of their mind, gunmen from the plantations are always afraid that, if the confrontation gets heated, these arms could be used against them. Cícero put it bluntly: 'the gunmen are cowards. They're doing the job for the money and they're badly paid. They don't want to die. We, on the other hand, believe in the justice of our cause, and we're prepared, if necessary, to die for it. That makes a big difference in these confrontations.' In these circumstances, MST's strategy of 'mass resistance' can prove remarkably effective.

The man in the trilby hat and the old mac, who had attracted our attention when he got on the bus, had been at the front, brandishing his fist at the gunmen. He turned out to be 71-year-old Antônio Severino da Silva. 'I lived near here as a child,' he said. 'My parents worked for Jorge Petribu's grandfather on a plantation. We used to visit this village, Nossa Senhora de Boa Viagem. We had to work very hard during the sugar harvest, from six in the morning to six at night. All they gave us to eat in the middle of the day was *cabaú* [a kind of syrup left over from sugar production], mixed with water. And they treated us worse than animals. The toilets were so filthy that not even vultures would go near them.'

They did not get paid in money, just in tokens, which they had to spend in the *barracão*, the only store allowed on the plantation. 'I can see the *barracão* now in my mind's eye', he said. 'It was run by a man called Zé de Alifate, who was blind in one eye. Because he'd lost one eye, he'd poked out an eye in his wife, his dog, his horse, his pigs and his chickens. They all had to be one-eyed like him.' Antônio Severino said that the only compensation was that they had their *sítios*. 'We weren't as hungry as people are today', he said. 'But I always hated it. The plantation owners could do what they liked with us. We had no rights. Today, at least, we have the law on our side, even if it is always a struggle to get the owners to respect it.'

Always a rebel, Antônio Severino had left the plantation when he was 15 years old, after working for eight years in the cane fields. 'I always thought that God had created the earth for us to grow our own food, not to work on for others like slaves.' He became involved in the struggle for land through the Pastoral Land Commission in the 1970s. 'I'm too old now, so I'm not going to sleep here under plastic, but I'll be back every day to help.' True to his word, he came back every morning with several large bags of bread rolls for the children.

We were still talking to Antônio Severino when the camp received its first visitors – José Servat, a French priest who has been living in this region for 35 years, and a nun, who immediately busied herself making sure that the children had enough to eat and were not ill. They had brought several sacks of rice and beans, which the women immediately began to cook. Father José had been delighted by the news of the occupation. 'Workers in these sugar plantations were organised in the 1950s and early 1960s but then they experienced dreadful repression and the movement collapsed', he said. 'They were abandoned by the Catholic Church. Just one or two of us struggled on. Some members of the Church are frightened by these occupations, but I'm not. The people are simply saying that they're not animals, they're humans. They want to be part of society. I've been hoping for years that something like this would happen.'

Although clearly unwell, Father José spoke to a hastily convened assembly. To much applause he said: 'this land does not belong to Votorantim or Petribu. It is the Saint's land. It belongs to the Church. There used to be a community around this church and, with God's help, you will build it again.' More cheers. 'I should like to make a proposal, that you christen this new community with its old name – Nossa Senhora de Boa Viagem.' At which point Cícero intervened so that the MST's democratic procedures for presenting a proposal and voting on it would be followed. The assembly voted by an overwhelming majority to accept the proposed name.

To our amusement, several members of the Communist Party of Brazil, who had also paid a visit to the camp that morning, endorsed the choice, even though the party is fiercely anti-clerical. More cheers and more slogans. Father José continued: 'I ask you to be prudent and to work within the law whenever possible. And with that I wish you a good journey into your new life.' Cícero was none too happy about Father José's final comments. 'He's a good man', he said, 'but we'd never get anywhere if we listened to everything that he and the Catholic Church say about working within the law. I'd be glad to have him back to hold a service when we inaugurate the new community, but I think we should restrict him to talking about religious matters.'

In the mid-afternoon, the camp held its third assembly, with people once again gathering under the MST flag. There was plenty of *mística*, but there was also more serious business, for the gathering elected the first two members on the camp's committee. The elections were not completely democratic. The activists had been busy talking to the families in the camp and had by then singled out a few people with the necessary leadership qualities. What they were looking for, they said, were people who were respected by the others, who could take decisions under pressure and who, if possible, had had previous experience in labour struggles. It was essential that the right people were elected, they said, because soon most of the militants would be going back to their own settlements or moving on to organise fresh occupations. The new leaders would have to take over responsibility for the running of the camp. So Cícero put forward two names – both men in their 40s or early 50s – to be elected, respectively, head of the camp's committee and head of the first of the commissions to be set up – for security, predictably enough. No other names were put forward. The assembly enthusiastically endorsed Cícero's nominations.

The head of the security commission immediately called on the men to volunteer for two shifts, one from 6 p.m. to midnight and the other from midnight to 6 a.m. A makeshift bell was quickly made out of a piece of metal. The head of the security commission said that, in the case of an emergency, day or night, the watch would ring the bell and everyone was to grab a farm implement and assemble under the flag.

It did not take long for the first emergency to happen. At about 10 p.m., as everyone was settling down to sleep in the tents, the bell rang out. The Toyotas – which by then for us, as for everyone else in the camp, had become a symbol of fear and violence, so different from their earlier image of smart modernity – had returned and were driving up and down the road. It was pitch black outside. The only source of light was a smouldering wood fire. A Toyota tried to drive in, to be confronted once again by 'mass resistance'. The villagers shouted their slogans and brandished their implements. Everyone in the camp was scared, knowing full well that people could be killed if the gunmen insisted on forcing their way in. But the vehicle finally backed off. After an hour or so of considerable tension, all the Toyotas drove away. It was a long night and few slept, but the gunmen did not return.

The next day was full of activity. The camp had survived the first crucial 24 hours and the news spread like wild-fire in the region. People began pouring in from the neighbouring villages. A delegation arrived from Cruz de Rebouças, begging the MST to send another bus to the shanty-town to pick them up, but Cícero was adamant: 'The bus came for you on Sunday morning, and you weren't there. If you want to join our camp now, you'll have to find your own transport.' Somehow they managed and a dozen or so families arrived a few hours later. More commissions were set up, with the people in the camp playing a more active role in the selection of their representatives. The MST's concern to promote women and young people to leadership roles also became more evident, now that the pressing problem of the physical survival of the camp had been resolved, at least temporarily. The new commissions were given a variety of responsibilities – to build more tents; to set up communal kitchens; to organise literacy classes for adults and children; to set up a women's collective; and to organise a young people's collective for collecting litter and for organising games. Everyone was busy.

The problems seemed immense. One activist was sent off to ask for food from MST settlements in the region. Another delegation travelled to Igarassu and other neighbouring towns to make contact with the local authorities. Quite surprisingly, several mayors promised to send in some supplies of rice and beans, even though they were not sympathetic to the MST's cause. Even so, it was clear that food would run out if the camp continued to grow rapidly. Cícero, who has organised dozens of occupations, was unperturbed. 'If necessary, we'll loot lorries on the highway', he told us. 'It all helps to raise people's awareness. People have been kicked around by the plantation owners since the days of slavery. It takes actions like this to make them aware that they can throw off oppression.'

During the day and sometimes at night the Toyotas would return. The gunmen didn't try to enter the camp but the threat of confrontation hung in the air. Few if any of the new recruits had ever stood up to authority before. Would the MST have the capacity to train people so that they would know what to do? Again Cícero was unruffled: 'People can change very quickly in these camps. They gain a sense of their own power and become fearless. As you saw, we don't need to encourage them. We even have to caution them against running unnecessary risks.' Cícero also said that everyone would have to respect the basic rules of camp life. People had to go to the two assemblies, one in the morning and the other in the afternoon and, unless they were very old or were caring for very young children, they had to take part in the commissions.

The MST believes that almost everyone – alcoholics, tramps, the homeless, and so on – can rebuild their lives. The MST instils two kinds of discipline in its camps: the external, almost military, discipline of getting up early to take part in the first assembly, of taking part in commissions, and of preparing for 'mass resistance', with singing, marching and the shouting of slogans; and the internal discipline of not drinking alcohol and of not behaving violently to your spouse or children. New recruits are given several chances to change their ways, but if they do not or cannot, they are expelled.

It was a novel experience. From the outside, the routine in the camps might appear harsh, even draconian, and the speed with which illiterate peasants were being drilled into shouting revolutionary slogans could be seen as brainwashing. It is certainly true that the left-wing slogans that the families were taught to chant had little meaning for most of them. But what was real and meaningful was the way in which people were encouraged to become actively involved in the democratic construction of a more participatory, collective culture. All this happens in the most difficult circumstances, in which people face the constant threat of violent eviction by gunmen. What was remarkable was the sense of fun and self-fulfilment. Although some people give up because of the hardship, many more seem to enjoy the life.

We left after a few days. By then conditions were even tougher than before, as the gunmen had infected with dead animals the only stream bringing water near the camp. Undeterred, several of the workers had begun to clean the old well that had been used in the past by the village but was now heavily polluted with diesel oil. Just before we went, we stood watching as the *sem-terra* marched around the camp – a long line of raggedly dressed rural workers, men and women, in a double file, left fists raised defiantly and right hands brandishing farm implements At the front, the red flag of the MST. Outside the camp, some 30 gunmen looked on. As the rural workers marched around the tents they had built for themselves a few days earlier out of branches and black polythene, they shouted out lustily the slogan: 'Agrarian Reform! When do we want it? Now! When do we want it? Now!' We counted them – 264 people, including 40 children in the front. A fortnight earlier very few of these largely illiterate people had had any contact with the MST.

We later learnt that by the end of the week there were 620 people living in the camp. Cícero had gone off to help organise yet another camp, set up spontaneously by families who thought that Nossa Senhora de Boa Viagem had become too crowded. It was an example of the permanent mobilisation that Jaime Amorim had spoken of. But, as so often happens in these land struggles, a major setback occurred. At 4 a.m. on the Saturday 100 policemen, accompanied by 200 gunmen, arrived at the camp equipped with an eviction order, issued by the courts in the name of Votorantim, to reoccupy the land and to expel the villagers. The families refused to move and a long stand-off ensued. The gunmen set fire to the tents and one labourer was seriously injured. Eventually, after mediation by the lawyer, Jessimar Pessoa Boracho, and a Catholic priest, a compromise was reached. The local Catholic bishop agreed to open the doors of the long-closed church and the families moved into the area immediately surrounding the church. As the families had technically moved off the land under dispute, the gunmen withdrew. The priest and the lawyer, still convinced that the land really belonged to the Church, promised to challenge the legality of the expulsion order in the courts. The scene seemed set for a long legal battle.

Early on Monday morning, watched by a small group of gunmen, the families, reinforced by seven MST activists brought in from other regions, reoccupied the plot. They had to start all over again. Many families had left, intimidated by the violence, so they had to send out word that they were now back on the land. They had to build new huts, bringing in fresh supplies of black polythene. They had to construct another communal kitchen, another open-air school. The long process of conquering the land – which could well involve further evictions and reoccupations – was under way.

CHAPTER 5

The Settlements

The most important and beautiful thing in the world is this: that people haven't been finished but they always go on changing, getting more in tune or getting out of tune. That's what life has taught me. And it's this that makes me happy.

Riobaldo in *Grande Sertão: Veredas* by the Brazilian novelist Guimarães Rosa

About 600 people are sitting along rows of trestle tables set up on the concrete floor of a huge, high-roofed hall, tucking into *churrasco*, the Brazilian term for barbecue. They are eating with the unrestrained relish of people who have known what it is to go hungry, filling their plates time and again with slices of beef, chicken legs and spicy sausages. Outside the hall, a dozen men are rotating some 40 giant skewers, each over a metre long, across glowing open fires. Fat dripping off the huge chunks of meat, previously marinated in a mixture of salt water and herbs, crackles in the embers. Vilmar Martins da Silva (*see* box 1.1), the indefatigable president of the cooperative COANOL, is still working while the others enjoy themselves. Perched on a stool in front of a tall desk, he is selling barbecue tickets, charging R$6 per adult (children are free). The cattle for the barbecue were donated by the settlers themselves and the proceeds will go on improving the present rudimentary installations of the hall – the settlement's sports and community centre.

There is no room here for the finer points of etiquette. Once they have eaten all the meat they can, people wipe their forks – and their fingers – on the sheets of rough white paper spread across the tables, and tuck into the puddings of crème caramel. Men and women wash down their food with beer and lemonade, drunk out of paper cups. As they feast and talk, laughing and drinking, their voices bounce off the bare walls. It is a festive occasion, but even now the worries of farming cannot be entirely forgotten. Many are complaining about the government's prolonged delay in releasing farm credit, which means that next year's harvest is threatened. Once this subject is exhausted, they return to their favourite topic – their epic struggle to conquer the land at Fazenda Annoni in Rio Grande do Sul. The families are commemorating the fourteenth anniversary of their community, Nossa Senhora de Aparecida, which was set up when they won the right to stay on Fazenda Annoni.

Once the *sem-terra* have won the right to the land, they establish a permanent community: their *acampamento*, or camp, becomes an *assentamento*, or settlement. Settlers return to a more normal way of life, without the harsh discipline of the camps. Rules are relaxed, for the dangerous period of violent confrontation with gunmen is over. Founded in 1984, the MST had by October 1999 (the last time it carried out a proper survey) set up 843 settlements in 25 states. About 100,000 families live in these settlements, which occupy 5.5 million hectares of land. Since then, the number of settlements is believed to have risen to about 1,200.

In national terms the MST is still small: its settlements cover just 1 per cent of Brazil's total farming area and make up about one fifth of the number of settlements in the country. The MST itself has not carried out a detailed breakdown of the geographical location of its settlements and the official land reform agency, INCRA, does not differentiate between settlements set up by the MST, the government or any other organisation. INCRA statistics for settlements in the country as a whole show that the region with the largest number of settled families is the northeast (with 45 per cent of the total), followed by the north (18 per cent) and the south (14 per cent)[1]. Not surprisingly, the southeast, which contains Brazil's most valuable farming land in the states of São Paulo, Minas Gerais and Rio de Janeiro, has the smallest number of settled families (10 per cent).

What makes the MST's settlements particularly interesting – and controversial – is the movement's claim that they can be a solution to the problems of social exclusion and environmental degradation that have become the scourge of so many developing countries. Whereas many of the other settlements are run by dispirited families struggling to fit into the pattern of increasingly globalised agriculture, the MST is attempting to prove that peasant agriculture offers a real alternative. On many of its settlements families are experimenting with ways of developing an environmentally sustainable way of life that may not bring wealth, but does bring self-fulfilment and personal happiness. It is this message that has turned the MST into a beacon of hope for similar movements throughout the developing world.

The History of the Settlements

The MST has been through various stages in its quest to build an alternative way of life for the excluded. In the very earliest phase, from 1979 to 1984, it paid little attention to how the land should be farmed. 'The conquest of land was the central question', an MST activist wrote in a recent publication.[2] 'The idea was: "the day I get my plot of land all my problems are over". It was a struggle for land not for agrarian reform'. The only forms of collaboration that the *sem-terra* practised were the traditional ones: *mutirão* (schemes for building houses or clearing land collectively) and helping each other out at harvest time.

The situation began to change in 1984 with the growing awareness that land alone was not enough. 'The number of settlements began to increase but there was little reduction in hunger and poverty. It became clear that unless the settlers sorted out their production problems they ran the risk of becoming indebted and losing their land, as had occurred to many of them in the past.[3] The settlers began to experiment with more organised forms of collaboration, generally with the encouragement of the progressive priests and pastors who had helped set up the movement. The groups were generally small, because the early Christians had lived in small communities (or, for the more politically militant, because Mao Zedong had said that small groupings could be an 'embryo' for great cooperatives[4]). These experiments were not yet very important for the movement. The participants at the First National Congress in Curitiba in January 1985 scarcely mentioned them. The MST's overriding concern was still to conquer land.

With time, the *sem-terra*, who were learning to think for themselves, outside the control of the churches, became dissatisfied with these forms of organisation. The Rio Grande do Sul leader, Vilmar Martins da Silva, who in 1982 participated in an experiment in collective living that the Catholic Church organised on a small area of land for families from the roadside camp at Encruzilhada Natalino, said that they found the ideology too paternalistic. 'We were not fighting for land to live out some rural idyll conceived by the priests', he said, 'but to grow food for our families and to improve our standard of living. It was all very well, in theory, to distribute food on the basis of need, not of hours worked, but it did not encourage people to work hard and achieve high levels of production. We were not the saints that some of the priests thought we were.'

Yet change came slowly, largely because there were so many other questions to resolve. In May 1986 the MST held the First National Meeting of Settlers, to which 76 settlements, from 11 states, sent representatives. The key issue under discussion was whether or not the *sem-terra*, once they became settlers, should remain part of the MST. A vociferous group argued that the settlers should set up a sister organisation, to be called *Pé no Chão* (Foot on the Ground), for the *com-terra*, the families that had won land. After a long discussion, the settlers voted to stay within the MST, a decision warmly welcomed by the leadership, who believed that the *sem-terra* and the *com-terra* were part of a single struggle.

By then the movement had moved beyond the idea of merely winning the land and firmly embraced the idea of agrarian reform, which it saw as a fundamental restructuring of the system of land tenure that would also redistribute power in favour of small farmers. While they campaigned for this, the settlers also sought more immediate gains, embarking on their long struggle to get the authorities to give them grants to build homes and roads and get electricity and running water installed in the settlements. In 1986 they set up the National Commission of Settlers and persuaded the government to create PROCERA, a special programme of subsidised credit for agrarian reform settlements. The first civilian government for 21 years was in power. While the backlash of the still powerful landowners had successfully blocked any real agrarian reform, many officials in MIRAD, the land reform ministry, and INCRA, the land reform agency, came from progressive backgrounds and were sympathetic to the MST's struggle.

Collective Production

In 1987 and 1988 the discussion over the organisation of the settlements gained momentum. Many settlers were keen to set up factories on their settlements to carry out simple processing tasks, such as de-husking rice, shelling soyabeans, producing cassava flour and slaughtering cattle. The basic idea, which was perfectly sound, was that the settlers should add as much value as possible to their produce on the settlement itself. Some *militantes* had recently returned from Havana and had far more ambitious plans. Excited by the way Cuba had eliminated malnutrition and built excellent health and education services, despite the US embargo, they suggested that the movement should adopt the Cuban model of collectivised production and big agro-industrial units. Infected by the *militantes'* enthusiasm, the leaders agreed, as a first step, to set up some fairly small collective farming cooperatives, to be known as *Cooperativas de Produção Agropecuária* (CPAs).[5] Over the next few years the MST duly set up the first CPAs – COOPANOR and COOPTIL in 1989 and then COOPTAR in February 1990, all of them in Rio Grande do Sul.

By then, the debate over how the settlements should be organised had moved to centre stage. In 1989 the MST undertook a lengthy consultation process and, at a conference on farming cooperation in June 1990, announced an across-the-board switch to a far more collective system of production. At first sight, it seems bizarre that the MST should have opted for this policy at precisely the moment when communist regimes in general were collapsing and Cuba in particular was experiencing the most severe recession in its history, with a contraction of at least one third of its economic output. The decisive factor was the sudden change in political conditions in Brazil in March 1990, with Collor de Mello's defeat of Lula in the presidential elections. Collor unleashed a violent campaign against the MST, which, cut off from all official assistance, had to rely exclusively on its own resources.

Just like Cuba, the movement adopted a 'war economy' strategy. It saw its settlements as 'liberated areas', which must be protected by a tough internal structure that would 'resist politically and economically'.[6] The basis of the new system was the network of CPAs, which would function as islands of socialist production, Cuban-style, within a sea of capitalism. The MST advised the settlers to form 'large associations, involving the maximum number of people' to carry out 'big productive activities ... in areas such as timber extraction, the processing of agricultural products, agri-business and so on.'[7] They should 'mechanise all possible activities' and 'achieve economies of scale'. They should use almost all their land for the production of cash crops, eliminating most subsistence agriculture. The emphasis was on big production, using modern inputs. The idea was that the movement would carry out 'primitive accumulation'; that is, the new units would produce a profit that could then be ploughed back into investment in industry and farming.[8] This would permit the MST to develop independently of the Brazilian state. The settlers were told to open communal restaurants and crèches so that women would not have to spend time cooking and looking after children. The leadership thought that, if the families worked and lived collectively, they would rapidly develop a 'socialist consciousness', and build, almost overnight, a socialist system.

There is no doubt that the MST needed to reorganise the settlements. As it said at the time, the old poorly administered associations were 'not responding to the needs of the settlers'.[9] Part of the problem was that the associations did not 'establish formal obligations and commitments among its members', which meant they tolerated 'petty vices', such as 'individualism, opportunism and self-sufficiency'. But, according to economist Horácio Martins de Carvalho, who has been a warm supporter of the MST for many years, the movement also committed a grave error. Instead of basing its new programme on 'the people in the settlements, their everyday lives, their work, their previous experience in cooperation, their social identities', it let itself be swayed by 'external influences'.[10] Because of its strong political support for Cuba, the MST failed to accept the painful truth that, without the Soviet subsidies, which came to an abrupt end in 1991, many of Cuba's collective farms and factories were economically unviable. The new collectivisation programme also failed to take into account the ecological degradation caused by modern farming methods.

The MST set up an impressive-looking organisational structure to back the new scheme. At state level all the CPAs were linked together in a body, called the Central Unit of Cooperation (*Central de Cooperação*), which had the role of promoting collaboration within the state. At national level, the MST created the Confederation of the Agrarian Reform Cooperatives of Brazil (*Confederação das Cooperativas da Reforma Agrária do Brasil*, CONCRAB), which was charged with the task of drawing up farm policies and providing technical guidance. The whole new structure was called the Settlers' Cooperative System (*Sistema Cooperativista dos Assentados*, SCA).

From the beginning, the new scheme faced resistance in the settlements. A few *sem-terra* embraced the idea of building a socialist system overnight, but others had serious doubts. It was not so much the ideology as the practical details. Many families, brought up in the conservative Catholic traditions of the Brazilian countryside, were horrified at the idea of collective living. Hard-headed peasant farmers questioned the economic viability of the new cooperatives. 'They wanted us to grow soyabeans on all of our land', said Oney Zamarchi, from COOPATRISUL in Rio Grande do Sul. 'But we knew how expensive food was in the supermarkets. It did not make economic sense for us to win land and then not use it to grow food. We thought each family should keep a small plot for their own subsistence. The *militantes* didn't like it very much, but we insisted.'

The new system was not a success. CPAs all over the country became heavily indebted, for the money they earned from their cash crops was not enough to cover all the expenses they incurred on farm machinery, pesticides, fertilisers, and even food. Hundreds of *sem-terra* voted with their feet, leaving the CPAs and reverting to some kind of subsistence agriculture, carried out by individual families. Oney Zamarchi says his cooperative's obstinacy was vindicated: 'our cooperative survived because we always had enough to eat. I don't know how we'd have managed without our vegetable plots.' Without this safety net many other cooperatives collapsed.

COOPTAR, located near the town of Pontão in Rio Grande do Sul, managed to survive but it went through a very difficult period. One of the co-op officials, Jesur Bertoli, known as Zuca, was painstakingly honest. With a frog croaking away in a hole in the wall of his tiny office – 'a sure sign of rain', he confided – he listed the mistakes they made. 'We set up the cooperative in 1990 with 29 families. We tried to be like the *granjeiro*, the big farmer. We bought a lot of farm equipment to cultivate soyabeans and wheat. It is true that we were unlucky – we had two awful droughts, in 1993 and 1994 – but it wasn't just that. Our scheme was basically unsound. With all the farm machinery we had, there wasn't enough work for us all. There were 35–40 people to keep busy. It only took two people to look after the soya plantations, and another two people to look after the 30 cows and two more to look after the pigs. That's all. People were fighting for work.' Some settlers had to find jobs outside the settlement. 'Some of us picked grapes and others helped with the maize harvest on neighbouring farms. We began to wonder why we'd conquered the land, if we were back working as labourers. And we still didn't have enough money.' Many families left the cooperative, which today has just 14 members.

The situation got so bad that the MST leaders had to take action. They visited settlements around the country and drew up a report, entitled starkly 'The Crisis in the CPAs and the Collectives'. In December 1994 the MST leaders presented a new plan of action. After admitting quite openly that they had made serious mistakes, they proposed important changes in strategy. The MST was not able by itself to generate enough capital to fund its own development, they said, so it should abandon the policy of 'primitive accumulation'. Instead, the movement should put pressure on the state to provide the services it needed – subsidised farm credit, schools, roads, electricity, health posts and so on. This was an important shift in policy: from then on the MST intensified its policy of mass mobilisations and marches in what was to become a very successful policy for extracting resources from state bodies. The decision to abandon the attempt to set up 'socialist islands of production' also re-rooted the MST in Brazilian society as a movement that depended on public support and that worked with other mass-based movements for reforms that would benefit the whole of society. The new policy was also the recognition of new political circumstances: by then, Fernando Henrique Cardoso had been elected President on a platform of economic stability and social reform. The MST had greater political space for expansion.

The MST reiterated its long-term commitment to collective production, saying that the CPAs were 'the superior form of organisation', but admitted that they would only work 'in well defined conditions'. In practice, this meant that the MST acknowledged that collectivisation could not be imposed in uniform fashion all over the country. From then on, it allowed the settlements to organise production however they wished, provided they remained faithful to the movement's goal of encouraging some form of cooperation and collaboration. João Pedro Stédile says that this was the single most important lesson from the experience. 'We don't have a model for anything today. Each time we have tried to do this, it has failed. Today we draw up "guiding principles" but we leave it to each state or each settlement to decide how and when these orientations will be implemented.'

Finding Their Way

In the immediate aftermath of the collectivisation fiasco, many settlements went to the other extreme, opting for individual farming with no collaboration at all between the settlers. As a result, the movement began to face political problems. Isolated on their individual plots, some families began to lose their day-to-day involvement in the movement (although most still turned up for demonstrations and marches). Men, who had learnt in the camps to help with childcare and to involve their wives in decisions over farming matters, started to revert to their *macho* ways.

Alarmed, the leadership took measures. One of the first decisions, taken in 1996, was to encourage settlements to set up service cooperatives. These cooperatives were far more popular among the settlers than the CPAs had been, for they brought clear economic benefits. The cooperative staff helped the families through the intimidating forms required for bank loans. The cooperative bought in bulk, which reduced the cost of agricultural inputs. The cooperative set up marketing networks, so the settlers could bypass the middlemen, getting better prices for their crops. Moreover – and this is what was most important for the leaders – the cooperative also brought political benefits. The settlers learnt to work together and to take collective decisions over the future of the cooperative.

It is still not easy to get people to turn up to meetings, to the annoyance of leaders like Vilmar Martins da Silva, president of the COANOL cooperative in the Novo Sarandí settlement in Rio Grande do Sul, who spends much of his day and every evening tearing between meetings in different settlements. 'People are often tired after working all day in the fields', he said. 'But they need to go to the meetings if they are to have their say in how the movement develops.' To make it easier for families to participate, the MST is giving more thought to the layout of the settlements. In the early days the land was shared out in chaotic fashion. Now, whenever possible, the settlers divide up the land like the spokes of a wheel so that they can form a community in the centre and reduce the isolation of the families.

Box 5.1 *Luís Fernando Santos da Silva*

I was one of 12 children. My parents never had land. They worked as day labourers in a sugar-mill in the Zona da Mata. They worked 12-hour shifts to earn the minimum wage. I started work in the mill when I was 10. I was 12 before I'd stepped into a school, and then I only went when I could fit it in around work. I stayed in the mill for five years. And then, in December 1983, Jaime Amorim visited our mill, inviting people to join the MST. At first I was against it. I'd heard about the MST on television. I thought they were radical, violent. It was my father who convinced me to go with him to visit a camp. It was, of course, very different from what I'd expected. In the end, my father and several of my brothers, we all joined the camp in a sugar plantation near Palmares. We were there for four years. My father and brothers won land, but by then I was a *militante*. I only wanted to work for the movement. I'd got very involved. I did a 'prolonged' course, for two months, in Sergipe. We studied in the morning and then we did practical things in the afternoon. I learnt how to drive a tractor, how to rear poultry and cattle.

I'd only been there for two weeks when I was sent to give lessons in a camp! At first I found it very difficult. I was very young and I was very shy. I'd lived in the countryside and wasn't used to talking to people. But I soon got the hang of it. The leadership helped me. I've been working for the movement for seven years now, organizing occupations, marches, camps. I suppose I've taken part in over 100 occupations. I find it very rewarding, winning land and seeing people get on with their lives. I've worked all over the place – Paraíba, Sergipe, Rio Grande do Norte, Ceará – wherever the leadership sends me. I arrived in this region in the *sertão* in 1995. I was one of six *militantes*, sent in to get the movement going here. Hundreds of people joined. There's so much unemployment and despair. The movement spread like wildfire. It's only been four or five years and we've already conquered 18 settlements.

I've been arrested twice. Once I was in a settlement, dividing up food sent in by INCRA. Thirty policemen arrived in three police vans and a passenger car. They had the names of three of us on a piece of paper. They said that a judge had ordered us to give evidence concerning an occupation. Three days before we'd been violently evicted from an estate. The police hadn't an arrest warrant, so we refused to go. We'd already guessed that they'd made up this story. It was a Sunday and no judge works on a Sunday! We realised that the landowner had paid the police to arrest us and beat us up. It was to be a warning to us not to re-occupy the estate. We were angry but what could we do? They pulled out their weapons and they shoved us into a van. They beat us up viciously for two hours. After I lost consciousness, they gave me some medicine to make me come round.

The police jeered at us. They said they were going to release us and then re-arrest us when they'd got the proper papers. They said they were going to brand us like cattle so they could recognize us later. They picked up a big, heavy stapler on the desk and put staples through our ears. It was so humiliating but we couldn't stop them. Then they took us to a police station, forced us to take off all our clothes. We had to stand there naked while they paraded us in front of visitors. Finally an MST lawyer arrived. We were taken to hospital where they took out the staples. By then, my ears were very inflamed. But we weren't intimidated. Two weeks later we re-occupied the estate and won it six months later. We also complained to the state commission of human rights. There was an investigation and the officer who'd arrested us was temporarily suspended. That kind of thing never happens here so it was a real victory!

4. Luís Fernando Santos da Silva (*João Zinclar*)

It's a real responsibility being an MST leader. I'm a member of the state leadership now. I'm doing an adult education course. And I need to be politically aware, to understand what's happening around me. I'm working with the poorest of the poor. It's perhaps their only chance to get out of poverty so I feel responsible. When it goes well, it's so rewarding. Joining the movement's made sense of my life. And I know now that wherever I go in Brazil, I'll find the red flag, people who treat me with the same respect, the same warmth. We're like a big family. That's what gives us strength.

The settlers are learning through their own experience to value cooperation. Maria José Bezerra, from a settlement near Promissão in São Paulo state, spoke about her experience. 'For six years we tried to be completely collective in the way we farmed, cooked and cared for children. But we found it difficult to reach a consensus. People are so different. What is really important for one person is neither here nor there for another. I don't think we'd prepared ourselves properly. People didn't really understand what it was all about.' The attempt was abandoned in 1998. 'For a year, we did everything on a completely individual basis but people found that didn't work very well either. There are quite a lot of things that are better done collectively. For instance, we cultivate tomato plants. We still use chemicals, though we're reducing the quantity. Some settlers know how to select the right pesticide and apply it properly. The others need their help. So, very cautiously and carefully, we're beginning to collaborate again. It's on a much sounder basis now, and I think it's going to be fine.'

The movement is encouraging this step-by-step approach, in which the community develops its own forms of collaboration instead of having an alien structure imposed from outside. In sharp contrast with its attitude in the early 1990s, when it spoke in crude Marxist terms of rapidly transforming 'peasant awareness' into 'working-class awareness' as part of the process of constructing socialism, the movement today is treading warily. In a recent document CONCRAB encouraged the settlers to look critically at their own behaviour: 'the struggle to survive has made us grasp at immediate goals. We haven't created social structures that help us develop our political awareness and change as human beings ... but we can change. We can learn to work together, beginning with very simple things and then advancing to more complex forms of cooperation.'[11]

While there is general agreement in the movement today that each settlement must find its own forms of collaboration and cooperation, a consensus does not yet exist over the kind of farming that the settlements should practise. Some settlements, particularly those being set up in regions recently conquered by the MST, are adopting modern farming methods and are trying to compete head-on with big capitalist companies, whereas other older settlements in the south of the country believe passionately that Brazil must develop its own sustainable way of farming, far more in tune with the needs and life style of the *sem-terra*. It is to this debate that we now turn.

Settlements along the São Francisco River

In 1995 the *militante* Luís Fernando Santos da Silva (*see* box 5.1), then 24 years old, was sent by the MST to help open up a big new front for the movement along the São Francisco river in the extreme west of Pernambuco. While his children watched television in his simple wooden house in one of the settlements founded by the MST as the result of this struggle, Luís Fernando explained why the MST had targeted this region. 'They knew that some of the fruit farms, set up with lavish government funding, were bankrupt. The owners had misused the money, buying luxury seaside homes and sending capital abroad, instead of investing it in their farms. In 1994, with the economic crisis, the Brazilian government had to cut back drastically in its spending. The supply of money to the farms came to an abrupt end, so the owners, who still had to service their debts, faced huge economic problems. Though many had installed irrigation pumps, most of them were working at less than 20 per cent capacity, which meant that the farms were officially classified as "unproductive". It was a wonderful opportunity for us'.

Luís Fernando and the five other *militantes* arrived by bus in the town of Lagoa Grande early one morning in June 1995. Lagoa Grande is a small town near the São Francisco river, about 650 km inland from the state capital, Recife. 'We didn't know any one in Lagoa Grande', said Luís Fernando. 'But we were pretty sure it would be easy to recruit because many of those living in the town's large shanty town had lost their jobs on the grape farms because of the crisis.' Luís Fernando said that they did what *militantes* always do when they arrive in a new region: they found out the names of left-leaning Catholic priests, Catholic lay groups and trade unionists and contacted them. 'We were lucky in Lagoa Grande. Dom Paulo Cardoso, bishop of Petrolina, was very sympathetic to our cause.'

The *militantes* started to hold meetings in the shanty-town. Maria Zilda da Silva Santos (*see* photo, p. 217), 57 years old, who uses her profound knowledge of medicinal plants to treat families in her settlement, was going through a very difficult period. 'I'd been to Maranhão with my husband and most of my 11 children in search of a better life, but it had been a disaster. There was little work and the weather was swelteringly hot. I weighed 75 kilos when I left, but I was only 50 kilos when we returned. We were desperate to improve our lot, so I was really interested by this talk of land. I went to the first meeting the MST held. There were about 18 of us there.' Soon word spread around. 'About 500 people went to the second meeting and then over a 1,000 people to the third. There were so many people that we couldn't all fit into the hall. The *militantes* divided us into five groups, according to the area of Lagoa Grande we lived in, and we held five separate meetings.'

After two months the *militantes* organised the first occupation. 'The local landowners knew we were active in the region and they kept on threatening us, but we didn't pay any attention', said Luís Fernando. 'The people in INCRA knew of the hardship in the region and didn't try to stop us. They even let us use their data so we could choose the most indebted and least productive farms as our targets.' The first occupation took place on 7 August 1995. As usual, the families were not told until the evening before. Somehow or other the MST organised 41 lorries, doing everything in an enormous rush. Maria Joaquina de Nascimento, known as Nazinha (*see* box 5.2), said that the lorries were so full that 50 families got left behind. 'They came later, most of them by car but some even by cart', she said. Manoel Nogueira de Lima, known as Adauto, then 22 years old, was also recruited in Lagoa Grande. 'The first families left at 4.30 a.m. By 6 a.m., there was a traffic jam along the pot-holed roads.'

Despite the MST's precautions, news of the planned occupation had spread. 'When we arrived at the Safra estate, there were already about 600 people there – police, state deputies, priests, journalists. By then we were arriving in our hundreds. The police didn't make any attempt to stop us. They wouldn't let us drive in through the main entrance, but showed us where we could cut the wire. We cut the wire in

Box 5.2 *Maria Joaquina de Nascimento (Nazinha)*

I'm 57 years old. I was born in Água Branca in Ceará. My father had a small plot of land. We were lucky because it had a spring, so we always had water. I was the only girl, but I had five brothers. I went to school for a short while. I had to get up, cook lunch for my parents and then walk the four kilometres to school. I really only learnt to sign my name. When I was 22 years old, I married. My husband didn't have land of his own so he worked with my father.

We all left Ceará because my father got ill. One of my brothers lived in Petrolina, so we went there. We had to buy everything, even gas for cooking. Before that we'd always used wood from the countryside. We found it strange to have to buy fuel to cook. It was difficult. I went hungry for the first time in my life in Petrolina. My husband got a job on a building site. I had seven children, but three died. My first-born died when he was eleven months old. Then I had twins, who were born dead. But the other four – three girls and a boy – survived.

We were living in Petrolina with all these problems when some lads came to the door and invited us to a meeting. They said they were from the MST and they could help us win land. We were so pleased! So we all took part in the occupation of Safra estate. We spent five months in this camp. But there wasn't enough land in Safra for all the families. So on 5 January 1996 we went with 105 other families to occupy Ouro Verde estate and that's where we won land. We were evicted once from here, on 31 January 1996. The police came and it was really frightening. But we reoccupied again, on 18 February 1996, and in the end we won the land. Everything is fine now. I've got a nice house, with a veranda. We sit out here in the evenings. It was my dream, to have a house like this. My parents had a house with a veranda. It was better than the one I've got, but I'm going to make this one as good as theirs one day. I've planted lots of trees in the garden and I've got flowers in pots. It looks like a real home.

We can grow all our food now. That's so much better. The only bill we have to pay is for the electricity – for the house and for the water pump for the grapes. We only have two crops to sell on the market – grapes and *azerola* (a tropical fruit). They don't really bring in enough money. We still suffer, but life is so much better.

three places.' Zilda looks back at that time with great nostalgia. 'It was such a good feeling. We were all so alive', she said. 'Even if I were to take part in another occupation today, it wouldn't be as good. We thought that by that single act we were solving all our problems. We didn't know of the difficulties that lay ahead.' According to Adauto, 2,204 families took part in that first occupation. By the end of the day they had erected about 800 tents. 'When we started chopping down trees

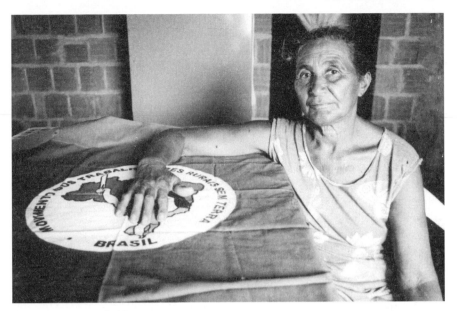

5. Maria Joaquina de Nascimento (*João Zinclar*)

to get poles for the tents, we disturbed rattlesnakes and armadillos. We even caught and ate an armadillo!'

The families stayed in Safra for nine months. The Catholic Church provided vital support. 'Dom Paulo was a tower of strength', said Luís Fernando. 'He arranged collections in the local churches and even went to police stations to demand our release after we'd been arrested on trumped up charges.' The police only made one attempt to evict the families. 'About 400 of us, all women, formed a barrier at the entrance to the camp', said Zilda. 'The police took one look at us and got back into their cars. They never tried again.' Adauto said that life was difficult. 'We had very little food. Men got day jobs on nearby farms, but they were often sacked when the landowner found out that they came from the camp. We stopped and plundered lorries about 15 times. I'll always remember the first time. We were a bit nervous, as we hadn't done it before. But the driver didn't mind at all. He drove the lorry into the camp and helped us unload the bags of cassava flour. The children were so hungry that they tore the bags open and ate the flour just by itself. Ten minutes later we stopped another lorry. It had 250 bags of beans. We were so happy, until the police came the next day and confiscated half the bags.' About 40 people were arrested, but the police did not press charges after MST lawyers, brought in from Recife, defended them forcefully by claiming their right, recognised by the Brazilian constitution, to *furto famélico* – the right of a starving person to steal food.

The Safra estate belonged to the Fenícia Group, which had produced tomato pulp before it went bankrupt. In April 1996 INCRA expropriated the estate and settled

250 families. There was not enough land at Safra for all the families, so the MST organised further occupations of neighbouring farms. 'Safra was the mother', said Adauto. 'It had five children'. On a few occasions the police managed to evict the families in these other camps, but each time they re-occupied and won the land eventually.

By then, the MST had moved on to new areas. Luís Fernando worked with the national leader, Jaime Amorim, to organise the occupation of the largest estate they have targeted so far in the region. Fazenda Catalunha belonged to the OAS construction company, part of the economic empire headed by one of Brazil's most powerful right-wing politicians, Antônio Carlos Magalhães, universally known by his initials, ACM. According to the MST, Fazenda Catalunha had obtained R$18 million (US$10 million) in subsidised government credits for the irrigation of tropical fruit, but had misused much of the money. At the time of the occupation, the farm had 22 water pumps, enough to irrigate 2,000 hectares of land, although only eight were in working order. With characteristic daring, the MST decided to invade the lion's den, and on 7 September 1996 about 700 families occupied the farm. The MST had expected fierce opposition from ACM, but, to their surprise, he made no attempt to evict them. Instead, he negotiated behind the scenes and obtained hefty compensation from INCRA. By 2000, the MST had set up 18 settlements in the region. It was an impressive political victory.

However, as Zilda suggested, their problems were just beginning. The settlers had taken over a small part of the 70,000 hectares of irrigated land that has turned the São Francisco valley into one of Brazil's main fruit exporting areas.[12] This kind of agriculture cannot be readily carried out on an individual basis, so the MST, perhaps not paying enough attention to the lessons that the movement should have learnt from its earlier attempt at collectivisation, told the settlements to set up production cooperatives. Once again, they failed.

Bartolomeu is a hard-working settler at the Ouro Verde (Green Gold) settlement, spawned by the Safra occupation. It is a pleasant hamlet with wide earth roads, which get very dusty in summer and are mainly used by mule-driven carts and horses. People enjoy sitting out on their wooden verandas in the late afternoon. While his wife made lunch of rice, beans and beef, washed down with mango juice, Bartolomeu said they had made three attempts among the 100 families to set up collectives. 'They all failed', he said. 'People didn't really know what collective production was and they were mistrustful. Another problem was that there were 60 sharecroppers living here when we arrived. We didn't want to evict them, so we told them that they could stay if they wanted to. Thirty-eight of them decided to and they've been a constant problem ever since. They're always complaining that they're short of money, although they shouldn't be, as they don't have to hand over half of their produce to the landlord now, as they did in the past. Far from joining in any attempt at collective production, they are often most reluctant to pay their share of the electricity bill.'

After the failure of collective production, the families opted for completely individual production. 'We divided up the grapevines', said Bartolomeu. 'It worked out at five rows per family. We even started buying our individual amounts of pesticide, fertilisers and so on. The only thing we shared was the electricity bill, which we had to, because we've no accurate way of calculating individual consumption.' After a year, the families began to realise that this, too, was an unsatisfactory way of working. Looking after grape vines is skilled work. 'Grapes can get 20 different kinds of disease', said Luís Fernando, who also lives in the Ouro Verde settlement. 'Many of us don't know which is the best pesticide to apply. We need to help each other.' Families also realised that they should work together marketing their grapes, as middlemen were playing off one family against another and sometimes paying as little as R$0.50 (US$0.28) for a kilo of grapes. 'Today we are at least making joint purchases of agricultural inputs and starting to sell our crop collectively. We've still got 50 hectares that we allocated for collective production when we first arrived. The area isn't irrigated yet, but it will be soon. If we plan it carefully, we can farm it collectively and make it work.'

The settlement has not even begun to tackle another serious problem: children applying pesticide without protective clothing. Thirteen-year-old João Neto Nascimento de Souza, dressed in shorts, a t-shirt and flip-flops, was by himself in the vineyard. He was applying pesticide by hand, often reaching up to grapes above his head, which meant that the poison could drip into his eyes. He said that he sometimes felt unwell after working long hours. 'We are planning to give people more training', said Luís Fernando, 'but we have few resources and we get little help from the authorities. Sometimes we go for months without receiving a single visit from a state agronomist.'

But the problems in Ouro Verde pale into insignificance compared with those being faced in the sprawling Catalunha settlement, home to at least 4,000 people. It is more like a frontier town than an agricultural settlement, with row upon row of mud houses stretching up and down over the hills. Chickens, pigs, dogs and mules wander between the houses and the bumpy earth roads are lined by bars with pool tables, tiny makeshift shops selling half a dozen grocery items, butcher's shops with scrawny cuts hanging outside, hairdressers, bike repair shops, bottled gas deposits, snack bars – anything that might bring in a bit of extra income. There are a few cars and tractors and many bikes, but most of the people have to rely on the ubiquitous rubber-wheeled carts pulled by sturdy mules that carry schoolchildren, nursing mothers, men and women on the way to the fields, drums of water, food, harvested crops, or whatever needs to be transported from A to B.

In the beginning the cooperative tried collective production but again it failed. In desperation, they divided up the irrigated land among the 800 families. This led to fierce disagreements and bitter squabbling, particularly over the electricity bill. Because there is no way of recording individual consumption, the MST has established rules. Each house pays R$10 (US$6) per month to cover electric lighting or R$15 (US$8) if the family has a refrigerator. People with irrigated land pay R$40 (US$22) per hectare. Not surprisingly, in a community where most are desperately poor, families find it difficult to pay. In August 2000 the newly privatised regional electricity company, now owned by a Spanish multinational, cut off electricity without warning after the community failed to pay a bill of R$80,000 (US$44,000). The company had insisted on charging the struggling settlement its business rate, although by law small farmers are entitled to a lower rate. Some of the families were in despair, afraid that their crops would die. The MST began hasty negotiations to reschedule the debt, and on the third day the company reconnected the supply.

An income gap between the families has already begun to emerge. This is a common feature of non-MST settlements, but is something that the MST has fought hard to avoid on its own projects. As the government's farm credit arrives late and erratically, the families that came to the settlement with some capital of their own have had a big advantage. They have been able to buy seeds, fertilisers and machinery, and get ahead. Some have even used their capital to grab business opportunities. Thirty-six-year-old Neide Souza Pinto noticed the lack of transport on the settlement and invested in three second-hand buses, which today carry passengers around the settlement and to neighbouring communities. While Neide has revealed herself as an astute businesswoman and is prospering, about 80 families who arrived penniless are still living in overcrowded rooms, without water or proper cooking facilities, in outhouse buildings that resemble old slave quarters and are, in fact, where the seasonal workers lived when Catalunha was still privately owned. Hungry, underemployed and disillusioned, these families complain endlessly about the settlement's shortcomings and have become a hotbed of malicious gossip about alleged – but as yet unproven – corruption among MST leaders.

Even some of those who arrived full of idealism are beginning to lose heart. Sitting at her kitchen table, with candles lighting her hut because of the electricity blackout, Maria Marta de Oliveira (*see* box 5.3) said that some of the people there were violent, 'bandits, that's what they are', who had taken advantage of the confusion to grab a piece of land. But she added, somewhat defiantly: 'I love the MST! With all its defects, I like Catalunha.' The settlement's oldest resident, 100-year-old João Justino Jorge Limus, puffing on his hand-rolled cigarette, disagreed. 'I had to come here because of my son, but I don't like it. We're not going hungry. It's not that. We're suffering hardship but not like the old days. My parents were slaves. When they got their freedom, they worked as sharecroppers. I remember that during one of those terrible droughts that ravaged the northeast we had to eat *palma* (a cactus plant). There were even people fleeing from the drought who threw bones and bits of leather on the fire, so they could chew and eat them. What I don't like here is the lack of discipline.' Marta concurred that the worst problem was the disorder: 'what we need is a good administrator. Someone who is honest, reliable and tough.'

Box 5.3 *Marta Maria de Oliveira*

I'm 45 years old. I was born in Mossoró in Rio Grande do Norte. We were brought up in the city. My father was a street vendor, selling candyfloss, things like that. I had six brothers and sisters. We were always hungry, and always squabbling over food. My mother had 13 children but seven died. We lived in a very poor area of the city. We hardly ever went shopping in a supermarket. We couldn't even afford rice and beans. We lived on scraps, things my father could get for nothing. Toasted pork tripe. Vegetables the market sellers threw away. Cassava flour bought cheaply. I went to school and I got lunch there. Not always but quite often. My parents were Evangelicals. They spent a lot of time in the Assembly of God temple. It was a comfort for them in their difficult life.

I went to Fortaleza to work as a maid. Then I got pregnant. I didn't marry the father, so it was all very difficult. At that time families wouldn't let you go on working for them if you had a young baby. My mother wouldn't help. Her faith was against it. The only person who helped me was the father's mother. She lived in Mossoró so I left my daughter, Luciana, with her while I went on working in Fortaleza. I wasn't registered with INPS (national health service), so when my daughter got ill her grandmother registered her as her daughter so that she could get her treated. I visited her whenever I could.

Then I tracked my father down in Petrolina. He'd separated from my mother and had a bar there. I decided to work with him so I went back to Mossoró to pick up Luciana. I was on my way back on the bus when the bus company asked to see her documents. Well, Luciana was registered as her grandmother's daughter and I had forgotten to get authorisation from her to take Luciana with me! I tried to tell them that I was Luciana's mother but they wouldn't listen. I had to take her back to Mossoró and by then I'd spent all my money. I had to leave her again. By the time I had the money to go and get her again, she was 6 years old and she didn't want to come back with me. I took her all the same for I didn't want to lose my daughter. But the first months were very difficult.

We lived with my father in Petrolina. I used to take in washing. Even though he helped me a lot, it was hard. Then I got a job on a grape farm. I stayed there for just over two years, but I left in the end because they paid so badly. At least I learnt to work with grapes, which is useful now. By then, one of my sisters had joined the MST and taken part in the occupation of Catalunha. She wanted me to join her but I always said: 'become a *sem-terra*? That's what vagabonds do. They're worthless people'. But then in 1997 I went to visit her. And do you know, I liked it from the very beginning! The atmosphere was so good. People helped each other. They divided up their food. They talked about their plans for when they conquered the land. I wish it was still like that today. There was even a woman in a wheelchair in the camp – Maria de Lourdes Cequeira. She brought her two children with her and slept in a hammock under the olive trees like the rest of us. She's dead now. It's not that life wasn't difficult. We used to run out of food, but then we plundered lorries. It was all very well organised. We spoke to the driver first to make sure he had insurance. And, if he had, we took the food and divided it up. None of the drivers tried to stop us. Most were happy to see the pleasure with which the children ate. It was lovely!

We learnt that we had to make demands if we were going to get anywhere. We had started irrigating the land and cultivating crops before we won the land. But the water pump broke down. So a whole group of us took over the room where the pump was at three o'clock in the morning and took the man hostage. We didn't hurt him and we all had fun. We cooked, we played the guitar, we sang. But we kept him there until they repaired the pump. We lived for over a year down by the river, sleeping in hammocks, before we won the land.

Things started to go wrong after that. There were already 650 families here and INCRA insisted on us taking another 150. It never worked out. These families weren't from the MST. They had different ideas and they made trouble. I tried hard in the beginning. I was on the coordination committee, the only woman. Just imagine it, nine men and me. There was a lot of resistance, even from the MST. But I proved myself. I worked in the health sector and got things well organised. Today it's much easier for women. There are a lot of women leaders now. But there are a lot of problems here. I love the MST and I always shall. But we need to sort out our problems.

To some extent, the MST leadership agrees with her. 'Catalunha is in a mess', admitted Luís Fernando quite candidly.

It has about 4,000 people. The camp leadership can't handle such a number. The MST fought hard at the beginning to have only 500 families but INCRA insisted on 800. It wanted to make up the numbers for the year so it would meet its target. We've got families here who'd had no previous contact with the MST and didn't take part in the occupation. They don't understand our project. But we will sort it out. We're just about to start a three-month training course. There will be 200 *militantes* in the settlement and one of their tasks is to sort out the problems. INCRA has finally agreed to bring down the number of families to 600, expelling those opportunists who registered but have never really lived there. We'll be changing the structure of the settlement, setting up six *agrovilas* [hamlets], each with 100 families. They will each have their own internal structures, as if they were separate settlements. And INCRA has also finally promised to provide a housing grant so we can get everyone in decent housing. We'll make it work.

In the longer term, Luís Fernando is even more optimistic. With his eyes gleaming, he says they are going to set up a food-processing plant that will handle all the produce coming from the settlements. 'We'll be making juice in cartons from all the tropical fruits we're going to grow – guava, mango, *cupuaçu* and so on. We're going to make jams and banana puddings. We'll export large quantities and we'll also sell on the domestic market, with special prices for the poor. We'll show the world that workers can produce as efficiently as businessmen and at the same time be humane.'

Perhaps ... but there are grounds for scepticism. After analysing the grape farms along the São Francisco, an economist recently concluded that their main comparative advantage was 'the low cost of both land and labour. Workers in the northeast earn R$0.75 per hour, compared with between RS$5 and RS$10 in California.'[13] To remain competitive on the world market, the big commercial farmers are always seeking to reduce costs further. One recently mechanised part of the production process on his farm, which allowed him to sack half his labour force.[14] Small producers do not thrive in this kind of set-up. The success of the São Francisco export initiative is due almost entirely to big farmers: 90 per cent of the family farmers who received plots went bankrupt.[15] They failed for a combination of reasons: lack of experience in grape cultivation, not enough members of the family of working age, unpaid bank debts, and lack of marketing experience.[16]

This is not a favourable environment for the MST, which conquered the land to improve the living standards of rural workers. It is extremely difficult to combine this goal with the ruthlessness required to succeed on the world market. The MST cannot adopt the normal range of actions undertaken by capitalist businessmen, such as using seasonal workers and paying them as little as possible. Yet in Catalunha the MST has not developed an alternative economic strategy. It has followed uncritically the example of the businessmen in the region and made the export of grapes the settlement's main economic activity. Although some settlers are producing a few food crops on non-irrigated land, this is a secondary activity. This makes it all the more difficult for the MST to improve the living standards of the settlers, for the families have to generate enough income to purchase goods on the market, including part of their food.

The unfortunate experience with large-scale cash-crop farming in the south of the country in the late 1980s seemed to have shown the MST that it could not simply copy the big capitalist farmers. Yet in the São Francisco it seems to be making a similar mistake. But change is afoot. The MST is very reluctant to lay down rigid norms for all its settlements, mindful of the problems caused by excessive centralisation in the earlier period, yet it has realised that it cannot afford to repeat the same mistakes each time it moves into a new region. Gradually it is establishing new policy guidelines. One of the movement's main thinkers, Ademar Bogo, said recently that, with hindsight, the MST's main error was 'to have copied an outmoded and unviable model of agriculture' and 'not to have had the courage to invent a form of agriculture adapted to our way of being and our conditions, with new methods of organisation'.[17] So the MST is now cautiously and somewhat reluctantly developing a new form of farming that combines the best elements of peasant agriculture, particularly its emphasis on self-sufficiency and sustainability, with the advances of modern technology. This new development, still embryonic, seems to contain within it the best chance for the MST's expansion in the modern world. It will be examined in greater detail in chapter 12.

CHAPTER 6

Education in the MST

To enlighten the people, to show the people the reason, the ground of all their sufferings; when a man works hard for 13 or 14 hours of the day, the week through, and is not able to maintain his family; that is what I understand of it; to show the people the ground of this; why they were not able.

A witness defining the aims of the Sheffield Society at a trial in England in 1794 of a shoemaker accused of treason, quoted by E. P. Thompson[1]

When you're illiterate, it's the same as being blind. With its schools, books and practice, the Movement teaches us to see the world.

18-year-old activist at the MST's Palmares Settlement

On the walls inside a big white house on top of a hill hang some of the letters of the alphabet, the MST alphabet: A for *acampamento* (camp), M for *marcha* (march), R for *reforma agrária* (agrarian reform), S for *seca* (drought), T for *terra* (Land), U for *união* (union), V for *vitória* (victory). That this house is now a school is in itself a victory. Until a few years ago it was the house of the boss, the sugar planter, who would sit here on the columned veranda, looking out over the green fields where his workers toiled all day cutting the cane. Now all this land, as far as the eye can see, belongs to the workers themselves.

At the foot of the hill, the 27 new houses of the settlement are going up on either side of a village street. There is no electricity yet, but the families have begun planting vegetable gardens behind their new homes. The settlement is named after Marcos Freire, a minister for land reform who was killed in a plane crash in 1987. At the moment the school is used only by children but soon there will be literacy classes for adults as well. Most of the *assentados* (settlers) in the northeast are illiterate, especially in sugarcane areas like this one, the Zona da Mata region of Pernambuco.

Hundreds of miles further west, the lush green countryside of the Zona da Mata gives way to the semi-arid *sertão*. On a treeless bank of the wide São Francisco river huddles a row of miserable mud-and-wattle huts, exposed to the harsh sun. This is the Riacho Fundo camp, where 28 of the 30 families are headed by women, because

Box 6.1 *Maria Ilsa Bezerra*

I was born in the *sertão* in the interior of Pernambuco. My parents had a small plot of land. But when I was 10 years old there was a terrible drought and we had to leave. My parents didn't want to, but there was nothing they could do. We had nothing to eat. I have nine brothers and sisters and we all went to Petrolina. My father got a job as a security guard but he didn't earn very much and we had to buy all our food. So we all had to get jobs. I became a maid and then a cook and then a hairdresser.

I met my husband in Petrolina. We married and had five children. Life was difficult and violent. I had to leave the children at home to go to work and I was always worried about them. When the MST *militantes* arrived here in 1995, they rented a room right next door. Imagine that! I didn't like it at all. I kept thinking, the police will come and we will all get into trouble. But then I started talking to them and I soon changed my mind. I'm going to join, I decided! I didn't go on the first occupation as the children were so small, but I went on a later one. My husband stayed in Petrolina, working as a waiter, so he could bring food. All the children came with me. My oldest is 11 and my youngest 6. That's enough! I've been sterilised so there won't be any more.

The occupation was fun. We arrived at about four in the morning. No one tried to stop us. It was pouring with rain and a lot of us had never really lived in the countryside before. We had 20 *militantes* with us. They showed us how to put up our tents. We had to go into the woods and cut down some branches. I remember there were a lot of snakes. I was quite scared! Then we brought the branches back and covered them with black plastic.

It was hard in the beginning. We were 87 families but a lot of people gave up. Now we're just 30 families. Most of us are women, without their husbands. Imagine it, 28 women by themselves! And we're getting on fine! We all help each other. I've learnt how to make a wattle-and-daub hut. It's much better than the plastic tent. We've dug a fairly small plot that we can irrigate with water from the river. We have to carry water in tins on our heads, as we haven't got a pump. I didn't know anything about planting but I've learnt. I'll have to teach my husband when he arrives!

I've been elected camp coordinator, but I haven't done the MST course yet. It's hard to leave the children. We're going to get this land because the owner wants to be expropriated. It's just a matter of time. If INCRA takes too long, we'll go and occupy their office. That'll speed things up! I want to get more involved in the movement. Next year I'm going to take part in occupations, even if there are gunmen. I want other families to have the same chance as us.

most of the men have stayed working in the town to buy food. Thirty-year-old Maria Ilsa Bezerra (*see* box 6.1) is here with her five children. Years ago a severe drought forced her family to give up their smallholding in the *sertão* and move to Petrolina. But the move did not work out and Maria Ilsa and her husband decided to join the MST and move back to the land. She and the children went on the occupation, while he went on working as a waiter, bringing them food once a week. In spite of the precarious conditions, she is amazingly cheerful and full of energy.

Maria Ilsa says that they were thinking of the children when they decided to join the movement. 'We wanted them to get an education and we wanted to bring them up properly', she said. 'As a farmer I have more chance of teaching my children the right things.' She went to school for only five years – the Brazilian average – but, even so, that is much longer than the others, so she is going to start literacy classes for young people and adults. She is also keen to continue her own studies. In exchange for her teaching, the other women show her how to work the land. Maria Ilsa's eyes sparkle with enthusiasm as she describes life in what is virtually a women's cooperative. 'We help one another. The women are very united. When a woman joins the movement, she becomes a man, she gets the strength of a man'. Next week a Cuban doctor is due to visit the camp to give everyone a check-up. Their only water comes from the river but they add chlorine to make it safe to drink. The women have begun sowing a few crops along the edge of the river, where the soil is rich.

The school Maria Ilsa's children go to is a short walk away in an older camp of 200 families, where the more solidly built huts are sheltered from the sun by a row of stately mango trees. Several years ago this area of 3,000 hectares was owned by a private farm, which produced asparagus for export, as the dried-up irrigation channels and spigots testify. The owner went bankrupt and abandoned the farm. Drug dealers moved in and planted 10,000 marijuana bushes. When the MST occupied the farm, the police evicted them and pulled up the marijuana plants. The families reoccupied twice and both times they were evicted, losing the crops they had planted. But after the third reoccupation the owner decided to sell the farm to INCRA and now the families are left alone. With only minimal help from the authorities, they are struggling to survive. At times they have been so short of food that they have resorted to looting lorries on a state highway.

Most of the population here is young, as in most camps, but Dona Rita (*see* box 6.2), who is swinging gently in a hammock under the trees, is 93, as her deeply wrinkled face suggests. A big hut with a thatched roof turns out to be the school. Twenty-five children aged 7–14 sit together in the single mud-and-wattle classroom. There is one small blackboard, and not everyone has a book. The young teacher, who is also called Rita, says she has to adapt the few books to the different levels of the children. It is an hour and a half's walk to reach the school but sometimes she is lucky and gets a lift on a mule cart, the local method of transport. Rita has been on a teaching course run by the MST, but she says the Pernambuco education authority moves teachers around to stop them getting too involved in MST schools.

Wherever there is an MST occupation, camp or settlement, there is a school. At the camp of black polythene tents, squeezed along the roadside verge in Pontal de Paranapanema in São Paulo, the *sem-terra* put the desks and blackboard in the road because there was nowhere else for them. At the dirt-poor Macaxeira camp in the Amazon state of Pará, near the road where 19 *sem-terra* demonstrators were killed by police in April 1996 (*see* Chapter 7), the school was an open-sided hut where the children sat on tree trunks under a roof of banana leaves and drank watery cocoa at break-time because there was nothing else. The struggle for land has also become the struggle for education, for schools, for the right to know.

Paulo Freire

The MST has become the main driving force for popular education in rural areas. Many of their schools and courses are named after Paulo Freire, the man whose revolutionary educational programme promised to eradicate illiteracy but was abruptly ended by the military government after the 1964 coup. Two years earlier Freire had launched his movement in the northeast, where 20 million of the region's 35 million adult inhabitants were illiterate and thus barred from voting. It was fiercely resisted by landowners and sugar-mill owners, who had a vested interest in the workers' ignorance. Even so, Freire's method – which could teach a person to read and write in 45 days – meant that hundreds of thousands of people joined the polling lists. He wrote in one of his books: 'Democracy and democratic education come together, precisely in their belief in man. In the belief that he not only can but ought to discuss his problems. The problems of his country. Of his continent. Of the world. Of his work. The problems of democracy itself.'[2]

The reformist government of President João Goulart was so impressed by the success of Freire's method that it decided to extend it to the whole country. In 1963 coordinators were trained to run 20,000 literacy circles, with the aim of teaching two million people to read and write. It was a time of great social mobilisation in rural areas. About 1,300 new rural unions had been organised. In Pernambuco almost a quarter of a million sugarcane cutters took strike action for the first time ever. The rural population was learning to read, write, vote, organise and strike. This turn of events alarmed Brazil's conservative elites and the result was the military coup on 1 April 1964.

Paulo Freire was arrested and exiled; other countries benefited from his methods while Brazilian education stagnated. When the military regime came to an end in 1985, over 20 per cent of the population was still classified as illiterate – they could not even sign their names. In 1988, as one of the most important gains in the new constitution, illiterates finally won the right to vote. By then illiteracy was concentrated in poor rural areas. When the MST reached the northeast in the late 1980s, 80 per cent of the adults in some of its camps were illiterate. 'There were

Box 6.2   *Rita de Souza*

I was born in 1907 in Paraíba. I had seven brothers and sisters. My father had a little farm. He kept a few head of cattle and we made cheese. We lived well. There was abundance in those days. But then in 1932 came the big drought. My older sister caught the fever first. She suddenly had a seizure. She shook and she trembled. She had a violent pain in her head and her neck. And she got so cold. She went yellow and she died. Then six days later my mother died in the same way. I caught it too. I went as white as this paper but I survived.

Only me and one of my brothers survived. We had to leave the land and look for work. I didn't go to school as a child. Even now I can't read or write. But I learnt how to work the land. We got jobs on farms but we were always travelling from one place to another. Eight years later I finally got married. My husband came from Ceará, so we went back there. It was hard. He didn't have land either. We had seven children. They're all alive today, thanks be to God. We came to Petrolina 30 years ago, looking for work. My husband died eleven years ago. Since then I've been living with my daughter.

I was so pleased when the MST appeared. I've spent so much of my life, looking for land. I want to leave my grandchildren something. We live from

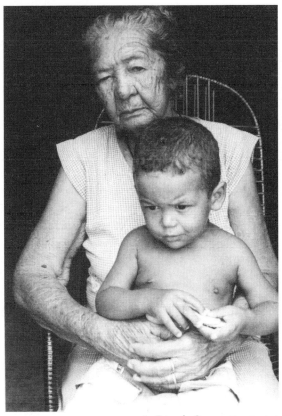

6. Rita de Souza (*João Zinclar*)

my pension today. But when I'm dead, they'll lose that. So I was stronger than my daughter, who was frightened. I said, yes, we're going on this occupation. One of my sons came too. And we're going to stay here and get settled on this land.

meetings when nobody could take the minutes, because not a single person present could read or write', wrote Roseli Caldart, an educationalist who is an adviser to the MST teacher-training programme and a member of the MST's education collective.[3]

The Fight for Education

Today education has become part of the identity of the MST. But – just as the key decision to create an autonomous movement, independent from the rural trade unions and the Catholic Church, was a conscious step that was taken only after long and difficult discussions – it was by no means obvious to the families that carried out the first occupations that the movement should take on another struggle. Bernadete Catona Choppe, who in 1996 was appointed education secretary in the rural district of Pontão in Rio Grande Sul, after a *sem-terra* candidate won the municipal elections for the first time, remembers how it happened. Just after she had trained as a teacher, she and her husband decided to take part in the Annoni occupation in 1985. There were a lot of children in the camp, so Bernadete and some other teachers and mothers in the camp began to organise playgroups. They started to explain to the children what was happening, why they were there, why the police surrounded the camp and kept them under siege. 'The children were there with their parents. They were taking part in the struggle and they needed to know what was going on. The police cameramen were filming them as well as their parents', said Bernadete, sitting in her office in Pontão. 'But not everyone agreed with us. They thought the children were too young. They thought it would worry them.'

Events gained a momentum of their own. When the families realised that there was to be no quick and easy solution to their demand for land, they began to wonder what they were going to do about the children's education. 'There were hundreds of children running wild, with nothing to do all day long, getting up to mischief', said Bernadete. 'We carried out a survey and found there were 760 school-age children in the camp and 25 qualified teachers among the women. It made sense to set up a school'. Even so, not all the families – or even all the leaders – agreed. Some said: 'we're here to get land, not a school. If we start demanding a school, it'll be a distraction'.

As so often with the MST, the issue was finally resolved through a vote in an assembly. A majority of the families decided that they should ask the authorities to set up a school. Even then at this early stage, they were clear on one essential point: education was the responsibility of the authorities. But the authorities replied that they were not prepared to help, as the camp was illegal. The MST counter-argued that the government still had a responsibility for the children's education. So, just as the *sem-terra* were taking action to conquer the land, so they began to mobilise to demand a school. They later used the same tactics to demand all the public services that they believed the government should provide – health post, running water, paved roads, subsidised farm credit and so on. Many *sem-terra* came to believe that it was just as important to knock down the barriers to these services as it was to break down the fences that kept them off the land.

As they talked, the families realised that they did not want the school in their camp to be the same as the schools they had known as children. They felt instinctively that the MST school had to be different. In her book *Pedagogia do Movimento Sem Terra*, Roseli Caldart said that many adults felt they had wasted a lot of opportunities in their lives because they had not understood how things really worked in society, and they did not want their children to have the same experience. The families wanted a school that taught their children 'to fight for their rights, to work together, to value the healthy life they could live in the country and to resist the lure of the city'.

In less than two years the demand for schools had spread to camps and settlements in seven states. By then the idea that they were fighting for the right to education as much as for land had taken hold. In the camps and settlements they organised their own schools, however precarious, and then demanded that they be recognised and that the local authorities appoint teachers for them. Sometimes they got the school before they got the land. They used the same tactics: first occupying government education offices, then negotiating, demanding audiences with the authorities. Sociologist José de Souza Martins considers this demand for schools to be almost as radical as the decision to occupy the land, because 'the school was also a right denied to the *sem-terra*, because of their very condition as rural workers, in a society whose development model did not require the education of ordinary people, especially in rural areas'.[4]

The Problem of the Teachers

The MST national leadership soon became aware of the importance of the new demand for education. In July 1987, in the town of São Mateus in Espírito Santo, the movement held the first national meeting of teachers from settlements. By then they faced a dilemma. Because the MST believed in public education, it had demanded that the local authorities accept responsibility for providing the schools; but, while succeeding in getting the local authorities to do this was a victory, it also created a problem. The teachers whom the authorities sent in were part of a city-based educational system that not only disregarded the different educational needs of the rural areas, but was also unsympathetic to the political objectives of social movements like the MST. Although some individual teachers came to admire and identify with the movement, most regarded being sent to teach in a settlement, especially in the more remote ones, as a punishment rather than a challenge. They were imbued with the prejudices of the town against the *sem-terra*, and they would often tell the pupils that their parents had committed a crime by invading land that belonged to others. This was very confusing for children who had spent months, sometimes years, living the precarious life of an occupation, maybe seeing the police attack their parents, their 'homes' destroyed by the hooves of police horses and their few belongings flung into the mud or burnt by gunmen.

In addition, many camps had been through a kind of cultural revolution, where traditional values had been turned upside down. Instead of individualism and consumerism, the families had shown solidarity with each other, sharing their food and their belongings. Although some men had resented it, women had become a powerful force, keeping morale high and taking responsibility for important tasks in running the camp. Even the children had often taken an active role in camp life. Teachers who did not, or would not, understand their pupils' background and experience caused problems. So the question was no longer just getting a school built and getting teachers, but what sort of school and what sort of teachers? It became the next logical step for the MST to produce its own teachers.

The MST had not originally intended to set up an alternative educational system but, once the need had become apparent, it accepted the challenge. 'It is the MST's way of doing things', said the academic Bernardo Mançano. 'It doesn't have preconceived ideas about what it can and cannot do. Everyday life throws up a need and the MST responds to it. And then the practice it acquires in meeting that need leads to the formulation of a strategy. It is this way of behaving that enables the MST to adapt and to survive.'

New Human Beings

There are no half-measures for the MST. Once it had accepted that it would get involved in education, it adopted an ambitious aim: to set up a school system that would produce 'new human beings'. To this end it created a National Education Sector and formed a new decision-making body, the National Education Collective. But, whereas in conquering the land the MST had the experience of earlier peasant movements to follow and to learn from, the new collective had no precedents to guide it in the field of education. No other social movement in Brazil had ever taken education so seriously. So the members of the collective had to develop new educational methods for the movement. They drew heavily on Paulo Freire for inspiration, but they also looked at the work of many other educationalists in other countries, especially socialist ones. They picked and mixed methods and educational philosophies, distilling them with the knowledge acquired from their own experiences.

In 1990 the MST began its first teacher-training course at a Catholic seminary in Veranópolis in Rio Grande do Sul. In the beginning it was the only course available for MST activists, and students came from all over Brazil, sometimes travelling for four or five days by bus. The MST began to produce its own textbooks and course material. It also began to think about the purpose of schooling in its settlements. In a discussion paper entitled 'What We Want From the Schools in the Settlements', it listed the aims of the MST schools:

- To train future leaders and *militantes* for the MST, the unions, the associations, the cooperatives, and other popular movements, because the struggle has to continue.

- To show the reality of working people, in the country and the city. To show the reason for all the exploitation, the suffering and the poverty of the majority. To show the reason for the enrichment of some. To show how society can be transformed. Teachers and pupils should also take part in the struggles of the popular movements and the unions.

- To think about how the new society that the workers are building should work. To compare it with what is happening on our settlements. The NEW should begin right NOW.

  Summarising: the school should teach pupils how to read, write and assess reality.

  Everyone in the settlement should be involved. As well as studying, the children should work, cleaning the school, helping to prepare school meals, looking after the school garden, and organising the library, games and parties. They should also do something linked to the land, growing vegetables and rearing small animals, and they must learn to work in groups.

Just as important as the actual teaching, it said, was the 'educational atmosphere', which meant the educational experiences present in the daily life of the movement: campaigns, marches, *mística*, and farming itself. Once it had set up its schools programme, the MST began to think about the younger children. The word *crèche*, used in Brazil for nurseries, was rejected because many state-run institutions were no better than dumps for children. Instead they took their inspiration from the word the Cubans used – circle – and chose *ciranda*, the name of a popular children's dance performed in a circle, because it transmitted the idea of both solidarity and having fun.

The Itinerant School

By the early 1990s the MST was well on the way to providing schools for the settlements, but the more intractable problem of providing good education for children in the camps remained. By their very nature, camps were temporary. They could last anything from a few weeks to ten years. They could be disbanded overnight by an eviction. Until then, the families had done as best they could. With the encouragement of the MST leadership, they had set up schools as soon as they could. But conditions were extremely precarious. The schools were often held in the open air, under the trees, because it was the only place available. It might seem romantic but there were problems. Children got stung by insects. They were exposed to extreme weather: in the south it could be bitterly cold and windy, while in the north and northeast it was often hot and humid. There was often a shortage of properly trained teachers.

7. Schoolchildren, Agro
Isa Camp, Pernambuco
(*João Zinclar*)

In 1996 a group of *sem-terra* in Rio Grande do Sul proposed an Itinerant School,
a flexible school suited to the conditions of camp life. The MST's national education
council in the state gave the go-ahead and the experiment began in 1997. The
organisers selected a state school in a settlement as a base. They then used the
travelling circus principle to send teachers and all their equipment – classrooms,
desks, chairs and blackboards, all of which had to be portable – to the camps. There
the teachers trained *acampados* (camp dwellers) as teachers and monitors, with the
base school providing teaching materials and support, as well as carrying out regular
inspections. To cope with the uncertainties of camp life, which made it difficult for
the children to follow the normal school year, they arranged the school work in
'stages', which could be completed in shorter or longer periods, as convenient.

The flexibility of the Itinerant School was put to the test in March and April
1998 when a group of *sem-terra*, who had occupied three large *latifúndios* in the
interior of Rio Grande do Sul, were evicted from their camps by the police, and

organised a protest march to Porto Alegre. The Itinerant School decided to go with them. One of the teachers describes how the school functioned during the march: 'our classrooms were all sorts of different places – the middle of the street, market stalls, football fields, pavilions at agricultural fairs, our own tents, parish halls, school yards'.[5] They learnt to improvise:

> our desks and seats were the hard, cold ground, the blackboard was a piece of paper taped to the wall, to the railings, to the trees or just held in the teacher's hand. We learnt by seeing, living and doing. We calculated the kilometres, metres, centimetres of the road we had to take, the number of days it would take to arrive in the capital, what was produced in the towns we went through ... We saw cars, horses, carts, trains, planes, a helicopter, boats, ships, so we studied means of transport. We sang in front of 2,000 people (at the teachers' union assembly in Porto Alegre). ... When we decided to write a letter to the governor, we talked about the theme, we wrote about it, each one giving an idea, then it was read and approved by the collective school.[6]

In Porto Alegre they held classes on the pavement in front of the building of the state government's financial department. The children visited ordinary schools to talk about the *sem-terra* experience, about why they were marching ('we are marching because we want land to plant and have a better life'). They had to overcome their shyness, and even found themselves being asked for their autographs. In spite of the novelty, it was not easy to keep the school going for nearly two months. Scarce resources and exhaustion took their toll. But the teachers managed. In 1998 fellow teachers in Rio Grande do Sul awarded the Itinerant School a prize for 'pedagogic innovation'. The idea was later adopted in other regions.

In the early years the families were so keen to get their children into schools that they neglected another problem – the widespread illiteracy among adults. While the MST held sporadic literacy courses in the camps, it was not until 1989 that it began to talk about a national literacy drive, and it was only in 1996 that it finally organised a campaign to train over 7,000 literacy agents to work in selected MST settlements. The MST persuaded the ministry of education (MEC) to pay for the campaign, which was considerably cheaper than most comparable government programmes. The Chancellor of Brasília University, João Todorov, was so impressed – even declaring the MST had 'done more for rural education than government programmes in the previous 500 years' – that he proposed that, at a cost of R$ 35 million, the programme should be extended to 21 states as a joint University/MST/MEC project.[7] The idea was to train monitors, who would then give literacy courses to 94,000 men and women. With the backing of the other university chancellors, Todorov was appointed coordinator of the programme.

At the end of 1997 Raul Jungmann, the minister of land reform, took over the programme, which was christened PRONERA (the National Programme of Land Reform Education), and promised to extend it further. Although the minister promised generous funding, only 10 per cent of the sum required had been disbursed by the middle of the year. Finally, in 2000, the government abolished the programme.

Training for Activists

As it developed and spread across Brazil, the MST also realised that the battle for land required the *sem-terra* to show not only the physical courage to stand up to gunmen but also the intellectual confidence to confront opponents in government offices, courtrooms and television studios. For many of them, the latter challenge was the more difficult. The earlier slogan, 'we are the *sem-terra* and we have a right to schools', became 'we have the duty to study because we are *sem-terra*', as they realised that they needed to be better educated to understand what was happening around them. They had to know what to say when the authorities said to them, as they had said to Darci Maschio, 'you're here to *beg* for land aren't you? Because here nobody's going to *demand* anything! You don't have that right!'

There was also a practical reason for wanting better-trained cadres. As the number of camps and settlements had multiplied, so the MST's need for coordinators, technicians and planners to take on the myriad tasks of a complex organisation had grown. At the beginning, Catholic seminaries in the south of Brazil had supplied the MST with many of its most enthusiastic activists, some of them firebrands who saw the new movement as a chance to carry out the long-postponed revolution. As the movement expanded, however, most of the *militantes* began to emerge from the rank and file of the *sem-terra* themselves, the sons and daughters of illiterate rural labourers and sharecroppers. These new activists needed practical and political training.

In the 1980s the MST and the left-wing trade union confederation CUT organised three joint training courses each year to respond to the needs of activists at different levels. The idea was to develop the *militantes'* critical awareness by teaching them the basic principles of economics, politics and sociology and by analysing the praxis developed in the struggle for land. The MST and CUT named each course after a man or woman murdered in the struggle over land: the rural trade union presidents Margarida Maria Alves and Eloy Ferreira Silva, and the priest Josimo Moraes Tavares. In 1990, as the unemployment crisis undermined trade union membership, the MST went ahead with these courses by itself.

The MST has also set up one-year courses for young people, aged 16 to 24, to allow them to complete their primary education and to learn the basic principles of organic farming. One of these takes place at the *Centro de Formação e Pesquisa Ernesto Che Guevara* (CEPAG), situated in northern Paraná. Perhaps because of its name, CEPAG has been frequently accused of 'training youngsters in Cuban-style guerrilla warfare'. It was a little disappointing to discover, when we visited it one hot afternoon in November, that it was no more than a boarding school for 21 young people – 16 boys and 5 girls. The youngsters were in the classrooms in the mornings, where they learnt all the normal subjects, spiced up with the MST's views on the evils of capitalism and the importance of revolutionary struggle, while in the afternoons they were being taught how to cultivate crops without the use of chemicals.

The young people proudly showed us their compost beds, their vegetable garden and their fields of maize, beans and rice. Many of them, like José Roberto Morais (*see* box 6.3), had had tough lives.

For US sociologist James Petras the emphasis on training is one of the things that distinguish the MST from earlier peasant and guerrilla movements. He lists several 'decisive aspects' of what he calls the 'new peasant movements in Latin America' (which includes both the MST and the Zapatista movement in Mexico) that are different from earlier movements: they are more democratic, in that peasants at the local level have a great deal of autonomy and are not just a conveyor belt for decisions taken by a central committee; the leadership is collective, not dominated by powerful individuals, which means that there are no personality cults; and the peasants are trained politically so that they can contribute to the internal debates.[8]

Not everyone, however, sees the MST methods with such positive eyes. The lecturer Zander Navarro accuses the movement of being authoritarian and says its leaders have become 'drunk with power'. He says that the system of organisation, through cadres, effectively blocks the 'mass' of the members from possessing any real power. He believes that young *militantes* are victims of 'ideological indoctrination' and are being offered 'the heady cocktail of adventure with the promise of power'. 'Young illiterate peasants, who had no prospects, go on a course and suddenly find themselves leading an occupation of over a thousand people', he said. 'No wonder it goes to their heads.' Navarro also accuses the MST of imposing 'military discipline'. 'The courses begin each day at 6 a.m. with the singing of the MST anthem and the running up of the flag'.

Some of Navarro's accusations are accurate. As will be discussed more fully in chapter 13, the MST is not always as democratic as its activists claim. Unsurprisingly, many of the founders of the movement, among them João Pedro Stédile, are still extremely influential. But, for all that, the grassroots democratic structure is not a sham. All members are encouraged to become active and to have their say. The leaders listen to what the base says and there are checks on the power of the inner clique. Other of Navarro's criticisms are less convincing. It does not seem to be inherently wrong for young people, who believed they had been condemned to a life of marginalisation and social exclusion, to be excited – or even inebriated – by the new responsibilities and opportunities that the MST opens up for them. And the 'militarisation' is a way that the movement has found to instil the external and internal discipline required during the first difficult months of an occupation. This strategy has the overwhelming support of MST members.

At a training camp in Diamantina in the state of Maranhão, where young *militantes* from the north and northeast go for courses lasting two to three months, we watched a new group begin their 'indoctrination'. They learned to march in step and to raise clenched fists as they sang MST slogans. They were even given 'little red books' containing MST teachings on a number of subjects. But the activists were also learning how to rear poultry, plant vegetable gardens and clean up litter. In the

Box 6.3 *José Roberto Morais*

I'm 17 years old. When I was very small, my father got the sack from the ranch he worked on in the north of Paraná. We all had to go to the nearest town, Colorado. We arrived in the bus station and had nowhere to go. I'll never forget it. We had to sleep under a viaduct and we had to beg. My mother couldn't take it, all the poverty and wretchedness. She left my father and all of her six children. A bit later my eldest brother went off to São Paulo. He worked as a male prostitute. Then, just a while ago, he was killed in a brawl in a bar. A man shot him, six times.

We lived on the streets for quite a long while. My three sisters got jobs as maids and then got married in the town. Life's hard for them but they're OK. They've got somewhere to live. It was harder for us men. We had to survive through odd jobs. It was hard.

Then my father got to know about the movement. And the three of us – me, my father and my other brother – we went on this occupation. I liked the life in the camp. I wasn't used to a nice home so I didn't miss the comforts of city life. I just liked the space and the chance to play football. It was so nice not to have pollution, violence, drugs, prostitution. It was so safe in the camp. My mother started visiting us. She didn't approve at all in the beginning, but now she likes it.

We got evicted once. Since we'd occupied the land, gunmen had been sniffing around. If we went out on to the road, they'd shoot near us, to scare us. But then one day – it was Christmas Day, 1999 – they came into the camp. We were all having lunch, sharing the little food we'd got. There were about 30 of them, military police and gunmen. I remember that a bullet whistled close by my head. They beat up a lot of people. One of my friends was so badly hurt that he couldn't walk for weeks afterwards. One pregnant woman was so hurt and scared that she lost her baby. And they set light to everything. We hadn't got many belongings and we lost them all!

We were about 150 families. Some were so frightened that they gave up. The rest of us, about 90 families, went to a neighbouring camp. And then we reoccupied again, with the help of some of the other families. The gunmen tried to stop us. They shot at us and we retreated, but then we advanced again. We just had scythes and knives. But there were a lot of us and we were determined. Most of us hadn't anything to lose. We hadn't anywhere else to go. That gives you courage.

The estate hasn't been expropriated but we've been told that we're going to get the land. The MST has already marked out the plots. I used to think that it was wrong for the MST to take land from estate owners. But I don't think that any more. They probably stole it in the first place. And who said that they could have such enormous tracts while we don't have anything?

I was a bit scared about coming to this training school. I hardly went to school when I was a kid. I only learnt to read and write at the school in the camp. I thought it would be too hard. But it isn't. I'm managing to keep up. We study in the morning and then learn about farming in the afternoon. It's great fun. My younger brother came last year, but he gave up. He was only 15 and he missed us all, particularly my dad, who's getting old and ill. But I'm older and I realise how much I'm learning. I want to train with the MST, become a militant and help with the revolution. There are so many people out there who need help. When I lived on the streets, I vowed that I'd get out of the violence and the wretchedness. And I have. But so many of the kids I knew then have become drug addicts or got killed. I was so lucky to meet the movement.

---

informal atmosphere typical of Brazil, the *militantes* were constantly laughing and clearly enjoying themselves. It was difficult to take too seriously the charge of 'militarisation'.

The conditions on the courses are often Spartan. Jorge Neri, an MST leader in Pará, told us that he had nearly left the movement during the first course he attended, because of the poor food, the hard mattresses, the lack of running water, alcohol and television, and the unrelenting pace of it all. About 200 young people due to arrive for the three-month course at the Catalunha settlement in Pernambuco were told they must each bring their own 'activist kit' consisting of a mattress, sheet, plate, spoon and glass, soap and toothpaste, plus a quantity of beans, rice, *fubá* (maize flour) and dried meat as a contribution to the camp kitchens. There was clearly no room for luxuries, like cigarettes or beer. But there are also compensations. As well as classes in political doctrine and the history and geography of Brazil, the *militantes* at Catalunha were also to have the chance of learning how to play the guitar, develop computer skills and become radio presenters. They would spend half of their time acquiring practical skills, such as farming organically and running a cooperative. 'I came back from my course a different person', said Jorge Neri. 'I'd given up smoking and stopped drinking heavily. I learnt that it isn't enough to have ideas about the transformation of society. You've got to begin with yourself.'

Many MST *militantes* are totally dedicated. Luís Fernando, 29 years old, lives with his family in the Ouro Verde settlement in Pernambuco, but his children and wife scarcely see him. He is out, day and night, working for the movement. His enthusiasm is evident from the very look of his house. The metal gate in front of his house is entirely covered with a painting of the MST flag. Inside, a poster of Che Guevara decorates one wall. On another hangs a photograph of Serra Pelada, the open-air goldmine in the Amazon, showing hundreds of mud-covered men toiling in search of the precious metal. Most of them had been landless rural workers who joined the 1980s goldrush. The picture was taken by the world-renowned photographer Sebastião Salgado, himself a fervent supporter of the MST. As Luís

Fernando talks, it is evident that without the MST his life would have been completely different. He is one of the 'fanatics' that upset Zander Navarro.

The MST's achievements are impressive. By 2001 about 150,000 children were enrolled in 1,200 primary and secondary schools in its settlements and camps. The schools employed 3,800 teachers, many of them MST-trained. The movement had trained 1,200 educators who had run courses for 25,000 young people and adults. It was running training courses for primary-school teachers in most states. It had set up partnerships with international agencies, such as UNESCO and UNICEF, as well as with the Catholic Church. It had reached agreement with seven institutes of higher education in different regions to provide degree courses in education for MST teachers. It was doing this not only because the Brazilian government was demanding better qualifications for its teachers, especially in secondary schools, but also because the teachers themselves wanted more education. Non-MST schools had adopted some of the movement's publications for use by their teachers. The movement has helped to organise a number of national and local conferences to rethink rural education. In perhaps its most ambitious project of all the MST has begun building the *Escola Nacional Florestan Fernandes*, also known as the *Universidade da Terra* (University of the Land), at Guararema near São Paulo. Each month, a brigade of volunteer *militantes*, men and women, comes from a different state to provide the labour. The bricks are made on the site out of baked mud. This college will run residential courses for *militantes* from all over Brazil.

Despite these initiatives, there is widespread agreement within the MST that much more needs to be done. Many activists believe that most teachers in their schools are still too conditioned by the dominant methodology of learning by rote and are too uncritical of orthodox views. The MST has made only limited progress in the construction of its own pedagogy. Though the movement constantly expresses admiration for Paulo Freire, it has not yet managed to apply his views systematically. This is not surprising. The MST wants its schools to be run by the *sem-terra* themselves. It takes time to train a new generation of politically aware and innovative teachers, recruited from illiterate, or barely literate, peasant families without a tradition of reading or studying. The MST is also cautious about imposing a single methodology. 'That would be against the MST philosophy of not having a model for anything', said Roseli Caldart. 'We prefer to provide guidelines and to help teachers develop the methods that work best for their particular school.'

The MST is taking measures to keep alive among the second generation the awareness that the education that they are receiving today is a right conquered for them by their parents. At the 29 de Outubro school (named after the day of the Annoni occupation) in the settlement of Novo Sarandí in Rio Grande do Sul, the teachers periodically erect a black polythene tent on the grass in front of the school. It is just like the ones the children's parents lived in for years to win their land. Inside the hut parents and teachers show photographs and tell stories about the camp. And in Porto Alegre in October 1999, during a meeting of several hundred *sem-terrinhas*, which is the term used for children from camps and settlements, some activists took the children to visit the city's shanty-towns. 'We wanted to show them where they would be living today, if we hadn't conquered the land', said one father, Oney Zamarchi, president of the cooperative at the Nova Ronda Alta settlement.

This is the formal side of the MST's educational system. But just as important in the MST's view are the occupations themselves, which are seen as a unique 'school of life' where men and women discover their own worth, acquire self-assurance and knowledge, and become citizens. Many of the men and women who now run cooperatives, meat-packing plants or schools, began their lives with no other prospect than that of being illiterate labourers or even becoming modern-day slaves, lured into debt bondage in remote areas of the Amazon forest.[9] In 1999 and 2000 over a thousand such slaves were discovered and set free in the Amazon region but the law that demands the expropriation of these estates, so that the land can be divided up among landless families, has never been enforced.

José de Souza Martins has recognised the wish of the *sem-terra* to be proper citizens: 'they want a social reform for the new generations, a reform that recognises them not only as workers but as people who have the right to the fruits of their labour. They want, in short, to be recognised as integral members of society.'[10] The *sem-terra* have learnt through their short history that this is a right that they will have to conquer for themselves. As their beloved Paulo Freire said: 'It is not through resignation but rebellion in the face of injustice that we affirm ourselves as human beings'.[11] For the *sem-terra*, true education not only teaches you how to read and write but also instils in you the courage to rebel.

PART THREE

This section looks at the forces pitted against the MST in its struggle. The most vicious opposition so far has come, predictably enough, from the old agrarian elites in backward states that are unwilling to cede a single hectare of land to the *sem-terra*, whom they regard as agitators and criminals. Clinging on to their vast estates, these landowners have waged ruthless war on the MST, sending in gunmen and gaining irregular eviction orders from pliant judges. Because the agrarian elites have a strong voice in Congress, the federal government has been reluctant to move effectively against them. Chapters 7 and 8 look in detail at the clash between the MST and the landowners in Brazil's most violent states – Pará and Paraná.

The MST, however, is not just fighting out-dated elites, which may eventually be forced to adapt to the modern world or face extinction. The movement also confronts more formidable long-term obstacles of a very different nature. The movement has gained its national (and international) renown from what it is learning to do well: conquer land and establish settlements. Yet the movement harbours much greater ambitions. Far from being a small movement that is willing to coexist with the major economic and political forces in Brazilian society, provided its members gain minor concessions, the MST dreams of leading a broad-based social movement that will bring wide-ranging reforms to the country's agrarian, social and economic structures and end the centuries-old inequalities.

In its struggle to revolutionise Brazilian society, the MST is swimming against a tide of structural changes that are sweeping over the farming sector and taking it in a very different direction. For Brazilian agriculture is being integrated into the world economy. Trade barriers are being swept away. Multinational corporations are moving in to monopolise sectors that are either highly profitable or of long-term strategic importance. Under the new rules of the game, Brazilian farmers, big and small, will have to learn how to compete in this new world or face bankruptcy. Chapter 9 looks at this whole painful process. The Cardoso government believes that the only role for peasant farmers in this new world is either to cultivate crops and rear livestock for the big economic groups, working as a kind of bonded labour, or to fill niches in the market, producing crops of no interest to the commercial farmers. Chapter 10 analyses the government's attempt, in uneasy collaboration with the World Bank, to develop a market-oriented programme of agrarian reform to fit in with this new reality.

The MST is struggling not just against this harsh new economic climate, for it also faces the political opposition of the government. In the early days the Cardoso government resented the MST's criticisms but refrained from outright confrontation, largely because it saw the movement as ineffectual. In 1997, however, the government became alarmed at the MST's growth and began to regard it as an ideological foe that it had to combat. Chapter 11 charts this process.

8. Friar Francineto faces the police (*Raimundo Pacco*)

CHAPTER 7

Massacre in the Amazon

On 17 April 2000, around 4,000 *sem-terra* and their supporters were coming to the end of a demonstration in Belém, the capital of Pará, to demand justice for the 19 *sem-terra* who had been killed in what has become known as the 'massacre of Eldorado de Carajás' in 1996. Four years had passed and, despite a lengthy investigation and a farcical trial that ended in acquittal and was later annulled, not a single military policeman had been convicted.

The *sem-terra* were tired. They had just spent an exhausting weekend in an occupied estate outside Belém. They had been discussing new, ecologically friendly ways of farming the fragile Amazonian soils and, in scrupulously fair elections, they had chosen a new state leadership. The hot sun beat down as the demonstrators, wearing their distinctive red caps and waving MST flags, walked down the avenue, bordered by colonial-style houses, that led into one of the city's central squares. Some *sem-terra* had gone ahead and set up temporary tents in the square. They had prepared huge cauldrons of rice and beans. It was half past one in the afternoon. 'I'm starving', confessed one middle-aged peasant woman, wearing a large straw hat tied with a ribbon under her chin, a red MST t-shirt, baggy shorts and flip-flops. 'I was up at 4 a.m. and I haven't had anything to eat yet.' As the procession began to move into the square, she added with a grin, 'I can already smell the beans.'

At that precise moment, lines of military policemen armed with riot shields, riot helmets, revolvers, tear-gas bombs and truncheons marched into the square from two sides. *Sem-terra* screamed as tear-gas bombs landed among the tents and shots rang out. People tried to flee but there was nowhere to go. A friar, Francineto Alves, dressed in a brown robe and sandals, knelt in front of the advancing troops. 'For the love of God,' he implored, 'no more violence.' A policeman grabbed him and threw him to one side. He was immediately arrested. A group of *sem-terra* women, anger blazing from their faces, formed a cordon to confront the soldiers, but a *sem-terra* leader, speaking through a microphone from a lorry, called on them to stop. 'This is no time for confrontation', he said. 'Walk backwards, slowly and carefully.' Showing the discipline for which the MST is renowned, the women obeyed. News of what had happened had by then filtered back to the part of the demonstration that could

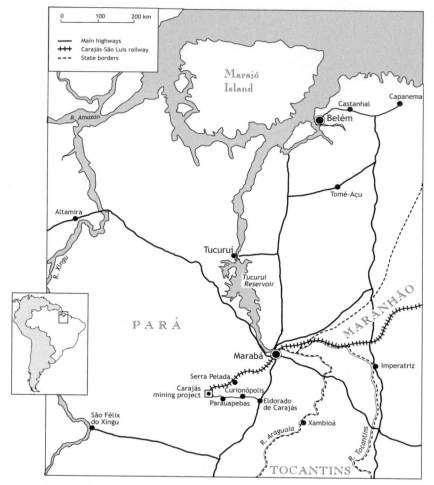

Eastern Amazonia

not enter the square. In their frustration at being separated from their comrades, some *sem-terra* began defiantly to shout MST slogans, while others set cars alight and invaded a building belonging to the department of public security.

Back in the square, the *sem-terra* were herded into a smaller and smaller space, as the troops advanced. Several demonstrators, including a child, were hit by plastic bullets. Tear-gas bombs injured others. A pale-faced man broke into convulsive sobs. It later emerged that his 18-year-old son, Oziel Alves Pereira, had been killed in the massacre four years earlier. Another woman fainted. She, too, had been on the highway at Eldorado de Carajás. Just as it seemed that another massacre was inevitable, the military policemen stopped. They lined up in front of the state tribunal of military justice, which stood on one side of the square. The *sem-terra*, huddled on the other side, carried on with their demonstration as best they could.

Along with some progressive local politicians, MST leaders stood up in their lorry and denounced what had happened through their loudspeaker. Just at that moment, torrential rain began to fall. Wet, hungry and miserable, the *sem-terra* listened to the leaders for over two hours. Over a dozen, who had been seriously injured at Eldorado de Carajás, sat inside a tent. Most were so traumatised that they could barely speak. Ambulances arrived, taking 18 people to hospital.

That night Paulo Sette Camara, a colonel who had collaborated with the military during the dictatorship and was at that time head of what was euphemistically called the Secretariat of Social Defence (but was really the department of public security), went on local television. Expressing more pain than indignation, he said in a soft, silky voice that Belém had once more been subjected to the 'uncontrolled violence' of 'MST radicals', who had 'burnt cars and invaded public property'. Some time later the civil police called for the arrest, without bail, of four MST leaders, accused of 'provoking public disorder'.

The State of Pará

Pará is a tumultuous state, twice as large as France, lying in the east of the Amazon basin. 'This region is violent, probably the most violent place in Brazil', said Carlos Guedes, the local Pastoral Land Commission (CPT) lawyer, sitting in his small office at his home in Marabá one Saturday in April 2000.

> Working with mercenaries employed by the big landowners, the military police is a law unto itself. In São Paulo, the military police carry out massacres, usually killing young black men they suspect of being criminals. And occasionally the authorities investigate and punish people for these crimes. Here the impunity is absolute. From 1988 to 1998, we know that these gunmen killed at least 488 people. In only one case were the assassins brought to justice. Two gunmen were sentenced to 50 years' imprisonment, but they escaped after three months. The federal authorities know very well what is going on, but don't do anything. They say that violence is inevitable in a frontier region. It will only end, they say, when the region is incorporated into the rest of Brazil. Their attitude is extremely irresponsible.

Carlos Guedes has a lonely life. He meticulously reports all crimes, without any hope of getting justice in an unwieldy and highly bureaucratic judicial system that is heavily biased in favour of the big landowners. 'I can only ever get anywhere when the crime is so outrageous that there are repercussions in the rest of Brazil and abroad', he said, sighing deeply and drinking glass after glass of iced water. He had had a long and unrewarding morning. While his wife looked after their young baby, of which he is inordinately proud, he had been down to the police office to report a break-in in the MST regional office the previous night. Ignoring other valuable objects, such as a photocopying machine, computer terminals and telephones, the thieves had taken the central computer, with all its floppy discs. 'It was clearly a politically motivated crime', said Carlos. 'The thieves forced their way in, smashing windows and breaking down doors. They did a lot of gratuitous damage, breaking cupboards and scattering papers on the floor. There are a lot of dogs in the house next door. Their barking must have disturbed the family, but no one admits to having heard anything. It even took me hours to get the bored officer in the local police station to take down the details.' The MST *militantes* are stoical. 'It was a warning', said Patrício. 'We were planning a big occupation for tonight. It's the landowners' way of telling us that they know and they're ready for us. We've decided to postpone the action for a more favourable moment.'

More clearly than anywhere else in Brazil, the MST and the landowners in Pará are waging war. The MST arrived in 1989, when the region was experiencing chaotic change. Since 1920 the local elite had been making huge fortunes through the export of Brazil nuts. It was wealth based on trade, not farming, which tended to reinforce the elite's scorn for physical labour, part of the legacy of slavery. Traditional families rented huge areas of tropical forest, immensely rich in Brazil nuts, from the government and for a few months of the year they employed migrant workers to gather the *ouriços*, the size of cannonballs, as they fell from the majestic Brazil nut trees, and then to break them open to take out the dozen or so Brazil nuts. The 'landowners', as they claimed to be, treated their workforce atrociously, paying very low wages and beating – or even killing – any workers who dared to demand better conditions. The region was remote and inaccessible. Very few reports of what was happening found their way out into the wider world. At the same time, a front of peasant families, known as *posseiros* (squatters), was slowly moving in to the region from Maranhão in the east. The families cleared small plots of land in the forest, planted cassava, rice and beans, and moved on when the land became exhausted.

All this began to change in the 1970s. 'The military government decided to integrate this region into the rest of the country', said Carlos Guedes. 'It set up a tax break system, so that big companies, both national and international, could use money that they would have otherwise paid to the government in income tax to set up huge cattle ranches. Volkswagen, for instance, set up a ranch the size of Greater São Paulo.' The companies arriving to open the cattle ranches found *posseiros* living on the land and sent gunmen to evict them. At the same time, they brought in labourers from the northeast to clear the land. From 1984 to 1986 Volkswagen had 700 or 800 labourers working on its estate in conditions of near slavery. 'Many federal government officials speak today as if the violence in Pará is a direct result of its backwardness', said Carlos Guedes. 'But history tells us differently. It was the arrival of the big capitalist companies that sparked off the surge in violence.'

The Catholic Church became profoundly concerned at the level of violence and in 1975 it set up the CPT – the body that was to play a key role in the foundation of the MST – to help the isolated families. What had also left a deep mark was the brutality of the 15,000 troops brought in to combat a small group of left-wing guerrillas who set up a base in the region at the end of the 1960s. The army wiped them out before they had a chance to carry out any operations. 'The fear of the army that peasant families still feel is remarkable', said Maria Célia Nunes Coelho, a geographer from the Advanced Nucleus of Amazon Studies. 'Many of them had sons killed or tortured. The dread is still there. It's being handed down from generation to generation.'

Even after the counter-insurgency operation had ended, the violence continued, now largely committed by the ranchers and their gunmen. To allow the old elite to sell its lands to the new influx of companies, a local politician, Jader Barbalho, at that time minister of agrarian reform in the federal government, had agreed to give them land titles for the vast areas covered with Brazil nut trees. Thousands of peasant families, evicted from the land, migrated to the towns. Some began to fight back. 'Unemployed men got together on the outskirts of towns', said José Batista Gonçalves Afonso, another CPT lawyer, who works closely with Carlos Guedes. 'They had no chance of getting a job and didn't even have the money for the fare back to their states of origin. So 20, 50, 100 or even 200 men would get together. They'd leave their families behind and go into the forest, with their rifles on their backs and their machetes in their hands. They would launch lightning attacks on the gunmen sent in by the landowners until they won the land or were defeated.'

The numbers of desperate men were swollen by hundreds of thousands of impoverished gold-diggers who swarmed to the region in the early 1980s to chance their luck in the huge opencast mine of Serra Pelada. This was discovered when in 1980 Brazil's largest state-owned mining company, Companhia Vale do Rio Doce (CVRD), set up a big mining project nearby to exploit the immense reserves of iron ore that had been found in the mountain range of Carajás. All these economic and social upheavals provoked violent conflicts. The worst year was 1985 when there were 134 registered assassinations, just in the state of Pará.

It was into this minefield that the MST arrived in 1989, with its very different strategy for conquering land. 'The MST is methodical', said José Batista. 'It lists the names of the landless. It works with the whole family – men, women and children. And it goes to great lengths to increase their level of political awareness.' At first, the activists were cautious, taking time to get to know the region. For a while they worked closely with the *posseiros*. On 10 January 1990, about 100 MST families occupied a ranch in the district of Conceição do Araguaia, in the southeast of the state. They were joining a group of *posseiros* who were involved in a fierce conflict with gunmen sent in by the ranch owner.

After a few months, however, the MST decided on a more spectacular action. With the support of the CPT, it spent seven months working with landless families around Marabá, which was already emerging as one of the most violent regions in the state. The MST was keen to introduce one of its trademarks – the mass occupation – into the region. It was a courageous decision. Brazil was being governed by the hard-line Collor, who had unleashed a fierce onslaught against the MST. Undeterred, the movement was fighting back. One of the most quoted slogans of that day was: Agrarian Reform – By Law or By Force.

The MST's telephones were bugged and informers wormed their way into the meetings. Not surprisingly, the information filtered out that the MST was planning a huge occupation, with 1,500 families, for the second half of June 1991. President Collor himself sent down a federal police officer to mastermind the anti-MST operation. On 17 June, the police blocked all the roads leading out of Marabá and arrested seven MST leaders, accusing them of being guerrilla fighters and promoting illegal land invasions. The development of the MST in the region was effectively barred – for a year. On 16 July 1992, the MST organised the occupation of a ranch in the nearby district of Parauapebas. Gunmen were already evicting the first arrivals before all of the 548 families had arrived. But by then the MST had realised that it must always have a second option if its planned occupation failed. The families mounted a temporary camp in front of the INCRA office in Marabá. The MST used the camp as a base for a never-ending series of demonstrations and mobilisations. After five months, an exhausted INCRA capitulated and bought a large area of land from the ranch that the MST had originally occupied and settled the families on it. The MST had truly arrived in Pará.[1]

Relations with the Catholic Church were not always easy. 'The Church had worked here in the 1970s. It had been here during the violent anti-guerrilla operation. It had made an "option" for the *posseiros*, offering them a great deal of support', said Maria Célia Nunes Coelho.

> Many members of the MST are old *posseiros* but there is a great deal of rivalry between the *sem-terra* and the *posseiros*. They don't mix. The MST is a new-style movement, imported, with an impressive know-how about organising land occupations. This makes it totally different from the *posseiros*, a movement that invades the land, leaves the land, enters again, but always in a disorganised fashion. The Church has an enormous difficulty in accepting the MST, because it appears as a tough movement, organised on military lines. The hierarchical structure created by the MST is, in fact, similar to military hierarchy. They don't do anything here without the backing of the national leadership. ... When you talk to people from the Church today, you feel their profound nostalgia for the old days of the *posseiro*.[2]

What made the MST's work in the south of Pará even more difficult was the kind of family it was recruiting into the movement. 'In the south of Brazil, in Rio Grande do Sul or in Pontal de Paranapanema, the families know how to farm', said Maria Célia Nunes Coelho. 'This is not the case in Pará. Here most of the impoverished, landless families have lost their direct link with the land. The men have dug for gold. They've worked for big companies, slashing-and-burning the forest. They've got to learn once again how to farm – and to farm in Amazonian conditions. That's a serious problem.'

The Eldorado de Carajás Massacre

In the early 1990s the MST developed a strategy for the south of Pará. They knew that one way or another they had to confront the big new power in the region –

CVRD – if they were to conquer land. They decided to cross the river Parauapebas and invade the large forest reserve, of over 400,000 hectares, that CVRD had created in the region. 'They knew that CVRD would evict them violently from its reserve', said Maria Célia Nunes Coelho. 'But they wanted a conflict. They knew that CVRD was powerful and had an image to preserve. They could force the mayor of Parauapebas, the state government's land institute (ITERPA), INCRA and the ministry of agrarian reform to sit down and negotiate with them.'

At first, the strategy worked well. About 200 families invaded the forest reserve and were evicted by the police. INCRA intervened, promising the families land in another area. For over a year the families waited, living in a temporary camp on the outskirts of the small and disorganised town of Parauapebas, full of bars and brothels, which had mushroomed, unplanned, beside the high fence that stops unauthorised people from entering CVRD's land. As always happens when there is the whiff of free land in the air, the camp acted as a magnet for all the desperate landless people in the region. Soon there were about 1,200 families living in the camp. INCRA finally offered the families land near the Tapirapé river, a remote area of virgin forest, about 150 km from Parauapebas. But some of the families had already lived in an isolated settlement. They knew that every year during the long rainy season, when the settlement becomes completely inaccessible, children died from malaria and other treatable diseases.

So the families turned down the offer and, in their frustration, invaded a nearby estate, called Fazenda Rio Branco, which, they said, was the kind of land they wanted. Fazenda Rio Branco belonged to the Lunardelli family, one of the most powerful landowners in Brazil, which had earned its initial wealth from coffee plantations in São Paulo but had then spread all over the country. Francisco Graziano, president of INCRA at the time, wrote later: 'Fazenda Rio Branco was reasonably productive. It reared good quality cattle. I couldn't expropriate it. ... But I called in the owners, young lads, who were very understanding, and in a few days I negotiated a price.'[3] Though only 250 families could be settled in Fazenda Rio Branco, the conflict seemed over. 'The families were so happy that they invited me to come to Pará the day they were to get the titles for their new plots. They wanted to hold a party.'[4] Graziano travelled to Pará in October 1995.

But the president of INCRA was in for a nasty surprise. He had failed to realise that for the MST Fazenda Rio Branco was only a stepping-stone.

Instead of thanking me for settling the families on Fazenda Rio Branco, the MST demanded the expropriation of a vast neighbouring ranch, called Macaxeira. I was standing on a raised platform on a lorry. Over 2,000 people, impoverished, miserable people, with suffering in their eyes, marched by. Under the guidance of young people, who didn't seem to me to be either northeasterners or rural workers, they lifted up scythes and machetes and shouted: 'Now Macaxeira! Now Macaxeira!' I had fallen into a trap. Up on that lorry, I felt afraid. Although protected by a cordon of military policemen, I was panic-stricken, seeing those sharp implements in the fists of the workers. They were expressing anger, social violence. Arms against repression. And I was representing the government.[5]

Graziano felt betrayed. 'I could remember what the *sem-terra* leader, Fusquinha, had told me in Brasília. He and the other leaders had made a public commitment not to invade any more land in the region, provided they received Fazenda Rio Branco.' But once back in Pará the leaders had broken their promise. 'I went to Pará with the hope of dismantling that camp once and for all. I travelled back to Brasília with the feeling that everything was beginning again. Where would it all end?'

Box 7.1 *Antônio Alves de Oliveira (Índio)*

I'm 40 years old. I was born in Lucilândia in Piauí. I had six brothers and sisters. My parents were sharecroppers. I liked studying and I wanted to carry on, but then, when I was 12 years old, my father left my mother. I became the main breadwinner and had to give up school.

In 1979 Jari [a large US-owned company] was recruiting labourers to work on the huge project it was opening up in the north of the Amazon. I went and started planting gmelina [an Asian species of tree]. But the work was too hard for me. I've always been small and thin. I think that's why people call me *Índio* (Indian). I spent three months there and for two of them I was in bed with malaria. People said it was difficult to leave, that they held you there like slaves, but they let me go alright. I think they thought I wasn't tough enough. Then I found another job in the Amazon, looking after black pepper plants for a Japanese man in Tomé-Açu. That was much better. The Japanese man didn't pay me much but he treated me well, almost like a son. I stayed there for a year and a half. And then I heard they were paying labourers well to clear land at Tucuruí, where they were building a dam for a hydroelectric power station. So off I went. It was January 1982, I think. But that didn't work out very well. We were applying chemicals to kill the vegetation. It made me feel ill.

I stayed for a while and then one night I dreamt of getting rich at Serra Pelada. The dream was so real that I left the next day, even though it meant losing quite a bit of money. When I got there, it was all exactly as I'd thought. Except that I didn't get rich! But it was good fun. There were 150,000 men there, all of us digging in the mud. Major Curió was in charge. He kept order. People respected each other and there were no robberies. I caught gold fever, I suppose. I got obsessed about striking lucky. I spent well over ten years in the region, working in lots of different *garimpos* [gold mines].

I was at Serra Pelada during the massacre. It was 1987, I think. There were about 15,000 of us *garimpeiros* [gold miners]. We were demanding our rights. The authorities wanted to close down Serra Pelada and we wanted to stop them. We were on a bridge when the police hemmed us in on both sides, just as they did at Eldorado de Carajás. There were helicopters flying above us. The police were shooting from all sides. I was lucky. I hadn't got on the bridge so I was able to slip away. I lay hidden in the undergrowth by the side of the river. The *garimpeiros* didn't have anywhere to hide. So they jumped off the bridge. I can see them now, jumping off like monkeys. Dozens and dozens of them. They didn't have a chance. The bridge was 50 metres above the river and the water was low. The bodies piled up in the river.

The authorities said that three people died. That's the biggest lie I've ever heard! I don't know how many there were. But it was well over a hundred. I didn't have a mature head, like I have now. Today we wouldn't let them get away with it, but then we didn't protest. There was no investigation and the police weren't punished.

So I went on working in the *garimpos*. I was in a small one, called Cotia, in 1996. I'd got a girlfriend by then and three children. The MST came to the mine, recruiting. I decided on the spot to join. I don't think too long before I do things. I act first. If I think too much, it never works out. But my girlfriend was horrified. She said: 'either me or them'. I woke her up at 3 o'clock the following morning. 'I've chosen the MST', I said. 'I've got to find a more decent way of life so that I can bring up my children properly'. She left with the children the next morning. She went back to her mother's house. And I joined the MST.

I adored the movement from the beginning. So many ideas, about justice, about building a new Brazil. We occupied Macaxeira estate near Curionópolis. We set up the Formosa camp. I joined the health commission. And I started doing courses and going on events. I started to learn so much. So, of course, when we decided to march to Belém, I was all for it. We were about 1,500 families.

I was hurt early on in the massacre. I got three bullets – in my left foot, right knee and right heel. It was terrible, the police shooting with machine guns. There were a lot of women and children on the march. I don't believe that none of them were killed. There were so many bullets flying about. I got shot early on. I dragged myself into the undergrowth about 400 metres away from the road. When it was over, one of the demonstrators helped me walk the two kilometres to his house in Eldorado. I was bleeding a lot. Once we got there, he bound up my wounds and the bleeding stopped. I couldn't sleep. All those images kept on going through my head. The next day I got him to help me get back to the place. I wanted to see what had happened. I wanted to help the MST tell the world what had happened. But when I got there, I fainted. The civil police were there by then and they took me to the hospital in Curionópolis. There were so many wounded people there.

I won my plot of land, 25 hectares, in the *17 de Abril* settlement. I can't work it properly but a friend helps me. I've got another son now, but I want my first three children to come and live on my land. Their mother can come, too. There's room for all of us. The problem is that I've lost contact. The last thing I heard they were in Imperatriz in Maranhão. As soon as I finish my treatment, I'm going to find them. That's the only thing I regret, losing my children. I've been lucky really. I've been through two massacres and I'm still alive. And I met the MST. That was the best thing that ever happened.

Though not at all sympathetic to the MST, Graziano, who is one of Brazil's lead-ing experts on agrarian matters, was aware of the underlying causes of the conflict.

> There is little employment. And wealth is concentrated in the hands of big farmers, generally men from the south and southeast of the country. Their ranches are enormous but they are not *latifúndios*. They are productive, with planted pasture and cattle of excellent quality. Their opulence, however, is an insult to the region's poverty. … It is a very unjust system. What right has anyone to occupy 40,000 hectares, let alone100,000 hectares? In whose name? Because of the sacred rights of capitalism? The net result: the impoverished workers, who have been suffering in poverty for centuries and dream of a better life, become vulnerable to deceptive promises and political manipulation.[6]

Shortly after his visit to Pará, Graziano was forced to resign from the presidency of INCRA after being unwittingly caught up in a phone bugging scandal involving other members of the government. The man who replaced him did nothing to defuse the increasingly tense situation. Negotiations stalled. The families moved to a new camp near the town of Curionópolis to be closer to the estate they were targeting. On 5 March 1996 some *sem-terra* began to occupy Macaxeira, while others set up another camp called Formosa, near the highway that goes from Parauapebas to Marabá. As the authorities still refused to negotiate, about 1,500 families decided to march to Marabá. They walked 40 km, getting as far as Eldorado de Carajás, an ugly frontier town of unpaved roads, rough brick houses, characterless bars selling soft drinks, beer and crisps, and giant filling stations for the massive lorries that thunder along the highway. On 16 April, about 9 km beyond Eldorado de Carajás, the families mounted a roadblock at the so-called 'S curve'. Stopping all traffic, they demanded ten tonnes of food and 50 coaches to take them to Belém.

The tension had reached breaking point. Never before had the power of the landowners in the region been so openly challenged. 'There is a very large group of extremely powerful and extremely rich landowners in the south of Pará, who are well organised and well armed', said José Batista.[7] 'They act as a state within a state', added Carlos Guedes.[8] 'It is difficult to imagine any area of public administration where they don't have their say. They interfere in everything from tax to police matters. They don't bother to use intermediaries. It's done quite openly.' On 23 March a group of these landowners had met the governor, Almir Gabriel, and the secretary of public security, Paulo Sette Camara, to demand that action be taken against the MST.[9] The landowners were even filmed handing over to the secretary of public security a list of MST leaders that they wanted 'removed' from the region. At another meeting on 28 March a leading landowner from Parauapebas said that they were going to take the *sem-terra* out of Macaxeira 'by the force of arms'.[10]

'After we'd blocked the road for several hours on 16 April, Major Oliveira and several other officers from the military police appeared', said Domingos dos Reis da Conceição, known as 'Garoto' (or 'Lad'), because of his slight, youthful appearance. Garoto was 19 years old at the time. 'There was a big tailback of traffic, several kilometres long. The major agreed to send us 50 coaches to take us to Marabá and then provide another five coaches to take a delegation to Belém. He said he'd send the coaches by 11 o'clock on the following morning, so we moved off the highway.' But by 1 p.m. on 17 April no coaches had arrived. 'Eventually a lieutenant arrived, to tell us that Major Oliveira hadn't been able to get the coaches', said Garoto. 'We thought they were fobbing us off yet again, so we reoccupied the highway.'

The reoccupation appears to have been the last straw for the landowners, who put further pressure on the state government. Colonel Fábio Lopes, commander-in-chief of the military police in Pará, personally informed Colonel Pantoja that he and his men were to go to the region immediately to unblock the highway. According to press reports, Lopes told Pantoja that it was 'a direct order from the governor'.[11] Pantoja planned a pincer operation: he would send in Major Oliveira at the head of police from Parauapebas, while he personally would head those coming from Marabá. According to later press reports, gunmen, disguised in military police uniform, were sent in by the landowners to identify key MST leaders.[12]

At about 4 p.m. 68 military policemen arrived from Parauapebas. Half an hour later another 87 military policemen came from Marabá. The *sem-terra* were hemmed in. There seems little doubt that the military police intended from the beginning to use a great deal of violence to clear the *sem-terra* off the road. There is no other explanation for the fact that, before they arrived at the highway, Colonel Pantoja told his troops to remove their identification badges. Marisa Romão, a journalist who worked for a local subsidiary of the huge TV Globo network and was covering the event, is convinced that the violence was premeditated. Before the shooting began, she became alarmed at the way in which the *sem-terra* had become boxed in and she went up to Colonel Pantoja to ask for the peaceful evacuation of the families; he told her to leave the area immediately, as 'I can't guarantee your life'. 'Though the violence clearly got out of control, they were intending from the beginning to teach the MST a lesson they would never forget', she said.

'The police from Marabá advanced silently towards us', said Antônio Alves de Oliveira, known as 'Índio' (*see* box 7.1). 'Then they started throwing tear-gas bombs and shooting in the air.' The *sem-terra* threw back sticks and stones. 'They were trying to intimidate us, but we're not easily intimidated', said Índio. 'We started marching towards them. One of us had an old rifle. He tried to use it, but it didn't go off.' The police got driven back to a line of lorries they had placed across the road. At this point, they appear to have panicked and to have started using their machine guns to fire directly into the crowd.[13] 'The first to get killed was a deaf mute, Amâncio Rodrigues dos Santos', said Garoto. 'He was walking towards them, waving an MST flag. He doesn't seem to have heard the shooting, so he didn't stop. They grabbed hold of him and started beating him. Finally, they shot him dead. I couldn't believe what I was seeing. It seemed unreal. We all loved Amâncio. He was a good person. He used to sing a lot in the camp. We didn't know what to do. We were desperate. We started to throw sticks and stones again, so that we could get hold of Amâncio's corpse, bring him back.'

The police responded with further tear-gas bombs and machine-gun fire, shooting now from both directions. All the *sem-terra* could do was try and scramble off the road. 'I was one of the first to be shot', said Jurandir Gomes do Santo.

> I was at the Marabá end. They'd kicked a child and I went to try and help her. I was shot before I reached her. They shot me in the right foot. Even so, I managed to get off the road. I staggered for 20 metres into the undergrowth, and then I fell down. I tried to hide under a Brazil nut tree. They shot at me. A bullet passed about five centimetres away from my head. An old man came up to me: 'if you stay here, you'll get killed.' He pulled me round to the other side of the tree. The police started firing at me with a machine gun. The old man ran off. I never saw him again. I pulled myself into a rice field. I lay there, watching it all. I think that's why I'm still so traumatised today. I saw so many people running away, being shot. I heard all the screams. Total confusion.

Garoto, too, was shot early on. 'I was at the Parauapebas end. They machine-gunned a 22-year-old lad, who was standing beside me. I saw him fall. Everyone started running. There was a lot of blood. A lot of dead people. I couldn't believe what was happening. I started running but then they shot me in the foot. I fell down. I remember the hot sun beating on my head. I tried to get up as the police got near me. I couldn't manage it. I fell down again. I saw the bone protruding out of my leg. I pulled myself up and hopped to the tent where the reporter was hiding.'

'I managed to hide in the same hut as Garoto', said Eva Gomes da Silva (*see* box 7.2). 'One of my sons was with me. We never felt more frightened in our lives. We could hear the bullets and the machine-gun fire. It was all so close'. With them in the hut was Rubenita Justiniano da Silva. 'I had already been shot. A bullet had knocked out seven teeth, shattered my jaw and got stuck in my neck.' 'Then a soldier arrived', said Eva.

> He kicked open the door with his boot and shouted: 'Get out!' Oziel [Oziel Alves Pereira, an 18-year old *militante*] was with us. He said: 'I'm going to find their commander. I've got to stop them'. I pleaded with him: 'Don't go, Oziel. They'll kill you.' But he didn't listen. As soon as he got out on the road, they seized him by the hair, handcuffed him and started hitting him. I couldn't bear it so I closed my eyes, but I heard the soldier sneering at him and telling him to shout: 'Long live the MST! Long live the MST!' Every time Oziel repeated these words, they kicked him and punched him. They killed him slowly. When I saw pictures of his corpse, I couldn't recognise him. His face was so swollen. They knew he was a leader and they wanted him to suffer for it.

The soldiers forced everyone out of the hut. 'They made us lie down', said Eva. 'The reporter, Marisa, shouted at them: "what are you doing? There are only women and children here!" One girl peeped from under her arm and saw them shoot her father. His name was Altamiro Ricardo da Silva. At last, a soldier came and held his rifle to my head. He said: "keep your head down. There may be a stray bullet." I felt so relieved, because I knew then that he wasn't going to kill me.' About 200 people lay on the ground. 'There was nothing we could do but wait', said Rubenita. 'I saw them kill people. They'd go up to injured men lying on the ground, and shoot them in the head. And they shot people as they were trying to escape into the undergrowth.' 'It seemed to last for a long time', said Eva Gomes da Silva. 'I was lying on the ground when a friend, Osioni, came up. He was bleeding very heavily. I was so scared that the police would come and finish him off, and us along with him, that I just screamed at him: "Go away! Go away!" In the end, a soldier came and told us to get up, look the other way, and run. He'd give us 30 seconds, he said. Rubenita was with me. Blood was streaming out of her mouth. We went as quickly as we could down the road. We passed several huts but the doors were all firmly closed. People were just too scared to help us.'

'I'm sure that more than 19 people were killed', said Garoto.

> I'd dragged myself out of the hut into the undergrowth. I saw them picking up our machetes and scythes and using them to kill injured people. I saw them hitting children. Then they divided the corpses into two heaps. They were robbing the bodies as they did so, taking anything of any value. They put one heap of bodies into a lorry and the other heap into a van. Those in the lorry reappeared, but those in the van were never seen again. Two soldiers came close to me. One was tall, black, with a rifle. The other was short, of Japanese origin. They went into the hut. It was only five metres away, but they didn't see me. I heard the Japanese man pick up a saucepan. 'I'm going to take this', he said. 'It's a good solid pan. I'm getting married next week. It'll be useful.' A young boy, Zé Carlos, who'd got a wound in the head, was in the tent with his mother. She implored the policemen not to kill them, and they let them go. As they were running away, they almost tripped over me. I told them not to say anything but the Japanese policeman noticed something. He came up with his machine-gun. He ordered me to get up. I told him I couldn't but he insisted. I got up, with the bone hanging out of my leg. I was shaking all over with the pain. He took me to the edge of the undergrowth and said: 'You're going to die, lad. Don't look at me while I shoot.' But I did go on looking at him. At that moment a sergeant arrived. The Japanese soldier told him that he was about to kill me, but the sergeant said: 'No. So many people have died.' He asked me how old I was. I said: '16 years old'. I lied. I was really nearly 20, but I knew I looked young. He asked me what I was doing there. I said I was trying to get a piece of land for myself and my brothers. He said: 'Run off, lad, or we'll kill you.' I went off, hopping. I was losing a lot of blood. I couldn't go far. A couple of comrades came and helped me. They carried me for about a kilometre. Then we stopped. They got a coconut from one of the trees and put slices of it on my wound. One of them tore up his shirt to make a bandage. Then we got a lift in a car to the hospital in Curionópolis.

When the highway was cleared, Colonel Pantoja phoned Major Oliveira. Oliveira told his superior that there were 'six dead men and a lot of wounded' on the road. By the end of the operation, there were 19 dead men and no wounded, which supports what *sem-terra* eye witnesses said: that, after the conflict was over, the police killed in cold blood the wounded men who had not been able to get off the road. Thirteen of the dead men were local MST leaders, which is consistent with the MST's allegation that, with the help of gunmen from the estates, the police targeted key people. Once the massacre was over, the police returned to base. The driver of one of the coaches that took them back said he heard Colonel Pantoja say to his men: 'mission accomplished. No one saw anything.' Another witness, a local teacher called Ana Azevedo, said that 'they started clapping when they got in the coach. For them it was a victory. … They seemed like soldiers returning from a war against an enemy country.'[14] But for the *sem-terra* the nightmare had not ended.

The Aftermath

Inácio Pereira, 53 years old, saved his own life through a subterfuge. When the police arrived close to him, he pretended he was already dead. The police dragged him by the hair into a lorry full of corpses. As they drove towards Curionópolis, one of the men started to groan and was summarily executed by the soldiers. So Inácio remained perfectly still until he reached the morgue in the hospital. A hospital employee, checking the pulses of the dead men, came across Inácio. 'Well, well', he said. 'There's one here who's escaped death'. Inácio later discovered that his 20-year-old son, Raimundo Lopes Pereira, who had only been visiting the camp to take his father some medication, was among the dead.

Others had equally traumatic experiences. 'When I arrived at the hospital, there were a lot of desperate people outside, looking for relatives. Everyone was shouting, crying', said Garoto.

> The doctors wouldn't let them into the hospital. My two brothers were there, but I didn't see them. There was a lot of confusion. They put me on a small mattress among a lot of dead people. I saw the corpses of Amâncio and Oziel. Then a doctor took one look at my wound and said: 'We can't treat you here. You must go to Marabá.' I had to go by bus. When I got there, a fat doctor put a plaster cast on my leg. When he'd finished, he looked me in the face: 'You should have all been killed, all of you. You invade private property.' I replied: 'Have we invaded land of yours? Or land belonging to a relative of yours? No? Well, then. As far as I know, your expertise is medicine. You have no authority to criticise us. Your duty is to treat us.' He was very angry with me but I didn't care.

The police even went on killing inside the hospital in Curionópolis. 'The police just walked in and shot one man dead, just like that', said Eva. Jurandir Gomes do Santo had a narrow escape. 'We were waiting to be treated. There were so many of us that a lot of people were lying on the ground. I was on a bed. A policeman came into the ward. He went straight up to me and put his revolver against my head. He said that he had a good mind to kill us all, as we were all "bandits" and "layabouts". I told him to go ahead. I just wanted it all to end. But at that moment the doctor came in. He told the policeman to go. I think that he would have killed us there and then if the doctor hadn't walked in.'

Box 7.2   *Eva Gomes da Silva*

I'm 47 years old. I was born in Pedreiras in Maranhão. My parents were share-croppers. They had 16 children but seven died young. When I was a child, the region had a terrible drought. We had to walk 12 kilometres to fetch water, bringing it back in cans on our heads. It was too difficult and we moved to Lagoa São Bento, also in Maranhão.

When I was 14 years old, my mother died in childbirth. The baby, too, died two months later. Nine months later my father died. I had a lot of younger brothers and sisters and we were all divided up, scattered to different relatives in different parts of the country. I got a job as a maid in the town of Xambioá on the Araguaia river. I was there when the rural guerrillas arrived. They did a lot of good. They provided us with medicines. They helped with transport. They weren't all Brazilians. Some were foreign, Cubans I think. I knew several of them quite well, particularly one woman.

It was the army who waged war on the guerrillas. They arrived one day in the village. You had to stay in your homes. If you went out in the street, the soldiers made you work for them. A poor teacher was going to his school, with his books under his arm. The soldiers said he had to work for them. He said he couldn't, as his students were waiting for him, but they knocked him over and forced him to help build their barracks.

They arrested a lot of people. They'd torture them, put them on the *pau de arara* (a kind of torture). Every one was very frightened. I had a friend, Flora. She told a soldier she'd met the guerrillas. He immediately took her off to the barracks. They stood her up against a wall. They fired shots all around her. She was terrified. She was only released because the mayor went there and said that she hadn't given any support to the guerrillas.

There were hundreds of soldiers. They killed a lot of people. They burnt houses. Soldiers went around disguised as salesmen. One came to my house, selling ham-mocks. I later saw him in uniform with the others. I didn't get into trouble because I didn't say anything. But you had to be careful. Even today people remember it all. They're still traumatised.

Then I got married. I went with my husband to Itapavas, which was a small place about 85 kilometres away. We were there for 16 years and had three children. But it wasn't a happy marriage. He drank a lot but that wasn't the main problem. He was a wicked man. That's what was worse. He threatened me. He humiliated me. I left him five times but each time he forced me to go back. He said he'd rather kill me than let me leave. I got desperate. So in the end I fled to my sister's house in São Felix do Xingu. It took me two days by bus. I left the children behind. I set up a bar in São Felix and then, after three months, I sent for the children. Unfortunately, my husband came too. It was awful. I was frightened the whole time. In the end we all fled to my sister's house and my brother-in-law got him to go back home.

I had my bar for seven years and then we all moved to Eldorado de Carajás. We'd heard that there were good opportunities for commerce. We were there when the MST arrived. I was mistrustful at first. Then I went to hear them at an assembly in front of the mayor's office. What they said made a lot of sense. Why should these landowners have so much land when we have none? I wanted land for my children, so I joined the movement. I took part in the occupation of Macaxeira with two of my children and helped to set up the Formosa camp.

After the massacre we went back to the camp. It was a sad place. A lot of people were crying a lot. There were gunmen on the road outside. Every time we went out, they threatened us. I was very frightened and thought about leaving. But a friend visited me. He said: 'Eva, the government won't allow another massacre. This one has done them enough harm. The gunmen are only trying to bully you into leaving'. What he said made sense and I decided to stay. I got involved in camp life and became a coordinator. And, sure enough, we won land very quickly.

Some of the wounded could not get treatment. 'I got a bullet in the head and then the police beat me round the head with a rifle butt', said Manuel Marcos Costa, who was 47 at the time of the massacre.

I lost so much blood that I thought I was going to die. When the shooting was over, I got a lift to Curionópolis. My head had stopped bleeding, but my shirt was completely covered in stiff black blood. A policeman on the road took one look at me and arrested me, taking me off to the police station. At about midnight an MST lawyer came and had me freed. Though my head was hurting dreadfully, I just wanted to get off the street to a friend's house. I was convinced that the police would kill me if they saw me. I changed clothes and early the following morning I forced myself to go to the hospital. But then the doctor wouldn't treat me. He said he was too frightened. The police had been there all night. They'd even killed people there, he said. So I finished up going to the chemist's and getting them to bandage me up. Then I went home and I treated myself with oil of *copaíba* [a tropical tree]. It's a natural antibiotic and it helped.

Many of the *sem-terra* thought that the government had succeeded in destroying the MST. 'I thought it was all over', said Eva Gomes da Silva.

We walked for five kilometres until we found a house where we could stay. Of course, I couldn't sleep. I kept hearing the shots, seeing all those people dying, and wondering what on earth we were going to do. We had nothing. And we couldn't even go back to my parents, as they were so hostile towards the MST. I felt so ashamed. It seemed as if they'd won and I'd lost. But a boy arrived the following morning. He said that there were a lot of people at the 'S' curve. So we went back. And there were a lot of people there, looking for relatives. Many of them didn't find the people they were looking for. Some people had fled, I know, but I don't think it's just that. I think a lot more people were killed than the government says. But what amazed me was the atmosphere. People weren't intimidated. They were more determined than ever to go on. They were saying: 'no. It's not all over. We're going back to the camp at Formosa and we're going to go on fighting'.

Repercussions

The massacre created a furore at home and abroad. The military police confiscated some of the early film footage, mainly, it seems, so that it could maintain the fiction that the *sem-terra* had attacked first. Even so, the cameraman salvaged enough film to give an idea of the violence. The scenes were shown widely on Brazilian television, though the accompanying commentary always repeated the official view that the *sem-terra* had begun the violence. Under pressure from human rights groups, President Cardoso went on television to demand that those responsible be punished. 'There can be no justification for the police shooting people just because they are expressing their opinions', he said. 'It is unacceptable. It is unjustifiable. It is an embarrassment for the country and for the President of the Republic.'[15] The federal government moved quickly to defuse the anger. President Cardoso detached INCRA from the agriculture ministry and created a brand new ministry – the Extraordinary Ministry of Agrarian Issues – to provide land for the landless (*see* Chapter 10). Raul Jungmann was appointed head of the new ministry. Within a month INCRA had expropriated part of the Macaxeira estate, creating the 17 de Abril settlement for the 690 families that had dared to return to the Formosa camp.

In contrast, the state government did little. The landowners scarcely bothered to conceal their involvement in the massacre. Caribaldo Ribeiro, president of the landowners' association in Marabá, was defiant. 'Massacre? What massacre?' he commented shortly after the event. 'Blocking a road is a serious thing. Considering what they did, few of them died.'[16] 'People say that the Eldorado de Carajás massacre was a turning point', said the lawyer Carlos Guedes. 'It was not. It may have affected the behaviour of the federal government but the state government here in Pará didn't change. The landowners continue to enjoy complete impunity.'

The state authorities were reluctant to provide help for the survivors of the massacre, who were severely traumatised. 'We had nowhere to go after the massacre', said Jurandir Gomes do Santo. 'We had to sleep in the streets, like pigs'. His wound eventually healed but he has not made a full recovery. 'I can't work any more because I'm too weak. People have to support me. My wife has been worrying so much that she's also become ill now. I've got three children, two girls and a boy. It's God's love that's keeping them alive. We had to send our youngest child to Maranhão to be brought up by her grandparents.' After a while the *mutilados* (injured) decided that, despite their poor health, they had to put pressure on the authorities. 'We went to Belém', said Jurandir. 'For two months we lived under black polythene, staging protests every day. And we got somewhere. Since December 1999, we've been getting free hospital treatment in Marabá. But it's still very difficult. My son had to leave school and start work. He'd wanted so much to study. His dream had been to go to university. It would have been possible if we'd got land and I'd been well. But now there's no chance. I think that's the thing I find most difficult.'

A few of the wounded did not recover. 'I was with my husband, Júlio, when he got shot', said Júlia Pereira da Silva, who was then 57 years old. 'His name was really Francisco, but everyone called him Júlio. We'd met in the camp. I'd been married and my husband had left me. I'd had such a hard time bringing up six children on my own. I was so pleased to meet Júlio. He was a kind and amusing man. Everyone liked him. I was so happy with him. I was the one registered with the MST, but I was often away, working in Parauapebas. So when there was an assembly and they called out my name, Júlia Pereira da Silva, he used to jump up with a grin and say: "I'm present". Everyone used to laugh and he acquired the nickname of Júlio'.

After the shooting was over, Júlia took her husband by bus to Curionópolis. 'But when we got there, the doctors told us to go by bus to Belém, where he'd get better treatment. We got as far as Marabá, when Júlio panicked. He was sure the police were going to kill him and he refused to go any further. We took him to hospital in Marabá, but when I went back the next day he'd discharged himself.' Eventually Júlio agreed to go to Belém but the doctors could not help him. 'He'd got an infection in the head by then. There was nothing they could do. He died exactly a year later, on April 17 1997. I've got land now in the 17 de Abril settlement but I'm too ill to farm it. God alone knows my suffering.' Júlio became the twentieth name on the official death register.

João Baptista Pereira Penha was 46 years old at the time of the massacre. 'My leg has never recovered', he said in a quiet voice in Marabá hospital in April 2000. 'It hurts a lot when the weather's wet. I get very tired and my legs swell a lot. I even gave up smoking, but it hasn't made me any better. The doctors tell me I'm improving but I don't think so.' Although his face was grey from the effort, he still wanted to talk. 'I've had a hard life. I've always been travelling, looking for work. It was just the same with my parents. They didn't even remember where I was born. They were always on the move. When I met the movement, I thought it the most wonderful thing in the world. I still do. Despite everything that's happened to me, I'll never leave it.' Shortly afterwards, on 7 May 2000, he died in hospital, bringing to 21 the official number of deaths from the massacre.

Though the MST has repeatedly called for justice, it has been careful to blame the officers and the authorities, not the policemen themselves, for the massacre. In a region with such a high level of unemployment, it is scarcely surprising that a few members of *sem-terra* families have joined the police. 'Soon after the massacre I was in Palmares camp', said Maria Célia Nunes Coelho. 'I interviewed a man who told me in great embarrassment that one of his sons was a military policeman and had taken part in the massacre. He'd told the MST leadership and was anxiously waiting their decision. In fact, the MST didn't send him away from the camp. And it wasn't just this case. A lot of rural workers join the police because there's so little work. ... For the MST, the soldiers were carrying out orders. They were not to blame.'[17]

After it had recovered from the shock of the massacre, the MST regained the initiative in Pará, carrying out a record number of occupations in 1998. The *posseiros*, too, increased their activities. Over the following four years, peasant families conquered 200 settlements in the south of Pará. 'The MST is growing fast', said Maria Célia Nunes Coelho. 'And I think it will grow much more, as a result of the unemployment and the lack of available land in the region. As the *sem-terra* say, it's the only solution!'[18] The high level of mobilisation clearly worried the authorities: in August 2001, the *Folha de S. Paulo* newspaper reported that, according to a classified report, the army had mounted an espionage operation in 1999 to monitor the activities of the MST and other non-governmental organisations in Pará.[19]

The landowners, too, were worried by the level of mobilisation and responded by setting up a new private militia. The same report quoted in *Folha de S. Paulo* had a table with the prices charged by local gunmen for assassinations: while the life of an ordinary peasant could cost 'no more than a glass of *cachaça*' (that is, less than a dollar), the life of an MST activist was put at R$5,000 (about US$2,000). On 26 March 1998 gunmen, with help of off-duty military policemen, assassinated two MST leaders – Onalício Araújo Barros ('Fusquinha') and Valentim da Silva Serra ('Doutor'). Several of the policemen accused of these murders are believed to have taken part in the Eldorado de Carajás massacre, which suggests that they were so confident of not being punished for their earlier human rights abuses they had not bothered to change their behaviour. So far, their nonchalance seems fully justified: in August 1999 a jury in Belém acquitted Colonel Pantoja, Major Oliveira and another officer 'for lack of proof'. The trial was later annulled because of its many irregularities, but human rights lawyers are not confident of a fair hearing when the retrial eventually occurs.

CHAPTER 8

Repression in Paraná

We were all very hopeful. We'd been told we were going to be given our plots very soon. INCRA had inspected the land, and said it was unproductive. We were so sure that we'd be settled over the next few days that we'd brought all our belongings into the camp.

But then everything changed. It was half past one in the morning, on 7 May 1999. We were all sleeping peacefully when the police arrived. They arrived shouting, very angry, beating on the plastic roofs of our tents. Many of them were wearing black hoods. I don't know if they were all policemen but they were all wearing uniforms. They had a lot of dogs, huge dogs. Two policemen, with a dog, went to each tent. One of them asked me if I was afraid of dogs. When I said that I was, he set the dog on me, laughing.

They didn't give us time to get dressed. Some women were just in their bra and knickers, and men in pants or shorts. The police separated the men from the women and children and then made them lie down on the ground. It was cold, and raining. They kicked the men, on the head and on the backside. But it wasn't really to hurt them. It was more psychological pressure. And they kept swearing at us, jeering at us. They kept telling us that we were stupid, that the leaders of the movement were making a lot of money out of us, that we were being used.

They were looking for my husband, Sebastião de Maia. They said he was a leader, and they didn't believe me when I said he was travelling. He'd only left that evening, and I think most people in the camp didn't know he'd left. They kept pointing their guns at me, and telling me that they'd kill us both if they found out that I'd been lying. They said that they'd already killed six people that night when they'd turned people off the neighbouring farm, Fazenda Bandeirantes.

They made all of us women sit on the concrete ground in front of the farm headquarters. All the children were crying. My daughter, Diana, who was 10 years old, spent the whole night crying. And my younger child, Gian, who was 3, was hungry. For hours they wouldn't let me make a bottle for him, so he got very upset. At about four o'clock in the morning they took me, with Gian, away from the other women. Diana got hysterical for she didn't know what they were going to do to me. They took me back to my tent. They said they were looking for arms. They turned everything upside down, stamped on things.

One of the policemen came towards me, leering. He said: 'we can rape you, now that your husband's not here. We've taken over the land and now we can take you over too. Your husband's not a man, he's a rat.' I began to tremble and cry, and he said: 'Now, you're frightened. When you invade someone else's land, you're not frightened then, are you.' I thought he was going to rape me, but he didn't. He just laughed.

At seven o'clock, they brought Diana to our tent. Her eyes were dreadfully red and swollen. They told me to get some cold water, make a compress for her. They were about to take her away, and they didn't want her looking like that.

The speaker is Adelina Ventura Nunes, 35 years old, from the Rio Novo camp, near Querência do Norte, Paraná

The eviction in the Rio Novo camp was not an isolated operation. During the evening of 7 May 1999, about 2,000 military policemen had arrived in the small town of Querência do Norte in the northwest of the state of Paraná. They had declared what amounted to a state of siege, with heavily armed policemen stopping all traffic on the roads. Using Querência do Norte as a base, large groups of military policemen had been sent out to destroy MST camps on six farms. In all the operations they used identical tactics to terrorise the families.

What perhaps scared the families more than the violence itself were the arrogance and insolence of the military policemen, who seemed confident that they would not be punished for their behaviour. 'The town (Querência do Norte) is reliving the time of the military dictatorship, with its doctrine of National Security', denounced Avanilson Alves Araújo, the MST and CPT lawyer for the region. 'I am not talking about isolated human rights abuses but about the systematic violation of the country's legislation. The rule of law has ended.'

We saw in the last chapter that the federal authorities in Brasília have been unable – and to some extent unwilling – to take the tough measures needed to impose the rule of law in unruly Pará. What is happening in the more disciplined state of Paraná is different and in some ways more sinister: the violation of human rights is part of a premeditated strategy. The most powerful groups in the state have decided, cynically and ruthlessly, to break the law. This has been possible because, in a paradoxical twist in the complex interplay of forces in Brazil's political system, the return to civilian, democratic government strengthened the might of the backward, undemocratic rural oligarchy within the state.

Land struggle in Paraná

Until the 1950s Paraná was sparsely occupied, but in the 1960s, as the land under coffee cultivation in São Paulo became exhausted, farmers rushed to the state, illegally taking over huge areas of public land. But the boom was short-lived, for in the 1970s Paraná's coffee plantations were devastated by frost. Some of the farmers switched to cattle rearing, while others moved into soyabeans and other cash crops. Neither activity required much labour. The construction of Itaipu, one of the largest hydroelectric dams in the world, also led to thousands more small farmers losing their land in the extreme west of the state. Altogether, hundreds of thousands of rural families were dispossessed, more than in any other state.

This rapid process of land expropriation created a wave of protests. In what was an unprecedented act of ecumenical collaboration, the Lutheran and Catholic churches worked together to help the families displaced by Itaipu to set up the *Movimento Justiça e Terra* (the Justice and Land Movement). In 1978 about 2,000 dispossessed peasant farmers camped for two months outside Itaipu and the government was finally forced to increase the value of the compensation they paid to the families and to create two land settlements for them. Elsewhere in the state landless families became involved in epic struggles. Perhaps the most famous – scored in the memory of the founders of the movement – was the clash with Giacometti, a company from Rio Grande do Sul that owned 95,000 hectares of land in the extreme south of Paraná. After reading in the local press that the estate was about to be taken over for agrarian reform, a group of landless families occupied the area in 1980. Giacometti immediately sent in gunmen. With the assistance of military policemen, they evicted the families with gratuitous brutality. Outraged by the treatment they had received, the families vowed to 'conquer' this estate one day.[1]

With the support of the Catholic and Lutheran churches, landless workers in the state created a host of new movements in the early 1980s: the Movement of Landless Workers from the West of Paraná (*Movimento dos Agricultores Sem-Terra do Oeste do Paraná*, MASTRO); the Movement of Landless Workers from the South-West of Paraná (*Movimento dos Agricultores Sem Terra do Sudoeste do Paraná*, MASTES); the Movement of Landless Workers from the North of Paraná (*Movemento dos Agricultores Sem-Terra no Norte do Paraná*, MASTEN); the Movement of Landless Workers from the Centre-West of Paraná (*Movimento dos Agricultores Sem-Terra do Centro-Oeste do Paraná*, MASTRECO); and the Movement of Landless Workers from the Coast of Paraná (*Movimento dos Agricultores Sem-Terra do Litoral do Paraná*, MASTEL).

While the activists who first thought of creating a national movement came from Rio Grande do Sul, they were keen from the beginning to work with Paraná's important and powerful movements. It was for this reason that the activists chose to hold the founding meeting of the MST in January 1984 in Cascavel in Paraná. The document drawn up at this meeting pointed out that 2.5 million people had been forced off the land in Paraná, far more than in any other state.

The Formation of the MST in Paraná

Under the impetus of the first National Congress in January 1985, the MST began to work intensively in the state of Paraná. Although the families were often evicted, they also won important victories and, with these, they gained confidence. One of the most celebrated conquests was the reoccupation of Fazenda Giacometti in 1986.

It was a triumphant event, with the peasants feeling that they had finally exacted retribution for the violence they had suffered at the hands of gunmen in 1980. The photographer Sebastião Salgado went on the occupation, and his photographs, published in the book *Terra*, made this event famous throughout the world. To accompany the photograph of the triumphal moment of entry into the *latifúndio* (reproduced on p. 37 of this book), Salgado wrote the following note:

> It was impressive, this column of 12,000 landless peasants, made up of 3,000 families, marching into the cold night in the beginning of winter in Paraná. The peasant army advanced in almost complete silence. The only thing you could hear was the regular breathing of people accustomed to making an effort, and the dull thud of feet on the asphalt.
>
> Peasants walk quickly: the 22 km were covered in under five hours. When we arrived, day was breaking. The early morning was wrapped in a thick mist from the Iguaçu river that runs close by. The mist slowly began to lift. And the river of peasants, which had flowed down the asphalt throughout the night, finally stopped, as it reached the gate of the estate, and then spread out, like the water of a dam. Children and women were sent to the back, while the men took up position at the front, placing themselves on an imaginary line where they thought a confrontation with the estate's gunmen could occur.
>
> But the small army protecting the *latifúndio* did nothing, so the men on the front line broke the padlock, opened the gates and entered. Behind them, the river of peasants began to move. They raised sickles, hoes and flags in an unrestrained avalanche of hope in this reencounter with life – and the repressed cry of the people without land rang out with a single voice in the clarity of the new day: 'Agrarian reform! A struggle for us all!'[2]

Faced with determined occupations like this one, the federal and state governments often negotiated with the MST. By 1999 about 15,000 families had won land in Paraná. They lived in 233 land settlements, which covered almost 300,000 hectares. By then, Paraná had become an important region for the MST. In only two other states – Pernambuco and Alagoas, where the MST was enjoying spectacular growth – had the MST expanded more rapidly. Within Paraná the MST was growing particularly strongly in the northwest of the state, where it was beginning to challenge the power of the outmoded and authoritarian agrarian bourgeoisie. For that reason it had to be stopped.

The Rural Oligarchy Fights Back

In the powerful assault it launched against the MST in May 1999, the military police clearly intended to drive the MST out of many areas into which it was expanding. The offensive ran roughshod over the more conciliatory strategy of the federal government body, INCRA, which was settling many families on the areas they had occupied, provided that a technical evaluation had shown the farm to be unproductive by the criteria established by the institute. Despite considerable press coverage of the atrocities committed by the military police, many questions remained unanswered. Who in the state government had decided on this tougher approach? Why had the federal government not intervened? What were the state government's long-term objectives? Who was protecting the police as they openly violated the law of the land?

We met Arlei José Escher, one of the MST leaders in Paraná, by chance. He was in hiding, as the police had issued a warrant for his arrest, and he unexpectedly turned up at the MST refectory one day while we were having lunch. A young fair-haired man of German descent, he was clear-headed and articulate, although he had had very little formal education. He was certain that the original decision to launch an offensive against the MST had been taken in June 1997 at a meeting that high-ranking state government officials held with MST leaders and members of the Catholic Church. Arlei, who was at the meeting, remembers that Cândido Martins de Oliveira, the Paraná secretary for public security, expressed outrage at the number of MST occupations in the region – 67 over the previous two years – and issued an ultimatum: either the MST stop its 'illegal actions' or face 'the consequences'. 'I left the meeting feeling very apprehensive', Arlei said. He felt sure that what was worrying the state government even more than the occupations was the way the MST was winning over public opinion and consolidating its presence in the region – 'territorialising', as Bernardo Mançano has called it.

At a press conference in July 1997, just one month after the meeting in Querência do Norte, Cândido Martins de Oliveira indirectly confirmed Arlei's hunch. He said that the MST was 'a problem for the government, because that region [Querência do Norte] is an MST republic and, to carry out the evictions authorised by the courts, we have first to destroy the workers' organisation. If we don't, we're not going to be able to evict anyone.'[3] The tone of the statement, so reminiscent of the language used by the generals during their period of rule, jars with the image that the federal government projects of a country that is trying to build a modern democratic society. Yet the lawyer Avanilson Alves Araújo said that the tone used by Cândido Martins de Oliveira was typical of the landowners he represents. 'They are backward, both economically and politically', he said. 'They're not modern farmers, producing for the world market. They occupy huge areas in the northwest of the state where they produce almost nothing, not even cattle in any quantity. And they're backward in their ideology. They believe in the absolute rights of property, just like landowners in France before the revolution. They don't accept the 1988 Constitution, which says that land should have a social function. And they reject the idea that workers – or landless peasants – have basic rights as human beings.'

The state governor, Jaime Lerner, is an urban architect, who believes most fervently in progress. So why did he form this alliance with these landowners? We put this question to Darci Frigo, an experienced and widely respected lawyer who works for the MST and the CPT in the state capital, Curitiba.[4] When we met him in his office, Frigo was tense. Over the previous couple of months he had received death threats, apparently from a faction within the military police. While he was determined not to give in to the blackmail and abandon his work, he was worried about the safety of his wife and two young children, aged 6 and 2. Frigo said that it was quite simple: Lerner depended on the votes of these landowners. 'Lerner himself knows very little about the rural areas. He is only interested in bringing industrial development to the state', he said. 'He needed to make an alliance with the landowners to get the votes he needed, so he did. Some 20 deputies in the state assembly are openly linked to the landowners, while another 10 or 15 can be persuaded to vote with the landowners' block, if lobbied. These votes are often crucial for Lerner.'

Frigo said that the landowners set only one condition for their support: that they should be allowed to use whatever methods they thought fit to deal with the MST. To this end, they demanded that Cândido Martins de Oliveira, a politician from Campos de Palmas, a traditional stronghold of landowners in the southwest of the state, be appointed State Secretary for Public Security.

However, said Frigo, there was another element that further complicated the issue: the autonomy enjoyed by a powerful group within the military police. Even before Jaime Lerner was elected governor, this group, headed by hard-line officer Major Valdir Cumpetti Neves, was arguing that the MST had to be stopped, as it represented a serious threat to Brazil's national security. Frigo said that, although Major Neves worked closely with Cândido Martins de Oliveira, he had an independent power basis, with a different set of priorities. While the Secretary for Public Security wanted to stop the MST challenging the political dominance of the landowners in the state, Neves was concerned by the threat to national security that he thought the MST represented. Neves backed tough action, and his name had been linked to the murder of several MST leaders, including that of Diniz Bento da Silva, known as Teixeirinha, who was assassinated in Campo Bonito in 1993. Frigo said that Neves became even more worried in 1997 when candidates from the PT were elected as governors in Rio Grando do Sul and Mato Grosso do Sul, both of which have borders with Paraná. Neves, he said, had started talking of a new 'left-wing axis' being formed by these state governments and the MST

Frigo said that Neves and Oliveira formed a tactical alliance and carefully planned their attack on the MST. Neves set up a special elite troop within the military police. At the same time, he arranged for each battalion within the military police to create a Group for Special Operations (Grupo de Operações Especiais – GOE). These groups were not formally subordinated to Neves, but, in practice, worked closely with him. A Centre for Special Operations (Centro de Operações Especiais – COE) was set up to help with the training. Frigo said that US military officers had helped at this centre. Detailed information about how these courses are run emerged after a policeman, shocked by the way in which he was being trained to regard the MST as a criminal organisation, decided to send the MST and the CPT a copy of one of the videos routinely made of the training sessions. The video showed the police being trained to arrive at the camps with powerful arms, dogs and tear-gas bombs and to use intimidation and violence in the evictions.

The new offensive began in early 1998, with actions spearheaded by UDR gunmen. In February they carried out two violent evictions. The expelled families said that Marcos Menezes Prochet, the local president of the UDR, led the operation and made a point of personally killing 65-year-old Sebastião Camargo Filho by shooting him in the back of the head at a distance of less than one metre. Another 30 peasants were injured. During another eviction, in Fazenda São Francisco, gunmen refused to let the families give medical assistance to 51-year-old Sétimo Garibaldi after he had been shot in the back; he bled to death.

The MST and the CPT decided to release the video to the press after the eviction on 9 July 1998 of the families camped in Fazenda Santa Gertrudes. This was one of the 'new style' evictions: about 700 soldiers, many of them hooded, arrived without warning in the middle of the night and, equipped with tear-gas bombs and dogs, used extreme violence to evict the families. Despite the intense cold, the men were forced to lie on the damp ground and the women and children, many of them shivering and crying desperately, were verbally abused by the police. Shots were fired. Many of the families accused the policemen of stealing money from their tents. The authorities, which had categorically denied the MST's version of events, were left without a leg to stand on when footage from the training video appeared on TV news programmes, including Globo TV's influential nightly news programme, *Jornal Nacional*. It demonstrated unequivocally that the military police had deliberately trained their troops to behave in the extremely violent way described exactly by the evicted families. The policeman who had provided the video was terrified that he would be killed. He was given special protection by the federal government and smuggled out of the state with a new identity. The state government, however, took no action.

All this was little more than a dress rehearsal for the much bigger wave of evictions in Querência do Norte in May 1999, an onslaught from the powerful alliance of landowners and military policemen that was to receive a vigorous response from the MST.

The Battle of Querência do Norte

The landowners and police planned their offensive carefully. On the night of Friday 7 May, 2,000 police arrived in the region with eviction orders for 34 areas, accompanied by two justice officials to oversee the operation. They also had with them, most conveniently, two officers from the civil police to serve arrest warrants if members of the MST were to commit offences during the evictions. As a first step, the police blocked the roads around Querência do Norte. They seized MST caps and

9. The Cobrinco camp   *(Dan Baron Cohen)*

t-shirts, burning them or cutting them into pieces, and telling the *sem-terra* that this was how they would be treated the next time they were found wearing MST emblems. Groups of about 200–250 policemen were then sent to clear MST families off six estates, including Rio Novo, where Adelina Ventura Nunes was camped. In clear breach of constitutional rights, the police allowed no one to travel to the areas, not even journalists or lawyers. Two weeks later, on the night of 21 May, the police repeated the operation and ejected families from another four estates, including one known as Cobrinco. Throughout the period the police also carried out other evictions of smaller groups of families. In all, they expelled about 2,000 people during the two months they were stationed in Querência do Norte.

The police used the same violent methods in all the evictions. At times, they invented additional forms of torture, such as forcing the men to eat cow manure, as occurred during the eviction at Fazenda Santa Maria. They arrested several men in each area, always selecting the detainees from a list of names in a notebook. They held the families in the area until about seven or eight o'clock in the morning, when finally a formal eviction order was read out. The police then took the families away in buses.

Cândido Martins de Oliveira blamed the MST for what was happening. In an interview with the magazine *Caros Amigos* at the height of the offensive, he said: 'From 1997 or 1998 the MST has been invading productive farms. There are 20 farms with MST camps for which I've got reports from INCRA that show that they are absolutely productive. ... People have started arriving from Mato Grosso, Bahia,

Minas Gerais, Santa Catarina, Rio Grande do Sul, as well as the *brasilguaios* [Brazilians who have lived in Paraguay]. They've set up a conveyor belt, with so many people arriving in the state that there's no way in which the demand for land can be satisfied.' He said the government's patience was exhausted. 'We spent almost three years talking to the families in the camps. Often they agreed to leave and then broke their word. This created an unacceptable situation, one of disrespect towards the judicial power. It is for this reason that the military police has acted – and will continue to act – when they encounter an irregular situation.'

After accusing the MST of 'subversive practices', Cândido Martins de Oliveira said that the police always respected the law: they only carried out evictions during hours of daylight, specified in the legislation to be from 6 a.m. to 6 p.m., and were always accompanied by a justice official with an eviction order. Quick off the mark as ever, the lawyer Avanilson Alves Araújo pointed out that this could not be true, as the police said that six evictions took place at exactly the same time and they only had two justice officials. 'I was only scoring points', he said later, 'for everyone knows that eviction orders are meaningless, because the local judges work very closely with the landowners, making politically expedient rulings. It is another way in which the landowners are able to use their local power, making a mockery of the country's legislation'. On this occasion the collusion was particularly blatant. Elizabeth Khater, the judge for the district of Loanda, who had issued numerous eviction orders in the run-up to the military police offensive, was out having dinner with some landowners on 7 May. A reporter from one of Brazil's national newspapers, *Folha de S. Paulo*, went up to her table. Mistaking him for a policeman, the judge complimented him: 'Congratulations! I was just praising your work to my friends here. We're celebrating. It could be the beginning of a new closer relationship between the military police and the landowners.' A report of the incident was published in the newspaper the following day.[5]

The police arrested 42 landless peasants during the first wave of evictions on 7 May. They claimed that the peasants had been 'resisting arrest' or had been 'abusive to authority', but this is not what the peasants themselves say. One of those arrested in Rio Novo was Orélio Lourenzino, a 43-year-old *brasilguaio*, who had first heard about the MST in Paraguay (*see* box 8.1):

> The police arrived at about one o'clock in the morning. I was lucky and managed to put on my trousers before I got hauled out. The couple of policemen who arrived at my tent weren't as bad as some of the others. They seemed to understand our situation, even feel sorry for us, while others arrived angry, shouting and swearing and beating on the tents. We were made to lie down on the mud for about five hours. It was very cold, and they wouldn't let me put a shirt on until the morning.
>
> Then they came around with a list. They asked my name and, when I told them, they looked at their notebook and said: 'That's one we want. Take him.' I don't really know why. I'm not a leader but I'd been one of the coordinators who'd helped organise the camp. They arrested three from our camp. They handcuffed us and put us in a van. By the end of the night, they'd arrested 21 men from various areas. They took us to

Loanda and I was accused of being the 'head of a gang causing public disorder'. I didn't really know what that meant. Then Avanilson came and found us. That was a relief. We were held in prison there about 21 days.

We received a visit from the head of public security, Cândido Martins. We chose five representatives to go and talk to him. They came back feeling much happier. He'd told them that he was going to Quêrencia do Norte and that he'd make sure things improved for landless families. But then later that day a lot of military policemen arrived. They divided us up. Nine of us got put in one van. We couldn't talk to each other and we didn't know where we were going. It was a time of great loneliness and fear. I'd never had any brush with the authorities before. I didn't know what to expect. We finished up in a prison in Maringá. A huge prison. There were 200 prisoners just in our wing. They were there for all kinds of crimes. A warden took us around. He shouted out: 'How many of you in that cell?' 'Six.' 'Then you can take one more.' And so on. We were all divided up. There were five prisoners in my cell. All there for violent robbery. I was very scared.

But they treated me well. An older man – Senhor Francisco, I'll never forget him – asked me if I'd eaten, for they all cooked for themselves in that cell. I said I hadn't, but that I hadn't any food, that I'd have to wait until my family brought some on Saturday. But Senhor Francisco told me not to worry, that they'd look after me. And he heated me up some food. All the prisoners had heard about the MST and knew about our struggle.

After a few days we received a visit from Senator Eduardo Suplicy. It meant a lot to us, that visit. Before I joined the movement, I never thought I'd meet someone important like him. And lawyers came, and priests and nuns. We realised that people out there cared about us. It gave us courage. It made us realise that the police can't just come to our camps and kill and torture us. We asked the senator to ask the prison authorities to put us all in a cell together. There were ten of us by then. And they did. It was better after that. Some of my comrades stayed in for 90 days, but I was released after 48 days. And I was never charged with anything. When you leave jail, you feel moved to see a dog in the street, a chicken, a tree. You don't see anything like that in a cell and you miss it.

The police robbed and vandalised during the evictions. The families in Rio Novo lost a lot. Worst affected of all were the *brasilguaios*, who had sold up everything they possessed in Paraguay and brought the money with them. Most of the families were too scared to complain but the feisty Adelina Ventura Nunes stood up to the police. She and her husband, Sebastião, had brought with them their most prized possession – a freezer. When the other families were taken out of the estate, Avelina, with her son, Gian, was left behind. She watched in anger as the policemen set about destroying the huts. At about midday the police finally decided that Sebastião was not hiding anywhere and told her to get in a bus with a group of policemen, but she refused, vociferously, to leave without her freezer. She claimed (falsely, she admitted to us) that she had kept the receipt at her mother's home and she would sue the police if the freezer went missing. The policemen jeered, saying that landless families had no right to have valuable possessions like freezers, but in the end they capitulated, probably intimidated by her threats, and put the freezer in the bus.

The policemen had instructions to send the evicted families back to their states of origin – Rio Grande do Sul, Santa Catarina, São Paulo – although it is illegal to move people against their will to another state, or even, for the hundreds of *brasilguaios*, to the border with Paraguay at Foz de Iguaçu. Avanilson Alves Araújo takes up the story: 'In a way, the whole operation, dreadful as it was, did some good. At that time the lawyers' network [a group of lawyers sympathetic to the MST] was just beginning to function. It was its first test and it was a real emergency. All the regional leaders of the MST had been arrested or were in hiding. There were only us to protect the evicted families. We managed to act very quickly. I personally helped stop five buses that were about to take landless families out of the state. I think that it had an impact on public opinion, seeing us standing up to the authorities on behalf of these families.'

The lawyers' network, however, was not infallible. When Adelina finally reached Querência do Norte, she saw Avanilson and the other lawyers on the road, monitoring the buses, but to her frustration they didn't see her. 'From the outside it looked as if there were just policemen in the bus and they let us through, without seeing me', she said. The bus travelled through the town and out to the other side. 'For the first time, I felt really frightened', said Adelina. 'They thought of me as a difficult person, and it would have been so easy for them just to have me and Gian disappear.' But on the outskirts of the town, they set her down, with her son and her belongings (including her freezer).

Adelina's troubles weren't over. She had never been in Querência do Norte before and knew no one. She left her possessions in a house and set out to look for somewhere to spend the night. 'I had enough money to rent a room for a few days', she said, 'but there was so much fear in the town that no one wanted to give me a room. As soon as they realised that I was from the MST, they turned me away. I was getting desperate, when suddenly an MST van went by. I flagged it down and they put me up in a room at the back of the warehouse at the COANA cooperative.'

Adelina's husband, Sebastião, had left Querência do Norte on the evening of 7 May. 'When I arrived to catch my bus, I realised something was up, because there were so many policemen in the town', he told us. 'But it never crossed my mind that they were going to evict us from Rio Novo. We'd been told by INCRA so many times that everything was going to be all right. The only reason why everything was taking time was that the land was not far from the border with Paraguay so the sale needed special authorisation from the federal government. But it was only a formality, INCRA had said.' When he got to Santa Catarina, Sebastião received a telephone call from the MST. 'I couldn't believe it', he said. 'And I got sick with worry when no one knew where Adelina and Gian were. I was so relieved when I finally got a call from her. She phoned me from a public phone, as everyone knew that the COANA phone was being tapped.' He went on: 'The MST told me that the police had been looking for me, that I'd been dubbed a leader, and they advised me to wait for a few days for things to calm down. But I just couldn't make myself wait. I only managed a day. On the Saturday evening I got a coach back. I decided to take off my MST cap to avoid trouble'.

The MST leadership knew that the only way to end the campaign of terror was by getting publicity nationwide. On 9 May Adelina and several other evicted peasants flew to Brasília. She described to a committee in Congress how she had been driven out of her tent in the middle of the night. Immediately after she had spoken, Cândido Martins de Oliveira rose to his feet and vehemently rebutted her account. He said that all the evictions had occurred in an orderly fashion during the day, with meticulous respect for the law, and that the 'notoriously subversive' organisation, the MST, had brought Adelina to Brasília to blacken the image of the Paraná government. It was the word of a powerful government official against that of a landless peasant. But then a federal deputy had an idea. As always, Adelina had her 3-year-old son, Gian, with her. Telling Adelina to remain silent, the deputy asked Gian whether it had been light or dark when they had been driven out of their home. Without prompting, the boy said it had been very dark, that the police had carried torches and there had been a lot of shouting and crying. Turning to Cândido Martins de Oliveira, the deputy asked: 'So the MST are now training 3-year-old children to lie on their behalf?'

Another event provided final confirmation of the MST's version of events. A military policeman had been filming the eviction in Rio Novo, so they would have a record of the families involved. Clearly unhappy with the kind of operation he had been forced to take part in, a policeman had handed over a copy of the film to the MST, which promptly made it available to national television channels. Clips were shown once again on Globo TV. Avelina saw the footage in Brasília at a special showing for 30 bishops and government officials, including José Gregori, then Secretary for Human Rights in the federal government. Avelina began to tremble, so vivid was her recollection of that dreadful night. After the film was over, the bishops called for the sacking of Cândido Martins de Oliveira, a demand endorsed by José Gregori. However, Jaime Lerner, the Paraná state governor, simply ignored this request.

The incidents around the Rio Novo eviction provide a fascinating insight into the complex nature of political power in Paraná, with two contradictory pressures at work. On the one hand, the return to civilian rule has actually strengthened the political power of the authoritarian landowners within the state, because politicians now need votes, which means that the control the landowners still exercise over the rural vote has gained in significance. So, paradoxically, the return to elected, civilian government has given rural landowners more clout than they had under the military. The power of the landowners is also highly significant in the National Congress where the *bancada ruralista*, the rural bloc, which has strong representation from Paraná, has consistently opposed democratic reforms, such as the proposal to restructure the military police. But this is only half of the picture. On the other

Box 8.1 *Orélio Lourenzino*

I was born in Paraná, but when I was 15 years old my parents lost their land and decided to move to Paraguay. The army officers in the local barracks encouraged us to go. I think they were quietly hoping to take over part of Paraguay. There were so many Brazilians where we went. We didn't really need to learn Spanish or Guarani [the Indian language]. We cleared the land and planted mint. You could make a lot of money from mint in those days. We'd have three harvests a year. You could just cut the leaves and leave the plant to sprout again. We used to take the mint in an oxen cart to the distillery. There they would beat the mint and boil it. The oil – and it's the oil that's the valuable part – would separate from the water. The distillery owners would export the oil to England to be used in medicines. People made quite a lot of money. Within two years you could earn enough to buy your own herd of dairy cattle.

It was too good to last. After a while the climate changed. It stopped raining at the right times. I think people had cut down too much forest and it drove the rains away. The whole industry collapsed. Even so, I stayed on. By then I was married to a Brazilian girl I'd met there. We had five children, all born in Paraguay. We were careful. Each time we had a child we went back into Brazil and registered him or her as Brazilian. That meant that we didn't have all those dreadful problems that most of the *brasilguaios* faced when they tried to go back to Brazil. It also meant that my children didn't have to do military service in Paraguay.

I spent 28 years in Paraguay. In 1998 we decided to go back to Brazil. Things were getting difficult in Paraguay. And we had friends who'd come back, joined the MST and got land very quickly. We thought it would be easy. But it wasn't. We came back and took part in the occupation of the Água da Prata estate here in Paraná. I liked the movement and everything seemed to be going well. But then, after three months, we were evicted. We took part in the occupation of Rio Novo and had all those problems there. I'd never been in conflict with the authorities before. It came as a big shock.

The police stole all the money we'd brought back from Paraguay. And, because we were in Paraguay so long, we don't have many relatives here. We get some help from people in the camp but it's difficult. Even so, we're going to press on. We're here in Rio Novo with my 19-year-old son. We want him to have a chance. Life outside is so difficult. When all three of us – my wife, my son and me – get jobs on a farm, then we get by. But when we can't get jobs, then it's really awful. Here at least we're struggling for something better.

hand, there has been real change, most notably in the sphere of political freedom, since the end of the military government. Despite setbacks, there is considerable press freedom and, just as important, a widespread belief among the public that it has the right to know what is going on. Many Brazilians, like the two policemen in Paraná who handed over the video footage, are prepared to risk dismissal – or even their lives – to get the truth out. Even though Brazil's media giants continue to censor information, they have had to adapt. Globo TV, though not at all sympathetic to the aims of the MST, felt obliged to show the clips or risk losing prestige among the public.

The MST Fights Back

More than half of the evicted families gave up because of the violence and repression, but the rest, with very little money and nowhere to go, were determined to struggle on. After a couple of weeks, the families held a secret meeting with some MST leaders to decide what to do. Adelina said: 'Of course, we were frightened, but we were also angry. We'd got so near to winning our land. We didn't want to give up now.' It was not ideological conviction but need, particularly the fear of going hungry, that was driving the families. 'We'd been so sure we'd win our land that we'd planted a lot of crops', said Adelina. 'We were just beginning to harvest them.' Sebastião remembered precisely how much they had planted. 'We had got together and planted 60 *alqueires* [132 hectares] of land, with beans, maize, manioc. We needed that food.' So the families, with the MST leadership, decided to reoccupy the land, even though they knew that there were still a lot of armed policemen there. 'We thought out our strategy', said Sebastião. 'We decided to get together a large group of people, men, women and children, and reoccupy the area in broad daylight. We thought that would give us the best chance'. Adelina decided, somewhat reluctantly, that she would remain in Querência do Norte with the children. 'They were just too upset to go through another ordeal. Diana was still getting nightmares, waking up in the middle of the night and shouting out: "The police! The police!"'

They decided to reoccupy the area on Saturday 26 June, 42 days after the eviction. Líria Fischer, a strong woman of German descent who had faced much adversity in her life (*see* box 8.2), decided to take part in the reoccupation with three of her children, aged 11, 7 and 5. She and her family had been out of the camp on the day of the eviction, and she was determined to get her land back. 'We brought together about 450 or 500 families. They weren't all from the Rio Novo camp. Some were from other MST settlements and camps, people who just came to help us. We arrived in a fleet of lorries at about two o'clock in the afternoon. There were about 60 policemen in the area. There was a football match on television and they had been drinking. They weren't expecting us and were caught off balance.'

Sebastião says that, as soon as the police in Querência do Norte found out what was happening, they sent military vehicles speeding to the area. But the families were ready for them: they had placed lorries across the road to bar access. The MST did not want violence. 'We got out of the lorries and went to talk to the police commander', Sebastião said. 'He told us that we must leave, but we said we couldn't, that we hadn't anywhere else to go.' Once he had heard about the reoccupation, Avanilson Alves Araújo also rushed to the area. 'I thought that the military police might react very violently and I wanted to do what I could to prevent people from getting hurt', he told us. However, it turned out that he, rather than the peasant families, became a target of police violence. As soon as he got out of his car, half a dozen policemen grabbed hold of him, twisted his arm brutally, and began dragging him towards a police van. Avanilson protested loudly, and one of the policemen threatened to kill him, pointing a gun at his head. At this moment, a group of peasants intervened, surrounding the policemen and forcing them to let Avanilson go. None of the policemen wore identification badges, and Avanilson demanded to be taken to their superior officer. After Avanilson had threatened to create real trouble for the commander in Brasília for breaking the law that requires all policemen on duty to be identified, the commander reluctantly gave Avanilson the name and the number of the policeman who had held a gun at his head. Since then, Avanilson has begun court proceedings against this policeman for abuse of authority, but he has very little hope of achieving a conviction.

Meanwhile, says Líria Fischer, the families were finding a way in. 'The police closed the gate, so we went in under the wire fence.' Sebastião takes up the story. 'The police came towards us, pointing their guns. But there were a lot of us, and we just carried on.' In the midst of considerable confusion, the families poured into the farm buildings and the surrounding area. Gilson dos Santos, a former electrician who took part in the reoccupation but is now living in Cobrinco, said that there was great excitement. 'The children rushed ahead, shouting and laughing. They'd got under the wire fence before the adults and were running all over the place. The police didn't know how to stop them.' The irony of the situation was captured by one of the local newspapers, which on the following day bore the headline: 'MST evict police and reoccupy farm'.

Manoel Oliveira de Campos, who works as a driver for the MST in Querência do Norte, had come on the reoccupation as an act of solidarity. A member of the extremely conservative Protestant church, the Assembly of God, he was an unlikely person to be taking part in what the government regarded as an illegal action organised by a militant socialist movement. But Manoel is an ardent supporter of the MST. And the Assembly of God is pragmatic. 'None of the pastors are critical of the MST in the settlements or camps', said Manoel, 'for they know they'd be driven out if they were'. Manoel was shocked at what they found, along with crates of beer, in the farm headquarters. 'Boxes and boxes of military arms – bombs, grenades, bullets. Lots and lots of bullets. Later the police took them away. They said they were plastic bullets, but they weren't all plastic bullets. I've done my military service and I know.'

Unknown to the MST, the military police had turned Rio Novo into a regional centre from which to direct operations in other areas. So how did defenceless landless families manage to eject 65 well-armed policemen?

The MST families had used their strengths to the best advantage. They had come in large numbers, men, women and children. They had come unarmed. They had built in an element of surprise, arriving at a time when many of the policemen were off their guard. And they had juggled this with the need for publicity: they had tipped off the press, but only after the reoccupation had begun. It was a well-devised strategy, which took advantage of the political freedom that exists in Brazil, even in a state like Paraná. However, as all the families knew, it was risky. The state government would not have wanted a massacre of unarmed peasant families, because of the outcry it would have created, but, as the deaths in Eldorado de Carajás showed, events can gain their own momentum. If military policemen are authorised to use repressive methods to control a social movement, there can be no guarantee that the violence will not spiral out of control.

The families were triumphant but they had only won the first battle in the war. Driven out of the farm, the police, too, thought fast. While the families were celebrating, they decided to close the entrance to the farm and to set up blocks all along the road back to Querência do Norte. Their strategy soon became clear: they would starve the families into submission. 'They locked us in', said Sebastião. 'The whole area was cordoned off. There were police blocks every 500 metres along the road. They arrested 17 people who went out to get supplies. We hadn't anticipated this. We'd come without enough blankets or food. We couldn't even get to the crops on our plots. The well pump was broken, so we didn't have any clean water.' Líria Fischer recalls the hardship. 'There was only cassava to eat. We had it for breakfast, lunch and dinner. The children kept on complaining. But much worse than that was the fact that the only water we could find was bad. We couldn't boil it because we hadn't got firewood. Children started to get ill, especially babies who were fed on bottles.' About 160 children had taken part in the reoccupation. 'I cried a lot,' says Líria. 'Not that I regretted coming, just that I found it so upsetting to see the children getting ill.'

The women started to organise activities to keep up their spirits. 'I'm a Lutheran', says Líria. 'Our pastor, Jorge Kaffer, has always helped us a lot, holding services in the camps and bringing sweets and painting books for the children. I know some of the hymns we sing, so I joined up with some Catholic women and we went with the children to the gate. We sang as loud as we could and we shouted MST slogans: Occupy! Resist! Produce! Occupy! Resist! Produce! Some of the women had sick children in their arms. The police didn't know how to react. They don't mind beating up men, but they don't like hurting women.' The police counter-attacked at night, shooting bullets into the air and lobbing in tear-gas bombs. Manoel remembers it well. 'Many of the families were sleeping on the ground in the open air, with mothers covering their children with leaves. But it rained a lot, and the children got ill from the cold. And when the bombs came in, all the children started crying. And we adults found it hard to keep our spirits up. We kept telling each other: "we're in the struggle. We've got to battle on."' One 6-year-old boy caught pneumonia. In the end his parents decided to leave the camp, but by the time they reached hospital it was too late and the boy died. The MST leaders paid little attention to the death, not even sending a representative to the funeral. 'I don't quite know what happened', said Adelina. 'I think there was such a lot going on that people just didn't have time to do anything else, not even important things.' The family was deeply hurt and left the movement.

'We eventually managed to make contact with the landowner in the next farm', said Sebastião. 'His house was very near, and we got him to rig up a pipe to send us water over the fence. We told him that if he didn't, he'd be next on the list of properties we'd occupy.' There was no way, however, that the families could find enough food. They persevered for five days, and then, with the situation deteriorating rapidly, they held an assembly. 'We realised we had to get help', says Sebastião. 'We decided that three of us should try and get out during the middle of the night. We'd lived there for nine months so we knew a back way. It was bit risky but worth a go. I went with two others.' They got to Querência and held a meeting with MST leaders. 'We decided to organise a caravan to Rio Novo, to bring in food and blankets. We'd get as many people as possible to take part – MST settlers, priests, nuns, politicians, the press.'

Because so many children were getting ill, the caravan had to be organised at short notice. On 1 July 1999 about 200 people left Querência do Norte, walking behind several lorries loaded with food and other essential supplies. 'The police tried to stop us leaving', said Sebastião. 'The commander drove at us in a military vehicle. One of us saw what was happening and drove his lorry across the road. If he hadn't, a lot of people would have been hurt. As it was, two women were injured and had to be taken to hospital.' The commander tried to convince them to go back. 'We argued with him', said Sebastião. 'We asked him what he'd feel like if it was his family going hungry. He didn't know what to say, particularly as there were priests and journalists there.' The commander reluctantly relented, but imposed some conditions. 'He wouldn't let us take in a pump for the well. And he said that the lorries could only carry food. We had to take the mattresses and the black plastic out of the lorries and carry them on our backs, but once we were out of sight of the commander, we put them back in the lorries.'

Finally, after travelling15 km, the caravan reached Rio Novo. 'They gave us such a welcome. There was a real party when we arrived. They had been getting so hungry and ill', said Sebastião. And, inevitably, they held an assembly. 'We thanked the people from outside for their help. And we sang our national anthem, hugging each other.' Clearly irritated, the police at the gate had a final trick up their sleeve: they refused to let any of the visitors leave. All of them, including the journalists and the priests, had to spend the night in the farm. But the blockade had been

Box 8.2 *Líria Fischer*

I'm 43 years old. My parents had a small plot of land in Rio Grande do Sul. It was enough for them but not for the children too. I used to help them on the land. Because I was a girl, my father wouldn't let me study at night but even so I went to school for seven years. It means I can help my children now with their school work when so many other parents can't.

When I was 18 years old, I married. My husband rented a piece of land from his uncle, but it was so stony that his harvests were always poor. We decided to move to Paraguay. We rented land there and grew a lot of crops. But then my husband's brother, who lived in Paraná, died in an accident. His wife wanted us back, so we went. We rented land and my husband worked for a while in a sawmill. But life was hard. By then, we had two daughters. So when we heard that there was land being sold very cheaply in Rondônia, we decided to go.

Our plot of land was very isolated, near the border with Acre. We were 80 kilometres from the highway. To get to it, you had to travel along a rough track which was impassable during the rainy reason. There was a lot of malaria. I got it so many times that it nearly killed me. And my children suffered. I remember my elder daughter caught it. She was only 3 or 4 at the time. I had to take her by ferryboat across the Madeira river to the nearest military hospital. She seemed dead in my arms, but, thank God, she recovered. We planted rice, maize and cassava. And I collected those big, round Brazil nut balls, breaking them open with an axe to get at the nuts. I'd never done anything like that, but I learnt.

Then a friend visited us and said the land was better in Acre. So we went up there and bought land directly from a widow. But the widow didn't tell us that she'd a lot of debts with the bank. And the bank foreclosed on the loan and forced us out. We went back to Paraná, but it was all very difficult there too. So when we heard of a new project in Acre, we decided to go back. It was an INCRA project, funded by the Inter-American Development Bank. They told us they'd support us for six months, while we cleared the land. But no one got the money. We had to get by on our own resources.

This area was even more remote. There were jaguars in the forest. I had six children by then, five girls and a boy. One girl had died. We had good harvests but then we couldn't sell our crops. The roads were so bad that the middlemen couldn't get in. We saw the produce rot. It was so frustrating. And everything we bought was so expensive. So back we came to Paraná. My husband got a job in a dairy and I worked as a *bóia-fria* [day worker] on the farms. I was mainly weeding soya plantations. It was hard work and badly paid. And we had to buy everything – food, electricity, water. My two eldest daughters had to work as maids. I got ill through so much work and worry.

> We got to know the MST through friends. My husband went on the first occupation of Rio Novo. I went on working as a *bóia-fria* to buy food for the children. After the eviction, we decided that we'd all go on the reoccupation. It was difficult when the police shut us in. My children were scared. But I'd do it all again. We can only solve our problems if we get land. It's wrong the image they give of us on television. We're helping to build Brazil. We want to cultivate food for the towns. And we're peaceful and orderly. We've organised the camp properly. No one can make any noise after ten o'clock and then we're up again at five in the morning.

broken. The families settled back in the camp, finding to their consternation that the policemen had destroyed most of their crops. There were, however, plenty of beans. 'We gathered 3,000 bags', said Gilson dos Santos with evident satisfaction. 'It was hard work, labouring out there in the hot sun with no shade. But it was worth it.'

The Offensive Continues

The victory in Rio Novo was an important psychological boost for the MST, but it did not stop the offensive. Time after time the lawyer Avanilson Alves Araújo tried to get the local courts to take action, but to no avail. 'The judges defend the interests of their allies the landowners with no respect for the law', he grumbled. 'I can only get anywhere when cases are referred to Brasília, and that doesn't happen often.' One of his few successes came in August 1999, when a higher court in Brasília found in favour of his appeal against the arrest of five MST members for carrying out a land invasion. In a highly significant ruling, the court decided that land occupations are not in themselves illegal, provided they are carried out as 'an act of resistance' in support of a social demand. Yet in practice this judgement changed little, for the authorities continued to arrest MST leaders, inventing the charges against them later.

The MST knew that its best chance of halting the offensive in Paraná was by mobilising public opinion. At the beginning of June 1999, the MST began The March Against Violence and in Support of Agrarian Reform. About 3,000 people walked from Ponta Grossa to the state capital, Curitiba, a distance of 120 km. They carried banners protesting against the arrests of the MST leaders and demanding that the state government settle 3,000 families before the end of the year. Avanilson Alves Araújo believes that it was this march, rather than his legal endeavours, which secured the release of most of the 42 people arrested during the wave of evictions in Querência do Norte.

Once the march reached Curitiba, about 1,200 people set up camp in the central square, opposite Iguaçu Palace, the seat of the state government. As usual in its camps, the MST organised a school and a pharmacy, and began making bread. The camp became a tourist attraction, with about 40 people visiting it each day. 'These visits are helping to combat the prejudice against us', said Luís Ivânio Born, one of the camp coordinators. 'Many people arrive here with one idea of what we're like and leave with quite a different view'. There was, however, opposition too. Many inhabitants of Curitiba thought that the tents disfigured their central square. Others criticised parents for bringing young children to the camp, particularly during the cold winter months of June and July. The controversy increased when an eight-month-old baby died from pneumonia on 1 July.

The landowners began a counter-offensive. In early November, Marcos Prochet, the president of the Paraná branch of the UDR, called a press conference after a meeting with 120 landowners. 'What generates violence are the constant land invasions and the theft of cattle, actions which the government does nothing to prevent', he stated. He said that the landowners had been forced to form their own private militias and that, from then on, he would be working jointly with another 34 farmers to evict squatters and to protect their lands from invasion.[6] Avanilson Alves Araújo pointed out – but again to no effect – that the decision by the landowners to set up their own armies was unconstitutional.

The UDR made rapid use of its militias. The MST still had 80 camps in Paraná, where some 8,000 families lived. Since the wave of repression in the northwest of the state, the MST had concentrated its occupations in the region around Marilena in the west, so the UDR decided to carry out its evictions there. On 21 November about 70 hooded men evicted a group of families living in Fazenda Santa Rosa. Francisca Pereira dos Santos, 59 years old, was hit by a bullet and interned in hospital in a serious condition. Two days later, on 23 November, Marcos Prochet and other leading members of the UDR went straight from a public meeting in Marilena to evict families in Fazenda Novo Horizonte. Through these actions, the UDR was showing the government that it would lock horns with the MST if the government did not undertake tougher action.

Worried by the impact at home and abroad of these clearly illegal actions, the state government capitulated to the landowners. On 22 November Cândido Martins de Oliveira signed a resolution that allowed the military police to evict peasants from a farm without an eviction order, provided they acted within 48 hours of the land invasion. Avanilson Alves Araújo immediately pointed out that this resolution both infringed the country's constitution, as it increased the powers of the police, which was something that the state authorities had no right to do, and was partial, as it gave to property-owners additional rights not shared by other rural inhabitants.

The landowners quickly followed up this initial victory, seeking support among national politicians to get the MST evicted from the central square. 'This is not an occupation but a provocation', proclaimed Divanir Braz Palma, the leader of the *bancada ruralista* in the National Congress. The pressure yielded results. The state government sent 750 military policemen into the square in the early hours of 27

November to eject the families. The lawyer Darci Frigo and seven MST leaders were arrested. Dom Ladislau Biernaski, auxiliary bishop in the archdiocese of Curitiba, called to the scene by the MST, was shocked by what he saw. 'Everything I've seen here has left me horrified', he said. 'If this is how they treat people in the capital, I can imagine how they carry out evictions in the countryside. It leaves me very sad.'[7] The eviction was entirely gratuitous, because the state government was on the verge of reaching an agreement with the MST by which the camp would have been dismantled by Christmas in return for a commitment from INCRA to settle more families. However, the landowners did not want a negotiated settlement. According to reports in the press, they had demanded a show of force from the government in return for their support in the state assembly on a key piece of legislation.

The MST reeled from this series of blows. It gained a partial reprieve, quite fortuitously, from a corruption scandal. In early 2000 evidence emerged that Cândido Martins de Oliveira was involved in a drug-trafficking cartel within the federal police. After fruitlessly attempting to deny it, he was eventually forced to resign in April 2000. The military police were not implicated, and Major Neves, who was quick to distance himself from Cândido Martins, may even have emerged stronger. However, the scandal weakened the whole state government, particularly as there were insistent rumours that the top echelons of the government, including the state governor himself, were involved.

The MST seized its chance. On 2 March about 400 peasants reoccupied Cobrinco farm in the northwest of the state, from which they had been evicted five days earlier. Manoel Oliveira de Campos, who took part in this operation as well as the earlier reoccupation of Rio Novo, said they arrived in the middle of the night, slept in the cassava fields and, at about 8 o'clock, surrounded the farm headquarters. Taken by surprise, the 65 policemen had at first shot at them, sending at least 40 bullets in their direction, but had then fled, after they had seen that they were heavily outnumbered.

The MST was particularly happy about the reoccupation of Cobrinco because the military police had injured 30 people, some of them quite seriously, during the eviction on 27 February. When we met 7-year-old Claudemar de Couto in the camp just over a month later, she showed us the wounds on her chest and mouth, still not completely healed. The families told us that they had not been expecting eviction because INCRA had been in the process of purchasing the farm from the leading Brazilian bank, Bradesco, which had acquired the ranch from the previous owner in exchange for bank debts.

So Who Won?

Neither side was victorious in the confrontation. The state authorities were clearly forced on the defensive, but the MST was also dealt a heavy blow. Dozens of its camps were dismantled. Many people, traumatised by the violence, left the movement. In 1999 the state government arrested 173 members of the MST and issued arrest warrants for many more, forcing them to hide. The absence of key people seriously disrupted the movement's work.

Where the families managed to cling on to the land, morale was not high. Many people, particularly *brasilguaios*, had joined the movement because they had heard from friends or relatives that they would win land in just a few months. The conflict made them realise that they had to be prepared for a long and arduous struggle, with no guarantee of eventual success. We visited Rio Novo in March 2000, nine months after the families had carried out their remarkable reoccupation. The 50 families were living in extremely difficult conditions, for even food was in short supply. The hunger in the camp had exacerbated internal divisions. The families coping best were those who used to live locally and still had relatives bringing them food. The *gaúchos* – people from the state of Rio Grande do Sul – had their own support networks, with the less impoverished families helping those in most need. The people suffering most were the *brasilguaios*, who were left absolutely destitute by the police thefts. 'We help when we can, but we're all facing such difficulties that it's hard', said Adelina. 'We've even had the odd case of one family stealing food from another, something we never had in the past.'

The hunger faced by the families – and their consequent anger at a society that had left them in such need – created problems with their neighbours. Local farmers, who used to employ the *sem-terra* as day labourers, were no longer doing so, as they found them difficult and unreliable. A farmer had caught men from the camp red-handed taking maize home to their families. Another farmer said they had helped themselves to cassava. The men were also less subservient than the average worker: they protested vehemently when a landowner paid them only half the agreed wage as they had finished the job by lunchtime.

The families also lived in fear of another eviction. 'We go to sleep in our clothes, just in case the police arrive again in the middle of the night', said Orélio Lourenzino. Despite these problems, none of the families was thinking of giving up. 'There's still a strong community spirit', said Adelina. 'Most of us feel that we're in it together and we'll win through together. And most of us had even more difficult lives before we came here. I often remember how I used to leave Gian with Diana, who was only small herself, when I worked as a maid. I used to be so worried. Now I'm with them all day. I really like that.' The camp was also beginning to grow. 'Families that left the camp after all the violence are coming back, even families that went back to Paraguay', said Orélio. 'And the MST leaders say they'll bring more people here soon. The idea is to build it up to 200 families. We'd feel safer then.' But the greater numbers did not ensure greater safety. On 21 November 2000, Sebastião was ambushed after leaving home. Gunmen shot him point blank, killing him on the spot. This death brought to 16 the number of rural workers assassinated since the state governor, Jaime Lerner, began his first mandate in January 1995. No one was arrested for Sebastião's murder.

The MST leaders were pessimistic of any meaningful change before the end of the Lerner government in December 2002. 'Jaime Lerner is treating land occupation as a criminal offence, not as the symptom of a profound social problem', said Roberto Baggio, one of the Paraná representatives on the MST's national executive. 'So rather than getting at the root of the problem and settling people on the land, he sends in the police.' He was afraid that the military police were using Paraná as a test case. 'We're experiencing repression of a kind never seen in Brazil before', he said. 'They're using new techniques, which they'll soon be applying in the rest of Brazil. We can only stop this through a huge mobilisation of public opinion.'

Lerner's refusal to settle families was building up pressure within the state. 'The MST has 9,000 families in camps, waiting to be settled', said Avanilson Alves Araújo. 'There are at least five times more families wanting land. There are more all the time, as the federal government's agricultural policy drives small farmers off the land. Tension is increasing. Unless the state government changes its policy, I'm afraid we could see a massacre, like the one in Eldorado de Carajás, as desperate families invade land and the authorities react.'

Paraná is a special case. The rural bourgeoisie is bitterly opposed not just to the MST but to any kind of change. As a result the federal authorities, which were promoting the modernisation of agriculture, along with a new form of market-oriented agrarian reform in which small farmers occupy market 'niches' left by agribusiness (*see* Chapter 10), made little headway in the state. According to the Catholic priest Roberto Kuriama, 'Raul Jungmann, the minister of agrarian development, told a group of landless peasants that Paraná was the only state in Brazil where it was impossible to make any progress with his plans for agrarian reform. He said that the UDR was simply too strong.'

CHAPTER 9

The Globalisation of Brazilian Agriculture

Ill fares the land, to hastening ills a prey,
Where wealth accumulates, and men decay;
Princes or lords may flourish, or made fade:
A breath can make them, as a breath has made;
But a bold peasantry, their country's pride,
When once destroyed, can never be supplied.

Oliver Goldsmith, *The Deserted Village*, 1770

While the MST has spread all over the country, enlisting thousands of landless peasants and conquering land through occupations, the farm sector as a whole has been going through enormous changes, as Brazil has become integrated into the globalised world food industry. The rural exodus has accelerated, with hundreds of thousands of small farmers being forced off the land. Many of those that have survived are rearing livestock or cultivating crops for multinational corporations, which pay them very little and demand complete control over the way they farm. Sebastião Pinheiro, one of Brazil's leading environmental campaigners, fears for the future. 'What we have seen so far is nothing,' he warns. 'The avalanche that lies ahead, as the global food and agriculture complex strengthens its control on Brazil, will be terrible'.

The 'Green Revolution'

Brazil's move into high-tech farming began, as in many other developing countries, with the 'green revolution' that swept the world in the 1960s. At the time, Brazil urgently needed to boost agricultural production both to feed the ever-expanding urban population and to increase exports to service the burgeoning foreign debt. For a while, before the 'green revolution' had made its mark, it had even seemed that, in order to increase output, the government would have to carry out radical agrarian reform to take away land from the rural elite and give it to more productive family farmers. But the green revolution provided the military rulers, who had seized power in 1964, with a 'technical fix' to the problem. Instead of carrying out agrarian reform, they formed an alliance with the international grain and chemical companies and promoted the modernisation of agriculture. The new 'magic' hybrids produced much higher yields, so a relatively small number of modern, efficient farmers, coexisting with the old rural elite, were able to bring in big harvests and boost exports. From a strictly economic point of view, there was no longer any need for radical agrarian reform.

The star performer was soya, the new 'wonder crop', for which there was a voracious demand from cattle breeders in Europe, anxious to satisfy the soaring demand for beef in their prosperous post-war societies. The area in Brazil under soya cultivation rose from 432,000 hectares in 1964 to 11 million hectares in 1992. Soya became the most important product traded on the world market, with Brazil the second largest exporter, after the United States. The soya complex – beans, meal and oil – became Brazil's chief export product. Sales of other export products – particularly coffee, orange juice and poultry – also increased sharply.

Small rural communities were inevitably affected by the green revolution, and almost always for the worse. The new technology, promoted by a barrage of publicity, began to erode their independence. In the past the farmers had grown all their own food, planting many different crops and saving seeds from one harvest to another. But hybrids require a great deal of fertilisers and pesticides, and their seeds cannot be saved from one harvest to another, so the farmers got sucked into the so-called 'technological package', by which they buy the seeds and all the appropriate fertilisers, herbicides and pesticides from a single supplier. Many farmers were lured into monoculture, believing that the higher yields from the hybrids would bring them in record profits. In practice, however, this strategy often ended in disaster, for monoculture left the farmers more vulnerable to adverse conditions – be it freak weather, pests or a sharp downturn in market prices – and this in turn could trap them in a spiral of escalating bank debt.

The Opening Up of the Farm Sector

While the green revolution increased the farmers' vulnerability, it was the opening up of the agricultural sector to the world market that delivered the *coup de grâce*. In the early 1990s, under sustained pressure from the industrialised countries, Brazil and many other developing countries were forced to dismantle the trade barriers that had previously protected their farmers from predatory global traders. The result was dire for farmers all round the world: 'The ability of agribusiness to slide around the planet, buying at the lowest possible price and selling at the highest, has thrown every farmer on the planet into direct competition with every other farmer.'[1]

In Brazil the situation was aggravated by conditions on the international financial market. To stop the Mexican currency crisis spreading to Brazil, the government increased real interest rates to over 40 per cent in late 1994. Although this had a disastrous impact on farmers, many of whom were heavily indebted to the banks, the government repeatedly refused to do anything to help them. Mário Bertani, president of Centralsul, a leading cooperative in the south, says that in August 1995, after thousands of farmers had gone to Brasília to protest over the near doubling of interest rates, President Fernando Henrique Cardoso, who had come to office in January 1994, called him to a meeting. The president told Bertani that other sectors of the economy were also suffering and that there was nothing the government could do. 'Take carburettor manufacturers', Cardoso said. 'They're all going bankrupt now that cars have electronic ignition and don't need carburettors any more. It's the law of the market. It's inexorable.' Bertani replied: 'Very well, Mr President. When Brazil no longer needs food, then you can let agriculture go bankrupt.'[2]

And that was precisely what the president did: he let agriculture – or, at least, a very large number of family farmers – go bankrupt. Figures from the agricultural census show that the number of family farms of less than 100 hectares dropped from 5.2 million in 1985 to 4.3 million in 1995, a decline of almost one fifth.[3] The area under crop cultivation fell from 48.1 million hectares to 38.3 million hectares during the same period.[4] At the same time, big farmers, encouraged by government incentives to cultivate export crops – particularly soyabeans and oranges – and a few food crops for the domestic market, sought to remain competitive through the greater use of modern farm machinery and chemical inputs. As a result, productivity increased – which meant that the size of the harvest increased for many crops, despite the marked decline in the area under cultivation – but levels of employment fell. Thousands of rural labourers lost their livelihoods. Overall, the number of people employed in the agricultural sector fell from 23.4 million in December 1985 to 17.9 million in December 1995, the biggest decline ever recorded in a ten-year period.

The government argued that there was no alternative to integration in the world market, however painful the transition might be. Brazil, it said, should export crops that it could produce more cheaply than anyone else and import food that it could not produce at competitive prices. The 'law of comparative advantage', it said, was the new logic of the capitalist market place. By 1999 Brazil was spending US$7.5 billion on food imports, mostly of rice, beans and maize, crops that traditionally Brazil had produced itself. And so the vicious cycle tightened: more imported food meant a larger trade deficit, and so a greater necessity to devote even more land to export crops, particularly soyabeans. By 1999 Brazil was earning about US$5 billion from the soya complex – beans, meal and oil.

While soya boomed, other crops were virtually wiped out. Before the changes in the world trade rules, Brazil's cotton industry had been the sixth largest in the world. But in the early 1990s huge quantities of imported cotton, sold at ridiculously low prices, flooded the Brazilian market. Many farmers went bankrupt and about 1.4 million rural workers lost their jobs. The area under cotton cultivation fell from 3.7

million hectares in 1985 to 900,000 hectares in 1997. Brazil went from being a cotton exporter, earning US$360 million a year, to becoming the world's second largest importer, spending US$650 million a year;[5] in all, the opening up of the cotton market cost the country about US$1 billion per year. A few years earlier, the government had started to provide textile manufacturers in the backward northeast with financial incentives to modernise their factories. It was part of a development plan to increase employment in what was then the labour-intensive activity of cotton cultivation. But the opening of the economy made nonsense of this plan, because local cotton farmers could not compete with the imported product: by 1997 Brazil's textile industry had indeed modernised but it was relying heavily on imported cotton.

The decline in rural employment took place at a time when industry, too, was shedding workers. The market reforms adopted by Brazil in 1990 had led to a drastic decline in industrial employment. From 1991 to 1997 the number of jobs in manufacturing fell by 34 per cent and in civil construction by 8 per cent. In 1998, for the first time ever, an official survey showed that there were more people working in the so-called 'informal sector' – which frequently disguises unemployment – than in the formal sector. By then few families expelled from the countryside were travelling to the metropolitan centres, for they knew they had little hope of obtaining employment there. Most scraped a living on the outskirts of rural towns, providing seasonal labour for the big farms and finding odd jobs in the informal sector.

Despite the huge social cost, the opening up of the farm sector to the world market brought benefits to some – and it is this that makes the debate so heated. A small group of farmers was able to become more competitive and survive. Even the battered cotton industry recovered, although on a very different footing. New, more efficient farmers began to cultivate cotton in the central states of Mato Grosso, Tocantins and Goiás, where production could more readily be mechanised. The agronomist Alberto Duque Portugal, director of Brazil's leading agricultural research institute, Embrapa, says they have developed a new variety of cotton that is far more resistant to drought. 'It is a hybrid', he said, 'that can grow with less than 200 mm of rainfall a year. A new cycle of cotton is beginning.'[6] Cotton is now 'set to become Brazil's next agro-industrial export hit, following the success of soyabeans, oranges and beef'.[7] As the new cotton industry is highly mechanised, it employs few labourers.

Multinationals Tighten their Grip

With Brazilian agriculture in turmoil because of these changes, multinational corporations have extended their influence. It is clear that for them Brazil is only one piece – though a fairly important piece – in a global jigsaw. All over the world the conglomerates are seizing control of what they see as strategic sectors of the huge global food industry, which stretches from the provision of seeds to farmers to the packaging of processed food for supermarkets. Farming itself is no longer seen as the crucial activity; what is important is strategic control of the industry as a whole.

One area that has attracted the multinationals is the export network for agricultural products. By 1999, 17 international trading companies were handling 43 per cent of Brazil's agricultural exports.[8] The same agribusiness conglomerates that control trade along the Mississippi river, which is the primary conduit for taking US soyabeans on to the world market, also dominate the Paraná–Paraguai river network, which is the main route for transporting soyabeans out of Argentina, Bolivia, Brazil and Paraguay. The authorities in both regions have been improving these export routes by building locks, and dredging and straightening river courses (all of which has caused considerable environmental damage in both areas) in the belief that this will make their soya more competitive on the world market. However, as a recent study pointed out, there is a fundamental flaw in this argument:

> Probably very few people have had an opportunity to hear both pitches and compare them. But anyone who has may find something amiss with the argument that US farmers will become more competitive versus their Brazilian counterparts, at the same time that Brazilian farmers will, for the same reasons, become more competitive with their US counterparts. A more likely outcome is that farmers of these two nations will be pitted against each other in short-cut practices that essentially strip-mine their soil and throw long-term investment in the land to the wind. ... So how can the supporters of these river projects, who profess to be acting in the farmer's best interest, not notice the illogic of this form of competition? One explanation is that from the advocates' (as opposed to the farmers') standpoint, the competition isn't illogical at all – because the lobbyists aren't really representing the farmers. They're working for the commodity processing, shipping and trading firms who want the price of soyabeans to fall, because these are the firms that buy the crops from the farmers. In fact, it is the same three agribusiness conglomerates – Archer Daniels Midland (ADM), Cargill and Bunge – that are the top soyabeans processors and traders along both rivers.
>
> Welcome to the global economy. The more brutally the US and Brazilian farmers can batter each other's prices (and standards of living) down, the greater the margin of profit these three giants gain.[9]

Another sector that greatly interests the multinationals is biotechnology, an area of growing strategic importance. In the mid-1980s the big pesticide manufacturers realised that the rapid development of genetic engineering of crops meant that the divisions between the different sectors of farming were becoming blurred. In the future, specially developed genetically modified (GM) seeds would have built-in resistance to pests (or to pesticides). There would no longer be separate manufacturers of seeds, pesticides and fertilisers: a single company would provide an 'integrated package'. So the companies renamed themselves 'life science' companies, which sounds very eco-friendly, and began buying up companies in the key sectors. This 'horizontal regrouping', as it is called, is leading to the formation of a few huge multinational industrial complexes whose interests spread widely across the agricultural sectors of many different countries.

One of the key sectors is seed production. Multinationals have been rapidly increasing their presence in this sector, particularly in the production of hybrid maize seeds (*see* Table 9.1). The biggest blow to the local industry came in 1997 when the biotechnology giant Monsanto bought Brazil's largest maize seed company, Agroceres, previously owned by Brazilians. By 1999 the multinationals' share of the hybrid maize seed market had increased to about 90 per cent, compared with 35 per cent in the early 1980s.[10] Monsanto, through its Brazilian subsidiary, Monsoy, was the absolute leader, with 60 per cent of the market. Next came Dupont, with a 14 per cent share.[11] Monsanto is now targeting the soyabean seed market: from a negligible presence in the early 1990s, it was already responsible for 18 per cent of sales by 1997.[12] Although the biggest market share is still in the hands of the state

Table 9.1 The Multinational Takeover of the Brazilian Seed Industry

Multinational	Name of seed company purchased	Crop	Year of purchase
Monsanto	FT – Pesquisas e Sementes	Soyabeans	1996
	Semente Hata	Soyabeans	1997
	Agroceres	Maize, sorghum	1997
	Cargill Internacional	Maize	1997
	Braskalh/Dekalb	Maize, sorghum	1998
	Delta & Pine	Cotton	1998
	Grupo MAEDA (to found MDM)	Cotton	1998
AgrEvo[1]	Cargill (US, Canada and UK)	Maize	1998
	Granja Quatro Irmaos	Rice	1998
	Mitla Melhoramento	Maize	1999
	Sementes Ribeiral	Maize, soya	1999
	Sementes Fartura	Maize	1999
Dow AgroScience	Dina Milho	Maize	1998
	Sementes Colorado	Maize	1998
	FT – Pesquisas e Sementes	Maize	1998
	Sementes Hata	Maize	1998
	Sedol	Seeds	1998
DuPont	Pioneer	Maize	1998
	Dois Marcos Melhoramento	Soya	1999

Notes: [1] Now merged with Rhône-Poulenc to create Aventis Cropscience
Source: Braspov; compiled by John Wilkinson

company, Embrapa, Monsanto is advancing: by 2004 it expects its share of this market to have increased to 35 per cent.[13]

This takeover of the local seed manufacturers is placing the 'life science' companies in a very strong position. If eventually the multinationals control the lion's share of Brazilian seed production, the farmers will have little option but to buy from them and accept their 'technological package'. Already farmers are finding it difficult to find old species. John Wilkinson, who has carried out a study into the Brazilian seed industry, says that 'the range of choices available to farmers has been significantly reduced.'[14] The economist Horácio Martins, who is an adviser to the MST, is fearful of the political impact. 'We are going back to colonial times, when our economy was controlled from abroad.' It is not by chance that the MST has decided to start manufacturing organic seeds (*see* Chapter 12).

A similar process is occurring in other parts of the world. A recent study observed: 'Only three companies (Cargill, Pioneer and CP–DeKalb) control almost 70 per cent of the Asian seed market.'[15] Just as in Brazil, this is leading to the disappearance of many crop varieties: 'Many traditional cultivated varieties of maize have already been replaced by modern varieties in many areas of Malaysia, the Philippines and Thailand. In Vietnam, numerous glutinous maize varieties important for human consumption and food security have already disappeared. Meanwhile, in Indonesia there are fears over the rapid disappearance of local varieties due to current government policies to promote new high-yielding varieties.'[16]

The 'life science' companies have not had it all their way in Brazil. For over three years a small group of committed environmentalists and consumer groups managed against all the odds to maintain the ban on GM crops. Monsanto, who had prepared large stocks of GM soyabean seeds for the 1999–2000 planting season, was caught on the hop. To its intense irritation, it could not sell the seeds and had to destroy most of them. The MST and Greenpeace collaborated in direct actions, pulling up GM soya being illegally grown in the south and raiding ships bringing GM crops into Brazilian ports. But it was a very unequal battle. Although in early 2002 the environmentalists and consumer groups were still holding out, it seemed only a matter of time before the powerful pro-GM lobby would prevail.

The 'life science' companies are expanding into other sectors. Through a series of mergers, takeovers and alliances, a handful of vertically and horizontally integrated 'mega-companies' are beginning to dominate global food production from seed production through to crop exports and food retailing. The blurring of distinctions, which began in the 1990s, is being taken much further. One indication of what lies ahead was an accord in 2001 between Cargill, the leading agribusiness conglomerate, and Monsanto, the huge 'life science' company.

Small farmers have, at best, a complementary role in this new world. Bill Heffermann, a rural sociologist at the University of Missouri, has warned that 'there is little room left in the global food system for independent farmers', who are, he says, being reduced to hired hands on their own land.[17] All over Brazil small farmers are turning into dependent, poorly paid contract labourers: they are producing seeds for Monsanto; they are raising chickens for Sadia, Brazil's biggest poultry exporter; they are rearing pigs for Perdigão, a producer of processed pork products; and they are cultivating and curing tobacco for Souza Cruz, the Brazilian subsidiary of British American Tobacco.[18] Very often the farmers are forced to adopt techniques that they find either disturbing, such as injecting chicks with growth hormones, or harmful to their health, such as using powerful pesticides in tobacco cultivation. And the contracts can be suddenly terminated: about 600,000 small farmers in the state of Santa Catarina in southern Brazil were rearing chickens and pigs under contract, when the companies suddenly decided to reduce costs by relying on fewer, bigger farmers. About 400,000 smaller farmers lost their livelihood. Not surprisingly, the MST expanded rapidly in this region.

The Brazilian government hopes that the multinationals, which until now have been advancing into all sectors of the food industry except the actual tilling of the land, will also move into this activity. Carlos Nayro Coelho, from the ministry of agriculture, said that the government has been taking farmers from the US, Japan and China around the country to look at the vast stretches of land currently up for sale. 'Brazil has 90 million hectares of good arable land available for purchase by foreign companies', he said. 'Foreign investment in agriculture will help boost economic growth and bring in the hard currency needed for servicing the foreign debt'. But others are sceptical. Largely because of the protectionist barriers it faces in the European Union and the US, Brazil has not been experiencing the boom in farm exports that the government had been predicting. With annual agricultural exports of around US$15 billion, it ranks seventh in the list of world agricultural exporters, behind the United Kingdom, which occupies fifth position.[19] With world commodity prices still languishing at very low levels, Brazil's farmers do not make the huge profits they have long dreamed of. Most multinationals may well prefer to remain in the other parts of the industry, particularly food processing and packaging, where much bigger returns on capital are possible.

The MST is a useful scapegoat for the lack of foreign investment. An editorial in one of Brazil's leading farm magazines put it bluntly: 'Land invasions, which are being undertaken with increasing brazenness and with absurd pretexts, under the complacent eyes of an insecure government, are causing great despondency in the rural area. Farmers are not investing and foreign agribusiness prefers to go to other Latin American countries, in view of the fact that property rights, guaranteed by the constitution, are not respected by the federal and state authorities.'[20]

The multinationals that have responded to the incentives offered by the Brazilian government usually arrive with a fully integrated operation. Smithfield Foods Inc., the largest pig producer and pork processor in the world, recently purchased land near Diamantino in the state of Mato Grosso, where it plans to rear about one million pigs a year. Smithfield has a global annual output of about 12 million pigs, produced in an almost identical way in many different countries.

Experience in these countries suggests that the benefits to the local economy from this type of investment are limited. Smithfield is a vertical producer, which means that it does not contract out work to independent farmers, but controls the whole productive process, from the birth of the piglets through to the marketing of the processed pork. The productive process is also highly mechanised, so few jobs will be generated. As most of the profits will be repatriated, local tradesmen will not benefit greatly from increased turnover. And the environment may suffer: in other countries Smithfield has concentrated such huge populations of pigs on small areas of land that the surrounding soil has been unable to absorb the vast amounts of slurry.[21]

The New Face of Brazilian Agriculture

The globalisation of Brazilian agriculture is far from complete, but even so it is possible to get an idea of the impact it is having. Perhaps the most obvious consequence is the fragmentation of farming into isolated 'islands' of prosperity in a sea of stagnation. A relatively small group of successful modern enterprises, some big and some small, has emerged, surrounded by a mass of technologically backward, near-bankrupt farmers, also big and small. The process is most marked in the poorest regions of the country, particularly the northeast. Speaking from his office in the Federal University of Pernambuco, on the outskirts of Recife, the political scientist Michel Zaidan Filho was emphatic. 'Whether in farming or other economic sectors, the dynamic enclaves are all linked to the world market', he said. 'They are the so-called "modern" sectors such as irrigated fruit cultivation, tourism, mining and oil exploration. The rest of the countryside, outside the global economy, is carrying on as it always has – impoverished, dominated by the old rural elites.'

However, Zaidan believes that the power of these elites is declining. 'Under severe budget constraints, the federal government has finally put an end to the huge subsidies, which it paid to the big landowners in return for their political support. It is a huge blow for the backward, corrupt and violent rural bourgeoisie that has ruled Brazil for so long. If the old landowners are to survive, they have to present a new face'. Some are doing just that. A number of landowners in the Zona da Mata in Pernambuco, who until recently ran their sugarcane plantations like feudal fiefdoms, are moving into 'modern' activities, such as planting large areas with eucalyptus and pine for export.

Most of these landowners are already heavily indebted to state-owned banks, which should bar them from more government finance, but Brazil's vice-president Marco Maciel, an old-style political boss who is probably the most powerful politician in the northeast, has promised 'financial engineering' to get around the legal obstacles.[22] Zaidan wryly pointed out that the Zona da Mata, with its high rainfall and fertile soils, would be an ideal region for an ambitious programme of agrarian reform but yet again, he said, the opportunity is being wasted, with the government encouraging export-oriented products that require little labour.

Table 9.2 Land Distribution in Brazil, 1992

Size of property		Number of properties		Area in hectares	
		Number	% of total farms	Area	% of total land
1. Over 2,000 ha,		19,077	0.6	121.9m	39.3
of which:	a) over 5,000 ha	5,095	0.2	41.9m	13.5
	b) over 50,000 ha	181	–	26.4m	8.5
2. Under 2,000 ha,		2,905,127	99.3	188.1m	60.4
of which:	a) under 100 ha	2,508,835	85.8	56.4m	18.0
	b) under 10 ha	907,764	31.0	4.4m	1.4
T O T A L		2,924,204	100.0	310.0m	100.0

Source: Estatísticas Cadastrais, INCRA, 1992
Note: The term 'property' refers here to land whose ownership has been registered with the National Institute of Colonisation and Agrarian Reform (INCRA). The area refers to that part of the property that can be exploited economically.

Table 9.3 Land Distribution in Brazil, 1998

Size of property		Number of properties		Area in hectares	
		Number	% of total farms	Area	% of total land
1. Over 2,000 ha,:		27,556	0.8	178.2m	42.8
of which	a) over 5,000 ha	7,436	0.2	62.4m	15.0
	b) over 50,000 ha	262	–	39.9m	9.6
2. Under 2,000 ha,		3,560,411	99.2	237.4m	57.2
of which:	a) under 100 ha	3,061,525	85.3	68.7m	16.5
	b) under 10 ha	1,144,642	31.9	5.4m	1.3
T O T A L		3,587,967	100.0	415.6m	100.0

Source: Estatísticas Cadastrais, INCRA, 1998
Note: The term 'property' refers here to land whose ownership has been registered with the National Institute of Colonisation and Agrarian Reform (INCRA). The area refers to that part of the property that can be exploited economically.

Another consequence of globalisation – one that is alarming both environmentalists and social movements – has been to step up the race to occupy what
remains of the still untouched hinterland in the Amazon basin. Brazil is one of the
few countries in the world to possess large stretches of unoccupied land that could
be farmed. Indeed, the agriculture minister, Marcus Vinicius Pratini de Moraes, says
repeatedly: 'Brazil is the planet's last agricultural frontier.' Now that Brazil forms part

of the globalised world market, there is an apparently unstoppable momentum to make this land accessible and to get it producing for the global market.

Government statistics show that 105 million hectares (*see* Tables 9.2 and 9.3) – an area four times the size of the United Kingdom – was brought within Brazil's agricultural frontier between 1992 and 1998. The figures refer to land registered with INCRA. This land grab is exacerbating Brazil's notorious problem of excessive land concentration. The share of registered farmland accounted for by properties of over 2,000 hectares increased from 39 per cent in 1992 to 43 per cent in 1998. And the number of very big properties – those over 50,000 hectares – rose by almost half, from 181 to 262 in the same period. By 1998 these monster properties covered 40 million hectares, almost 10 per cent of total farmland. This area of 400,000 square km is half as big again as the US state of Texas or the United Kingdom. Remarkable as it may seem, this further concentration was happening while Brazil's minister of agrarian reform, Raul Jungmann, was frequently appearing on television to say that he had carried out 'the biggest programme of agrarian reform in Brazil's history', which paradoxically was in some senses also true (*see* Chapter 10).

Who is occupying this new land? Much of the expansion can be attributed to the soya front, which has occupied the fragile soils of the *cerrado* (savannah) region in central Brazil and is now expanding into the Amazon basin, the world's largest remaining area of tropical forest.[23] Brazilian farmers, headed by the new 'soya king', André Maggi, have been the main actors, setting up 'farms so enormous that they dwarf even the biggest operations in the US Midwest',[24] but the indirect beneficiaries are multinational conglomerates. Headed by Cargill, these companies are building grain terminals and improving port facilities to ensure that they control the export networks in the new areas. Logging, too, has attracted interest. Asian companies, which have exhausted most of the forests in their countries of origin, are now moving into the Amazon. There have also been reports of multinational companies buying up areas of tropical forest to carry out bio-prospecting for new drugs and to be in a position to control what is expected to become one of the key commodities of the twenty-first century – fresh water.

The Future

The characteristics discussed so far – the enclaves of dynamic growth, the modernisation of the rural elite, the expansion northwards of the agricultural front and the increase in land concentration – fit in with what in practice seems to be the government's vision for the future, even if it is not always reflected in government rhetoric. What was not planned – and is very worrying for the authorities – are the signs that a large part of the farming community is failing to adapt to the modernisation of agriculture. The modern enclaves, which should be kick-starting the local economy around them, remain isolated outposts of prosperity.

In March 2000 one of the government's top advisers, the economist Guilherme

Dias, gave a lecture in the ministry of agrarian development's head office in Brasília. For several years the agriculture ministry has been forecasting a grain harvest of over 100 million tonnes, regarded as a psychologically important barrier. Dias was unequivocal. 'It's not easy to expand agricultural output in the present scenario of an open economy and stiff competition from abroad', he said. 'I don't believe in the government's projection of 100 million tonnes. To be frank, we haven't the slightest chance of reaching that target.' Dias continued, 'The opening of the economy to the world market has meant that those farmers who don't have the technology to compete have been thrown to the wolves.'

The figures given by Dias are startling. They show that just 858,000 farmers – 18 per cent of the total number – generate almost two thirds of the country's agricultural income. All farmers in this charmed circle share a common characteristic: they employ sophisticated farming methods. But the similarity ends there, for this elite consists of two quite separate sub-groups. One is made up of a few extremely prosperous rural entrepreneurs. Numbering about 88,000, they account for less than 2 per cent of the total number of farmers (*see* Table 9.4), but they own more than 20 per cent of Brazil's farmland and account for more than 60 per cent of the country's total agricultural income (*see* Table 9.5). These are the successful big farmers, who bring in large harvests of soya, coffee, oranges, sugarcane and now cotton too, or intensively farm chickens, cattle and pigs. They are responsible for most of the country's agricultural exports.

The second group, which is much larger, consists of successful family farmers. They account for about 16 per cent of the total number of farmers and 13 per cent of the land. Although individually they earn much less than the 'big boys', together they account for almost 40 per cent of the total agricultural income. This group – which makes a much bigger contribution to rural prosperity than the agribusiness entrepreneurs, who tend to spend their income in the cities – is made up of well-to-do market gardeners, tropical fruit growers, black pepper farmers and so on. Their success shows that family farming can be profitable.

Dias, however, is much more interested in what these figures reveal about the farmers who are failing than the success stories. He is startled to find that there is a huge group of 3.3 million family farms and 700,000 rural businesses that generate very little income and are, as he puts it, 'sick'. 'It's very clear that the healthy segment is very small', he said. The rest of the sector – which accounts for 82 per cent of the farms – 'is technologically out-dated and economically old-fashioned. ... There is no way in which these producers can survive a transition as violent as the one we're going through. ... Such is the scale of the social problem created by this transformation that the country's productive structure is threatened.'

The government expected the farming sector to bounce back once it had recovered from the 'shock' of foreign competition. But this was always an illusion. Although Dias puts all the 'sick' farmers in a single category, there are two groups, just as there are two groups of successful farmers. On the one hand, there are members of the old rural elite who, vehemently opposed to progress of any kind, are clinging on to their political power. These landowners have swelled the ranks of the UDR, and their private militias have been responsible for most of the violent

Table 9.4 The Farm Sector, by Income Share and Size of Property

	Farms			Area		
	No.	% of total	% of segment	Hectares	% of total	% of segment
1. Rural businesses:	784,539	16.1	100.0	224,041,817	63.4	100.0
a) income above average	88,201	1.8	11.2	76,707,776	21.7	34.2
b) income between						
average and median	188,846	3.9	24.1	43,799,633	12.4	19.5
c) income below median	265,539	5.5	33.8	31,190,945	8.8	13.9
d) negative income	241,953	5.0	30.8	72,343,463	20.5	32.3
2. Family farms:	4,075,325	83.9	100.0	129,569,425	36.6	100.0
a) income above average	769,341	15.8	18.9	45,648,751	12.9	35.2
b) income between						
average and median	921,798	19.0	22.6	23,909,178	6.8	18.5
c) income below median	1,634,033	33.6	40.1	30,034,328	8.4	23.2
d) negative income	750,153	15.4	18.4	29,977,168	8.5	23.1
TOTAL	4,859,864	100.0		353,611,242	100.0	

Source: IBGE, Censo Agropecuário, 95–96; compiled by Guilherme Dias

Table 9.5 Rural Producers, by Share of Gross Agricultural Income

	Gross agricultural income		
	R$ millions	% share of total	% share of segment
1. Rural businesses:	8,976	53.6	100.0
a) income above average	10,422	62.2	116.1
b) income between average and median	1,893	11.3	21.1
c) income below median	472	2.8	5.3
d) negative income	–3,810	–22.8	–42.4
2. Family farms:	7,768	46.4	100.0
a) income above average	6,534	39.0	84.1
b) income between average			
and median	1,408	8.4	18.1
c) income below median	641	3.8	8.2
d) negative income	–814	–4.9	–10.5
TOTAL	16,745	100.0	

Source: IBGE, Censo Agropecuário, 95–96; compiled by Guilherme Dias

repression employed against the MST. Because of their continued political power in Brazil's out-dated electoral system, the government has been reluctant to move forcibly against them, although it has been encouraging them to transform themselves into part of the modern elite. On the other hand, there is a far larger group of 'sick' small farmers. Without the education, technical support or capital to manage their farms efficiently, they have, not surprisingly, been unable to compete with imported food, sold at knockdown prices.

So the rural exodus continues. About 4.2 million people left the countryside between 1996 and 1999.[25] Beatriz de Albuquerque, coordinator of the government research programme Progesa (*Programa de Estudos Sobre Agricultura e Desenvolvimento Sustentado*), believes that others will follow them. Including in her figures *posseiros* (squatters) and other unregistered rural families that don't even enter the official figures used by Guilherme Dias, she says that there are over 6 million small farmers with such low levels of productivity that they cannot even guarantee their own subsistence. 'If we include the members of their families, we are talking about at least 12 million people', she warns.[26]

Other countries are facing a similar crisis. Thomas Homer-Dixon, director of the project on Environment, Population and Security at the University of Toronto, sees the expulsion from the land of the world's farming community as one of the major security threats in coming decades. Such dislocation, he says, accounts for roughly half the growth of urban populations across the Third World, and is leading to further overcrowding of shanty-towns already straining to meet the basic needs of their residents. 'What was an extremely traumatic transition for Europe and North America from a rural society to an urban one is now proceeding at two to three times that speed in developing nations', says Homer-Dixon.[27]

The MST has long argued that the only way of stopping the displaced families from moving to the towns and cities is through radical agrarian reform, which would reverse the trend towards further land concentration. Yet because the Cardoso government saw globalisation as an immutable fact of modern life, it regarded such a programme as completely unworkable. Saying that peasant families, like everyone else, must accept the logic of the market-place, it came up with a market-driven programme of agrarian reform in which rural workers would be allowed to purchase marginal areas of land not wanted by the successful modern farmers.

CHAPTER 10

Agrarian Reform Through the Market

In Brazil, since the second world war, all powerful social pressures, with real possibility for far-reaching transformation, have been readily changed out of recognition into projects and solutions which have achieved exactly the opposite of the original objectives of the social struggles. The political system has demonstrated a notable capacity for appropriating pressures and proposals, assimilating and integrating disruptive elements which in other societies have become an essential element in the process leading to profound social and political transformations.[1]

José de Souza Martins, Lecturer in Sociology, University of São Paulo

In his spacious, comfortably furnished office on the 8th floor of the Ministry for Agrarian Development, Minister Raul Jungmann glanced out of the window at the twinkling lights of the Brazilian capital. 'The MST is moving away from being a legitimate social movement', he said, carefully choosing his words. 'It's becoming a political party, dominated by radicals, which is using the despair of landless families to achieve its own political ends. This is very bad', he added, sighing deeply. 'Conservative forces are exploiting the fears caused by the MST's radicalism to prevent agrarian reform.' Jungmann did not say it, but the implication was clear: the MST must be stopped. That conversation took place in August 2000. By then the government was already implementing a two-pronged strategy: on the economic front it had developed a new programme of market-oriented agrarian reform to provide rural workers with a real alternative to the MST's 'radicalism', and on the political front it was beginning to move energetically to contain – or even destroy – the MST. In this chapter we will be looking at the first stage in this process – the development of the alternative – and in the following chapter we will look at the government's political initiatives.

Raul Jungmann was appointed head of the Extraordinary Ministry for Land Affairs in the wake of the political furore caused by the death of 19 members of the MST in Eldorado de Carajás (see Chapter 7). His mandate was to defuse public discontent by breathing life into the dormant programme of agrarian reform, a challenge that the ambitious and energetic Jungmann relished. A member of Brazil's

Communist Party, he also believed in the justice of the agrarian reform cause. In the early years he thought only of increasing the numbers and creating what he was later to call 'the world's biggest programme of agrarian reform'. His decision to introduce radical changes into the programme seems to have been motivated originally not by ideological commitment but by irritation at the inadequacies of the old system. At that time INCRA, the federal government's agrarian reform agency, obtained the land it required for agrarian reform through the legal mechanism of forcible or compulsory purchase (*desapropriação*). This mechanism, enshrined in the 1988 Constitution, allowed the federal government 'to acquire for the purposes of agrarian reform rural properties that are not carrying out their social function, through the prior payment of just compensation in agrarian debt bonds'.[2]

However, the system was not working as originally intended. Just as Souza Martins said, Brazilian landowners have over decades developed enormous skill in turning to their advantage measures originally intended to bring them into line, and they had managed to transform the process of agrarian reform into a scam for bringing them huge profits. The scheme worked as follows: the legislation governing forcible purchase gave landowners the right to appeal to the courts for a higher compensation payment than the one offered by INCRA, so the landowners routinely appealed to judges who were notoriously biased in their favour and authorised absurdly high payments, on average five times the market price of the land. The rewards were so attractive that there were reports of landowners encouraging landless peasants to invade their estate so that they could get their hands on the compensation.[3] Jungmann, who had become understandably annoyed in seeing his budget used up in these compensation payments, began to rethink the whole procedure. 'I became aware that it wasn't just a case of finding a way of reducing the compensation to a reasonable level. I realized that the whole principle of forcible purchase was out-of-date', he said. 'It was authoritarian and it concentrated power in the hands of the federal government. Brazil had adopted a market economy, so it had to find modern market mechanisms for agrarian reform.'

In late 1998 Jungmann announced a new programme of agrarian development, called *Novo Mundo Rural* (New Rural World), which took power away from Brasília and delegated it to local bodies. 'It's a democratic form of decentralisation in which social movements, as well as landowners and local politicians, have influence', he said. 'In the past, INCRA and the federal government have expropriated land without consulting local interests. That is anti-democratic.' Under the new scheme, Jungmann said, groups of landless peasants would negotiate directly with landowners and the market would establish the price to be paid for the land. To make sure that the landowner did not exploit the landless families, he created special Councils of Sustainable Agrarian Development, one at the state level and others at the municipal level, which would have to approve the deal before it went ahead. Landowners' associations, government bodies, trade unions and popular movements all had the right to have representatives on these councils.

The minister stated, in his first draft of the new programme, that 'the guiding principle' was 'that land has to be paid for'.[4] It was a clear break with the old system in which the government had always paid lip service to the requirement that families paid for their plots, but had never actually enforced it in practice.[5] All this was to change, said Jungmann, for under the new scheme the families would have to sign a binding agreement to pay for their land before they were allowed to move in. To provide impoverished rural workers with the resources they needed, Jungmann created the *Banco da Terra* (the Land Bank), which was to make loans to the families. The aim of the programme, Jungmann went on, was to create a new class of 'small rural entrepreneurs'.[6]

Although Jungmann denies that he deliberately intended to harm the MST with his new programme, this is scarcely credible. National MST leaders have long been fiercely opposed to decentralisation. In 1998 a director of INCRA had commented ironically: 'To talk about decentralisation with the MST is like showing the crucifix to a vampire.'[7] It is easy to see why the MST is so keen to keep the federal government in control of the agrarian programme. The movement's first step in targeting a new region, dominated by landowners, is to recruit local families and to occupy a large estate, usually one that is involved in a wrangle over ownership. Once the estate has been occupied, the MST mobilises its disciplined and committed members to put pressure on the state and federal governments, through demonstrations, marches and the occupation of government offices, to expropriate the area. This element in the strategy is essential. Without this ability to lobby the politically sensitive federal government, the MST cannot defeat the authoritarian and violent landowners, who maintain themselves in power through political patronage and are impervious to outside pressure. Once this first estate has been conquered, the MST can build its own political base, but it needs a foothold in a region to start the process off.

Banco da Terra

By late 1998, when Jungmann officially announced *Novo Mundo Rural*, he had already carried out some preparatory work. Although he ought to have realised that he would need support from civil society, he did not involve any non-governmental organisation or representative body in the discussions. Only the World Bank – which was offering half of the US$2 billion budget for the *Banco da Terra* – was involved. As a first step, the World Bank and the government began in 1997 to implement a pilot programme, entitled the *Cédula da Terra* (Land Bill), to try out their proposals. They decided to settle 15,000 families in five states in the northeast over a three-year period.

The new market mentality imbued all aspects of the programme. Groups of landless families had to get together in their region and negotiate directly with the landowner. Only when they had reached agreement in principle could the families approach the authorities. The deal then required the approval of both the state and municipal Councils of Sustainable Rural Development. Before they set foot on the land, the families had to sign an agreement with the *Banco do Brasil* over repayments. They were given a three-year grace period but if, after that, they failed to make the repayments, the bank would foreclose on their loans and they would lose their plots. Once they had the credit, the families, many of whom are illiterate, had to contract private construction companies to install basic infrastructure, work previously undertaken for free by INCRA. Indeed INCRA, which had previously played the central role in agrarian reform, was virtually excluded from the programme.

The *Cédula da Terra* had a mixed reception. The northeast was undergoing a severe drought at the time. After hearing publicity on the radio, desperate families, attracted by the idea of bank loans and land, flocked to the *Cédula da Terra* offices. The programme was over-subscribed in every state and 8,000 families, considerably more than had been anticipated, were settled in the first year. However, this did not mean that the programme was well received by those who knew most about the issues. To the obvious discomfiture of the World Bank – which was still embarrassed by the fallout from a disastrous road construction project in Rondônia in the Amazon – rural trade unions, NGOs and social movements, brought together in the National Forum on Land Reform, universally condemned the programme.

The Forum made several shrewd observations. First, it said that the government was deliberately misleading the public by calling the *Cédula da Terra* a 'programme of agrarian reform'. Real agrarian reform, it said, demanded not only the distribution of land to the landless, but also a set of public policies to redirect the thrust of rural development by strengthening peasant agriculture and by combating the inequality and social exclusion created by decades of capitalist development.[8] The Forum said that, instead of deceiving the public, the government should be calling the *Cédula da Terra* what it really was: a programme of loans for land purchase.

Second, the Forum believed that the *Cédula da Terra* was unsatisfactory even as a programme of bank credit. The cost of the land was far too high for poor rural families. A rural trade union body calculated that, even if everything went as well as anyone could reasonably hope, farmers would have to spend up to half of their income for 17 years to cover the repayments. 'Such high levels of payment are not viable', the study concluded. 'It would be much cheaper for the farmer to rent land.'[9] The Forum was also critical of the way in which the government and the World Bank had declared the programme a success just because it was over-subscribed. 'It would have been surprising if the project funds had not been fully spent, given that there was a severe drought in most of the project area in 1997 and 1998, the years the programme began. Families that were already poor became completely destitute. Any chance of access to land and money became an exceptionally attractive option', concluded Stephan Schwartzman, from the Environmental Defence Fund in Washington, who has worked closely with the Forum.[10]

Third, and most important of all, the Forum was highly sceptical of the idea, central to the success of the programme, that groups of poor, badly educated peasant farmers could select the land best suited to their needs and negotiate as equals with landowners whom they had been brought up to fear and defer to. In support of their argument, the Forum cited an evaluation that the Nucleus of Agrarian Reform and Rural Development Studies (NEAD), an institute linked to the Ministry of Agrarian Reform, had commissioned from two economists at the University of Campinas (Unicamp). The evaluation, which Jungmann tried hard to suppress,[11] found that most of the associations set up by the peasant farmers to negotiate with the landowners 'originated from the populist tradition, in which representation is based on co-option, subordination and social and political control over poor families'.[12]

The evaluation also concluded that land prices were not being set in an open market, as the government had hoped, and that many of the peasant farmers who had gained land did not even appear to know that they had taken out a bank loan and could lose their land if they failed to make the repayments. In his analysis, Stephan Schwartzman concluded: 'Whatever else it may prove to be, *Cédula da Terra* is an effective source of support for local and regional interests ideologically opposed to the MST and organisations aligned with it, and is a way of stopping the MST organising and of potentially undermining its membership at a local level.'[13]

The Forum was not alone in its criticisms. Osvaldo Russo, a former INCRA president, was vehement in his condemnation.

> It was wrong-headed from the beginning. It was an attempt to bring in neo-liberalism to solve a historical problem. The market can be a solution for many problems but it can't resolve the problem of social inequality. The *Banco da Terra* would have led to the further pauperisation of rural workers. It is clear that both the government and the World Bank intended to make the *Banco da Terra* the only way in which the rural poor could obtain land. Though there may be a case for using the *Banco da Terra*, or something like it, to enable richer, better-educated rural families in the south to gain access to the land, it is simply the wrong instrument for carrying out a programme of agrarian reform for intensely poor, illiterate and long-exploited families in the northeast.

Jungmann denies that he ever wanted the *Banco da Terra* to become the only – or even the main – way in which rural workers could obtain land. The government's own figures, however, tell another story. The expenditure projections that INCRA published in early 1999 showed that the outlay on agrarian reform through the traditional route – forcible land purchases – was to decrease from R$1.2 billion (US$700 million) in 1999 to R$300 million (US$160 million) in 2002, while the expenditure on agrarian reform through the new market-oriented route – *Banco da Terra* – was to increase from R$360 million (US$200 million) to R$720 million (US$400 million) in the same period.[14] Moreover, the government slowed down the pace of land expropriations in the first half of 1999, signalling a move towards the new scheme.

Popular organisations began a powerful orchestrated campaign to get the *Banco da Terra* scrapped. Osvaldo Russo says that the force of the reaction took the government and the World Bank by surprise. 'The rejection by the popular organisations was universal', he commented.

> Even the rural trade union confederation, CONTAG, joined the campaign. The organisations felt that the creation of the *Banco da Terra* ran counter to hard-won democratic practice in Brazil. By trying to decentralise this power and hand it over to state governors and mayors, the president was abdicating his responsibility. He was trying to get the market – with all the unequal relations that the market reinforces – to take over responsibility for resolving a secular social problem. It was a wrong-headed decision since democratic practice demands the political space for social pressure. Luckily, the president failed. The reaction was just too strong.

Second Thoughts

The first to crack was the World Bank. The authorities in Washington were clearly alarmed by the repeated requests from the Forum for an investigation. Sitting in his air-conditioned office in the plush Corporate Finance Centre in Brasília, Joachim Von Amsborg, a German economist working for the World Bank, put a brave face on it. 'The *Cédula da Terra* was a pilot project, which means that it was intended from the beginning to be a learning experience', he said. 'We have an open mind, a learning-by-doing approach.' Gobind T. Nankani, the director of the World Bank's office in Brasília, adroitly shifted the responsibility to the Brazilian government. 'Our aim is poverty reduction', he said. 'Once it became clear that the Brazilian government had a different focus for the *Banco da Terra*, we decided that we would fund a different programme.'

The new programme, which the Bank initially called *Crédito Fundiário* (Land Credit), is being negotiated with CONTAG. Perhaps to save face, the World Bank presents the new programme as a continuation of the *Cédula da Terra*, even though it contains crucial differences. 'The *Cédula da Terra* experience showed us that the community-based focus does work', said Joachim Von Amsburg, 'but we will be introducing important changes. We will be providing more support for the communities in the negotiation process. We will be greatly improving the financial conditions so that the programme really is accessible to the very poor. We are retaining the principle that in a market economy communities must learn to run their own affairs, not have everything done for them by state organs, but we are increasing our assistance. The resources for infrastructure and the technical assistance will be provided as grants, not loans.'

Even more important for CONTAG than these changes in the programme itself has been a fundamental shift in the attitude of the World Bank: it has accepted that market-oriented schemes, like *Crédito Fundiário*, should not become the principal form of access to land. 'Even though we now believe that forcible land purchase should remain the main route, we think there is a role for the market-oriented scheme when, for instance, small groups of 15 to 20 families get together to purchase a fairly small plot of land', said Von Amsburg. 'About one fifth of the families will get their land this way. The rest will go through the old expropriation route.' Moreover, the World Bank has accepted that *Crédito Fundiário* is not carrying out agrarian reform, at least in the way this term is understood by the Forum. 'We will be financing small family farms to occupy niches in the market left by the big farmers', said Von Amsburg.

He gave what he called a 'textbook success story'. 'The cacao plantations on the coast of Bahia in the northeast have been devastated by witches' broom disease', he said. 'Big plantation owners are abandoning the region. There is a cure, but it is very labour-intensive. The families have to treat each tree manually, pulling off the affected leaves. It doesn't make economic sense for the big farmers to do this work, as they would have to pay such a lot for labour. The work would also have to be very closely supervised. But groups of poor farmers, who got loans under the *Cédula da Terra*, have managed to get the cacao plantations back in production. They put in a lot of free labour, but now their income has gone up to R$5–6,000 [US$2,800–3,300] a year. This is the kind of poverty reduction project we're looking for.'

Faced with opposition from popular movements, NGOs and finally even the World Bank, Jungmann has been forced to accept that, for the foreseeable future at least, INCRA will continue to play the principal role in the agrarian reform programme and that forcible land purchase will be the chief mechanism by which landless families gain land. He is pressing ahead with the *Banco da Terra*, but on a far smaller scale than he originally planned, now that the World Bank has pulled out. He said that he expected the *Banco da Terra* to be most active in the south of the country, where rural families have more resources and a greater understanding of the market economy. 'It's being very well received at the grassroots', he said. The minister poured scorn on CONTAG for accepting *Crédito Fundiário*, while remaining firm in its refusal to take part in *Banco da Terra*. 'Today there isn't really much difference between the two programmes', he said. 'We've also learnt from experience and improved *Banco da Terra*.' But he does not expect the popular organisations to get involved in the *Banco da Terra*, because it would mean admitting that they had been wrong. 'The real reason why CONTAG carries on opposing the *Banco da Terra* today is because it attacked it so vociferously in the past', he commented somewhat bitterly.

Jungmann has also 'modernised' the old-style programme of agrarian reform. He has completely restructured INCRA, rooting out corruption and making it more accountable. He has invested heavily in computers, so that staff in Brasília can now communicate instantly with INCRA personnel all over the country. He has scaled down the operations in Brasília to release 12,000 'counsellors' to be sent to the settlements to help the families to set up economic activities geared to the market. He has informed thousands of settlements that they are to be 'emancipated'; that is, he will issue each family in the settlement with a land title and with instructions to start paying for the plot. He is trying to make it easier for families looking for land to bypass the MST by authorising the country's 12,000 post offices to accept postal requests from individual families for enrolment on a land settlement programme.

Jungmann's reforms have undoubtedly made the system work more efficiently. Although the MST is critical of the government's statistics, saying that the figures are artificially inflated by the inclusion of *posseiros* (squatters) who have been living on their land for many years, Jungmann says he settled about 80,000 families on the land in 2000 and another 80,000 families in 2001. These numbers bring together all the families settled through the various programmes – forcible land purchase, *Cédula da Terra* and *Banco da Terra*. At the end of 2000, more than half a million families were living on 3,800 agrarian reform settlements. About one fifth of the families in the settlements are members of the MST. While Jungmann may have artificially inflated the numbers, it is clear that the Cardoso government has settled more families on the land than any previous administration.

Yet doubts exist as to whether this really adds up to effective agrarian reform. Although on a few occasions the MST has conquered valuable land in prestigious locations, the government has usually allocated the settlers marginal land in regions of little interest to commercial farmers. The agrarian reform programme is driven by political and social considerations, particularly the need to defuse discontent among landless families. The government does not assign small farmers an important role in its economic plans for the development of the country. This has created a fundamental contradiction in the government's policy. While Jungmann has been settling thousands of families on the land, the government as a whole has been pushing ahead with tough macro-economic policies that are extremely harmful to small farmers. About four million people were driven off the land from 1995 to 1999,[15] while only about a quarter of this number (260,000 families) were settled on to the land by the government during this period.

As a result, the outlook for the families on the agrarian reform settlements is extremely bleak. As we saw in chapter 9, one of the government's own advisers believes that only 18 per cent of Brazil's farmers will survive. Almost all the families in the settlements must be included among the farmers he classifies as 'terminally ill'. Because the government does not see settlers as key economic actors, it provides them with completely inadequate support. It was this that led Francisco Graziano, once a top Cardoso adviser, to comment angrily: 'Brazil has produced the largest and the worst agrarian reform programme in the world'.[16] Unless the government changes its policies, many of the settlers will soon join the rural exodus.

Confronting the Rural Bourgeoisie

As part of his vision for modernising the Brazilian land situation, Jungmann also wants to break the power of the backward, unproductive landowning elite. It is a position shared by President Cardoso who, in a seminar on the 'third way' attended by Bill Clinton and Tony Blair, said that, while Brazil, like the US and Britain, had to confront new social problems, such as the 'digital divide', it also faced other difficulties, 'such as our outdated agrarian structure, a problem which the US resolved in the nineteenth century'.[17] Perhaps the most effective way to weaken the old rural bourgeoisie would have been for Cardoso to have supported the MST in its land occupations and to have reformed the judicial system to stop local judges from finding, repeatedly and irregularly, in favour of the landowners. But such a course of action was anathema to the president. Apart from the personal hostility he felt towards the MST, Cardoso depended in Congress on the support of the Liberal Front Party (PFL), the party of the big landowners. So Jungmann had to find a more devious, indirect form of attack.

The minister opted for a legal approach. He decided to speed up the work initiated by an earlier INCRA president, Francisco Graziano (the same man who today is critical of Jungmann's programme of agrarian reform), who began the long and difficult process of challenging in the courts the legality of many of the land titles held by the big property owners.[18] The procedure used by Jungmann was straightforward: in early 2000 he warned all owners of properties over 10,000 hectares that he would cancel their land register with INCRA unless they were able within four months to present a land title legally proving their ownership. Without a register from INCRA, landowners cannot obtain bank loans, sell their properties or leave them to their offspring in their wills. In effect, it means they lose control over their land.

Jungmann issued this warning to 3,065 landowners who together owned – or claimed to own – 93 million hectares of land, over one tenth of the total area of Brazil. As he expected, most of the owners did not even try to prove ownership. It seems that in some cases the land did not actually exist, but had been invented by the landowner to be used as collateral for heavily subsidised bank loans, while in other cases the landowners did not have land titles or knew that their land titles were poor forgeries. The owners of another 30 million hectares of land decided to argue their case in the courts. In all, Jungmann said, INCRA would probably cancel the register for about 70 million hectares, an area somewhat larger than Spain. Once this was achieved, said Jungmann, the political power of the *latifundiário*, the old landowner, would finally be broken. 'Just by this measure alone, we are reducing dramatically the level of land concentration in Brazil', said Jungmann with evident satisfaction. 'We will have a huge new area of land available for agrarian reform.'

Jungmann was proud of the success he was having: 'It is the most important intervention ever into the country's land structure and the most severe blow ever dealt to the *latifúndio* in Brazil's history.' Although Jungmann's achievements on this front are impressive, these claims are overblown. First, as Jungmann admitted, some of this land did not exist, and unreal land is of no use to very real landless families. Second, much of the land he hoped to reclaim lay in isolated, inaccessible regions.

Three quarters of the 93 million hectares were in the Amazon region (22.8 million hectares in Mato Grosso, 20.8 million hectares in Pará, 13.9 million hectares in Amazônas, 4.1 million hectares in Maranhão, 3.9 million hectares in Acre, 1.4 million hectares in Rondônia, and 1.3 million hectares in Goiás). Most of this land was covered by tropical rain forest, so it should not be used for agrarian reform settlements but turned into ecological reserves. And third, Jungmann had not yet got the landowners off the land. 'Jungmann may have shown that some of them don't have legal titles, but he hasn't got the land back', said Osvaldo Russo, the former INCRA president. 'He'll have to go to the courts for an eviction order. That is not easy, given the power of the landowners within our judicial system. The landowners will play for time, expecting Jungmann to lose office at the end of the Cardoso government. Attempts like this have been made before, but they've never succeeded.'

By a wave of his wand, Jungmann took Brazil out of the international firing line. Indeed, he announced on several occasions that his reforms meant that Brazil no longer ranked as a country with a heavily skewed system of land distribution. Yet it remains a virtual reform. Until land claimed by the land barons is handed over to the rural poor, the achievement is more apparent than real. Taking out of the equation non-existent land may have improved the statistics but it did nothing to reduce land concentration in the real world. And, in the real world, the concentration of land was increasing.

As we showed in chapter 9, the land occupied by properties of 2,000 hectares or more rose from 122 million hectares in 1992 to 178 million hectares in 1998. These figures undoubtedly included much non-existent land and many properties with forged titles, but the stock of fraudulent land was nearly all accumulated in the old days of *grilagem* and was unlikely to have increased much in recent years. The big new properties registered in the 1992–98 period are far more likely to have reputable land titles and to exist on the ground. This means that, unless Jungmann is able to redistribute to landless families over half of the land he is claiming back from the *latifúndios* – which is an extremely ambitious goal, given that much of the land may not even exist and that he will almost certainly have to go to court to get the landowners off the land they are illegally occupying – he will fail even to stem the growing concentration.

Because the government came forward with its own strategy for Brazilian agriculture, which allocated peasant families a role (albeit a modest one), it felt increasingly justified in repressing the MST as an outmoded and dangerous social movement. The government's political offensive against the movement, which ran parallel with the development of its alternative programme of agrarian reform, is described in the next chapter.

CHAPTER 11

The Government's Counter-Offensive

It is easy to blame the violence and the fury on the water, but why not call into question as well the banks that hold this water in.

Bertolt Brecht

On 17 April 1997 1,300 footsore *sem-terra* arrived in Brasília after walking more than 1,000 km, timing their arrival to coincide with the first anniversary of the Eldorado de Carajás massacre. The impact of the march, the first important action organised by a social movement opposed to the Cardoso government, was huge. When the weary marchers reached Brasília, crowds flanked the road to cheer them on and thrust food and water into their hands. Children gave them flowers. The massed ranks of red flags poured into the capital, past the towering, impassive glass and chrome buildings of the banks and the ministries, like triumphant Roman legions entering a liberated city. This march, in which the MST demonstrated its considerable capacity to mobilise society outside the constraints of normal parliamentary politics, alarmed the Cardoso government. It marked the moment when Raul Jungmann ended his uneasy attempt to work with the MST and embarked on a drive to demobilise, criminalise and perhaps even destroy a social movement involving thousands of poor rural families, which had seemed at first his strongest card in his campaign for agrarian reform. This chapter tells the story of this rupture.

The Early Years

In October 1994 Fernando Henrique Cardoso was elected president, winning by a comfortable majority in the first round of the elections. He was riding on the crest of a huge wave of support from a public still celebrating the end of runaway inflation, achieved by an imaginative anti-inflationary package introduced by Cardoso in July 1994 when he was finance minister in Itamar Franco's government. The economy was still reeling from market reforms, particularly the dismantling of trade barriers, carried out by Fernando Collor de Mello. The social cost of these reforms was high, with a surge of unemployment in both the cities and the countryside, but, such was the relief at the end of inflation, this had not affected the new president's rating with the public.

Perhaps because of his high personal popularity, Cardoso at first believed that he should allow the market reforms complete freedom to take their course, even though they were creating such a serious crisis in the countryside. Jungmann recalled a conversation that he had with the president in 1995, before he was minister, in which they had both agreed that there was little the government could do to ease the pain of economic modernisation. 'We decided that there was little point in trying to intervene in the process of agricultural modernisation, which was destroying so many jobs in the countryside', he said. 'In the developed, capitalist world, the towns are full and the countryside is empty. We thought there was simply no point in trying to keep rural families in the countryside. We weren't as arrogant as to think we could revert a tendency of capitalism!'

In some ways, this meek acceptance of capitalism's implacable laws might seem surprising, for Cardoso had once been well known as a left-leaning sociologist. In the 1960s he and the Chilean sociologist Enzo Faletto had elaborated the theory of dependent development, in which they discussed the constraints on the development of countries in the periphery because of their structural dependence on the central economies. Cardoso's ideas were considered subversive by the military and he had to spend several years in exile. However, even before he came to office, Cardoso had dashed any hopes that he might lead a Third World movement against globalisation. In an article syndicated around the world just before he came to office, he said that Brazil would find the solution to its problems in 'integration and participation in the international system'.[1] In a notorious interview with Brazilian journalists, he commented jokingly: 'Forget everything I've ever written'.

Ironically, the British Marxist historian Eric Hobsbawm helped to convince Cardoso that nothing could be done to stem the rural exodus. In 1994 Hobsbawm had come to Brasília to take part in a brainstorming session organised by Cardoso just before he took office. At that time, Hobsbawm was just completing his masterly study of the twentieth century, *The Age of Extremes*. In a controversial passage in that book, which sparked fierce debate in Brazil, he wrote:

> The most dramatic and far-reaching social change of the second half of this century, and the one that cuts us off for ever from the world of the past, is the death of the peasantry. For since the Neolithic era most human beings had lived off the land and its livestock or harvested the sea as fishermen. With the exception of Britain, peasants and farmers remained a massive part of the occupied population even in industrialised countries until well into the twentieth century. ... At the very moment when hopeful young leftists were quoting Mao Tse-Tung's strategy for the triumph of revolution by mobilising the countless rural millions against the encircled urban strongholds of the status quo, these millions were abandoning their villages and moving into the cities themselves.[2]

Changing Tack

After a couple of years in office, Cardoso began to change his mind about allowing the law of capitalist development to take its toll. What brought about the change was the growing mobilisation of the MST, which was expanding rapidly as a result of the crisis in rural employment. The agronomist Francisco Graziano, at that time Cardoso's top political aide, recalls the atmosphere: 'The MST, demanding agrarian reform, had its foot on the accelerator. Thirty years after the defeat of the Peasant Leagues (a powerful movement of rural workers in the northeast), sickles and hoes were on the front pages of the newspapers once again.'[3] And the government was floundering:

> The agriculture minister, José Eduardo [de Andrade], and Brasílio [de Araújo Neto – head of INCRA] were experiencing more and more difficulties with MST and the rural workers' trade union, CONTAG. Things were not going at all well for the government, which had even stopped talking to the leaders of the main popular organisations. The situation was reaching boiling point. Agrarian reform was becoming a stick with which to beat the government, a banner used by the opposition to discredit Fernando Henrique. This was obvious to everyone, just as it was only too evident that José Eduardo didn't have the ability to deal with the situation.[4]

During the heat of his election campaign Cardoso had promised to settle 280,000 landless families on the land during his government but, once in office, he had done little. INCRA had been reduced to an ineffectual department, with little political clout, within the ministry of agriculture. The minister, himself a banker and landowner, had close links to the big farming groups and, far from promoting agrarian reform, he had actively campaigned against it. It seemed that, like his predecessors since the return to democratic rule in 1985, Cardoso would fall far short of his goals. But in a climate of growing rural discontent, Cardoso, wishing to present himself at home and abroad as a modern and democratic president, had been unwilling to endorse the only real alternative to agrarian reform – the systematic use of violence to silence the noisy and demanding *sem-terra*.

The federal government's dithering raised the political stakes. The *sem-terra* became more convinced than ever that they would get land only if they occupied estates; and the landowners, because they heard the government repeatedly criticising the MST, felt encouraged to take more energetic measures against the *sem-terra*, counting on the support of the local state authorities. The result was two massacres, carried out in different parts of the Amazon basin. In both cases the state military police force was responsible for the violence and some of the policemen involved also worked as security guards on landowners' ranches.

The first massacre took place on 9 August 1995 at Corumbiara in the state of Rondônia. Some 500 families had occupied a forest area belonging to the Santa Elina ranch. It was not an MST camp, but for local ranchers *sem-terra* and the MST were synonymous. Under pressure from the ranch-owner, the local judge issued an eviction order. He established one condition – that the military police should not use excessive force, as there were many women and children in the camp – but the ranch-owner paid no attention. He covered the transport costs for 200 well-armed military police to travel to his estate from the state capital, Porto Velho, and he arranged for the security guards from his ranch, some of whom also worked as policemen, to join these troops.

The police arrived at the camp on 8 August. They held talks with the *sem-terra* leaders and assured them they would not use force in the eviction. But at 4 a.m. the following day, under cover of darkness, the police launched a surprise attack. They threw tear-gas bombs and set fire to some of the huts, causing panic. In the dark no one could identify the attackers and some of the men fired back with hunting guns and old rifles. Two policemen were killed and their colleagues started a frenzy of killings and beatings. Survivors, quoted in an Amnesty International report, told how a policeman said 'We'll exterminate you like rats. The rancher has money to buy off or to kill everyone'.[5] Eyewitnesses said policemen forced the men and the boys to lie on the ground, and then kicked and stamped on them. The police killed ten *sem-terra* in the camp, and fired on others as they tried to flee, killing a 7-year-old girl and three adults. The police arrested 730 people, about 100 of whom were injured, 30 so seriously that they had to be taken to hospital. After the massacre was over, the police set fire to the camp in what appears to have been an attempt to destroy evidence that could have been used against them.

Without the discipline and organisation of MST families, the traumatised survivors fled all over Brazil. The policemen, who justified the high number of casualties by claiming that the *sem-terra* had ambushed them, were not arrested and continued to work normally. Despite considerable press coverage of the massacre, it took human rights lawyers five years to get the authorities to prosecute those responsible for the killings. Eventually in 2000, 12 policemen and 2 *sem-terra* were tried in Porto Velho. Nine of the police officers were acquitted, and the other three, along with the two *sem-terra*, were given prison sentences. During the trial a state prosecutor, paraphrasing a well-known saying about the locust-like *sauva* ants, said: 'either Brazil finishes off the *sem-terra* or the *sem-terra* will finish off Brazil'. Meanwhile the delay in prosecuting the policemen at Corumbiara had given the green light for a second and larger massacre, which took place eight months later in Eldorado de Carajás (*see* chapter 7).

President Cardoso's first reaction to the Eldorado massacre was to dismiss it as part of 'archaic' Brazil, which had nothing to do with the modern globalised country that he was promoting, but the storm of outrage at home and abroad forced him to take action. As other presidents had done at times of crisis, Cardoso created a new ministry – the Extraordinary Ministry for Land Policy – that was to take its orders directly from the presidency, not from the minister of agriculture, and selected Raul Jungmann, a shrewd and tireless political operator, to head it. Agrarian reform was back on the political agenda and, backed by a generous budget, Jungmann was going to make it happen.

Relations between the MST and Jungmann were not hostile in the early years. 'We needed each other', said Jungmann. 'Without the constant pressure from the MST, I would never have got the funds for agrarian reform, especially at a time of IMF-imposed budget cuts. And, though they don't like to admit it, the MST bene-fited from having as a minister a man who was profoundly committed to agrarian reform.' Jungmann's first objective was to defuse the social unrest by getting landless families on to land, and he set about this task with the single-minded determination and energy that were to characterise his years in office. By the end of Cardoso's first four-year term, about 260,000 families had been settled on over 8 million hectares of land. By contrast, only 140,000 families had been given land in the ten years before Cardoso came to power. Many MST families benefited from the programme.

Even so, the agrarian reform fell well short of what the MST wanted. The government had largely resisted the MST's endeavours to win fertile land near the main consumer centres. According to a report published by a parliamentary commission of enquiry, three-quarters of the 8 million hectares allocated for land reform lay in the Amazon basin. The commission concluded that the Cardoso government was using its land reform programme in much the same way as the military governments in the past: 'The present government is carrying on with the old policy of using agrarian reform as a way of alleviating social tensions in the south, southeast and northeast regions of the country by transferring impoverished families to the Amazon basin.'[6]

By early 1997 the tension was growing. The MST was using its by now well-established tactics – land occupations, marches, mobilisation – to conquer land, while at the same time bitterly attacking the government for not delivering 'real agrarian reform'. Conservative sectors within the Cardoso government felt that the MST was getting out of hand. After visiting five states where land conflict was acute, the minister of justice, Nelson Jobim, urged state governments and public prosecutors to take a 'harder line' against the MST and those who organised land occupations, which he described as 'criminal acts'. He said that the MST was a 'political apparatus being used by other groups' that had no commitment to land reform as such.[7] Such views had been aired before. What caused the government to listen to these complaints was the march on Brasília.

On 17 February 1997, the MST started what it called a National March for Agrarian Reform, Employment and Justice. Leaving from three corners of the country, the 1,300 *sem-terra* reached Brasília on 17 April, the first anniversary of the Eldorado de Carajás massacre. 'It was not just that people flocked in their thousands to express support for the movement', said the former president of INCRA, Osvaldo Russo. 'It was also the quality of the mobilisation. The MST captured the mood of the moment.' The MST spoke a new language of idealism, optimism and commit-ment, values that shone through the statements of those taking part. Cardoso had no option but to receive the MST leaders in the Planalto Palace and listen to their demands.

An opinion poll carried out at the time showed that 94 per cent of the population supported the MST's campaign to achieve agrarian reform and 85 per cent thought they were right to occupy land. Political scientist Clovis Moura says that the march showed that people identified strongly with the MST's objectives. 'For the first time a political movement went to the federal capital and [spoke] to the government on an equal footing', he wrote. The MST placed on the table, above the arguments of party politics, 'a global project for solving the most acute social problems'.[8] The scale of support for the MST shocked the government. Osvaldo Russo believes that the march was a turning point. 'For the first years in power the government was not particularly concerned about the growth of the MST', he said. 'It might even have seen it as an ally in its drive to modernise the old agrarian elite. But the MST's march on Brasília changed all that. The government became scared. For the first time it became worried that the MST might actually overthrow the government. They felt they had to stop it.'

Taking on the MST

Over the next year and a half Raul Jungmann painstakingly constructed a different kind of agrarian reform, one that was decentralised and operated with market mechanisms. The model left no role for a national movement like the MST. Not surprisingly, the MST fiercely opposed the new strategy, which it believed had been deliberately engineered to undermine it. Relations deteriorated, exacerbated by a growing personal animosity between Jungmann, an atheist and ex-Communist Party member, and MST leader João Pedro Stédile, a former Catholic seminarian. On one occasion Jungmann described Stédile as 'the product of the hatred that Catholic immigrants in Rio Grande do Sul feel for modernity, technology and the uncertainties of capitalism',[9] and on another he accused him of 'trying to destroy the democratic left'.[10] In turn, Stédile once commented bitterly: 'The worst conservative is a former Communist',[11] and another time he accused Jungmann of being an 'inveterate liar', who knew nothing about agrarian reform before he took office, 'as all he'd done was spend eight years at university studying psychology and even then he left without a degree'.[12]

There was more to the conflict than personal animosity. Jungmann sees himself as a pragmatist. 'I am not carrying out the agrarian reform programme that the left has dreamed of', he said. 'But I am carrying out the only kind that is possible in today's world. To think that a classic programme of agrarian reform is possible today is dangerous nonsense.' Stédile, however, believes in this 'nonsense': he says that the enormous inequalities in wealth and in land distribution that are arising in Brazil as a result of globalisation will eventually lead the country to adopt an entirely new 'model of development' that will include wide-ranging agrarian reform. The two men stand for profoundly different visions of Brazil's future.

Despite the growing tension, Jungmann refrained from attacking the movement while he was elaborating his new strategy. Instead, he let conservative forces in the countryside spearhead the offensive. One of the first targets for police harassment and intimidation was José Rainha Junior, the charismatic MST leader who had emerged as the main spokesman for the *sem-terra* families in the Pontal da Paranapanema region of São Paulo state. In June 1997 the jury in a small town courtroom in Rainha's home state of Espírito Santo found him guilty of the murder in 1989 of both a landowner and a military policeman. The prosecution lawyers produced no incriminating evidence because there was none: Rainha was 2,000 km away in the northeast at the time of the murders. Instead, the lawyers melodramatically knelt before the members of the jury, almost all of whom were linked to local landowners, and in tears pleaded with them to convict Rainha 'for the sake of God and your children'. Amnesty International concluded that Rainha was falsely convicted 'on the basis of his activism in the MST in organising land occupations rather than on the basis of evidence presented in the trial'.[13] Even the judge admitted that Rainha's name had been 'tacked on' to police reports. He expressed his unease with the conviction by giving Rainha a heavy prison sentence (26 years and six months) thus ensuring that Rainha would be retried, since under Brazilian law this right is automatically granted to anyone sentenced to more than 25 years.

During the trial proceedings José Rainha was subject to harassment in the Pontal region. Local police carried out at least 12 separate investigations into Rainha's activities. Arrest warrants were issued, but Rainha always managed to evade imprisonment. In 1995, in a move interpreted by many as a form of pressure on Rainha to give himself up, the police arrested his wife, Deolinda, while she was baking a cake for their 2-year-old son's birthday party. The police repeatedly arrested other Pontal leaders, charging them with 'the violent seizure of land and the organisation of a criminal gang'. For the local policemen, the MST was a 'social cancer' and MST leaders ought to be arrested 'in the name of God' because they were the 'tools of tyranny'.[14] Ignoring the procedures laid down in their own national human rights plan, the federal authorities remained silent throughout these events.

However, the MST was not completely isolated: it received the support not only of sympathisers but also of many other Brazilians who did not necessarily approve of the MST's left-wing ideology but believed that the movement should be given the political space to mobilise. The MST gained the backing of a small but influential group of lawyers who, while recognising that the MST's main strength came from its capacity to organise mass struggle, believed that it was also important to press forward on the institutional front. These lawyers helped the movement to overturn judgements that were blatantly unjust. One of the country's most prestigious barristers, 88-year-old Evandro Lins e Silva, came out of retirement to lead Rainha's defence in the appeal court and in April 2000 the MST leader was acquitted. About 3,000 *sem-terra* waited outside the courtroom in Vitória, the state capital, ready to take to the streets in protest should the verdict have gone against him.

10. *Sem-terra* marching   (*João Zinclar*)

These lawyers have also begun to press for a fundamental reorientation in judicial interpretation, so that new ways of understanding the law can be established.[15] In a groundbreaking judgement on 31 August 1999, Brazil's Federal Public Ministry, a new body set up by the 1988 Constitution to be independent of both executive and legislature, established that land invasion was not necessarily a crime, saying: 'we believe that, in this context, the act of bringing people to invade land, with the objective of putting pressure on the authorities for a social change, can be viewed as a legal act'. Brazil's Supreme Court of Justice also ruled that a campaigning movement, which mobilised its members to put pressure on the government, could not be considered the equivalent of a 'criminal gang', which organised its members to commit crimes.[16] This new thinking occurred almost exclusively in the higher courts, so a pattern emerged in which the MST was frequently subject to harassment and intimidation by police, prosecutors and judges at the local level but often won its appeals in the higher courts.

On 10 November 1999 the MST and other member organisations of the Forum for the Struggle for Land, Work and Citizenship held a national day of stoppages. Demonstrators also occupied tollbooths on several national highways in protest at high road charges. Several busloads of MST settlers from the Nova Canudos camp arrived at the tollbooths on the Castelo Branco highway in São Paulo state. The protesters spread out across the road, stopping the traffic. After the police had arrived, firing into the air, some of the demonstrators broke open the tollbooths and set fire to them.

This action was clearly illegal but the authorities reacted with disproportionate heavy-handedness. Over 100 people were detained and six *sem-terra* activists were held for six months before being brought to trial. Although none of the prosecution witnesses was able to identify the accused, the activists were given sentences of between 8 and 11 years of imprisonment. In her ruling, the judge accused the MST leaders of being 'anti-democratic' and of taking advantage of ignorant landless workers to create public disorder and further their revolutionary cause. The MST appealed, and their requests for bail were initially turned down. It was a higher court, the São Paulo Appeals Court, which in December 2000 ordered the immediate release of the prisoners, pending the result of their appeal.

Undermining the MST

For a long while President Cardoso refrained from direct action to repress the MST. In June 1998, he had spoken of the need to get the balance right in his treatment of the movement. 'If the state reacts with brute force, with repression, it will not resolve the problem', he said. 'But, on the other hand, it has to do something. There are clearly people in the MST who imagine they're going to carry out a socialist revolution. Some are even thinking of armed revolution. I know there are. But there's no way they're going to carry out a revolution. The conditions for this don't exist. If action isn't taken, they could threaten democracy. We have to maintain a difficult equilibrium.'[17]

In early 2000 Cardoso decided that the MST's growing momentum required a firmer response. Flushed with its success in taking its struggle to almost every region of Brazil, the MST had entered a new phase, in which it had broadened its struggle to mobilise the whole of society around a new 'popular project'. Jungmann and Cardoso began to see the MST as a dangerous foe bent on sabotaging their programme of market-oriented agrarian reform. The first signs of the new policy came in Jungmann's public statements, which acquired a far tougher tone. After the MST had occupied an INCRA building in March 2000, he commented: 'I will not negotiate with those who disrespect human rights and invade public buildings. ... Those who infringe democracy favour totalitarianism.'[18]

The offensive soon moved beyond verbal attacks. In April the MST carried out a wave of land occupations and then, a week later, about 5,000 *sem-terra* occupied public buildings in 14 state capitals and another 25,000 took part in demonstrations all over the country. Even though the MST had frequently taken over public buildings in the past, it had never before organised such a comprehensive and well-planned day of action. The state governments reacted calmly to the land occupations, which shows that the MST had managed to get this tactic accepted as a legitimate form of pressure. But their response to the demonstrations and the mass occupation of public buildings was far more extreme. Only two state governors – Itamar Franco of Minas Gerais, and Dante de Oliveira of Mato Grosso – sent representatives to negotiate with the MST. The others immediately resorted to force, sending in heavily armed military police to evict the *sem-terra* and to repress the demonstrations. Predictably enough, the toughest response of all came from Jaime Lerner, the governor of Paraná, who ordered 800 policemen to stop MST members, heading for Curitiba in 40 coaches, from taking part in a demonstration. When the unarmed demonstrators got out of the coaches, the police forced them back with considerable violence, injuring about 50 people and shooting dead a 38-year-old MST settler, Antônio Tavares Pereira, the father of five children.

The federal government responded just as energetically to the MST actions. For the first time it treated the MST not as a legitimate social movement exercising its right to bring pressure on the government but as a potentially criminal organisation that warranted police investigation. In an unusually tough speech, Cardoso said that the MST 'had overstepped the limits of democracy' and that this was 'unacceptable'.[19] He even blamed the MST for the death of the settler, which, he said, should be 'a warning to all those who have opted for provocation and for disrespect for democracy and citizenship'.[20] This statement, coming from a president who in the past had been an outspoken opponent of the military regime, was greeted with dismay by several prestigious commentators. 'The warning issued by the presidency is an overbearing, anti-social and anti-democratic threat', wrote the well-known journalist Élio Gaspari, former editor of the influential news magazine *Veja*. Even though Gaspari has little sympathy for the MST, he was vehement in his criticism of Cardoso: 'His statement means that anyone who does something that the government (perhaps correctly) sees as an attack on democracy can be given a shot in the belly. It was not the MST and its rabble-rousers who infringed democracy. It was Paraná's military police, with the backing of the presidency. ... Antônio Tavares Pereira's death is not an alert to the masses. It is an alert to Professor Fernando Henrique Cardoso. It shows that he is adopting the authoritarian military views he criticised in the past.'[21]

Paulo Singer, an economist who had worked in a left-wing think-tank with Cardoso in the 1970s, argued that the freedom to organise and to demonstrate lies at the very heart of the democratic system. 'The MST's "anti-democratic" demonstrations reflect the despair of many thousands who have lost their livelihood and cannot find another one. ... Those who point an accusatory finger at the MST ought to consider what other forms of pressure they can use: civil disobedience, with passive resistance like Ghandi? Setting themselves alight, like Buddhist monks did during the Vietnam War? Hunger strikes?'[22]

But Cardoso was in no mood to listen to his critics. Admitting he had been 'taken by surprise' by the MST's offensive, he held emergency talks with Jungmann and then announced what became known as 'the anti-MST package'.[23] In a determined attempt to deprive the MST of its main tactic – land occupations – the president announced a two-year ban on INCRA expropriating an estate invaded by landless families for the first time, and said that if the estate was occupied a second time – as often happens after families have been evicted – the ban would be increased to five years. Cardoso also decided to give the police and intelligence services a more prominent role in dealing with the MST. To the dismay of human rights lawyers, he decided that the old National Security Law, introduced by the military and still on the statute books, should be dusted off and invoked against *sem-*

terra. Until then most *sem-terra* resisting eviction had been charged with 'disrespect for government employees', a crime carrying a maximum sentence of one year's imprisonment. Under the National Security Law *sem-terra* could be charged with 'threatening the functioning of the established powers' and receive sentences of up to ten years. It was an extraordinary step for Cardoso. In exile in the 1970s, he had expressed outrage when the generals had used this law to crush opposition, and his own justice minister, José Gregori, was at that very moment encouraging Congress to revoke the draconian law as part of the 'authoritarian rubble' left by the military government.[24]

The federal police used the law for the first time in May 2000. Once again it was in Paraná, where its hard-line governor authorised this controversial step. For 14 years 36 families had peacefully occupied an estate in Espigão Alto do Iguaçu in the south of the state. But when INCRA placed a compulsory purchase order on the estate, the owners appealed to the Supreme Court and won. The families resisted the attempt to evict them and nine *sem-terra* were charged under the National Security Law with 'impeding the course of justice, resisting arrest, and forming a criminal gang'. The decision to use the law was widely criticised by lawyers, including the minister of justice.

At the same time Cardoso set up the Public Security Intelligence Subsystem, a replica of the old National Intelligence System (SNI), which had formed part of the military government's system of repression. He also instructed the federal police to organise a new department to co-ordinate police operations against the MST. Established in July 2000, the Agricultural and Land Conflict Division (DECAF) had by October begun 32 separate inquiries into episodes involving the *sem-terra* all over Brazil.[25] The government also adopted a tougher attitude on other fronts. In September 2000 the president ordered the immediate arrest of 14 MST leaders, after several hundred demonstrators cheekily occupied the road in front of the Cardoso family ranch in Buritis in Minas Gerais.[26]

As the MST came under increasing attack from the authorities, the national media, which had often reported sympathetically on occupations and marches, began to adopt a much more aggressive attitude towards the movement. To a large extent, this was a reflection of the close relations between the government and mainstream media, particularly television, by far the most influential medium in Brazil. TV is a public concession and the authorities also provide a sizeable chunk of the advertising revenue through official commercials, so it is not difficult for the government to influence the output. In fact *Rede Globo*, the country's biggest TV network, run by the Marinho family, has always been seen as the government of the day's unofficial spokesperson, whether the government in question is military or civilian. As a result, it was scarcely surprising that its main news bulletin, *Jornal Nacional*, began to run stories alleging corruption or intimidation on MST settlements. As *Rede Globo* has a virtual monopoly on news audiences, stories shown on *Jornal Nacional* have a huge impact.

Unread by most of the population, newspapers are none the less influential with opinion formers. At a time when Brazil was racked by corruption scandals involving the misuse of millions of dollars of public money by the authorities, bankers and businessmen, they ran headlines about 'MST extortion', claiming that the leadership forced each family on the settlements to contribute to the movement. To fund many of its basic activities, the MST relies on what the press began to call a *pedágio* (literally a toll). This is a contribution, usually of 3 per cent, which each settler makes to the movement from the loans he or she obtains from the *Banco do Brasil*. On 15 May, *Folha de S. Paulo* ran the headline: 'MST seizes part of government funds destined for land reform'.[27] It seemed as if the MST had committed a serious crime, comparable with the crimes of illicit enrichment that many politicians were being accused of at the time. The subliminal message was clear: for all its high moral tone, the MST was no different from anyone else; indeed one journalist, writing in *O Estado de S. Paulo*, one of the country's leading newspapers, claimed that the MST was 'worse than the Mafia'.[28]

In May, too, Andrea Matarazzo, the federal government's communications minister, phoned from Brasília to demand the cancellation of a live studio discussion with João Pedro Stédile that São Paulo state's *TV Cultura* was about to broadcast and other educational television channels were due to retransmit. Claiming to be passing on a request from the president, the minister said that a person who incited the wrecking of tollbooths and who had been charged by the federal police under the National Security Law could not give an interview on educational TV. To its credit, *TV Cultura* went ahead with the interview, but the other channels, dependent on federal government funding, cancelled the programme.

During the same month, the influential news magazine *Veja*, which in 1995 had sent a reporter to Corumbiara and carried a detailed story on the massacre, ran a cover story entitled 'The Tactic of Rioting – The MST Uses the Pretext of Agrarian Reform to Promote Socialist Revolution'.[29] The title stood out against a blood red background. Inside there was a photomontage which showed João Pedro Stédile's head attached to the body of James Bond, gun in hand. The story was prompted by the death of the unarmed MST demonstrator in Paraná, and the magazine turned the facts on their head by implying that it was the MST, not the authorities, that had guns and was violent.

Many months later *Veja* was found guilty of libelling Stédile and fined, but by then the media onslaught had had an impact on public opinion. An opinion poll carried out in October 2000 showed that, while two thirds of the population of the city of São Paulo strongly favoured agrarian reform and almost half approved of the MST, 70 per cent thought that the movement was using the wrong tactics to support its demands.[30] Only a handful of independent publications, particularly the monthly magazine *Caros Amigos*, regularly sent reporters into the field so that they could see for themselves what life was like in the camps and settlements and obtain first-hand accounts of evictions and massacres. It is these small, underfunded publications that have provided the most objective and detailed reports on the MST's activities.

Accusations of Corruption

With the media reports on alleged MST corruption, the federal government felt justified in launching an extensive investigation into the movement's economic activities. As a first step, it began an audit into the accounts of the MST cooperatives. It had been known for some time that Jungmann was unhappy with the arrangements by which the MST settlements benefited from *Lumiar*, a technical assistance project set up by INCRA. Although INCRA paid the wages of the agronomists, the settlements had won the right to select the agronomists, saying that they could work only with people who broadly supported the movement. The 'financial scandal' was a golden opportunity to change this set-up. Orlando Muniz, INCRA president, accused the agronomists of aiding the MST in 'irregular' financial operations.[51] Before any of the accusations had been substantiated, Jungmann summarily sacked the 1,300 agronomists working on the project, causing severe problems for the settlements. He said that *Lumiar* would be placed under tight federal control and, in the future, municipal councils, many of which were hostile to the MST and sympathetic to Jungmann's views, would be empowered to select the agronomists.

The 'restructuring' of *Lumiar* was only the beginning. In what was to prove a much more damaging policy, Jungmann then moved to cut off almost all financial support for the MST. Until then, despite the hostilities, the authorities had directly and indirectly supplied the MST with much of its funding. Under the terms of the country's agrarian reform legislation prior to the *Banco da Terra*, INCRA had provided all settlements, including those run by the MST, with basic infrastructure – roads, electricity, running water and building materials for their homes. The state-owned Banco do Brasil had also supplied the settlers with subsidised farm credit. The system was far from perfect, for the money was insufficient and often arrived late, but for all its failings this government support was absolutely essential for the survival of the settlements. Jungmann decided that the *Banco do Brasil* would no longer make bulk payments to MST associations or cooperatives for them to distribute the money to the settlers but, instead, would disburse the loans directly to individual farmers. The sudden changes caused serious disruptions. Some settlements received no farm credit at all in the 2000/2001 planting season. On other settlements some families received their bank loans while, for no good reason, others did not.

For a few weeks the government's investigations into the MST made a big splash in the press, but then the newspapers lost interest. However, on 11 August – which happened to be the opening day of the MST's five-yearly national congress, when 11,000 activists from all over Brazil had gathered in Brasília – 'MST irregularities', still unproven, were once more headline news. In October INCRA said that early investigations suggested that the MST had 'irregularly deducted' up to R$600,000 (US$340,000) from the bank loans. 'The government will demand that all this money is paid back', said Muniz.[32] In February 2001, the INCRA president said that they would no longer be lending money to any cooperative that charged a commission.[33]

Ideological Confrontation

The government justified the measures it took against the MST by saying that it needed to drag the movement, kicking and screaming, into the twenty-first century. It insisted that *sem-terra* had to accept that they were ordinary small farmers like all others and that they had to learn to live by the harsh laws of market economics. Yet this explanation is not convincing. The offensive against the MST ranged from connivance with state authorities in the use of violent repression to the cessation of almost all financial and technical support. It seemed like a witch-hunt, designed to maim the movement, if not destroy it.

In late 2000 José Maschio, a journalist at *Folha de S. Paulo*, published an open letter entitled 'The Satanisation of the MST in the Media'. In it he attacked the conservative elite for portraying the MST as 'the Great Satan to be exterminated, in one of the most radical campaigns ever waged against a popular movement'. It is significant that *Folha de S. Paulo* did not publish this letter, although it was widely circulated on the internet. In another letter, three university lecturers and Bishop Tomás Balduino, president of the CPT, accused the government of orchestrating a campaign 'to demoralise the MST by unfairly accusing its leaders of embezzlement'.[34] They went on: 'the objective of this strategic operation is to liquidate the MST, just as the Peasant Leagues were liquidated during the first months of the military regime'.

What really lay behind the conflict was a profound ideological confrontation. In his office in Brasília Jungmann did not hide the personal venom he felt towards a movement which, by defending 'out-dated socialist ideals', had dared to challenge the basis of the government's whole economic and social programme. The MST gave as good as it got. It regularly accused the government of wide-scale corruption and of becoming a lackey to international capital. There was no longer any middle ground. It was a 'holy war' with no truce nor victor expected before the end of the Cardoso government in December 2002. In its short but troubled history the MST has learnt to be resilient. Though the movement was damaged by the government offensive against it, it was not destroyed. In November 2001 Darci Frigo, the human rights lawyer in Paraná, was detecting a new surge of support for the MST: 'Landless peasants are getting very frustrated. They're realising now that the government's promise to give them a plot of land if they merely send in a request through the post is a trick. So they're going back to their old tactic of land occupation. They're putting the land question back on the national agenda. And this time they're doing it with greater force than ever before.'[35]

PART FOUR

This Part looks at the ways the MST has been responding to the challenges described in the previous three chapters. The movement has been making progress, if somewhat erratically, in its efforts to find a successful way of farming the land in a hostile world. Some experiments in forms of organic peasant farming are beginning to prove successful. This process is described in chapter 12.

The movement is advancing more slowly on another front. MST leaders are aware that to maintain mobilisation they need to create a new revolutionary ideology that is powerful enough both to break their members' allegiance to the conservative peasant way of viewing the world and to withstand the onslaught of modern consumer values. Chapter 13 charts the movement's as yet unsatisfactory efforts in this area.

The MST is not the first peasant-based movement that has sought to transform the world. Chapter 14 looks at earlier movements in other countries, particularly England, the United States and elsewhere in Latin America, and compares them with the MST.

CHAPTER 12

The Green Option

We found that sustainable agriculture can lead to substantial increases in food production per hectare. The proportional yield increases were remarkable: generally 50–100 per cent for rain-fed crops, though considerably greater for a few crops, and 5–10 per cent for irrigated crops. It shows the extraordinary productive potential of small patches on farms, and the degree to which they can increase food security.

Jules Pretty, Director of the University of Essex Centre for Environment and Society, whose centre carried out the largest known survey into worldwide sustainable agriculture.[1]

The biting *minuano* wind blows straight across the rolling open fields in the extreme south of Rio Grande do Sul, on an afternoon in September 2000. The sun is shining, but it is bitterly cold. A 15-year-old girl, Adriana Fischer is spraying rows of onion seedlings with *biofertilizante*, an organic fertiliser. She works methodically, carefully, because she is helping her parents to 'purify' seeds. After two harvests, tended only with natural products without a whiff of chemicals, they can be classified as organic and her parents, who live on the Conquista da Fronteira settlement near the town of Bagé, will be able to sell them to the MST's own organic seed producer Bionatur. The fertiliser is homemade. Gilmar Paulo Zanovelo is mixing his in a plastic drum in a shed behind his wooden house. 'About 20 ingredients go into it', he said. 'Cattle manure, calcium, phosphate, milk, sulphur, honey, all natural ingredients. It only costs about R$20 (US$11) to produce 200 litres, so it's much cheaper than a chemical fertiliser. Plants that are fed with it grow slowly but sturdily. They become very resistant to disease.' The Bionatur company was set up here because the climate makes it an ideal region for growing seeds. The biotechnology companies also run all their seed operations in this region.

Bionatur sells organic seeds to other settlements all over Brazil, and at the MST shop in São Paulo. Production is still small, but it is an important step in the movement's slow, often hesitant, move to *agro-ecologia*, or sustainable farming, which it has come to see as far more compatible with the needs of the *sem-terra* than modern chemical farming. The driving force behind this change is environmental degradation, which has exacerbated the settlers' economic hardship. The big landowners have often been able to get away with keeping their most fertile land, while giving up for land reform exhausted soils in inaccessible areas, far from towns and markets. The settlers have realised that, unless they can return the land to a state of ecological health, the long-term economic viability of their settlements is threatened. It is a bonus when they discover, as many have, that this kind of sustainable farming brings them much greater personal satisfaction.

Pontal de Paranapanema

Perhaps the most environmentally damaged land that the MST has ever conquered lies in the Pontal de Paranapanema in São Paulo state. When the MST conquered this region, serious environmental problems were already emerging: rivers were silting up, soils were becoming exhausted and the region had become vulnerable to prolonged droughts. The MST's political satisfaction at settling 6,000 families on this land after many violent confrontations with the land-grabbing ranchers and their gunmen blinded it at first to the gravity of the situation. The MST wished to prove that it could be as successful as the big farmers in Brazil's economic heartland. José Rainha, the MST leader in the Pontal, predicted a future of great prosperity: 'we are going to become the new businessmen. Yes, we are. Why not? We want to come out from under our black polythene. We want to stop being hungry and become producers. We are going to industrialise and market our products. We are going to stop being poor. ... We're going to have money so that our children can go out, and enjoy ourselves at least once a month and can eat at restaurants like the middle class', he said in an interview with a São Paulo newsletter. [2] José Rainha, who comes from a poor family, was expressing the wishes of the mass of the *sem-terra* he leads, but his attitude, with its clear endorsement of consumer society, undoubtedly annoyed the group of much more austere former Catholic seminarians who helped to found the movement and are still very powerful within it. It also seriously under-estimated the scale of the environmental problems, as the history of the settlements is proving.

As in so many other settlements, the most dedicated *sem-terra* first attempted collective production and, after it failed, set up a service and marketing cooperative called COCAMP. It proved successful in recruiting members. 'We started off with 280 members in 1994 and today we have almost 3,000', said Walmir Rodrigues Chaves, known as Bill, who is the president of COCAMP. As well as providing financial and marketing services to its members, COCAMP runs a fairly large cassava flourmill and is able to pay its members a better price for their cassava crop than they would get from middlemen. The cooperative will shortly be opening both a sizeable dairy to produce milk, cheese and yoghurt, and a large fruit-processing factory.

COCAMP should be an MST showcase and yet somehow it is not. The cassava flourmill is often closed for lack of raw material and the co-op directors are clearly worried about the long-term viability of their processing plants. 'Our farmers aren't producing well', said Zelitro Luz da Silva, a member of COCAMP. 'We've inherited devastated soils. Today they're not even fertile enough for cassava. We've got to get our settlers to rethink their farming methods. We need to get a real debate going in the settlements so we can start developing sustainable ways of farming. We've formed a *coletivo de agro-ecologia* but it's not enough. We've got 80 settlements in our region and we haven't got enough activists and agronomists to work with the settlers.'

COCAMP is constantly clashing with the agronomists from ITESP, the São Paulo state rural extension agency. 'ITESP thinks that we're interfering in their area of expertise', said Zelitro. 'The MST's job, they say, is to win land and, once we've done that, to hand it over to them. But the problem is that they don't do a good job. At the moment they are encouraging all the settlers to opt for dairy cattle. They arrive in a settler's house and get him to fill in a form for a bank loan. It's all done in 30 minutes and the agronomist can tick that family off his list. But the problem is, it won't work. The soil here is far too poor to sustain dairy cattle. It's a recipe for disaster.'

MST settlers are finally moving, somewhat belatedly, to avert impending ecological catastrophe. José Lourenço lives in a rudimentary wooden shack in one of the settlements. All around, the land is devastated. A few head of cattle graze on pasture that shrivels up during the prolonged drought in the summer. The only reminder that this land was once covered by dense forest is the Morro do Diabo ecological reserve, one of the few remaining fragments of the Atlantic Forest, about 20 km away. José and his wife, Maria Aparecida, have made a valiant attempt to plant flowers in the ground in front of their house but the plants struggle dejectedly in the dry and sandy soil. José's pride and joy is the small greenhouse beside his house where he is raising seedlings. 'I've got a lot of different kinds of trees', he tells visitors. 'Some of them, like eucalyptus and acacia, grow quickly and provide good wood for construction. Others are old native species, like brazilwood and *ipê*. We're going to plant these trees and leave them to grow. Through them we're going to start rebuilding the forest.'

José has a tough life. 'The soil on my land is exhausted. I've got a few head of cattle and I plant a few crops, but it's not the life I dreamed of when I won land.' Maria Aparecida works as a health agent for the municipal government. 'I haven't been paid for months', she confesses. 'I have to hitch lifts as I can't afford the bus fares. I'm really doing the job for love!' José says that his greenhouse is proving a great success. 'The families here in the village are always asking me if the seedlings are ready to plant out. They want to have trees on their land. They provide shade and protection from the wind, and they're going to help us to recuperate this wrecked land. They're also providing a benefit we never imagined. Families from miles away are bringing chickens and maize to exchange for seedlings. I think we can build this up into a little business, which will bring some resources into the community. And we certainly need them!'

José is taking part in a groundbreaking partnership between COCAMP settlers and the non-governmental environmental agency, IPE (which stands for Environmental Research Institute, as well as being a native tree species). José Lourenço gets his seedlings from a centre run by IPE in the Morro do Diabo reserve. One of their botanists is a young woman, Inês Morato, who bubbles over with enthusiasm. 'It's been an important learning experience for us too', she said. 'We came here to help protect the golden lion tamarin, a lovely little squirrel monkey which is an endangered species. You still find it in the Morro do Diabo reserve. We realised that to prevent endogamy, or excessive inbreeding, we needed to create links with other fragments of forest so that the monkeys could travel more freely and interbreed with other groups and that, in order to do that, we had to get help from the families in the settlements. That's how it began.'

The first of IPE's projects is called 'Islands of Diversity'. In order to link the Morro do Diabo with other forest fragments, IPE had to create small patches of forest that, like stepping stones, would be close enough together to enable the golden lion tamarins, together with the other animals, birds and insects that require forest to survive, to make the journey. IPE selected 20 families whose lands lay between the reserve and the first forest fragment it was targeting and set about developing a way of encouraging these families to plant small patches of woodland with different kinds of trees – fruit trees, native species, cashew and others. Inês said IPE realised from the beginning that the project would only work if they got the settlers involved and to do this they had to make sure that they, too, benefited. 'We began to think of our tree planting programme as part of a much broader project to help the families recuperate their devastated land and improve their lives. We started thinking about the people as well as the animals.' It was soon clear that a lot could be done. 'We realised that families could grow other plants, ecologically useful plants, in consortium with their normal crops', said Inês. 'There were many possibilities. They could plant maize with a legume called *leocena*. *Leocena* improves the fertility of the soil by capturing nitrogen from the air, and it can also be fed to cattle. They could bring real benefits to their pasture by planting a variety of trees – eucalyptus, pine and others. Eucalyptus has a bad reputation but there are 20 different varieties. If you select the right ones, it's fine. These trees would help stop erosion, provide shade and improve the quality of the soil. All these things are very easy for the settlers to do.'

As a first step, IPE invited the families to spend a day at their centre in the reserve. 'We had a great time', said José Lourenço. 'In the morning we talked about new ways of farming and in the afternoon we looked around the centre, particularly the nursery. Some of us recognised trees that we'd seen in the forest when we arrived here as children but never again.' 'The families were very receptive to our ideas', said Inês. 'We let them choose the species they wanted and started providing them with seedlings. In the beginning, most of them wanted eucalyptus. They know it grows quickly and is resilient. I was a bit disappointed.

But now I realise that we need to give them eucalyptus to get the project going. It's something safe that the families know and don't find daunting. Once they have planted eucalyptus, they gain confidence and are keen to experiment with native species.' All but two of the 20 families started to plant patches of woodland on their plots. 'Now even those two families who were reluctant in the beginning have seen the benefits and have said they want to get involved', said Inês with evident satisfaction.

Spurred on by this success, IPE encouraged families in other hamlets to come to the centre for short courses. 'The response was overwhelming', said Inês. 'We could have expanded far more quickly, if we'd had the resources. We had to be quite tough, selecting communities of strategic importance for our project. Later we'll help the others.' There are now 12 nurseries, like the one managed by José Lourenço, and many more in the pipeline. IPE is also carrying out a further project, called 'Green Embrace', in which it is encouraging families that live beside the reserve to plant eucalyptus at the edge of their plots, so they will not be tempted to 'nibble the edges' of the reserve to get timber. Again IPE makes sure that the families benefit by showing them how to plant food crops – rice, maize and beans – in between the eucalyptus seedlings. Families are also developing their own associated projects. 'Eucalyptus starts flowering after just one year and the trees are already attracting a lot of bees', says Inês. 'Without any encouragement from us, families are beginning to make honey.'

In the first full year of the IPE project (1999), the families planted 100,000 trees. 'The families have become much more environmentally aware', said Inês.

> And we've changed, too. We no longer see the families just as a means to achieving our goal of protecting the golden lion tamarins. We want to help them in their own right. The problems are serious, particularly because the ranchers used such powerful defoliants, including Agent Orange, to clear the land, but I'm hopeful that we can turn the situation around. *Agro-ecologia* is the way forward. What we've done is already making a difference and the families have seen this for themselves. The settlers, particularly the young people, are taking the project over, which is just what we want. They're finding new ways of moving forward. They've got quite a trade going in seedlings, exchanging them for piglets, chicks, grains and so on. It's having an impact on the local economy, something we'd never imagined. And old people are remembering the old ways. For instance, ants are a real problem here. It makes it difficult to abolish completely the use of pesticides because applying insecticide seems to be the only effective way of controlling them. But then one of the old settlers remembered that his parents used sesame. And we're trying and it really helps.

What the families still need is support from the authorities. It seems absurd that they can get farm credit to rear cattle and plant sugarcane, both activities that are very damaging to the exhausted soils, but they find it almost impossible to get financing for the mixed farming that is the basis of the agro-ecological approach.

Settlements in the South

The new, more ecologically friendly approach has been developed even further in the older settlements in the south. Forty-nine of the CPAs – the collective production cooperatives – survived the fiasco of collectivisation, but each of them had to adapt. Most opted for a mixed system, combining individual and collective forms of production. One of the most successful is Oney Zamarchi's COOPATRISUL in Trinidade do Sul in Rio Grande do Sul. After refusing even to attempt the full collectivisation that the movement recommended, these settlers did not suffer as much as families in many other cooperatives. Today their community is doing well. The verandas in front of their spacious wooden houses, which look something like Swiss chalets, are a mass of colour, with flowers growing in pots and old tins in every available niche. Chickens and pigs scratch around in the backyard. Tucking into his lunch and looking around at his wife and two children – it is rare for a family in this settlement to have more than three children – Oney Zamarchi remarked: 'We live well but we have very little money and we buy very little. The good quality of our lives is based on subsistence farming. Let's take what we're eating now – lettuce, onions, pancakes stuffed with minced beef, fried chicken, rice, beans, papaya juice. We produced it all, except for the salt, the flour for the pancakes, and the olive oil for the salad. We don't even buy oil for cooking, as we use lard. That's the only way *sem-terra* can live well, being self-sufficient.'

This cooperative still has problems. It earns most of its modest cash income from raising chickens for Sadia, the biggest Brazilian poultry exporter. 'We raise 330,000 chickens a year. Sadia gives us the chicks when they've just hatched and we have to rear them just as they say, giving them growth hormones and not letting them sleep properly at night so they don't stop feeding. They've got to grow quickly, reaching their full weight in 46 days, so that the meat is tender. We don't like doing it very much, but we need the money. We keep chickens in our backyards to eat ourselves.' This reliance on Sadia worries them. The company could unilaterally decide to terminate the contract, as it did in the neighbouring state of Santa Catarina, where 400,000 families suddenly lost their livelihoods. Some families also dislike the idea of producing poultry to be eaten by city dwellers (and abroad, for Brazil is one of the world's leading chicken exporters) that they themselves do not really believe is fit for human consumption.

The settlers in the nearby cooperative COOPTAR have got out of this predicament by devising a way of earning money that does not involve contract labour for a big economic group. 'We had a very tough time for a few years', said co-op official Jesur Bertoli, known as Zuca. 'When families began to leave the cooperative in quite large numbers, we realised we had to rethink our project. We had to change our mentality, working harder and gossiping less, and we had to reorganise production. We started to grow our own food, with a proper vegetable garden. We began integrating our production, so that we could start processing

11. Zilda tends her medicinal plants   (*João Zinclar*)

products on the settlement, because that's where the profit is. We still grow soyabeans and maize, but now we feed them to our pigs. We have our own slaughterhouse so we can sell sausages and other processed pork products. It took two years to sort out the paperwork and get authorisation but we got there.' They introduced other changes too. 'We've begun to work more closely with other settlements. We give them piglets to rear for us. They get a better price and we can increase our output.' Most recently of all, they have started to go organic. 'It takes time to recuperate the soil after it's been heavily contaminated with pesticides for soyabeans, but we're getting there. We planted half of the area organically this year. We're beginning to rotate crops and to create green manure, planting special crops that enhance the fertility of the soil. We're also reforesting some areas, as trees help prevent soil erosion. They also attract birds, which eat pests. This helps us to use less pesticide.'

One of the driving forces behind the changes in these Rio Grande do Sul settlements has been the Centre for Popular Alternative Technologies (CETAP). It was founded near the town of Sarandí in 1985 with funding from foreign NGOs, but it was 10 years before the MST took its recommendations seriously. 'We got very worried by what was going on around us', said José Armando de Oliveira, an agronomist at the centre. 'Small farmers, including MST settlers, were moving into soyabeans in a very big way. They were beginning to use a lot of chemicals, particularly something they call *secante*, which is a pesticide that they apply directly on the land so that they can plant soyabeans without ploughing. We could see it was ruining their land and damaging their health, but for a long while farmers wouldn't listen to us. The propaganda in favour of chemical farming was so strong that people didn't believe that an alternative model was possible'.

What changed the attitude of the settlers was the logic of the marketplace. Claudemir Mocellin, who as an 8-year-old child went with his father on the occupation of Macali estate in September 1979, is today a qualified agronomist. He remains a committed *sem-terra* and has his own plot of land, which he won by going on another occupation when he was an adult. For several years he was employed by *Lumiar*, the government's technical assistance programme for the settlements,[3] to work with families in the COANOL cooperative, set up on land conquered after the occupation of Fazenda Annoni. Firmly shutting the door of his office to escape from the horde of settlers who have come to talk to him, he says that in the beginning the MST got it very wrong. 'We reproduced the system. We wanted the most modern hybrid seeds. We used the most lime, the most fertilisers. We wanted to have the biggest machines and the largest harvests.' But it did not work. 'Families found that, as their soils got exhausted, they were spending more and more on fertilisers and pesticides. Their purchases of these modern inputs started absorbing 60–70 per cent of the price they got for their crop. It didn't make any sense.' Claudemir said that he decided to study agronomy because of his growing concern. 'The course didn't help me very much. It was so uncritical of modern farming. It was only in 1992, when I went to work at CETAP, that I started to find answers to my questions. By the time I left, in 1996, I was a committed ecologist.' Today he believes passionately that the only way forward for the MST is organic farming.

The pressure for change, says Claudemir, came from the families themselves.

> We didn't wait for the leadership to alter its policy. We started to do the sums. If a family plants 10 hectares of soyabeans, it might produce 400 bags, which sounds a lot. But then it would have to use the proceeds from 200, or even 300 bags to cover all its costs. It might have just 100 bags left. That would bring in R$1,500 (US$830). And how can a family of four or five people live on that for a year? Especially if it has to buy all its food and is paying at least half as much again for beef in the supermarket than if it had reared a few head of cattle at home and could eat them? I was getting really worried about the ecological problems – farmers were applying five litres of poison to every hectare of farming land. Imagine what that was doing to the soil! But what made people start changing were the economic arguments. We started to do cost–benefit analyses. People began to realise that they didn't necessarily get better off by having a bigger crop if they were spending a lot on their inputs. With organic farming, your output can decline somewhat in the beginning, but your costs fall much more sharply. And after a year or two yields get bigger than they were before.

Groups of settlers started visiting CETAP's model farm, run by the peasant farmer Ademir Sá and his wife, Luci. They and their two children are brimming with energy and vitality, perhaps not surprisingly as they eat only organic food. They have used no chemicals on the land for 12 years and they have good harvests of rice, maize, beans and green vegetables. They have a dozen dairy cattle and a couple of dozen pigs. With the guidance of the agronomists, they have developed ways of increasing the fertility of the soil through crop rotation, green manure and organic composts. 'Organic crops are much tougher than people think', said Ademir. 'Because we grow a lot of different crops together, they protect each other from pests.' There are often a dozen or more round cheeses drying in the sun in front of Ademir's house. Their flavour is perhaps a bit bland for the European palate but they sell very well in the street market in a nearby town. He and his wife also make salami and sausages. Their cash income is fairly low but their standard of living is high.

'The settlers always come back impressed with what they've seen', said Claudemir. 'We never tell them what to do. They have to make up their own mind, but more and more families are planting food crops and reducing their use of chemicals. I don't like calling it subsistence agriculture, because that suggests that they're "sub-existing", "under-existing", whereas in fact they're improving the quality of their lives. And I refuse to accept that chemical farming is "modern". Organic farming is the real modern farming, in that it is the farming of the future. Chemical farming is doomed, as it exhausts the soils so rapidly. It is just not sustainable.' Claudemir says that organic farming has taken off in the region. 'Most of the settlements are moving that way today but you can't do it overnight. It takes time for the chemicals to leach out of the land. And you have to build up other ways of replenishing the soils, through crop rotation, composts, green manure, companion planting, fallow periods and so on. It takes five years to complete the transition. I should say that we've achieved 30 per cent of our goal at the moment.'

The new ecological awareness is spreading into other activities. Paulinho Freitas, a vet at COANOL, is encouraging the families to adopt preventive medicine for their animals. 'We encourage families to feed their animals very healthily and to rear them free-range whenever possible. Like Claudemir, I appeal to people's pocket. Healthy animals don't get ill very often, so by taking more care of their livestock they can reduce their outlay on medicines and cut the mortality rate. The loss of just one cow or pig is a terrible blow for a peasant family. And they can get a better price for good quality, healthy meat.' Paulinho is also developing homeopathy for animals. 'It exists in Brazil, but only for rich people's pets. I am learning as I go along, but we're getting results.'

In the beginning, the families received little help from the authorities. 'It is ridiculous', said Augusto Olson, another MST technician. 'The families can get bank loans to buy fertilisers and pesticides, but no one will give them money to help them switch to organic farming.' The situation began to improve, however, in 1996 when a *sem-terra* was elected mayor of the nearby town of Pontão. Nelson José Gracielli, who had taken part in the occupation of Fazenda Annoni, faced a great deal of hostility from the local landowners – a school bus and school were even set on fire – when he tried to change the administration's priorities. Even so, he managed to take some positive measures during his four years in office: one was a contract with the settlements to supply fresh food for school meals.

Since then, progress on the political front for the MST in the region has been uneven. In 1998 the victory of Olívio Dutra of the Workers' Party in the elections for the Rio Grande do Sul state governorship benefited the MST. For the first time, the MST settlements began working with a state administration sympathetic to their aims. Though he stressed that the Rio Grande do Sul administration was not carrying out what he called 'real, radical agrarian reform', because of the limits to what a state government can achieve, João Pedro Stédile said at the second World Social Forum in Porto Alegre in February 2002 that, compared with dealing with the Cardoso government, 'it's as different as day is from night to be working with the Workers' Party'.[4] Yet there have also been setbacks. Largely because all the other political parties except the Workers' Party backed a single anti-MST candidate, Gracielli failed in his attempt to be re-elected as mayor of Pontão in 2000.

COPAVI

Perhaps the most advanced of all the CPAs is the *Cooperativa de Produção Agropecuária Vitória* (COPAVI), located near the small town of Paranacity in the northwest corner of Paraná state, near the border with São Paulo. It is a small cooperative, made up of 29 families. When we arrived one Sunday afternoon, some members were seated at a table in their communal hall, passing around the *chimarrão*, the *mate* tea which they drink from a leather gourd, discussing a report on their community drafted by a Finnish psychotherapist, Pertti Simula. Some of its conclusions were hard-hitting: 'many of the members of the cooperative lack confidence and are afraid of expressing their views at meetings and of taking on responsibilities. It is as if they had an internal block. In part, this may have been caused by the very authoritarian, or even violent, way they were brought up. Social factors, such as the way Brazil was colonised by the Portuguese, patriarchal authority and *macho* attitudes, may also have contributed.' Some of the settlers were rejecting the ideas in the report or having difficulty in understanding the concepts, while others were cautiously welcoming its conclusions.

COPAVI has been lucky to find Pertti Simula. He spends three months of the year in Helsinki, where he earns well as a consultant for multinational companies and, as a result, he is able to charge only a fraction of his normal rates to COPAVI and the other progressive bodies he works with. He hopes that the settlers will start thinking about the way they treat their children so that they can break the vicious circle through which one generation hands on to another its authoritarian patterns of behaviour.

COPAVI has shown the same spirit of innovation in other areas. Just after our visit, COPAVI learnt that it had won the International Prize for Technological Innovation from the Catalan Association of Industrial Engineers. What particularly caught the eye of the judges was COPAVI's new unit for processing bananas and other tropical fruit, fuelled by solar energy. Apart from technical excellence, the judges said they had looked for social commitment, sustainability and local development in the projects they had assessed.

COPAVI is one of the few cooperatives in which farming is organised in a completely collective fashion. The people live in wooden chalets, evenly spaced out along broad avenues in a well-planned hamlet. There are very few cars, so the children fly kites and play football on the unpaved roads. They have a communal kitchen where they eat breakfast and lunch. On the walls is a big poster, bearing the slogan 'To make Revolution, Get Educated'. The families serve themselves from large pots, weigh their plates, and write down in a notebook the amount they have taken. At the end of the meal, they wash their own plates, knives and forks in the big sinks. Each month the cost of their meals is deducted from their wages. They pay very little, as most of the food is produced on the cooperative itself. The settlers, who are allowed to opt for the task they most like, be it preparing food or cleaning out pigsties, record the hours they work and are paid on this basis. Although it is small, the cooperative covers the living expenses of two members who are working full-time for the movement.

These settlers' struggle to win the land was similar to that experienced by hundreds of other groups of *sem-terra*. Back in 1988 the Paraná state authorities had decided to expropriate the estate for being unproductive, but the landowner had fought back, renting out the land to sugarcane farmers so that he could claim that it was being used productively. For years the case dragged on in the courts, while a group of landless families who had been promised the land waited patiently in Paranacity. Not surprisingly, they were irritated when the MST, with its more aggressive tactics, moved into the region and quite soon afterwards, in January 1993, occupied the estate and won the right to the land. Instead of squabbling with the other families, the MST helped them to occupy and conquer another area. This friendly act also made it easier for the MST to overcome the initial hostility they faced among the inhabitants of Paranacity.

When the families arrived, the soils were exhausted. 'We had to pull out the sugarcane by hand. It was the only way of eradicating it', said Antônio Natalino Gonçalves, the president of COPAVI. 'For several years we didn't grow enough food to feed everyone, and some of the men had to work as labourers on neighbouring farms.' However, the families did not get dispirited. 'We'd talked a lot in the camp', said Natalino. 'We knew we wanted to farm the land collectively and we'd worked out exactly how we were going to do it.' Collective production was not imposed on these families, as occurred in many other cooperatives, but was a decision they took themselves (at a time when many other settlers were rebelling against the idea).

In the beginning, COPAVI made some of the same farming mistakes as the other cooperatives. The cooperative bought modern machinery and planted large fields of cassava and maize with the idea of selling these cash crops to finance part of their own food consumption. 'After a while, however, we realised that we were never going to support ourselves like this', said Edson Borges dos Santos, one of the settlers, who recently completed his university training as an agronomist. (Because he is black and there are very few black people in the state of Paraná, he is universally known as Zumbi, after the slave who led a revolt in Pernambuco in the seventeenth century. 'It is a racist nickname, but I've got used to it', he said. 'I was the first black man to have studied at the university in Maringá for 25 years. It wasn't easy. And even here on the settlement people are sometimes racist, though they don't always realise it.') 'We decided on a radically different course of action – product diversification', said Zumbi.

Today COPAVI earns most of its modest cash income from selling milk, yoghurt and cheese. Four times a week a settler loads up a horse and cart and goes to Paranacity. Again they made mistakes. 'At first, we were so keen to sell our products cheaply to impoverished families that we let them buy on credit', said Natalino. 'The bad debts we accumulated nearly made us bankrupt. Now we still visit the poor neighbourhoods but we insist that everyone pay cash.' Once the dairy cattle were established, COPAVI branched out into poultry, not the force-fed chickens that COOPATRISUL rears for Sadia, but COPAVI's own chickens which, although still reared in chicken sheds, take 55 days to reach 1.5 kg (compared with Sadia's 46 days for a 2.5-kg chicken). 'We feed them on organic maize', said Zumbi. 'The meat is firmer and less white than Sadia's chicken, and the taste is better. We sell 3,000 chickens a month.'

COPAVI has started taking its produce to a street market in Maringá and is discovering that there is a big demand for an even healthier chicken – the *caipira*, or free-range country chicken, which is reared in the settlers' back yards and takes 80–90 days to be fully grown. 'It is far tastier and we can charge three times the price', said Zumbi. 'If we could produce more, we could sell more. I know it is a luxury product for the middle classes. We would like one day to sell it cheaper to poorer people but we can't afford to do that at the moment.' COPAVI is slowly becoming completely organic. 'We haven't used any chemicals in our vegetable garden for five or six years', said Zumbi. 'The longer we've been doing it, the easier it becomes. Plants reach a natural equilibrium. It's chemicals that upset this balance and make the plants vulnerable to disease.' They are also taking measures to conserve the soils, such as mixing crops and planting hedges to act as windbreaks, and are planting crops, such as clover, that they can plough into the land to increase its fertility. They put a lot of effort into recycling everything, keeping compost beds for waste from the kitchen and rearing free-range pigs, not for the price they can get on the market (which is very low), but because they need the manure to complete the production cycle. 'Our motto is: Let nothing be wasted', said Zumbi.

Now that it produces almost all its own food, COPAVI is trying to process more products and to sell small quantities on the market. The settlers did not eradicate all the sugarcane on the estate and in 1997 they started producing treacle, *rapadura*

Box 12.1 *Marcelo José da Silva*

I'm 28 years old. I was born in Água Preta in the Zona da Mata in Pernambuco. I come from a family of sugarcane workers. One of my uncles was president of the rural trade union for nine years. He was combative and he influenced me a lot. From the beginning my father said to us all: 'children, this isn't the life I want for you. I know how it destroys people'. So my parents scrimped and saved to get us children a proper education. They had six children. Two of us trained as agronomists and three as teachers. Only one of us gave up studying.

I remember once I needed school materials and my father hadn't any money. So he sold his only cow. When things got very difficult, my mother used to remember what life was like in her parents' home in the *agreste* (drylands). 'We had our own plot of land, so we had all the food we needed – cassava, breadfruit, bananas. We never went hungry like this.' It still brings tears to my eyes, remembering how she suffered.

I finished my formal training in 1993. The technical college taught us in the orthodox way. They showed us how to maximise profits and increase productivity. They didn't talk about the quality of life, about human values, about helping each other. I never liked it but I didn't really understand why. I was always a bit of a radical. At that time there were gunmen in this region. They'd been in control for 12 years. When the MST arrived and started occupying land, they fought back. There was a lot of violence. The local Catholic priest, Father Vinicius, and I used to help the *militantes*. We'd take them out soup, bread, anything we could lay our hands on. We'd go secretly at night in Father Vinicius's car, a Beetle.

Things got so hot I had to leave. I was qualified as an agronomist by then and I went to work on a large, modern farm in Barreiras in Bahia. The company had 12,000 hectares of land, where they planted coffee and soyabeans. I was in charge of 120 men. I didn't like the way the company exploited the labourers. I used to encourage them to plant vegetable plots by their houses, though the company told them they couldn't. I'd get hold of seeds and take them to them. There was no MST there. It was all I could do by myself.

I went back to Água Preta in 1996. It was then that I decided to join the MST and get my own plot of land. I became an ordinary settler, thinking that all that I had learnt as an agronomist was useless, as it only helped the big companies. Even so, I did a few things, like setting up a nursery for seedlings. So many of the settlers didn't even know how to do these things. They'd just worked in sugarcane and knew nothing else. But then one day we held an assembly. An MST regional leader came and we started talking about the need for a new kind of cooperative and a new kind of farming. I talked quite a lot and he came up afterwards and asked me where I'd learnt all that. I told him I'd been to technical college but it hadn't helped much. What I knew that was useful, I said, I'd learnt from everyday life. He asked me if I'd like to join their technical team and become a member of *Lumiar*. So that's how it began.

When I was a settler, I'd realised that the families needed help in planning their plots. So that's what I started doing, visiting the plots and talking to the whole family. 'Now what do you want to grow? How would you like your plot to look in ten years time?' I talked to a man the other day who said that he'd always wanted to plant grapes, mango and *caquí* (persimmon). I looked at his plot and we talked about the need for trees so that the plants would have shade. I said I thought the climate was too hot for grapes but that the other crops would be fine. I can give advice but they have to decide. If they reach their own decisions, they're far more committed.

We have to start in the camps, talking about conserving the soils and creating green manure, so that they arrive in the settlements with some knowledge. We've made a lot of progress in the last five years. People are learning how to cultivate organically and to participate in the cooperative. We need to get the women more involved. Of the 47 members of the co-op, only six are women. My wife is reluctant to get involved. She comes from a family in the *agreste* where the men decided everything. Now we've got two children, she just wants to stay at home with them.

My father didn't understand why I'd joined the MST. He's not 50 but he's worn out after all those years in the plantations. He and my mother come here every Sunday. They arrive at six o'clock in the morning. They're so used to getting up early. At first, my father used to complain to me: 'why have you joined the MST? That gang of troublemakers? Those criminals?' He watches *Jornal Nacional* and that's the image they give of us. He's started changing his mind now. My mother was always pleased to see us with a plot of land, with our own crops, so we won't go hungry. I keep saying to her, 'but it's not just that that's important, mother. It's a way of life too. It's helping other people.'

(raw brown sugar) and *cachaça* (white rum), feeding the waste products to the pigs. 'Everything we produce is of a high quality. You can drink quite a lot of the *cachaça* and it doesn't give you a hangover', said Zumbi, sipping the fiery yet wonderfully smooth rum. COPAVI recently inaugurated its award-winning fruit-processing plant, which will be able to handle a variety of different fruits. It intends to export dried bananas to Europe, if it can eventually find its way through Brazil's administrative labyrinth and obtain an export certificate.

Despite all these activities, COPAVI's members are poor. 'We only earn R$150–200 (US$80–100) each a month', said Natalino. 'It's still a real struggle to make ends meet, especially as we nearly all have young children and we have to buy school materials. We are registered to sell milk in the local district, but we are selling all our other products illegally. It is just so difficult to get through the bureaucracy.

Everything is geared to the big companies.' Despite their low cash income – which means that the cooperative would be classified as 'ill' in the government statistics cited by Guilherme Dias (*see* chapter 9) – the families do not seem particularly worried about their poverty. When Pertti Simula asked members of the cooperative to rank goals in order of priority, most put 'earning more money' in third place, after 'having more contact with people outside the settlement' and 'studying more'. (It is possible that some of the settlers were giving the answers that they thought the interviewer most wanted to hear – which would, incidentally, be further evidence of the need for the work that Pertti Simula is doing in getting the settlers to question the authoritarian culture they were brought up in.)

A New Model of Sustainable Farming

Although the ecological awareness is most marked in the older settlements in the south, it is beginning to be visible, too, in the much newer settlements in the northeast. Young agronomists, like 28-year-old Marcelo José da Silva (*see* box 12.1), from the Ourives-Palmeira settlement in the Zona da Mata region of Pernambuco, are encouraging the settlers to go into new activities, such as fish farming. 'We've got funding from the Inter-American Development Bank to build 40 fish tanks', said Marcelo. 'We're trying to do it in an ecologically friendly way without the use of chemicals, giving the fish healthy food that we produce ourselves from organic cassava, maize and potatoes. We're also producing organic vegetables for the local street markets.' Marcelo says that some of the settlers are uncooperative. 'They only know how to grow sugarcane. So when they conquer their land, they want to plant sugarcane on it, with the profits going to them, not the plantation owner. We advise them against it, but if they really want to, they can. It's their land after all. And then they learn the hard way that their plots aren't big enough to make money from sugarcane and that sugarcane ruins the soil.'

Other settlers, however, hate sugarcane, which they know has destroyed their lives, making them old men at 40. 'They know how they've suffered in the sugarcane fields', says Marcelo. 'They know there must be a transformation, but they don't know how. It can be very moving. You talk to the men about the new ways of farming and you see them "wake up". Sometimes they even say: "this is what I've been looking for all my life but I didn't know it before". It makes the work so rewarding.' Marcelo says that it can be an advantage that so many of the settlers have had little farming experience. 'They've never used chemical fertilisers or pesticides on food crops, so they don't miss them. They can move directly to organic farming without experiencing the problems caused by chemical farming.'

A similar process of growing ecological awareness is beginning to happen, belatedly, about a thousand miles to the west of Pernambuco in a region of the Amazon basin where the MST has not always displayed environmental sensitivity. In April 2000 some 1,200 *sem-terra* from the state of Pará sat under palm trees by the swimming pool of an estate they had occupied near Belém. They were drinking milk from the coconuts they had collected from the dozens of palm trees that surrounded the luxury farmhouse and were listening to an MST activist talking about a new model of ecologically friendly farming. It was not easy for some of the families to grasp the ideas and some were fidgeting or even dozing.

The MST's record in the Amazon has attracted criticism. The environmentalist Noé von Atzingen, who runs an ecological and cultural centre in Marabá in the south of the state, had earlier expressed horror at the MST's decision to build a cassava flour factory in the 17 de Abril settlement created for the survivors of the Eldorado de Carajás massacre. 'I know why they did it', he said. 'The government was embarrassed by the international furore over the massacre and wanted to make amends. It was willing to fund a development project and this cassava flour plant seems to have been the first thing the *sem-terra* thought of.'

Von Atzingen said that the decision showed that the MST was still thinking according to the same short-term, self-defeating logic as the cattle companies that it so bitterly opposes. 'Amazonian soils are very poor, despite their deceptive fertility for two or three years after the felled forest has been burnt. By building this plant, the MST is encouraging the settlers to plant cassava. This kind of annual crop does just as much ecological damage as the big companies' cattle-rearing. And it doesn't make sense for the settlers themselves. By planting cassava the settlers are ruining the soil, which means they will have to leave the settlement after a few years. This shifting agriculture is bad for the settlers and even worse for the forest.' Von Atzingen said that alternatives do exist. 'It is possible today to earn a living in the Amazon forest without causing devastation. You can clear tiny areas for your food crops and plant perennial crops, such as coffee and cacao, in the middle of the forest. The problem with the 17 de Abril settlement was that the settlers were all poor, illiterate families. The only technique they knew was slash-and-burn. The MST didn't have the resources to give them proper guidance and the settlers got little technical assistance from the authorities.'

The MST settlers are beginning to listen to the ecologists. Elizvaldo Costa de Souza, a former president of the settlers' association at 17 de Abril, stood in the rain and pointed at a slash-and-burn clearing beside the 20-kilometre earth road linking the settlement to an asphalted highway. It was the beginning of the four-month rainy season and the road was already getting impassable. It was a desolate scene. Just a few blackened tree trunks, too massive to burn, remained standing in the sparse pasture on which a few head of listless cattle were grazing. 'This land was cleared a couple of years ago and its fertility's already going', he said. 'Before, there were 20 or more Brazil-nut trees here. It didn't make sense at the time to cut down these trees, for the nuts would have provided an annual income. But you have to understand the pressures the families are under. Many of the settlers worked in the region before they won the land. They cleared forest for the big landowners or they were gold-panners. They didn't know anything about farming, let alone sustainable farming in the Amazon. The timber companies came in and offered them R$20 (US$11) for a Brazil-nut tree. It's peanuts but the man's family was going hungry.' Elizvaldo said the settlers were changing. 'We're getting them to plant perennial crops like coffee and cacao in the middle of the forest without cutting it down. We're getting them to clear smaller areas and to stop using powerful defoliants such as Tordon. It's a slow process. It's the most difficult thing of all to change the attitude of the settlers.'

And this is what the MST activist was trying to do, under the palm trees in Fazenda Taba: change settlers' attitudes. After discussing in small groups practical ways of farming more ecologically, the families were listening to the activist as he spelt out the views contained in a provocative paper written by one of the movement's leading thinkers, Ademar Bogo.[5] Bogo said that the MST had set up processing plants in the settlements to improve the income and the quality of life of the settlers. 'But of all the factories we have set up', asked Bogo, rhetorically, 'how many have achieved this? Big companies are profitable for these reasons: they only employ labour when they need it, they buy inputs in large quantities, they operate without ethical principles, they use machinery whenever possible, they don't get involved in social welfare. Even so, these companies don't always survive.' Further on, he puts it more succinctly: 'The capitalist doesn't control capital, but serves it.' The MST cannot do this, he says, so it is time to rethink its approach.

Some 4,000 km to the south, Darci Maschio, the veteran MST leader in Rio Grande do Sul, was grappling with a similar issue. Darci is a member of the MST's state leadership and he spends part of his time working for CREHNOR, the MST's credit cooperative, which deals with 7,000 families on 160 settlements ('all conquered through occupation', he said proudly). 'It is very difficult for our settlements to compete with agri-business', he explained, sitting at his computer in his office in the cooperative, the table covered with official reports on interest-rate movements and crop forecasts. 'We could perhaps become as efficient as they are, but we could never become as exploitative as them. Capitalist farmers pay a pittance to their workers. They don't care whether or not their employees earn enough to eat properly and live decently. They use seasonal labour, which means that many of their workers go through great hardship during the dead season. We aren't prepared to do that.'

Because they are not prepared to exploit their members, MST settlements are beginning to experiment with new commercial activities that allow them both to increase their cash income and to promote the kind of sustainable farming they approve of. One of the most interesting initiatives along these lines is the Bionatur organic seed company, mentioned earlier in the chapter.

Organic Seeds

Gilmar and his wife, Romilda da Silva Vargas (*see* box 12.2), met in 1990 when they both arrived with relatives to live on the Conquista da Fronteira settlement. 'We were the first couple to get married in the settlement', laughed Romilda, as she stoked up the wood stove, the only source of heat during the bitterly cold winter. Although hoarfrost covers the fields, their two children, 9-year-old Gian and 2-year-old Jacqueline, wearing only t-shirts and open sandals, are playing happily outside. The family grows most of its own food and keeps a few cows, which provide them with milk and cheese. 'I had some pigs, as well', said Gilmar. 'We fed them on maize. But then last summer one of our neighbours saw a snake and, silly woman, she set fire to her field to frighten it away. Everything was so dry that the fire got out of control and destroyed my maize plantation. I had to slaughter my pigs, because I couldn't afford to buy food for them. But I'm going to start again with pigs next year.' Gilmar said that he always liked the idea of organic farming. 'About three years ago I was on a tractor applying *secante* (a pesticide) to prepare the land for planting maize. It was windy and some of the *secante* blew back into my face. When I got home, my face started swelling and itching terribly. I couldn't sleep at night. I thought I was going to die. I kept thinking: "I'm never ever going to touch *secante* again". So when Bionatur came with this proposal for growing organic seeds, I leapt at the idea.'

The settlers had not planned to move into organic farming. When they joined the MST, they were all landless rural workers. They knew that they wanted land, but they had not thought a great deal about how they would use it. Many of the families had taken part in the occupation of Fazenda Santa Elmira in the northwest of Rio Grande do Sul. In March 1989 these families, who had refused to accept a court order to leave the estate, suffered one of the most violent evictions in MST history: UDR landowners sprayed the camp with tear-gas, using two agricultural planes, and 1,200 military policemen invaded the camp with machine guns. Four hundred *sem-terra* were injured. The incident caused a furore and, after more marches and demonstrations, INCRA bought areas of land all over the state to settle the families. Several of the areas were located in an isolated cattle-rearing region, not far from the small town of Bagé, where land was still cheap. Ninety-one families went to one of these areas and set up the Conquista da Fronteira settlement.

The first years were arduous. None of the families had visited the region before, and they found life difficult, particularly the very cold winters. Some of the families set up a cooperative, COOPTIL, to cultivate the land collectively. As in so many other cases, it did not work out, so the families started cultivating individual plots. They turned COOPTIL into a service cooperative and also founded a regional cooperative, COOPERAL, to work with all the settlements in the region. The move into organic farming was almost accidental. Gilmar's brother, Amarildo Zanovelo, who helps run Bionatur, takes up the story. 'This is the best region in Brazil for growing seeds. There is a lot of sunlight and not too much rain. The winters are very cold, so the pests get killed. All the big seed companies, including the multinationals, produce seeds here. So we started to cultivate conventional seeds for the private seed company Agroceres. It was integrated production. They gave us the seeds, told us what to do, and we did it. We didn't really like working for a big company after all we'd been through to get out own land, so we were sympathetic to the idea of setting up our own seed company.'

The idea for the organic seed company developed in talks between two local men: João Rockett, a self-educated agronomist in Bagé, who gave up his university agronomy course because of the lecturers' refusal to take organic farming seriously, and the well-known environmentalist Sebastião Pinheiro. Rockett says he got to know the MST shortly after they arrived in 1990:

> I was pleased to see them arrive, as our region has been dominated for so long by *latifúndios*. They had so few resources that I lent them my tractor. I would have visited more often if it hadn't been so difficult to make the journey along the unpaved dirt track. They invited me once to visit a plantation of hybrid maize, which was demanding a lot of water. I made some criticisms of the way they were farming and they took it so well that I asked if I could come back and make another proposal. The whole of COOPERAL's management council came to listen to my ideas about organic seeds. At the end, no one said anything. I felt quite nervous. And then one of the oldest settlers commented slowly: 'Well, there's no point in our having a cooperative if we don't support this project.' I felt so relieved!

João Rockett said he started by selecting 12 farmers – 'the twelve apostles of organic production', as they were nicknamed. 'All of them had had experience in growing seeds for the seed companies and all of them liked the idea of organic farming', said João Rockett. 'We began with just two varieties – carrot and onion.' 'In the beginning, it was difficult', said Amarildo. 'We had very little money. João didn't even have his own car or motorbike and the roads were very rough. And when we harvested our crop, it was difficult to find a market.' Gilmar said they proceeded cautiously.

> For a while, I went on using chemicals on the rest of my crops, though I always made sure they were at least two kilometres away from my seeds, but now I've gone over completely to organic farming. I used to plant hybrid maize but now I plant an old species, creole maize, which we got from a farmer who'd been growing it for 40 years. We've had really excellent harvests and we don't have to pay for the seeds, for we just keep them from one year to the next. We're starting to do our own genetic selection, so our results are getting even better. We're collecting the old species of other crops, though some we're hunting for seem already to have disappeared. We've got more than 20 varieties of *feijão* (beans) and we've even managed to get hold of 22 old varieties of wheat, which the government research institute, Embrapa, had stored but wasn't using.

João agrees. 'People have become really keen to recover old varieties. We're already producing three varieties of wheat – one that's good for noodles, another for bread and another for biscuits. The other day one of the settlers visited his father and came back with an old variety of wheat that produces excellent straw for hats, and people have started planting it. Imagine trying to get a multinational company to let you do that! But people love it. It fosters their sense of community. And that's what the MST is all about.'

Box 12.2 *Romilda da Silva Vargas*

I was born in Redentor near Tenente Portela in the north of Rio Grande do Sul. My father had a small plot of land. I was only two-and-a-half when my mother died in child labour. My father was left with six children to bring up. The oldest was a 12-year-old girl, with crippled feet. She was still going to school so, even though she could hardly walk herself, she had to carry me on her back, as I was too young to leave alone in the house.

My father married again after a year. My stepmother was a lovely woman but she had bad health. To cover the medical bills, my father had to sell his plot and buy a small piece of land in another district. It was difficult for him to make ends meet. When one of my elder sisters was 21 years old, she married and I went to live with her in a nearby town. I looked after the house, washed the clothes, made bread and looked after my nephew. And soon there was another child too. I went on studying for a while, but it wasn't easy. My sister and her husband had to rent a plot of land, giving half of their produce to the landowner. Money got so short that we had to buy food on credit in the local shop. After harvest, we'd pay off our debts and have hardly anything left. I remember one year we wanted to buy a chair for the house, but there wasn't even enough money left for that.

At the time, my father was renting land from a widow. But then the government confiscated her land and settled some *sem-terra* families on it. It was 1986, and the MST was only beginning. I was 14 or 15 at the time. We saw the way the families progressed. They lived in black plastic tents when they arrived, but soon they'd built proper houses, bought furniture, got electricity. We'd been there all those years and we hadn't even got electricity! At first, my brother-in-law got angry. He said: 'Here we are, killing ourselves with work and paying all that rent. And these vagabonds get all this help from the government.'

But after a while we started making friends with them. They joined our Church. They were active in the trade union. We were still very poor. We never had any money for clothes, for anything. So my brother-in-law decided to join the MST. One afternoon he and my sister went off to an MST meeting. I stayed at home with the children. They were coming back in the afternoon. It was the planting season and it was raining heavily. They were walking, holding an umbrella, when they were both struck by lightning. There was a man nearby, up on a ladder, putting back the tiles that had been blown off his roof by the wind. He heard this cry, a desperate cry, from my sister. Her husband was unconscious, lying in a deep puddle. She was afraid he would drown. My sister was paralysed from the waist downwards, but she managed to put the umbrella handle under his head and pull it up a bit.

The man from the roof took them straight to hospital in his car. My brother-in-law was unconscious for many hours but then he came round. The doctor was amazed.

'I thought you were dead', he said. 'You've been born again.' One of my brothers came to help, as I couldn't manage by myself. My brother-in-law kept having very bad headaches and my sister had trembling fits. So the doctor told them to dig a deep hole near the orange trees and bury themselves alive, with just their heads sticking out. They said it was horrible, with all that heavy earth on them, but it seemed to help. Even so, my brother-in-law often used to shudder all over and shout out. They had to tie him down at night, in case he hurt himself.

About 30 people, men, women and children, from a nearby MST settlement heard about this. They came over one weekend to help. They spent two days clearing our land, planting, mending fences, doing everything that needed to be done. Although they were still ill, my sister and brother-in-law decided to go on the occupation of the Palmeira de Missões estate on 26 November 1986. The children went with them but I stayed behind to look after the cattle, the chicken and the pigs. Three months later I joined them. By then my father was living in the town of Novo Hamburgo near Porto Alegre and he told me I could either live with him or stay in the camp. I preferred the camp. I was 16 or 17 years old at the time and I loved the camp. It was a wonderful experience.

But the owner of the estate got an eviction order from the courts and we all had to leave. Eventually, on 9 March 1989, we occupied the Santa Elmira ranch in the northwest of the state. The landowner got his gunmen together and launched an attack. First of all, his planes sprayed tear-gas on the camp. And then the gunmen tried to take the children away from their mothers. They'd brought a bus to take them to a home. The mothers screamed and wouldn't let go of their children. The men grabbed them by the hair, the clothes, anything. By chance, I wasn't there that day. My sister had gone to town to have another baby and I was with her. But I heard all about it.

They took all the men away. They made them lie down, they beat them, they trampled on them. A lot of them had their ribs broken. They accused the men with beards of being priests, the bigger men of being leaders. They put revolvers in their mouths and knives under their nails. They stripped off their clothes and put them on anthills. There was a priest there – Frei Sérgio Gorgen. They broke his teeth with a blow to his mouth. And then they arrested 30 men, including Frei Sérgio. On the way to prison in the town of Sobradinho, they pulled them all out of the police van and threatened to throw them into a gully. And in the jail they treated the men like criminals, shaving their heads and beating them. There was a huge uproar. Lots of mobilisations and marches. The state governor, Pedro Simon, had to back down. He had to free the men and give land to all the families that had been in Santa Elmira. It all happened quickly, in just two weeks. That's how we got the land for our settlement, Conquista da Fronteira. It's in a very remote area, right down near the border with Uruguay.

We arrived at 10 o'clock at night on 14 June 1989. We were 91 families. We'd

12. Romilda da Silva Vargas (*João Zinclar*)

travelled by bus and our belong-ings had come by lorry. The owner of the land was still there. He saw us as a band of criminals. He thought we would steal or break everything. He made us sleep in a barn, where he was still keeping animals. We had to clean out the horse dung before we could put the mattresses down. Some of the women had young babies. We asked for water but he wouldn't give us any. He said we had to use the dirty water he'd left for the animals. We boiled the water and then sieved it. And still the powdered milk curdled in the babies' bottles! The water was so salty that we just couldn't use it.

The next day we put up our tents under the pear trees and the men dug a well to find water. The owner covered the windows of the house with newspapers so we couldn't see in. His employees said that he was intending to take everything out of the house, even the glass from the windows. So we went and negotiated with him. We told him he could take all the furniture, even the light fittings, but he had to leave the farm installations and the window fittings with the glass. We gave him one month to move out.

That first winter was very difficult. We were very isolated and we had absolutely nothing. Although most of our neighbours wouldn't have anything to do with us, a few felt sorry for us. One man gave us three cows so that we could give the children milk. Luckily, we didn't have many children on the settlement, for we were mostly young people.

I married Gilmar in 1991. We had our first child in 1992. It wasn't planned, as life was still so difficult, but we managed. I had the baby in hospital. It was a difficult birth. Gian weighed 4.6 kilos and I'm quite small! I had 16 stitches. Gilmar was there for the birth but then he had to go back to the settlement. When Gian was eight days old, I was discharged from the hospital. I went by bus to Bagé. That took me two and a half hours. And then I didn't know what to do. The Catholic Church had a house not far from Bagé. I had no money at all so I couldn't take a bus. I walked there in the hot sun. It took me over two hours. My legs were so weak that I was trembling all over. I had to keep stopping. But I got there and someone in the house gave me money for a bus to Hulha Negra, the village nearest our settlement. I went there the next day, still not knowing how I was going to travel the last 23 kilometres home. In the end, someone gave me a lift in a tractor. I was so sore from the stitches that I couldn't sit down as we bumped along the track. Then it started raining. I covered myself and Gian in a plastic sheet. By the time we got home I was shivering but Gian was fine. Gilmar was so pleased to see us.

It was even worse for some women. They had to walk all the way home, wading across streams. It's not like that any more. Today everyone has their own home and plenty to eat. The settlement's even got its own transport. We look back at those early days and feel like real pioneers.

Bionatur has begun to grow rapidly. In September 2000, people were thronging to its colourful stand at EXPOINTER, an agricultural show in Porto Alegre still dominated by the big farmers. Bionatur now produces 20 varieties of organic seed, with an output of four tonnes in 2000. About 50 families are producing the seeds in various settlements. 'Today we've got our seeds registered as organic, which took a lot of doing', said Amarildo. 'People know us today and we're selling well, particularly to other settlements. We could even export. Cuba, which is developing organic farming in a big way, is keen to buy from us. And some cooperatives in Venezuela have expressed interest. We've sent them both some samples but we can't do any more until we get an export licence from the agriculture ministry. That's going to be another long struggle.'

The impact is being felt in many settlements. 'We could have a dozen families in one settlement producing all the seeds', said Amarildo, 'but that's not the way the MST works. We want to spread the benefit. The families make a good profit. Because they produce almost all their inputs, they spend only US$28 per hectare, whereas the families working for the seed company, Agroceres, have to spend US$500–700 per hectare! And we pay them a bit more for their seeds than the private companies.'

Amarildo says that the seed venture is generating a whole process of change. 'People are adopting organic farming methods for their other crops, too. We can already see the difference that this is making. We've got far more birds than we had before. You should hear the dawn chorus! I always liked nature but I never imagined that we could preserve it as we are. For me it is a dream come true.' The settlements are also having a political impact. In the municipal elections at the end of 2000, the candidate from the left-wing Workers' Party was for the first time elected mayor of Hulha Negra, the rural district in which many of the settlements (including Conquista da Fronteira) are located. He owed his victory to the massive support he received from the settlements.

Despite this flurry of change, the environmental campaigner Sebastião Pinheiro, who helped João Rockett to think up the original proposal, believes that progress has been too slow. Munching brown rice and fried vegetables in a popular vegetarian restaurant in Porto Alegre and speaking at breakneck speed between mouthfuls, he commented:

> the MST has changed a lot. It all began when it realised that it was going to be crushed by the multinational agro-industrial food complex. It needed an alternative model, which *agro-ecologia* gave it. But even so the MST isn't moving fast enough. Many of the settlements now think they can survive outside the market, but they can't. That's utopian socialism. The MST settlements need to have a cash income and to do that they need to develop a strong local market for organic products that offers consumers a real alternative. All of us need to join forces to face the frightening, powerful avalanche that is being unleashed by the multinational corporations. Bionatur should be growing far more quickly. The MST should be ordering all its settlements to use its seeds! They wouldn't even have to do this. All they need do is stand up and say: 'This is our seed, not Monsanto's! Support our product!' That would be enough, but the leadership doesn't do this. The problem is that it is still divided over the importance it gives to sustainable farming. Some leaders still see it, quite wrongly, as a diversion from the more important, political struggle. Support for *agro-ecologia* has been growing very rapidly at the grassroots over the last three years but we could have achieved a lot more if we had had the firm support of the MST leadership.

While they understand Pinheiro's impatience, many settlers believe that he underestimates the very real difficulties that the settlements face in making the change to *agro-ecologia*. One of the most frustrating problems that the newly literate settlers confront is the labyrinth of Brazilian bureaucracy. Clarinda Ernestina da Santa, 55 years old, who spent five years in an MST camp before winning a plot of land for herself and her five children, was perspiring as she stirred a gigantic cauldron of *doce de leite* in the kitchen of the tiny cottage industry that she runs with two other women in an MST settlement near Promissão in the state of São Paulo. Apart from the *doce de leite*, they make sweets and desserts from seasonal fruit. Their products are pure and extremely tasty.

Over the last couple of years, they have tried to register their products so that they can sell them in the local towns. 'It hasn't been easy', said Bernadette Silva Calagari, 44 years old, who works with Clarinda, in what proved to be a considerable understatement. 'First we discovered that we couldn't make the *doce de leite* in the same kitchen as the fruit desserts, as one product is of animal origin and the other of plant. So we built that other kitchen over there.' But then came problem two. 'We were told that we had to have three toilets – one for women, one for men and one for the health inspector.' This absurd requirement was made of three women who do not yet have running water in their homes. Problem three is perhaps the most intractable. 'We have to get three different certificates – one to sell our produce locally, another to sell it nationally and yet another to export it', said

Bernadette. 'What's worse, the whole system is at standstill at the moment'. The Brazilian government says that the current delays – which have already lasted two years – stem from its efforts to push through Congress a package of reforms that would simplify the system, which was set up with the needs of the large economic conglomerates in mind.

If the reforms are finally approved, the MST should benefit greatly. It is already getting ready for a big increase in the sales of its products. With the help of the British development agency War on Want, with whom it has won funding from the British National Lottery, the MST is setting up a marketing network based in São Paulo city. The MST already has its own trademark, *Sabor da Vida* (Taste of Life), and is selling some products in its small Agrarian Reform Shop in São Paulo. It hopes to develop a flexible system that can allow the settlements to work together to supply products to the local supermarkets. 'The bureaucratic problems are horrendous', said Maria José Bezerra, one of the administrators. 'Just because our office is located in São Paulo, we have to pay the São Paulo state government's valued-added tax (ICMS) on all the processed goods we sell, even if they don't physically come into the state. For instance, if we are arranging for several settlements in Paraná to put together their output to satisfy a bulk order from a supermarket in Curitiba, the state capital, we still have to pay this tax. It's absurd. There are ways round some of these problems, but it takes time to learn.'

Medicinal Plants

Another initiative that, like the cultivation of organic seeds and the production of *doces*, allows the families to increase their income in a way that they find compatible with their aspirations is the cultivation of medicinal plants. The *sem-terra*, like all rural people, value herbal medicine, which taps into traditional indigenous and peasant knowledge. In 1992 a group of 18 women in an MST settlement in Itapeva in the interior of São Paulo planted a herbal garden. Their main objective, they said, was to reduce expenditure on pharmaceutical products. With the encouragement of a Swiss nurse, Isabelle Plomb, who lived in the community for three years, they set up Farmácia Viva (Living Pharmacy). Though they are still not officially registered, they produce 60 herbal remedies, providing them free to members of their own cooperative and selling them to other settlements. Their remedies have become widely known in the region, with visitors frequently travelling some distance to purchase them.

Such experiences have been common throughout the settlements. In 1998 the national leadership began to think of bringing together these isolated initiatives into a national network, and called in the charismatic guru of alternative medicine, Celerino Caricondi, to help them draw up a national health programme for the MST camps and settlements. There was an instant rapport between Celerino and the MST leaders. Celerino, who runs the Northeast Centre for Popular Medicine, has long been a thorn in the side of the local authorities for his forthright attacks on pharmaceutical companies and his staunch defence of local customs and culture. This was something that MST leaders instinctively liked. Celerino had long admired the MST for its stubborn independence and the courageous way it confronts the rich and powerful.

Sitting in the small office of his centre in the old city of Olinda, near Recife, Celerino spoke enthusiastically about the project. 'I'm developing a new health paradigm with the MST. Just like the new paradigm they're developing for education, it's based on the ideas of Paulo Freire. The system of health for the poor has to emerge from their concrete experiences in their communities. It cannot be imposed from outside. The new paradigm must be built around the idea of health, not illness, and the basis must be the community, not the hospital.' Picking up one of the numerous pamphlets on medicinal plants that his centre produces, Celerino carried on: 'People in the countryside still have a profound knowledge of the curative power of plants. Peasant families use medicinal plants to keep people well and to nip illnesses in the bud. They are our natural allies in the struggle to develop an alternative paradigm. The dominant health paradigm is rooted in the logic of capitalism. The biggest companies in the world today are no longer the arms manufacturers but the pharmaceutical groups. The main cause of illness in today's world is medicine. We've got to put an end to this madness.'

The first step in setting up a national health programme for the MST was to make an accurate diagnosis of the health situation in the MST's camps and settlements. Over the following year, *sem-terra* all over Brazil filled in 40,000 questionnaires about the health of their communities. 'Many of the people we were working with were barely literate. We had a few technical problems but on the whole the process went remarkably well.' There were fewer regional differences than Celerino had anticipated. 'What emerged was a huge difference between the level of health in the camps and the level of health in the settlements. There are far more problems in the camps. They don't have a regular water supply. They don't treat their waste properly. The plastic tents they live in are very cold in winter and very hot in summer. Far more people are infected with worms and other parasites. Many more people are illiterate. It is scarcely surprising that there is much more illness.'

The MST began to prepare for the introduction of the new structure. 'Perhaps the MST was a bit slow in taking up the health challenge', said Celerino. 'For the *sem-terra*, health came a poor second to education. Because so many families were winning land to give their children a better chance in life, they always gave an enormous priority to education. But now they are taking health seriously. I'm increasingly convinced that the MST is the only force in the country that can create a new health paradigm.' One reason why the MST has changed has been the Cuban influence. 'After the collapse of the Soviet Union, Cuba no longer had the hard cash to buy pharmaceutical products', said Celerino. 'The Cuban health service was forced to change its approach. It had to go back to using medicinal plants, and with that came a change in attitude. Today it has a far more holistic approach, with a much greater emphasis on health, not illness. This has had a big impact on the MST. It has sent 25 youngsters to study medicine in Cuba. It is a six-year course, and the whole of the first year is spent studying sociology, psychology and anthropology. Doctors need to know how people function.'

Agro-ecologia is the basis of Celerino's new health programme. 'It's not a case of each settlement setting up a medicinal herb garden while it carries on with chemical farming', said Flávio Duarte, an agronomist who works with Celerino. 'It's far more fundamental than that. We're talking about a new form of organic agriculture, in which the settlers cultivate medicinal crops as part of their mixed farming. So, along with their cassava, maize, lettuce and radishes, they plant camomile. The medicinal plants work very well in this set-up. They often produce a lot of organic matter, which helps to provide green manure. But it's a radical change in approach, and many of the MST settlements aren't ready for it. The change is coming more quickly in the south of the country than here in the northeast where we work. But even here we've had stirrings. We expect to move more rapidly, once the new health programme is completed and endorsed by the leadership.'

Communities of Peasant Production

The MST's switch into ecological farming changed the way the ecologist José Lutzenberger, who was Minister of the Environment for a brief period in the 1990s, viewed the movement. Basking in the sun on a raft on the lake he made out of a disused mine on his small farm outside Porto Alegre, he said that there had been an 'avalanche' of interest in organic farming in the region. 'It's been good to see the change in mentality in the MST', he said. 'It's been driven by economic factors. The MST was an emergency movement, set up by desperate rural labourers who had lost their livelihoods. Now that they are back on the land and farming their own plots, they have begun to realise that they have to question the whole basis of modern farming. It's encouraging but not enough. The MST needs to be at the forefront of efforts to forge a much broader alliance to stand up to destructive modern farming.'

Lutzenberger believed, like Claudemir Mocellin, that peasant farming was the agriculture of the future. 'What we call modern agriculture is unsustainable', he said.

> It works with resources that do not grow back. It uses absurd amounts of energy, more energy in the inputs than it fixes in the photosynthesis, and it causes tremendous social and ecological havoc all over the world. But unfortunately technocracy today wants to eliminate the independent small farmer. It wants only monoculture to survive. Among the small farmers it sees a role only for those who are 'vertically integrated', that is, those who work for the big companies, like many poultry and tobacco farmers do, here in the south of Brazil. These farmers receive all the inputs from the big company. They have to do everything just as the company tells them and they can sell their product only to the company. The farmer may have the illusion of being a self-employed entre-

preneur but, in fact, he is a labourer who doesn't have a guaranteed wage, who works extremely hard, often at night, and who doesn't get holidays or social benefits. He is really a new form of indentured labourer.

Lutzenberger gave courses in sustainable farming to MST settlers.

It is not really a question of teaching them new things, but of recovering knowledge that they or their parents had in the past, techniques such as painting fruit trees with whey from cheese-making to prevent fungus. Modern technology can help, of course. I'm not in favour of returning to the backbreaking labour of the past. We can use machinery, when it makes sense, and we can take advantage of the knowledge we have accumulated on how plants work. But the families themselves have all the basic knowledge they need. We just have to give them conditions to develop what they know and to get society to respect their knowledge.

Lutzenberger said that the multinationals put out a great deal of misinformation.

They claim that modern agriculture in the developed countries is so productive that only two per cent of the population need work in agriculture to feed the whole country. In contrast, they say, 40 per cent of the population has to work in farming in a peasant economy. But this is an illusion. They are comparing chalk with cheese. The old peasant family was a self-contained system for the production and distribution of food. It produced all the inputs – from the collection of seeds for the following year's harvest to basic processing jobs, such as de-husking rice and cheese making. The family even produced its own energy, as it worked with draft animals that fed from its pastures and ate its silage. The old peasant delivered his food to the consumer in the weekly market. But the modern farmer is only a tractor-driver or a poison-sprayer. He is only a tiny cog in an enormous and highly complicated techno-bureaucratic structure that begins in the oilfields, goes through the whole chemical industry and the huge agri-business industry – I'd rather call it the food manipulating, denaturing and contaminating industry – and ends up in the supermarkets. If you include the whole of this infrastructure, it employs something like 40 per cent of the population or even more. Another lie that they spread is that peasant farming is unproductive. They say that the Indians in the south of Mexico have a yield of 2,000 kilos of maize per hectare compared with 6,000 kilos of maize on the modern farms. But that, too, is a false comparison. The Indians are using this land to produce other crops, including all the food they need. They space out the maize so that they can grow beans, cucumber, tomatoes and other crops mixed in with it. You can't compare this with monoculture. If you take the whole of the Indians' output, they are just as productive and they are conserving the soil.

Convincing though he was, Lutzenberger was a lone voice in a world increasingly dominated by agribusiness. To survive in this hostile world, the MST has to come up with a viable economic alternative. Some analysts believe quite bluntly that the MST has not done so and that its settlements do not have a future. Zander Navarro, the sociologist from Rio Grande do Sul, is one of these. He believes that the MST settlements will not prove efficient enough to survive. He wrote in a recent unpublished paper: 'The settlements, as a general rule, will provide no more than a temporary afterlife to families who lost their plots of land earlier and gained a reprieve in the settlements. To opt either for subsistence agriculture, as many settlements have done, or for modern agriculture, with agro-industrial inputs and large productive structures that leave the settlers heavily in debt, does not provide the settlements with economic or productive viability.' To sum up, Navarro believes that within a few decades most of the *sem-terra* will be driven off the land by bad debts and find themselves back working as day labourers on the big farms or living in shanty-towns in the towns and cities. His forecast is in line with the analysis made by the economist Guilherme Dias.

Although, not surprisingly, the MST does not accept this gloomy prognosis, some of its leaders have taken on board the points made by these analysts and are arguing that, in order to survive in the globalised world, the MST will have to make a more radical break with modern farming and actively promote an alternative model, going back on its earlier decision to let each settlement decide for itself the kind of farming it wants. Ademar Bogo has suggested that the way forward may be to create what he calls 'communities of peasant production' in which the settlers view the land, not as a factor of production for generating income, but as a resource for improving the quality of their lives. At times, Bogo says, the families should learn from their grandparents. 'In the past, quite a lot of peasant farmers planted sugar-cane and had a small unsophisticated sugar mill, which they had built themselves, in their backyards. They made their own brown sugar and all kinds of different puddings. They didn't make these products to sell on the market but to save themselves money and to improve the quality of their lives.'

The policies recommended by Bogo are popular at the grassroots. While the catalyst for change has been economic hardship, settlers also enjoy returning to a healthier and more creative way of farming. The enthusiasm these initiatives are generating is remarkable, in marked contrast with the almost universal mistrust the settlers felt towards the experiment with the collectivisation of production. One of the two motions to come from the floor in the fourth National Congress in Brasília in August 2000 was a demand that the leadership should embrace *agro-ecologia* more enthusiastically. Several participants in the Congress said that the leadership should back unequivocally the 'communities of peasant production' as the main direction the movement should take.

CHAPTER 13

From a 'Culture of Resistance' to a 'Culture of Liberation'

> Oppressed and bound to the land, the peasant is like a stick of dynamite waiting for a fuse. But it's no simple thing to get the charge to explode: it needs patience, and the peasant's mistrust and shyness won't succumb to mere words. If words are not followed up with action, he stays withdrawn and goes on waiting, just as he will wait for the sun or the rain or harvest.
>
> Meanwhile he goes on working the land for little or nothing, because the land is his stomach and his life. And freedom is like the wind in the trees: he can feel the land under his feet and strike it with his hoe; it is the blood in his veins, flesh of his flesh. But freedom is like the wind he cannot touch but which he knows exists.
>
> Francisco Julião, the leader of the Peasant Leagues[1]

'Land is more than land', says Dom Pedro Casaldáliga, the bishop of São Felix in the Amazon basin, with his unerring ability to state important truths simply. Though the *sem-terra* may say that all they want is a plot of land, this plot of land has always been a symbol of their yearning for a different life in which they and their children will have a far greater chance of fulfilment and be accepted as full citizens. Land for them is the promised land and to achieve it the *sem-terra* have been willing to face hunger, repression and persecution. Since its foundation, the *sem-terra*'s desire for land and for inclusion in society has coexisted, at times uneasily, with the objectives of many of the leaders, who wish to turn the MST into a revolutionary movement in the Leninist tradition. These men were not manipulating uneducated peasant families, as right-wing commentators have suggested; they simply believed that the *sem-terra* would not conquer the land they wanted in the conditions they wanted without redistributing power. And that required a revolution of some kind.

This determination to turn the MST into an effective revolutionary force is particularly clear in the case of six key founding members – João Pedro Stédile, Jaime Amorim, Edgar Jorge Collink, Ademar Bogo, Adelar Pizetta and Neuri Rossito. They all trained for the priesthood within the Catholic Church – four of them in the same class in a seminary in Santa Catarina – but gave up their studies, because they wanted to be involved directly in the political struggle for revolutionary change. These ex-seminarists knew that they could readily recruit members into their new movement, for agricultural modernisation had left hundreds of thousands of families in complete penury. Their main challenge would be to develop the political awareness of these exploited people, so that they would have the courage, discipline and determination to take on the powerful *latifundiários* who had dominated the countryside for centuries. Working together, the founding members and the *sem-terra* recruits developed an extraordinarily effective methodology for welding the disparate (and desperate) families into a highly effective movement run by dedicated and politically aware activists. The transformation of the families begins with the very act of occupying the land (*see* chapter 4) and is reinforced by the experience of living collectively in a temporary camp during the fight to conquer the land.

The Camp

Taking advantage of the initial impetus created by the occupation, the MST leaders seek to turn the temporary camp, where the *sem-terra* live after the occupation, into 'a laboratory for creating social awareness'.[2] Conditions in the camps are uniquely suited for such an exercise in social engineering. Deprived of their normal sources of entertainment, particularly television, and anxious to grasp with both hands the new opportunity that they have been given, the *sem-terra* are willing to 'think the unthinkable' in a way that they have never been before.

The MST's achievements in these camps are remarkable. People who have been pushed around and exploited all their lives begin to vote in assemblies and to take charge of their own lives. The MST has developed an effective daily routine for getting people involved. 'In the camps the MST introduces an organic structure that, through sectors, commissions and other forms of organisation, brings people together, distributes power and constructs democracy',[3] said Ademar Bogo, the movement's leading thinker on cultural matters. Everyone in the camp, from the very young to the very old, has to take part in one of these bodies, be it a young people's brigade to keep the camp clean or a health commission to deal with routine ailments. Through these activities people learn to behave responsibly.

The MST does not offer easy 'salvation'. The *sem-terra* are constructing the camp in the most difficult circumstances, in which people often go hungry, get ill and face the threat of violent eviction by gunmen. João Pedro Stédile put it bluntly: 'life in a camp is hell'. 'It is the form of struggle of last resort', he said. 'People only turn to it if they are really desperate. When they've run out of options, with nowhere to go, they decide to give the devil a taste of his own medicine. That's the situation of the *acampado* (person living in a camp).'[4] Yet 'hell' is not how a camp feels. What is remarkable is the sense of fun and self-fulfilment in many of the camps. People seem to need very little sleep and talk and laugh a great deal. The camps are usually bustling with activity. The *acampados* are usually keen to open a primary school,

Box 13.1 *Gerson Antônio da Silva*

I was born in the city of São Paulo in 1966. My father was a car mechanic but when I was 7 he went bankrupt. We had dreadful economic problems and I had to work. I washed cars. I carried people's shopping home from the street market. Though I went home to sleep at night, I spent a lot of time by myself on the streets and I got to know all the vices of street life. It wasn't long before I was taking drugs – marijuana, crack and others. I still managed to go to school for a while and almost finished the eight years of primary education.

Then my parents separated. I stayed with my father but he didn't pay much attention to me. For a while I was OK. I got a job as a shop assistant and I got married. I've got a 7-year-old son. But my marriage didn't last. I got more and more dependent on crack. It destroyed me. I used to shake all over and I lost my short-term memory. I lost everything because of it – my home, my marriage, my son. I haven't seen my wife for a long while.

My younger brother joined the MST before me. That was three or four years ago. I was angry with him. 'Don't do this', I said. 'These people are using you. You'll get into serious trouble.' But my brother replied: 'They're not like that, Gerson. Come and spend a few days with me and you'll see.' I was in a bad way. I'd been addicted to crack for about four or five years. At that time crack didn't come ready-made, as it does today. You had to prepare it at home. I used to work a bit in the morning, doing non-jobs like looking after cars. I'd get a bit of money and then I'd go home, prepare the crack and then take it for the rest of the day. I knew it was gradually killing me, so in the end I decided to visit my brother. I thought it might give me a chance to break the addiction.

Today my brother is a MST *militante*. He'd taken part in the occupation from the beginning. He'd help set up this camp of Nova Canudos. So I came to pay a visit. And, do you know, I liked it from the beginning. You're busy all day. The MST gives you things to do all the time. I'd never ever farmed but I'd always been interested in farming. I'd read a lot of books. I knew a lot of theories. And now I'm trying them out on the patch of land we're cultivating. We talk a lot among ourselves. I really enjoy it.

I've been here for six months. I haven't taken any drugs. It was hard to begin with. I used to shake a lot. And even now I haven't completely recovered. I still haven't got my short-term memory back properly. But I've met this wonderful woman here. She helps me through the bad times. I get very upset sometimes, very angry. And she helps me control my temper. I've started studying again. I work in the camp in the mornings and then I go by bus to college in the evenings. I've already made up that bit I missed of primary education. I don't get back until midnight. And then sometimes I can't sleep. I get tense, thinking of the things I've got to do. At times, the wind blows very fiercely and tears the black polythene on our tent. I start panicking and she calms me down. She's the good side of the coin.

This camp has had its problems. It was organised with a lot people from the city. There were addicts, like me, and alcoholics. When I first arrived, it was more chaotic, 'organised disorganisation', I called it. People were trying to give up alcohol but they couldn't. They'd smuggle it in. It was difficult. Today it's better.

The MST is the only organisation that's ever tried to help me. It gives you hope again. There's a man here, 72 years old. He'd never been given a chance to achieve anything. And now you only have to look in his eyes. They've got back their fire, their brightness. He knows he'll get a plot of land in a year or two. And then, he says, he's going to carry out his dream and cultivate his food for the first time in his life.

---

even if there are no properly trained teachers in the camp. Very often they hold adult literacy classes at night. And there is much political debate. At times, this can seem like political indoctrination, with the *militantes* trying to get scarcely literate peasant farmers to grapple with Marxist concepts such as 'surplus value' or 'mode of production'. More frequently, however, the discussions are firmly rooted in everyday reality, with the *militantes* attempting, in honest and straightforward fashion, to explain to the families the underlying reasons for the poverty and exploitation around them.

What is most important of all for the families, however, is the concrete experience of trying to live a different way. Inês Maria Tchik, who took part in the very first occupation organised by Father Arnildo Fritzen in Rio Grande do Sul in 1979, lived in the camp for eleven months, before gaining her plot of land. 'I changed a lot. You remember that I come from a German family. We'd been taught to put ourselves first. Well, camp life altered all that. I learnt that you live better when you share things. And that lesson has stayed with me.'

As a result, despite all the difficulties, people often look back with great affection at the time they spent in the camp. Maria Rodrigues and her young children arrived in a camp in the interior of São Paulo several days after the initial occupation. 'When I first arrived there, I took fright. Everyone had conjunctivitis. The tents, made out of black polythene, were really hot. But the day-to-day life in the camp, the activities, they got me involved. I didn't notice any more that life was so difficult. And I made friends with the other women. Everyone went together to the river to do the washing. When I had health problems – my children got very ill – there were a lot of other women, who also had sick children. So we went to hospital together and we came back together.'[5] Younger people adapt even more quickly. Dulce joined the same camp when she was 15 years old. 'It was a lot of fun. Some people say they hated it, but I really liked it. We had to walk a long way to get water. We had to cook in the open air. ... It was very hot in the tents, but it was nice. I helped to look after the children because there was a conjunctivitis epidemic soon after we arrived in the camp. I was part of the health team and I put drops in the children's eyes. I also helped in the pharmacy. It was great.'⁶

Simone de Graça, a 14-year-old girl still living in the Cobrinco camp in Paraná, shares Dulce's enthusiasm. 'I have so many friends. Everyone is so pleasant. We're all as poor as each other. I don't feel inferior, as I did in schools in the towns, where everyone else had got so much more than me.' Further north in the same state, 17-year-old José Roberto Morais, who is currently being trained in organic farming in one of the MST's agricultural schools, said that he was happy for the first time in his life. 'My father lost his job when I was very young, so we ended up living on the streets. I often went hungry and I didn't go to school. I suffered a lot. ... After the occupation, we lived in the camp. I thought it was great. Everyone was so friendly. And there wasn't any pollution or bad smells or prostitution. We just had fun, pure, healthy fun. And no one told us off.'

Others, such as 34-year-old Maria Sônia Franca, who lives in the Cobrinco camp in Paraná, have found unexpected advantages in camp life. She did not want to go to the camp, telling her husband she would leave him if he went. 'I would see the *sem-terra* people coming into town, and I would run away from them, so that they wouldn't talk to me. I was afraid of them. I thought they would rob me.' But, in the end, Maria Sônia agreed to go. 'We ran out of money and started to go hungry', she said. 'There wasn't anything else we could do.' Once in the camp, she started to enjoy it, although even then she did not take on completely the *sem-terra* identity. 'I realised that most of the people were just like me. I liked them, but it still took me a long while to tell my friends. When I went back to the town of Terra Rica, I'd make excuses, saying that we'd been away because my husband was working on a ranch. I was still ashamed. It took me months to find the courage to tell them.' Her 11-year-old daughter, Diana, loves the life in the camp. 'She wasn't happy in the town. We were so poor and I never had time to give her affection. I was working all the time. Here I'm much closer to her. We talk a lot.'

People also begin to adapt skills learnt elsewhere. A group largely composed of shanty-town dwellers set up a camp, called Nova Canudos, not far from the city of São Paulo. Some of the *acampados* had worked on building sites in the capital and they brought their urban skills to a rural setting, working out a way of building two-storey tents out of the poles and black polythene so that the families could have 'bedrooms'. Several of the people in the camp were previously drug addicts, like Gerson Antônio da Silva (*see* box 13.1). There are failures, particularly in camps set up with shanty-town dwellers. About one third of the families in Nova Canudos have returned to the city, having found it more difficult to adapt to rural life than they had expected. There has also been an explosion of teenage pregnancies. A perplexed young doctor, who provides medical assistance free of charge at weekends, said only half jokingly: 'I'm beginning to wonder if I'm going to have to put contraceptives in the drinking water!' The *acampados* themselves laugh about it, saying that with no television young people have no other distractions, but, as the doctor says, it is clear that the movement is not giving young people enough orientation. Yet, for all the difficulties and deficiencies, the camp is progressing, with its assemblies, commissions, *místicas* and schools.

The *militantes* quickly detect potential leaders among the *acampados*. They invite them to attend a special course that can last anything from a few days to several months. Some urban recruits, like Jorge Neri, now a committed *militante* in Pará (*see* box 13.2), can find these courses arduous. If the recruits show aptitude, they will soon be entrusted with important tasks. Paulo Venâncio (*see* box 3.1), who as a young man had a very tough life in the northeast, took part in the first occupation in Pernambuco in 1989. 'Two months later, I was invited to become a *militante*', he said. 'I was 19 years old and very excited by what was happening. I readily accepted, so off I went for a two-day course on how society works and how to organise an occupation. And then I was sent to the district of Escada to organise, single-handed, my first occupation. To begin with, I found it very difficult to talk to a group of people. I was really shy. But I learnt, and today I don't mind speaking to 5,000 people. No problem.' Sebastião de Maia, a leader in the Rio Novo camp in Paraná, was also sent on a course. 'I went on a 15-day course in Cantagalo in Paraná. It gave me another vision. It's made me think about what I see on television more critically. It taught me how to talk to people and how to control my own temper, which I've always found difficult to do. It's helped me run this camp better. I feel I'm learning, growing.' In November 2000 Sebastião was ambushed and killed by gunmen.

Forging Sem-Terra *Identity*

The MST activists realised that, in the struggle to conquer land, the capacity of the *sem-terra* families to resist cultural domination was even more important than their ability to rebut physical attempts by gunmen to evict them from their camps. To give the families the confidence to defy the status quo, they needed to create a 'counter-culture' and to get the families to identify strongly with it. The MST activists thought long and hard about the symbols they should adopt. At first, the *sem-terra* in the south of Brazil wanted the typical peasant straw hat to be the official emblem of the movement and for a while the families adopted it. In 1988, however, the MST activists decided that the straw hat sent out the wrong message, as it implied that the movement was old-fashioned and conservative. They wanted a more defiant symbol, something more militant and outspoken. After lengthy discussions, the families opted for a package of new symbols to 're-brand' the movement – a distinctive red flag, with a green map of Brazil in the centre, out of which step a woman and a man brandishing a machete, and a red baseball cap to go with it. The red t-shirts, stamped with the MST flag, soon followed.

Today these images have transcended their origin and become in themselves very powerful instruments of *sem-terra* identity. For thousands of *sem-terra* the red cap is important, not because it stands for socialism, which for many of them is a meaningless concept, but because it defines the person wearing it as a *sem-terra*.

Box 13.2 *Jorge Neri*

I'm 34 years old. My mother was born in the countryside. She came to live in Belém in the 1970s because she thought she'd be able to get an education. She was wrong. The only work she could find was as a maid. And maids are like slaves. They work day and night. Worse still, the young men in the house exploit them. A young man told her he was in love with her. She believed him and had an affair. As soon as she was pregnant, he left her. And a young woman with a child has few options. She got deceived again and got pregnant again. She was left on her own to bring up two small children. I was one of them. She lived in a shanty-town near the river, which often got flooded. When I was four, my mother married. My father, a black man, worked on a building site. He became my real father. He registered us as his children and I started to call him Dad. He's the grandfather of my children.

My family was hurt by the economic crisis in the early 1980s. My father couldn't get work. We were very short of money. One bright spot in my life were the visits I occasionally made with my mother to her parents' home in the countryside. They had a *sítio*, a plot of land. They lived from hunting, fishing and collecting Brazil nuts. During the dry season, they grew cassava. I loved it there.

But then they started to build roads and the landowners arrived. My grandfather wasn't evicted by guns but by sweet talk. The landowner told him that he had no rights, he'd have to go. He offered him a trifling sum and my grandfather accepted. He went to live by the road and started working for the ranch. It was a big shock for him. He soon died from a heart attack. My grandfather had 17 children. In the old days children used to leave home and travel around, but they'd always come back to the *sítio*, at least for visits. Once the *sítio* had gone, there was nothing left to hold us together. I've lost contact with a lot of my cousins. Before the roads arrived, people had a different set of values. They showed solidarity, they helped each other, they shared food. All that ended.

And there was more. Once the road was built, the Evangelicals arrived. Before that, we'd all been Catholic. And this divided my family. The Evangelical branch of the family wouldn't talk to the Catholics. I was emotionally close to an aunt, who was an Evangelical, but politically I was closer to the Catholics, who were more combative and fought to stay on the land. Today it's getting better. Everyone who went to the towns is in desperate straits. There's so much crime, unemployment, violence. The problems are bringing people closer to each other again.

I completed the eight years of primary education. I liked studying. During this time, I got active in the Catholic Church. I was influenced by liberation theology. I got involved in the radical student movement. That's why I stopped studying. I thought college was bourgeois. Since I've joined the MST, I've started studying again. But I'm still resistant to the idea of going back to college. I'm studying to get a better understanding of reality and to use my studies as an instrument in the liberation struggle. So I'm doing an internal MST course. There are 30 of us, studying philosophy and political economy. It's much more useful than going back to college.

I've been working since I was 7. I've done a lot of things. I've sold popcorn and lollipops in the street. I've cleaned cars. I've carried shopping for customers in supermarkets. I've worked in street markets. I've worked on a building site. I've worked for a trade union, helping to produce a newspaper. At the end of the 1980s I got tired of life in the city and went to work on an educational project with *posseiros* (squatters) in Marabá. It was my first contact with land conflict. It was a difficult time and leaders were being killed. The *posseiros* were brave and determined. I have a lot of respect for them and still have good contacts with them.

Then the MST appeared. I already knew about them. I remember reading an article in *Veja*. It was a critical story, under the headline 'The Last Radicals'. I can remember grinning and thinking 'they sound like my sort of group', so I was pleased when they appeared. It wasn't long before I decided to leave everything and join them. It was easier then, because I wasn't married. In 1994 I did a course for *militantes* in Maranhão. I'd acquired urban habits, got a bit soft. I was smoking heavily and drinking a lot so the discipline came as a bit of a shock. I had to get up early every day, at 5.30 a.m. I had to stop drinking (though I continued a bit, secretly). And I gave up smoking.

There was also the *mística*. It made me realise that I was sexist, that I needed to rethink my ideas about women. I realised that it's not enough to have ideas about social transformation. I had to change too. At times, it all seemed too much and I thought of giving up. What made me go on was seeing the others. They were always so good-humoured, always ready to face the challenges. I was 27 years old. Many of them were much younger than me. I felt ashamed. I thought, 'how can I fight a war, a revolutionary war, if I can't even put up with a bit of hardship?' So I persisted. I was there for seven months. And at the end, of course, I was very glad I'd done it.

Many, like 20-year-old Dirce, from a settlement in Rio Grande do Sul, have assumed wholeheartedly their new identity. 'It was in the movement that I learnt to be someone, to live, to think about other people. The MST today is my family, my life. I'll do anything for it, go anywhere for it. I am very fond of my parents, but if I had to go anywhere in the world for the movement, I'd go.'[7]

Many *sem-terra* are still moved to tears to see that in the most famous photograph of Roselí Nunes, a well-known woman leader from Fazenda Annoni who was killed in 1987, her tiny daughter (the first child born in the camp) is wearing a sticker saying 'sou *sem-terra*' (I am a *sem-terra*). This proud affirmation of *sem-terra* identity is also evident in a much-loved song composed in 1997, which begins: 'Sou *sem-terra*, sim senhor! Sou *sem-terra* com amor!' (I am a *sem-terra*, yes sir! I am a *sem-*

terra, with love!). MST supporters recognise the value of these symbols. Despite working for Globo television, the well-known publicist Carlito Maia was a fervent MST supporter. On 17 April 1997, a year after the Eldorado de Carajás massacre, the MST leaders José Rainha and his wife, Diolinda, presented Carlito, who was already seriously ill, with an MST flag and cap in recognition of the help he had given the movement. 'Carlito embraced the flag and put the cap on his head. From that day onwards, he always used it. He never left the house without putting his MST cap on his head. It became part of him. It became his trademark.'[8]

The *sem-terra* instinctively use their caps and their flag as a way of affirming their identity in the face of opposition. In March 1997, when a public prosecutor accused José Rainha of killing a landowner in Espírito Santo, a large group of *sem-terra* had gone to the courtroom to hear the charges. In his speech, the prosecutor began to make serious accusations against the MST. Without any kind of prior agreement, the *sem-terra*, who had taken off their caps as a sign of respect when they entered the courtroom, put them firmly back on their heads. They were saying: the MST is here. 'Sou *sem-terra*, sim senhor!'[9]

The authorities, too, are well aware of the importance of these symbols. On many occasions, the police have deliberately torn or destroyed caps, shirts and flags. Lisiane took part in a demonstration in Gravataí in Rio Grande do Sul. 'The police beat us all up. A lot of people were wounded. My mother and some of the other women tried to get in the way, to stop the police from hitting the men, but the police just carried on. One woman had her arm broken. The police gave our flags to the dogs to tear up, saying that the sight of the MST flag made them feel sick. They threw a tear gas bomb at our feet, and we had to get out quick, with the dogs chasing us.'[10] Adelina Ventura Nunes and her husband, Sebastião de Maia, from the Rio Novo camp in Paraná, both remembered that, at the height of the conflict they were involved in, military policemen seized their caps and tore them up.

Other social movements in other parts of the world have displayed the same need for symbols to represent their identity. In a discussion about the making of the English working class, Eric Hobsbawm talks about the way in which manual workers adopted the peaked cap as their badge of identity.

> By 1914 any picture of masses of British workers anywhere, on or off duty, reveals the familiar sea of flat peaked caps. ... Herbert Smith [a leader of the miners] was famous for his cap. ... He wore it like a flag. There is a photograph of him in old age, as mayor of Barnsley, with Lord Lascelles in the elongated elegance, bowler and furled umbrella of *his* class and the Chief Constable in a frogged uniform. Herbert Smith, a stocky, rather fat old man, wore the Mayor's chain and insignia, but above them he wore his cap. One could say a lot about his career, and not all of it complimentary, though I defy anyone to withhold all admiration from the man who, in 1926, sat at the negotiating table in his cap, minus his false teeth, which he had put on the table for comfort, and said 'no' on behalf of the miners to the coal-owners, the government and the world.[11]

Partly because the founder members of the MST set out to learn from the achievements – and the failures – of earlier social movements, they deliberately forged the identity of the MST, in a way that would have been alien to Herbert Smith. In some ways, a closer parallel is with the 'little red book' and the 'Mao suits' devised by Mao Zedong. However artificial the process of creation, the identification of the *sem-terra* with the symbols of their identity is extremely strong, just as it was for the millions of cadres of the Cultural Revolution in China.

But what exactly does it mean to be a *sem-terra*? The movement bears proudly its history of resistance and defiance in the face of persecution. Almost all *sem-terra* families have experienced severe deprivation and physical violence, and most have emerged more determined than ever to conquer the land. So this has become a key element in the *sem-terra* profile. Cida, a *sem-terra* woman in São Paulo, never forgot the eviction she suffered in 1983 and the anger it provoked in her.

> The military police began to knock down the first hut, built with so much sacrifice by someone who had never had a house before, just to please a minority who have more than the rest of us put together. The house had a banner hanging from it, which read 'Agrarian reform now! This country is ours!' I asked myself: is this country really ours? If the land belongs to God alone, how is that someone can come and take the land from us? I grabbed the banner and said: 'Come on Dali, help me!' And I began to shout: 'Agrarian reform now! This country is ours!' The justice official and Father Israel came running up: 'Cida, are you mad? They'll beat you up!'
>
> But I thought it was absurd what they were doing. They came and took the banner away from me. But this just gave me strength, ever more strength, and more and more people were joining me. We picked up the bread that was left over, for the hut hadn't yet been destroyed, and we tried to offer it to the soldiers, for they were poor too, they should be on our side, but the justice official and the sergeant stopped us reaching them. A child got through the barrier. It was Luciana. She went running ahead and handed over the bread. There were people who saw it, the soldier crying so much that he couldn't put out his hand to take the bread. Then the priest called her, because he was afraid that the other soldiers would hit her. It was something that marked me deeply.[12]

Another element in the *sem-terra* identity is mental agility. The *sem-terra* are proud of their ability to see through the attempts by the authorities to fob them off. This is evident in the amusing anecdotes the *sem-terra* recall from their early history. In July 1985, a group of *sem-terra* occupied a building in the town of Campinas that belonged to the São Paulo state government's agriculture department. Such action was unprecedented and the regional coordinator for the department hastily organised a meeting with *sem-terra* representatives and a director of Fepasa, the São Paulo railway company, which owned the land the families were demanding. The railway director offered to employ the *sem-terra* to cut eucalyptus in a plantation belonging to the company. The *sem-terra* turned down the proposal outright. 'The coordinator then turned to us somewhat nervously and asked us what we wanted, if this work wasn't enough. Then Leonor spoke. "I don't know if you don't understand the way we talk or you don't want to understand. We've occupied the agriculture department to ask for land. If we wanted jobs, we'd be in the labour department.'"[13] After six hours of talks, the *sem-terra* got their way.

The ability of the *sem-terra* to see through deception is also evident in another much-told story. After a group had occupied Fazenda Timboré in the interior of São Paulo state in 1989, they were called to a meeting with INCRA. The *sem-terra* Geraldo José da Silva picks up the story: 'INCRA proposed that we should do a swap, that we should go miles away to Fazenda Itassul in Mato Grosso do Sul, which belonged to the same man who owned Fazenda Timboré here in Andradina. The superintendent of INCRA told us that the estate was much more productive, that the land was flat, that it had lots of water, that it was far better than Fazenda Timboré. So we turned to them and said: let the owner have that estate then if it is so much better, because we're quite happy with Timboré.'[14] Eventually, after a long struggle, the *sem-terra* won this land too.

The *sem-terra* are also proud of their capacity to outwit the landowners. In the same conflict over Fazenda Timboré, the families, who at that time were camped outside the estate, organised a four-day party to distract the guards who had been sent in to protect the property. While many of the *sem-terra* enjoyed *forró*, a lively, noisy dance from the northeast, others were quietly dismantling their tents. On the last night, while some of the families were still dancing rowdily, others quietly cut the barbed wire and occupied the estate. The gunmen realised belatedly what was going on and shot wildly. One *sem-terra* was killed and others were injured, but the occupation was successful.[15] On another occasion, a 12-year-old girl, Lucimar, helped to set free thousands of ferocious bees from their hives in order to stop military policemen from beating up the families during a land expulsion.[16]

The MST leaders are constantly reinforcing *sem-terra* values in the *mística*. Reflecting the Catholic tradition of suffering and redemption, the *místicas* often recall the stories of the movement's martyrs. Because so many families have experienced repression and seen friends die, they find these enactments extremely moving. In April 2000, 1,200 activists from the Amazon state of Pará held a meeting in Fazenda Taba, a luxury country mansion, which had belonged to a rich airline executive before it was occupied by the MST. On the last night of the four-day event, the *sem-terra* held their evening meeting in a banqueting hall built by the businessman for his wild parties, renowned throughout the region, at which scantily clad dancers brought from Belém used to dance on the tables. The floor and the walls were made from hard timber, which glowed magnificently in the candlelight. Almost all of the MST activists at the meeting had known some of the19 *sem-terra* killed in the Eldorado de Carajás massacre. After scrupulously fair elections to select the new members of the state council, the *sem-terra* held a *mística*. Down the central aisle of the hall lay 19 newly elected leaders, draped in the movement's flag and covered with flowers. In the candlelight a *sem-terra* woman read out one by one the names of the 19 martyrs. As each name was pronounced, one of those lying on the floor stood up and said '*sou presente*' (I am here). By the end, most people in the hall were silently crying. It was a cathartic healing for a community still traumatised by the deaths, as well as a collective expression of determination to carry on with the struggle.

Because the *mística* is such a powerful weapon, the leadership controls its use quite firmly. Even the *mística* commemorating the martyrs of Eldorado de Carajás, which was so appropriate for the state meeting in Pará, had been conceived in the MST's head office and was enacted in many settlements throughout the country. There are reasons for this procedure. Many *sem-terra* lack the confidence to think up their own *místicas*. It is easier at a busy meeting for the *sem-terra* to copy a blueprint than to think up their own event. It also permits the leadership to use the *mística* to drive home particular political messages. In the fourth National Congress of the MST in Brasília in August 2000, the delegates spent an evening paying homage to the 250 people who had been killed by gunmen and the military police in the 16 years of struggle. The *místicas*, which deeply moved the *sem-terra*, were clearly intended to stiffen their resolve to stand up to the offensive unleashed by the Cardoso government.

Internal Democracy

The aim of the MST's whole methodology – the occupation, life in the camp, the creation of the *sem-terra* identity and the *mística* – is to make new recruits feel part of the movement and to get them to participate in the struggle. But what does this mean? Is the MST constructing a genuine democracy in which people freely decide the key issues governing their lives? Or are the leaders cynically manipulating ignorant peasants to gain support for an alien revolutionary cause? In other words, is the MST a democratic movement? Zander Navarro, the sociologist from the university of Rio Grande do Sul, had no doubts. He said that the MST had a 'policy of indoctrination in the worse sense of the word'. 'The middle cadres are inculcated with Marxist ideology', he said. 'For them the movement brings an intoxicating mixture of adventure with the promise of power. They are recruited from the very poorest sectors of society and, without the MST, they would have had very little chance of education, let alone power. They do a course with the MST and are then put in charge of perhaps 1,000 people. The leaders control these cadres in draconian fashion. If one of them expresses doubts, he is expelled.' MST *militantes*, however, vehemently reject this charge. For them the MST is the most democratic body in Brazil because it is always consulting its base and encouraging members to participate. 'The leadership listens to what the grassroots say', claimed Itelvina Maria Mazioli, a leader. 'We get things wrong and we change the policy after protests from the base. We did over the collectivisation of agriculture. And we did over gender.' So who is right?

The families' first contact with the MST's system of democracy comes in the camps. On the very first day, the *militantes* encourage the *acampados* to elect a camp coordinator, who is often a new recruit to the movement and someone who is known to at least some of the families. If the camp is made of up a lot of different families who don't know each other, the *militantes* handpick a man – and again it almost always is a man – whom they know or who they believe shows leadership qualities. With the help of the *militantes*, this coordinator then organises the day-to-day life of the camp. He first divides people into cells (*núcleos*), generally grouping together relatives and friends. Each cell then elects two representatives to the camp coordination committee, which runs the camp. The movement encourages the cells to send a man and a woman, but in many camps women are reluctant to come forward. This committee then supervises the formation of commissions to take care of every aspect of everyday life: health, education, security, hygiene, tent construction, crop cultivation, and so on. The cells send representatives to each of the commissions and everyone in the camp, except for the very young and the very old, is expected to take part. Apart from being an efficient form of organisation, these commissions help to break down barriers between groups of people recruited in different regions. An assembly is held every day to report on developments and to resolve grievances.

As we mentioned earlier, the activists are trained to spot potential leaders within the new recruits. These people, who are generally teenagers or young adults, are sent off for training as *militantes*. Some analysts do not like this set-up. Maria Célia Nunes Coelho, from the Advanced Nucleus of Amazon Studies in Belém, dislikes the division between the *militantes* and the *massa*. 'One of the things I criticise a lot is the idea of the *massa*', she told a São Paulo magazine. 'That's the expression they use. The *massa* is usually made up of older people who have followed their children into the movement and can't become *militantes*, because there is no room for older people among the militancy. And the *massa* doesn't have a voice.'[17] This criticism has been valid in the past. When in 1989 the MST took the decision to carry out mass occupations as a way of accelerating the expansion of the movement, *militantes* were sent from one state to another to organise occupations rapidly with huge groups of people. Insufficient time was spent integrating the new recruits and many families left, feeling that their voices were not being heard.

Since then, the MST has changed strategy. While it still organises mass occupations in some parts of the country, it takes more care to involve the families. Even so, it is clear that leaders put more time and energy into training youngsters than their parents, largely because they find young people more open to new ideas and more likely to show the dedication and commitment that the movement requires from its activists. There is, however, no ban on the involvement of older people; many of them are active in the coordination committees in the camps and a few quickly emerge as leaders. The fact that not many old people are *militantes* stems as much from the reluctance of older people to rush around the country as from any veto on their participation from the national leadership.

From the beginning, the camps have considerable contact with the *assentamentos*, the settlements. *Assentados* (settlers) pay frequent visits to the camps, bringing food and other supplies. They also offer shelter after an eviction and often take part in reoccupations. The camp is quickly integrated into the MST's overall structure. The coordination committee elects two representatives – and again the leadership encourages them to choose a man and a woman – to form part of the regional coordination committee, which in turn elects two more representatives to the state coordination committee. The state coordination committee is too cumbersome to be effective, so it elects a smaller and tighter group to form the state council (*direção estadual*), which in practice runs affairs in that state. Stédile says that the most important forum for discussion within the MST is this state council. 'The discussions at these state meetings are more profound than anywhere else, because the leaders are dealing with problems that are specific to that region. There is also more time for discussion than at the national meetings.'[18]

Each state council elects two representatives to the national coordination committee, but again it is the smaller national council (*direção nacional*), made up of 21 people, which is the more powerful body. Eighteen members of this council are elected by the national coordination committee from the delegates sent by the state councils. These members, who have a two-year mandate, can be re-elected but, in order to make sure that new ideas from the grassroots are fed into the council, the movement encourages a turnover of about one third at each election. There are another three members – João Pedro Stédile, Neuri Rossito and Gilmar Mauro – who have been on the council since its formation. They could, in theory, be thrown out, because they have to be re-elected each time by the national coordination committee but, in practice, they are permanent members. Members are unapologetic about what could be seen as an undemocratic practice: they say it is important to have continuity and to have leaders not involved in the day-to-day running of the organisation who have the time to develop long-term strategies.

The movement says that this basic organisational structure is the MST's circulatory system, which carries oxygen around the body. It is seen as a two-way system in which ideas flow up and down. Before an important decision is taken, the national council sends a proposal to be debated at all levels and waits for feedback. Apart from this basic structure, there is a host of other bodies. Over the last few years, the movement has set up 12 *coletivos* to handle specific issues: production, education, training, health, gender, human rights, culture, environment, communication, international relations, youth and *frente de massa* (recruitment). These *coletivos* come forward with proposals that, if adopted by the national council, become MST policy.

Does this add up to a democratic structure? It is true, as Itelvina says, that the leadership listens to the base and that the grassroots have at times forced the leadership to change policies. It is also true that the settlements have great freedom to organise their activities as they see fit, from the kind of farming they adopt to the type of school they want. 'We decide on guiding principles, not norms', says Stédile. Most *sem-terra* come from a world of abusive exploitation and extreme poverty, where, despite Brazil's formal democracy, they had no influence whatsoever over key factors in their lives. They were not consulted over the running of the school their children attended or the hospital where they got health care. They had little say over what they ate, where they lived or how they worked. Almost without exception, the *sem-terra* say that the MST has offered them their first real chance to give their opinion and to participate in the construction of their community.

Even so, this does not add up to a completely democratic structure. The old guard – particularly the six former seminarists who played such a fundamental role in setting up the movement – have great power and influence. No one yet has seriously challenged their leadership. At most, a few young *sem-terra militantes* will admit to some unease with the fact that the leaders, none of whom came from *sem-terra* families, do not live with their families in camps or settlements (though they visit them frequently) but have homes in the towns or cities. The real test of the MST's internal democracy will come when there is a serious leadership contest. Will the old guard eventually hand over power to a new generation of democratically elected leaders? Or will João Pedro Stédile, like Fidel Castro, see himself as irreplaceable and decide that he cannot step down?

Revolution or Reform?

Linked to the issue of internal democracy is the question of the MST's revolutionary project. The ability of the MST to transform people impresses everyone who visits its camps. José de Souza Martins believes that the MST is the 'most effective movement for the modernisation and re-socialisation of rural populations in the history of Brazil'. 'It takes people who have lost their way in life and are living in absolute poverty and transforms them into citizens who are living in a state of well-being.'[19]

Yet other aspects of the MST greatly worry Souza Martins. He argues that the *sem-terra*, like peasants in other societies, are essentially conservative: 'whether or not they are members of the MST, the peasantry, especially the *acampados* and the *assentados*, act in defence of classic conservatism: land, work, family, religion and community'.[20] What they want, he says, is to be accepted as full citizens in the modern world. This, he says, is not the aim of the leaders of the MST, who, applying 'the Leninist concept of the revolutionary role of the working class', are mistakenly attempting to turn the *sem-terra* into agents of revolution. As a result, Souza Martins says, there is a profound contradiction 'between the revolutionary project of the *militantes* of agrarian reform and the conservative project implicit in the struggle and Utopian hope of the rural workers'.[21] Souza Martins says that by trying to enlist the *sem-terra* as soldiers in a revolutionary army, the MST is embarking on a project that is doomed to failure and is betraying the very people it claims to be defending.

There is some truth in what Souza Martins is saying. The *sem-terra* are not revolutionary by nature. Brought up in the profoundly conservative Brazilian countryside, they were taught to think of themselves as inferior and to regard the *latifundiários* as their natural overlords. Despair drove them into the MST, where they learnt to 'think the unthinkable'. This break with the past is not always permanent. Once they have conquered their plot of the land, some of the men revert to their earlier conservative behaviour, particularly with respect to their wives and daughters. Yet this does not mean that MST *militantes* are wrong-headed or manipulative in their attempt to mould the *sem-terra* into a revolutionary force. As we saw in chapter 9, Brazil's globalised agriculture leaves little room for small farmers. One of the government's own advisers is predicting that, in face of fierce competition from imported food, only 18 per cent of Brazil's farmers will survive the next decade. Very few of the underfunded and unskilled settlers in the agrarian reform projects have a real chance of belonging to the small group of survivors. In these dire circumstances, the MST *militantes* may be justified in joining ranks with dispossessed farmers in other countries in the world in a last-ditch effort to limit the power of the multinational corporations and to force through far-reaching changes in global food production that will leave space for small-scale sustainable farming. This endeavour may fail but it seems to be the *sem-terra*'s only chance of survival.

For this strategy to have any chance at all of success, there must be a high level of political awareness and revolutionary commitment throughout the movement. While Souza Martins is right in saying that peasant culture is profoundly conservative, he appears to be underestimating the MST's impressive capacity to effect change. As we have seen, the MST did not develop this ability by chance: it worked hard at developing a methodology to be applied in the camps for freeing the *sem-terra* from the domination of the *latifundiários*. Perhaps the main problem that the MST faces today stems from its failure to have developed a comparable methodology for the settlements, where the problems are very different. Instead of an external enemy, the *assentados* need to overcome the more insidious foe of profound cultural conditioning.

A 'Culture of Liberation'

At present, the MST is living two contradictory moments. In some regions, particularly in the north and the northeast, the movement is still very young and is expanding rapidly. Thousands of youngsters are drinking deep the exhilarating cocktail of occupation, confrontation and political awareness. For the first time in their lives they have the chance to prove themselves as individuals. In a conversation in March 2001, Dan Baron Cohen, a British activist who has also worked in Northern Ireland and South Africa, calls this culture, with its emphasis on personal sacrifice, collective suffering, resilience and absolute unity, the 'culture of resistance'. During the difficult struggle to conquer the land, this 'culture of resistance' is still a source of great inspiration. But in other regions, particularly in the south, where this culture was first forged, the movement has entered a new phase. The second generation of *sem-terra*, brought up on the settlements, has not experienced the extreme poverty, humiliation and despair that drove their parents to risk all in a dangerous land occupation. Young people do not identify with the 'culture of resistance'. It is not uncommon to hear them say: 'The MST, that's my parent's movement, not mine.'

Dan Baron Cohen thinks that the movement needs a new culture to deal with the second phase. 'Offering people the chance to participate in the creation of a new community may be empowering', he says. 'Implementing it, building a new collective culture in which people jointly take decisions, is an entirely different struggle. Many rush to occupy the land but few transform the legacy of their past. It is extremely demanding to make the transition from what I call a "culture of resistance" to a "culture of liberation". I've seen movements founder at this stage in Ireland, South Africa and Palestine. I don't want it to happen with the MST.'

In Brazil the problem of creating a new and relevant culture for the second generation of *sem-terra* is exacerbated by the wave of sophisticated neo-liberal propaganda that has been swamping the country since it opened its economy to the world market. 'It is a moment of great ideological confusion', said Baron Cohen. 'Neo-liberalism is presenting the technological revolution of the twenty-first century as the means of achieving individual freedom. It is replacing the socialist revolution as the depository of Utopian dreams. New e-commerce companies are even appropriating the language and imagery of the left to bolster the idea that they represent the revolution of the coming century.'

To illustrate his point, Baron Cohen refers to a couple of billboards commonly seen in Brazil's cities.

> Outside the MST's lodging house in São Paulo is a huge billboard, advertising *Mercado Livre* (free market), an e-commerce company. A contented Fidel Castro addresses the consumers of the billboard: '*Companheiros* (comrades), I've just deposited 20 boxes of cigars on the *mercado livre*'. A smiling Bill Clinton, facing him, ruminates: 'And now I know where I can find my cigars'. The images don't only suggest that the greatest living icon of the Latin American revolutionary dream has capitulated and entered the neo-liberal marketplace. They also simultaneously satirize and appropriate the traditional language of the Left, implying that there is no longer any reason for resisting – or even the means to resist – the cultural and technological revolution we are living. But it is a confusing image for *sem-terra* families who have heard MST leaders denounce US imperialism against Cuba and know that the MST has sent 25 youngsters to Cuba to train as doctors. Even the MST's own language is vulnerable: another billboard and advert on television promotes *Terra Livre* (Free Land), which promises new ideas, new products, new symbols, new life.

The world that the adverts portray is mythical: behind the billboard representation of healthy and happy teenagers is a real world of exploitation, poverty and violence, where millions of poor Brazilians are condemned to a barbaric struggle for survival. Yet it is the unreal world, heavily promoted by television, which is capturing the hopes and desires of millions of young Brazilians. The young *sem-terra* are not protected: outside many of the houses in the MST settlements in the south are satellite dishes for feeding TV Globo into the settlers' living rooms. Television is turned on from early morning until late in the evening in many MST houses. While the *sem-terra* all over Brazil have grown expert at extracting hard information from the heavily biased TV coverage of MST activities, they are far less skilled at examining critically the inherently conservative values embedded in the barrage of consumer propaganda.

The MST can counter this bombardment but it needs its own space in the settlements to put forward its alternative vision. The movement needs to confront some of the problems that were pushed aside during the exciting days of the 'culture of resistance'. 'Many of the leaders speak in a discourse of suffering, commitment, collective self-sacrifice and postponed fulfilment', says Baron Cohen. 'Through their extraordinary dedication to the development of the movement, many have spent very little time with their own children. This can be rationalised in terms of the values and principles of necessary sacrifice – the language that they brought to the MST from the Catholic Church – but it means they have little practical understanding of the psychology of adolescence.' As a result, they do not regard the problems faced by young people as important.

One obvious example is sexuality. Most of the first generation of *sem-terra* are Catholic and, formally at least, accept the Catholic Church's attitude towards sexuality, including its belief that sex outside marriage is wrong. Yet, in practice, their behaviour often clashes with their professed beliefs. Because they spend so much time away from home, many *militantes* have clandestine affairs. Inevitably, there are problems but these are rarely discussed openly, because so many *militantes* still regard personal relations as something secondary that should be subsumed to the revolutionary struggle. This contradictory behaviour makes it difficult for young people to deal with their own growing sexual awareness. Because sexuality is not discussed properly in MST schools, huge numbers of teenage girls get pregnant in the camps and the settlements. Even the MST's heroes are treated as totally dedicated asexual monks, who spent their whole life serving the movement. Che Guevara is adored throughout the movement, but no mention is made of his notorious sex life.

Young people, many of whom do not share their parents' Catholicism, do not want to behave in the same repressed way as their parents. 'They have – and *need* – a different language, the language of the twenty-first century, in which to talk about love, desire, sexuality and the questions that will define their dreams', says Baron Cohen.

They need the space to experiment with their own identity, and to discover the language of their own individual experience. The movement was built around the symbol of the *facão*, the knife in the MST's flag for bringing in the harvest and for promoting the struggle. Young people are not even represented on the flag. A profound cultural transformation is now needed. It is particularly difficult at the moment, with government waging war on the MST, but along with the clenched fist of resistance and unity, the MST needs the open palm of questioning, dialogue, empathy, sensitivity and decentralization. These concepts are already in place. If they are not implemented, the base of this unique movement will disintegrate.

It is possible for the movement to tackle these issues. Baron Cohen and others have carried out successful cultural and educational projects in which they work with hundreds of young *acampados* and *assentados*. 'We cultivate motivation through intimacy, affirmation, critical reflection and artistic experimentation', said Baron Cohen. 'We encourage people to develop as confident individuals and community activists who can explain, demonstrate and develop creative and collective decision-making'. These projects, as yet occasional events, have been greatly appreciated by young people, but some traditional leaders have been resistant. Much more is needed. A new generation of women leaders, who had to fight their own battle against entrenched *machismo* to get their views heard, may be the people to take the lead on this issue.

Gender

Peasant life was extremely restrictive for women. Girls were kept at home, while their brothers often went to school, at least for a few years. Married women were expected to obey their husbands without question. As well as doing all the domestic and child care tasks, the women worked long hours in the fields but were not consulted over farming matters. Though peasant families in the south were generally less impoverished than those in the northeast, the repression of women could be even worse. Isabel Greem, from the MST's state leadership in Paraná, said that most of the immigrant families that arrived in her state in the nineteenth century came from Europe, particularly from Poland and the Ukraine. 'Family structures were very rigid. Women were expected to work very hard and say very little. The men imposed harsh discipline.'

During the second half of the twentieth century there was an additional source of suffering. Throughout this period Brazil had one of the highest rates of internal migration in the world. As the agricultural frontier expanded into isolated areas, rural labourers were constantly on the move, clearing land for big property-owners and working as sharecroppers in the newly opened areas. Wives were expected to follow their husbands, even though this entailed the huge emotional wrench of leaving their mothers and sisters. Women in the MST frequently look back at their mothers' lives with great sadness. Lurdinha from an MST settlement in Promissão in São Paulo says she scarcely knew her mother: 'Since a tiny child, I remember my mother as a person whose life was finished, as an old person, even though she was still quite young at the time, 45 or 46 years old. ... She had a worn face. She was constantly ill.'[22] Illness was so common among poor rural women that Dulcinéia Pavan, in her study of MST women settlers, believes that it may have been a defence mechanism they subconsciously created to deal with the constant upheavals and traumas of migrant life. 'As it was impossible for them openly to oppose the traditional practice of following their husbands or fathers, illness was a recourse, a kind of passive resistance. It was used as a justification for staying where they were.'[23]

Life in an MST camp was a revolutionary experience for women from this background. Cresi Gobbi Machado, 41 years old, now a teacher in an MST settlement, recalls her days in the Fazenda Annoni camp in Rio Grande do Sul. 'There were a lot of problems – not enough food, constant illness, such inadequate accommodation that we often had to sleep four or five couples in a tent', she said. 'But we women just got organised. We actually enjoyed ourselves. We talked so much, something we'd never been able to do before. It wasn't so good after Rose [Roseli Nunes] died. She was such a great person and a great leader. But, even after her murder, we went on learning and growing.'

Women often stiffened the resolve of their husbands. Nazaré, now settled in the Pontal do Paranapanema region of São Paulo, said she showed more determination at a critical moment. 'When we arrived here, my husband weakened. When we came under attack, he said: "this isn't the place for us. We only came here to win land. Let's go back to the town." But I said: "No. We're here. We came here to do a task and we're going to stay here until the end." Even today, he says that if it hadn't been for what I did, as a woman, he wouldn't have got his land.'[24] On many other occasions, as in Fazenda Annoni, it was the women who banded together and faced down the gunmen sent in to evict them.

The women's contribution to the movement has always been recognised by the leadership, yet, despite this, women faced a long struggle to be treated as equals. Many women faced hostility from their families when they started to get involved in political struggle. Itelvina Maria Mazioli, a fair-haired woman of European descent, who is today a 36-year-old single parent with a 3-year-old daughter, remembers what it was like. 'My father had a small plot of land in the north of Espírito Santo. We were a big family. I had seven brothers and five sisters. We were strong Catholics and I was in the church's youth group. It was there that I gained my political awareness. I was rebellious. I couldn't understand why all the sons could do exactly as they pleased but the girls had to stay at home until they married.' In 1985 Itelvina took the momentous step of leaving home, even though she was still unmarried. In 1994 she was elected to the MST's national leadership.

Itelvina was the second woman to be elected to the national leadership. The first was 34-year-old Maria de Fátima Miguel Ribeiro, a slight, dark-haired woman with a quick smile. Also born in Espírito Santo, Fátima did not face the same hostility from her parents. 'After working for many years on a cattle ranch, my father was sacked', she said. 'The cattle rearer was afraid that he would go to court to demand compensation, so he made sure that he was given a good beating before he left. My father ended up in hospital, and never really recovered. Even so, he decided to go to court and, with the help of the local trade union, he eventually won, though he got very little money.' With the family facing so many problems, Fátima had to fend for herself from an early age. 'I was very angry about what had happened to my father. It was that, I think, that turned me into a rebel. First, I was active in the Catholic Church and the local trade union. Then I encountered the MST and I knew straightaway that it was the movement for me. I went to the MST National Congress in 1985 and came back, really fired up. With José Rainha, I helped organise the first occupation in Espírito Santo in 1985.'

Fátima organised scores of occupations and then in 1989 the MST sent her all by herself to set up the movement in the backward state of Ceará in the northeast. It was a tough, violent life and one of Fátima's colleagues was the victim of gang rape carried out by military policemen. Since then, Fátima has been sent as a trouble-shooter to many difficult areas. Rather surprisingly, she was looking after a small baby at the fourth National Congress. Another single mother? Yes, but with a difference. Someone left a two-day-old baby on Fátima's doorstep in April 2000. 'At first, I didn't mean to keep the baby', she said. 'I knew it would be difficult, without a father, and with the life I lead. But I got attached to her so quickly, that I found I couldn't give her up. I knew nothing about babies and I had lots of problems in the beginning, but I've learnt.'

In the early years, there was resistance within the MST itself to the involvement of women in leadership roles. Itelvina recalls:

> The movement always recognised the importance of women in the occupations, the marches and the demonstrations, but it wasn't so keen about having women as leaders. The MST wasn't nurtured in a goldfish bowl, separate from the rest of society. It is part of peasant culture and reflects the *machismo* in this culture. At first, men looked at us strangely when we spoke at meetings and stood for election. It was quite intimidating. We found it relatively easy to be elected to the health and education *coletivos*, as they are seen as suitable areas for women. It was much harder to get elected elsewhere. Many men still believe that some sectors, such as farm production, *frente de massa* and security, are 'naturally male'. Change doesn't come easily. We have to confront men. We have to come up with our own proposals and show men that we too can think.

The difficulties are not just caused by the *machismo* of male activists. Many women, particularly in the more remote rural areas, find it difficult to break with ingrained sexist customs. At the meeting in Fazenda Taba in Pará in April 2000, two or three confident women leaders repeatedly called on the other women to put forward their views and to stand for election, but very few responded.

Change is gathering pace. In March 2000 some 3,000 women from the MST and a sister organisation, the Small Farmers' Movement (*Movimento dos Pequenos Agricultores*, MPA), met in Brasília for a two week conference. Along with the themes routinely discussed at such gatherings, such as farm credit and the political situation, the women talked about their own problems, particularly their difficulties in speaking publicly and in demanding help from their husbands in child care and housework. Many of the women had never travelled alone before. 'Many unexpected things happened at this meeting', said Isabel Greem. 'Women spoke far more readily than they would have done if men had been present and felt far freer to speak about feelings. One of the speakers asked everyone in the audience to look at her right hand and the right hand of the woman sitting next to her. She said that you could tell so much of a person's history from her hand – her work in the fields, her constant washing of clothes, her sensitivity in comforting her children, her intelligence in using her hand to respond to her brain's demands. It was moving and empowering. It wouldn't have happened like that if men had been running the meeting.'

In the 2000 elections nine women were elected to the national leadership of 21 people. That was the largest number of women ever elected, exactly half of the leaders chosen by the bases. Women were also much in evidence at the fourth National Congress in August 2000. They organised events and participated fully in the imaginative and moving *místicas*. Yet it was notable that the women were still in a subordinate position. Though several women spoke and chaired discussions, men gave all the keynote addresses. Itelvina was quite candid: 'Women have made great strides in the movement, but we haven't yet had the experience of the men. Our development within the movement has to be organic, not forced. When we are ready, we will play as full a role as the men.' There is a groundswell of support from women in the movement for greater gender equality. At the fourth Congress, only two additions came from the plenary when the leadership requested feedback to the strategy of political struggle that it had presented for the following five years. One called for a more explicit espousal of gender equality. (The other asked for a stronger endorsement of *agro-ecologia*.)

There have been frustrations as well as advances for the women. After the failed attempt at collective farming, many families started cultivating individual plots. The culture of collective resistance and community spirit, which flourished so strongly in the camps, weakened. Many of the men, forced to allow women a say in the running of the camps, slipped back into their old *macho* ways. Maria Rodriguez, a settler in São Paulo, is angry. 'We all know that men are sexist, but the peasant farmer is much worse than the rest', she said. 'He feels that he is the owner of his plot, his cows, his wife, of everything, even the thoughts of his wife. If a wife is going to vote, she has to vote as her husband tells her.'[25]

The leadership is worried by the setbacks in the settlements and believes that the greater participation of women can help. It is encouraging the settlements to set up *coletivos do gênero* (gender collectives), made up of men as well as women. It is exhorting the settlers to elect as many women as men on to all the movement's councils. Though there are no quotas and most women do not want quotas, this is leading to a notable increase in the number of women in leadership roles. Although men always say in public that this is what they want, they are not always so supportive in practice. 'At the last meeting of the education collective, there were four women breast-feeding young babies', said Isabel Greem. 'It was a bit disruptive and the men got irritated. But the movement's got to learn to live with this.'

There are already signs that the women's sensitivity and perceptiveness will bring other changes. Almost all of the women leaders are authentic *sem-terra*, in that they were born into families of landless peasants and still live in the settlements or camps. Many of them have children and are managing, with difficulty, to bring them up. They have a lot of contact with young people. Although they understand the older leaders' fear of abandoning the MST's tried-and-tested monolithic political culture precisely at the time when the government seems more determined than ever to destroy the movement, they are profoundly worried by the lack of motivation among the young *sem-terra* in the south, and are looking for solutions.

Prospects

The MST has faced serious problems in the past, and one of the movement's undoubted strengths has been its capacity to reformulate policy after setbacks. The MST has an agenda that could readily be used to inspire the young. Its project for sustainable farming is an extremely powerful proposition for the twenty-first century. As well as turning the MST into a symbol of opposition to the excesses of intensive chemical farming with its barbaric exploitation of people and the environment, its 'communities of peasant production' with their organic farming could become a flagship for the world. If the MST could bring together its proposal for sustainable agriculture with an equally daring revolution in personal relations, its agenda for change would be unbeatable.

There is support for such a programme of action within some sections of the movement. Before the fourth National Congress, one of two slogans under discussion for adoption as the movement's watchword for the following five years was: Agrarian Reform – A Way of Life (*Reforma Agrária – Una Opção de Vida*). This slogan, proposed by a settlement in the south, expressed the movement's concern to improve the quality of life in its settlements and was in tune with the 'culture of liberation'. In the end, the movement opted for the other slogan: Agrarian Reform – For a Brazil without *Latifúndios* (*Reforma Agrária – Por um Brasil sem Latifúndios*), which, in line with the old 'culture of resistance', expressed the movement's commitment to political struggle. The two slogans represent the conflicting pressure within the movement, as the *sem-terra* move from one stage of their development to another. By the time of the next national conference in 2005, the balance of power of the movement may well have shifted, as more land is conquered and more *sem-terra* grapple with the problem of making the settlements work. Particularly if the young women leaders gain ground, the movement may by then be prepared to turn its attention to the issues of personal and cultural liberation. But such an optimistic scenario faces two linked threats, one external and one internal: from outside the movement, there is the risk that the unfavourable economic climate for small farmers, together with the government's offensive against the MST, will damage the movement's capacity to grow and to develop; inside the movement, there is the danger that the present leadership, driven into a corner by the external onslaught, will retreat into a monolithic political culture. What is encouraging, however, is the growing awareness among the membership of the urgent need to rethink the movement for the second generation. Although the MST has not yet resolved the problem, it is turning its attention towards it.

CHAPTER 14

The MST in Historical Perspective

It is childish to expect ever to see Small Farms again, or ever to see anything else than the utmost screwing and grinding of the poor, till you quite overturn the present system of Landed Property. For they have got more completely into the spirit and power of oppression now than was ever known before. ... Therefore anything short of total Destruction of the power of these Samsons will not do. ... Nothing less than the complete Extermination of the present system of holding Land ... will ever bring the world again to a state worth living in.

Thomas Spence, 1800, quoted in E.P. Thompson, *The Making of the English Working Class*[1]

Three hundred and thirty years before Brazil's *sem-terra* made their appearance, hungry Englishmen were occupying unproductive land and digging it up to sow corn and plant carrots and beans. England was in desperate straits in the 1640s, for the disruption of the civil war had been compounded by disastrous harvests, rising food prices, heavy taxes and low wages. Enclosure was beginning to take away much of the common land where the poor had traditionally grazed their animals and planted their crops. In *The World Turned Upside Down*, his book on radical ideas during the English Revolution, Christopher Hill quotes a pamphlet of the time: 'Necessity dissolves all laws and government, and hunger will break through stone walls'.[2] Many resorted to looting. 'The poor did gather in troops of ten, twenty, thirty in the roads and seized upon corn as it was carrying to market and divided it among themselves before the owners' faces, telling them they could not starve.'[3]

On 1 April 1649 a group of labourers began digging up an area of wasteland at St George's Hill, outside London. It was one of the first acts of a radical group of non-conformists who became known as the Diggers. 'It was a symbolic assumption of ownership of the common lands', wrote Hill.[4] By claiming that the poor had the right to cultivate land to produce food, this group was carrying out the same kind of defiant direct action that the MST was to turn into an organised strategy three and a half centuries later. The Diggers were confident that their movement would spread across the land. A chronicler of the time wrote: 'they invite all to come in and help them ... and promise them meat, drink and clothes ... They give out they will be four or five thousand within ten days. ... It is feared they have some design in hand'.[5] Gerrard Winstanley, the best-known Digger leader, claimed that one-third of England was 'barren waste, which lords of manors would not permit the poor to cultivate'. If this land was used properly, he said, it could feed the population ten times over, so that begging and crime could be abolished. England would become 'the richest, the strongest and the [most] flourishing land in the world'.[6] The Diggers knew that the landowners would not voluntarily give up this land, so 'they called on the poor to organise themselves for practical action'.[7]

The Diggers, under the leadership of Gerrard Winstanley (who refused to doff his hat to a superior, rather as the *sem-terra* use their red caps as a symbol of defiance towards the authorities), deliberately defied the power of the landowners. Not only did they demand an end to the enclosures, which were taking common lands away from the rural poor, they also challenged the authority of the landowners to use the commons for their own ends. 'The Diggers had ordered the lords of the manor to stop cutting down "our common woods and trees ... for your private use". It was intended, as all the Diggers' actions were, to be a symbolic challenge as well as an economically necessary step.'[8] When the lords of the manor refused, the Diggers began to cut the timber for their own use. It was an open act of defiance: 'Squatting and cultivating the earth could be deemed to be done by courtesy of the lord of the soil; but cutting wood against his wishes was a direct assertion of a property right which could not be overlooked.'[9]

The Diggers were only one of a host of groups of common people, who at the time were trying, in Hill's words, 'to impose their own solutions to the problems of their time, in opposition to the wishes of their betters who had called them into political action'.[10] Like the MST centuries later they were not just mobilising to get land to solve their economic problems. As part of the republican movement which had overthrown the monarchy, they also wanted a freer and more democratic England, where all men would be equal, where the aristocracy, the lords of the manor, the church and the clergy would no longer wield huge power over the mass of poor people. They wanted a form of what we today would call communism. They believed that 'the poorest man hath as true a title and just right to the land as the richest man ... True freedom lies in the free enjoyment of the earth.'[11]

Hill writes that for brief periods these groups were strong. 'There had been moments when it seemed as though from the ferment of radical ideas a culture might emerge which would be different both from the traditional aristocratic culture and from the bourgeois culture of the protestant ethic which replaced it.'[12] If the culture of the Diggers, the Levellers, the Ranters and the other radical groups had prevailed at that turbulent time, when the King was beheaded and England came the nearest it ever has to overthrowing the power of the aristocracy and the church, then a very different society would have emerged. Instead of the Protestant work ethic, which paved the way for the industrial revolution, English history might have followed another course. 'Rejecting private property for communism, religion for a rationalistic and materialistic pantheism, the mechanical philosophy for dialectical science, asceticism for unashamed enjoyment of the good things of the flesh, it might have achieved unity through a federation of communities, each based on the fullest respect for the individual. Its ideal would have been economic self-sufficiency, not world trade or world domination.'[13]

This ideal, which was most enthusiastically supported in Digger communities, never really came close to realisation. 'Coolly regarded, we must agree that this was no more than a dream', wrote Hill. 'The counter-acting forces in society were too strong.'[14] Even in Cromwell's New Army, which had fought and defeated the Royalists, the Army leaders rejected the demand of the Leveller soldiers for a greatly extended popular franchise; men without property were not seen as important enough to have a say in the running of the country. In 1647, after the generals had turned down their demands, the Leveller leader, Edward Sexby, commented bitterly at Putney outside London: 'There are many thousands of us soldiers that have ventured our lives; we have little propriety in the kingdom as to our estates, yet we have a birthright. But it seems now, except a man hath a fixed estate in this kingdom, he hath no right. … I wonder we were so much deceived'.[15]

After their fright, the landed classes regained power and the established church reasserted itself as an instrument of social control over the poorer classes. In 1660 the monarchy was restored and, by the end of the seventeenth century, the Diggers and all the other radical movements had disappeared. But their legacy lived on: just over a century later radical groups re-emerged stronger than ever. They were inspired now by the French Revolution of 1789 and by Thomas Paine's *Rights of Man*. Once again, the appearance of these groups greatly alarmed the ruling classes. In his masterpiece, *The Making of the English Working Class*, E.P. Thompson wrote of the 'frightened gentry who had seen miners, potters, and cutlers reading the *Rights of Man*'.[16] Fearful of where it might all end if they loosened their control, the authorities cracked down on attempts by the poor themselves to improve their conditions and to open up the political system. When a group of men met in a tavern called *The Bell* near the Strand in London in January 1792 to found the London Corresponding Society to campaign for parliamentary reform and universal suffrage, the authorities saw it as a threat. They grew even more alarmed when similar societies were formed in other parts of England.

The members of these societies, who described themselves as 'tradesmen, shopkeepers, and mechanics', met in taverns and homes and corresponded with each other by letter. One of the London Corresponding Society's key decisions was 'that the number of our Members be unlimited'. For E. P. Thompson this apparently innocuous rule was 'one of the hinges upon which history turns. It signified the end to any notion of exclusiveness, of politics as the preserve of any hereditary elite or property group' or 'identification of political with property rights'.[17] Moreover, the societies began to organise themselves to achieve their aims. It was precisely because of this decision to coordinate and plan their actions that Thompson regards the Corresponding Societies as the first working-class political organisation.

The powers-that-be were quick to grasp the significance of the new development. If the idea that the 'swinish multitude'[18] could demand the vote was anathema to them, the decision by ordinary men to organise themselves outside the control of the educated classes to further this demand was alarming. It all smacked of revolution; and in May 1794 the secretary of the London Corresponding Society, a shoemaker named Thomas Hardy, was arrested and charged with treason. It was a very serious crime, for which he could have been hung, drawn and quartered; somewhat unexpectedly, he was acquitted by a jury. But the authorities took other measures: the societies were outlawed, Tom Paine's *Rights of Man* was banned and meetings were prohibited. Even so, the authorities were not able to eliminate all the rumblings of discontent. The thirst for new ideas continued.

It was not only in the towns that the lower classes were getting organised. Times were even harder for the poor in the countryside. They had suffered a series of blows: 'high rents ... taxes on malt, on windows, on horses; Game Laws', with tough controls over poaching, including 'mantraps and (after 1816) sentences of transportation: all served, directly or indirectly, to tighten the screw upon the labourer'.[19] But what hurt most was the continued loss of the common land where families had been able to graze their animals. 'The groundswell of rural grievance came back always to access to the *land*.'[20] For the enclosure of public commons had intensified since the seventeenth century, creating widespread hardship. Just as some 200 years later families in the northeast of Brazil were devastated by the loss of their *sítios*, the plots of land for subsistence farming, so for the English poor 'the loss of the commons entailed ... a radical sense of displacement'.[21] Moreover, like the *posseiros* (squatters) in the Amazon basin, the dispossessed families almost never received compensation: 'In village after village, enclosure destroyed the scratch-as-scratch-can subsistence economy of the poor. The cottager without legal proof of rights was rarely compensated. The cottager who was able to establish his claim was left with a parcel of land inadequate for subsistence and a disproportionate share of the very high enclosure cost.'[22]

The big landowners were interested not just in grabbing more land; they wanted a permanent reserve of cheap labour to work, when required, on their estates. The highly influential *Commercial and Agricultural Magazine*, which represented the point of view of the propertied class, opined that labourers should never have 'more land than he and his family can cultivate in the evenings', because he would not be available to the farmer for 'haymaking and harvest'.[23] Many labourers became seasonal workers, losing their employment as soon as the harvest was over; during the winter they and their families had to depend on the parish poor law to get food to eat.

E.P Thompson was struck by the degree of exploitation: 'How was it possible, when the wealth of the landowners and farmers was rising, for the labourers to be held at brute subsistence level?' He believes that the greed of the landowners is not by itself an adequate explanation: 'We must look for an answer in the general counter-revolutionary tone of the whole period. ... [T]he reflexes of panic and class antagonism, inflamed in the aristocracy by the French Revolution were such as to remove inhibitions and to aggravate the exploitive relationship between masters and servants.'[24] Similar factors help to explain the violent wave of repression against the MST. Landowners and the authorities feel particularly viciously towards the movement, not because it represents the landless, whose cause they often admit is just, but because it has dared to mount an ideological challenge to neo-liberalism, the economic orthodoxy that brooks no opposition.

The poor in England were also badly hurt by mechanisation, just as was to happen to the *sem-terra* in Brazil many generations later. When the new threshing machines began to appear on the big farms, many farm workers became superfluous. In the cities, too, artisan workers were replaced by large machines that could be tended by a handful of workers, even by children. The poor fought back as best they could. Desperate mobs wrecked many of the new machines, both in the countryside and in the towns. Luddism, as the machine breaking was called, was more than a protest against progress by an ignorant mob. The Luddites had wider concerns: they believed the machines were eroding standards of craftsmanship by producing shoddy goods; and, angered by the factory owner's brutal exploitation of his labour force, they called for a legal minimum wage and better working conditions, particularly for the women and children employed in the new mills. Though the movement rarely admitted, even to itself, the real significance of its demands, 'Luddism was a *quasi-insurrectionary movement*, which trembled on the edge of ulterior revolutionary objectives'. [25]

The discontent of the rural and town workers made redundant by mechanisation fed into the continuing campaign for parliamentary reform, with secret meetings and 'seditious' pamphlets passing from hand to hand all over the country. The reformers claimed the right to hold open public meetings and in 1819 decided to organise a mass meeting at St Peter's Field in Manchester. Contingents marched in from many surrounding towns and villages, carrying flags. The protesters were unarmed and there were many women and children, which all suggested that they were planning a peaceful action. But the ruling class was worried. More than the numbers involved, it was 'the *discipline* of the sixty or a hundred thousand who assembled on St Peter's Fields which aroused such alarm', for it was 'evidence of the translation of the rabble into a disciplined *class*'.[26] Even middle-class reformers were alarmed. A Yorkshire property-owner who regarded himself as progressive, warned the government: 'Armed or unarmed, Sir, I consider such meetings, as that held at Manchester, to be nothing more or less than risings of the people; and I believe, that these risings of the people, if suffered to continue, would end in open rebellion.'[27]

The local magistrates gave orders for the demonstrators to be dispelled with force. Local factory-owners and shopkeepers pointed out the leaders to the soldiers. Sabre-wielding troops rode into the crowds from all sides, and after several hours of chaos and panic, 11 people had been killed and another 412 injured, 161 from sabre wounds. The empty field was strewn with caps, bonnets, shawls and shoes. The massacre became known as Peterloo, after the Battle of Waterloo four years earlier. One hundred and seventy-seven years later, Peterloo was eerily re-enacted in the Brazilian Amazon, at Eldorado de Carajás, when police fired on unarmed MST demonstrators, killing 19, injuring more than 60, and leaving the road strewn with shoes and personal belongings.

The Populist Movement in the United States

The United States also experienced an agrarian revolt, which stemmed in large part from the difficulties small farmers encountered in adapting to the new economic order that emerged after the end of the Civil War. In the second half of the nineteenth century, the US was industrialising and urbanising rapidly. To respond to the cities' growing demand for food, big commercial farmers were taking over land earlier owned by subsistence smallholders. Small family farmers in the south, already reeling from the defeat of the Confederacy, were affected with particular severity.

The problems were exacerbated by the government's tough monetary policy. During the Civil War the government had funded the war effort by issuing treasury notes (which soon became known as 'greenbacks' because of the colour of the ink used to print them). Over the years the government printed such a large number of these notes that it was forced to abandon the gold standard (by which the value of the new money was fixed in gold). As a result, the 'greenbacks' progressively lost their value, eroded by inflation. Once the war ended, the government, under pressure from bankers, decided to restore the value of the 'greenback' by exercising very tight control over money. For more than a decade the government refused to issue new notes. As both the population and production were rising, less money was chasing more goods and prices fell heavily. The prices paid for staple agricultural products, such as cotton, corn and wheat, dropped particularly sharply.

Farmers tried, at first, to cover the shortfall in their income by producing more, but it soon became clear that this only exacerbated the problem. Many, particularly vulnerable small farmers in the south, became engulfed in a massive social crisis. They sought to borrow their way out of their predicament but, as unscrupulous moneylenders took advantage of them, their debts snowballed out of control and 'thousands, then millions, descended into the world of landless tenantry'.[28] Some went in search of a better life on America's expanding agricultural frontier, with almost 100,000 families migrating west each year throughout the 1870s.

In 1877 a group of farmers decided to form a new self-help organisation. Using language that recalled the ideals of the Diggers in seventeenth-century England

(and prefigured those of the *sem-terra*), one of the founding members said that their overriding purpose was to 'more speedily educate ourselves in the science of free government' and to construct 'a grand social and political palace where liberty may dwell and justice be safely domiciled'.[29] This pioneer organisation collapsed but another movement, called the National Farmers Alliance and Cooperative Union, was formed shortly afterwards and it was initially a spectacular success. One of the organisers sent a rhapsodic account of a recruiting tour: 'I met the farmers in public meetings 27 times and 27 times they organised. … The farmers seem like unto ripe fruit – you can gather them by a gentle shake of the bush.'[30] The historian Lawrence Goodwyn says that the pattern was much the same everywhere. 'The word spread … that the Alliance meant what it said about "doing something for the dirt farmer".'[31] About 40,000 branches, known as Sub-Alliances, were formed, with altogether about a quarter of a million members. Because very few former slaves owned land, the vast majority of the Alliance members were white.

In Texas the Alliance sought to free the farmers from debt peonage by setting up its own marketing cooperatives and a system of rural credit, known as the exchange, an initiative it hoped would eventually be adopted nationally. As local bankers sought to crush the farmers' exchange, the Alliance called on its members to meet on a certain date in local towns throughout the state to discuss ways of defending their organisation. 'The farmers came by the hundreds, and in some cases by the thousands, to almost 200 Texas courthouses on June 9th 1888. Townspeople … watched with puzzlement the masses "of rugged honest faces" that materialised out of the countryside and appeared at the courthouses of the state. In scores of county seats the crush of farm wagons extended for blocks in every direction, some beyond the town limits. Reporters remarked about the "earnestness" of the efforts to save the exchange and the "grim determined farmers" who were making pledges of support.'[32] At a later meeting in the same year, reporters noted that the farmers paid 'the most intense interest' to the address given by the main speaker, although it was 'tedious and exceeding complex'.[33]

The Alliance gained its own momentum, outside the control of the original organisers. ' "It is not an organisation", noted one participant. "It is a growth".'[34] Just like the MST a hundred years later, the Alliance gave the oppressed farmers the confidence to think for themselves: 'Populism is the story of how a large number of people, through a gradual process of self-education that grew out of their cooperative efforts, developed a new interpretation of their society and new political institutions to give expression to these interpretations. Their new ideas grew out of their new self-respect.'[35] 'This [the Alliance's] culture was in the most fundamental meaning of the word "ideological": it encouraged individuals to have significant aspirations in their own lives, it generated a plan of purpose and a method of mass recruitment, it created its own symbols of politics and democracy, and it armed its participants against being intimidated by the larger corporate culture.'[36]

For all the support the Alliance generated among the impoverished farmers, the movement failed. One factor that contributed to its demise was the premature decision to move into mainstream politics and to form a new political party – the People's Party – which would bring together the rural and urban poor in a common struggle against what it saw as a 'massive conspiracy' by bankers and big business. By this stage the movement had become known as Populism. Paradoxically, the creation of the party was both the high point of the movement, for thousands swarmed to join, and the beginning of its decline. According to Goodwyn, the Alliance failed to make the transition from an issue-based rural movement to an all-encompassing national political party. Its members never learnt to speak the language of the urban poor and they did not have the knowledge – or the confidence – to develop a radical programme for the cities. Little by little the People's Party was co-opted by the far less radical Democrat Party. Populism did not even manage to save the livelihoods of its early supporters: by the time of the New Deal in the early 1930s, half of the farmers in the cotton belt – the Alliance's heartland – had long since lost their farms.

Historians disagree over the ideological content of the Populist project (just as today analysts in Brazil argue over the political significance of the MST). Some see it as a backward-looking, nostalgic movement established by outdated farmers unable to come to terms with modern industrial society. Others see it as the only political movement to offer Americans a different kind of society, in which the good of the community was considered more important than company profits. Goodwyn is a forceful spokesperson for the second camp. 'Agribusiness began to emerge as early as the 1920s … The collapse of Populism meant, in effect, that the cultural values of the corporate state were politically unassailable in 20th century America.'[37] Goodwyn values the legacy left by the Alliance: 'As a movement of people, it was expansive, passionate, flawed, creative – above all, enhancing in its assertion of human striving … The Populist essence was an assertion of how people can *act* in the name of the idea of freedom.'[38]

'Dislocation of the Social Order'

Although it is true that unsuccessful attempts at revolution tend to be written out of history ('The blind alleys, the lost causes, and the losers themselves are forgotten'[39]), revolutionary movements of the kind described here are not frequently encountered in England, the US or Brazil. Do they have any common underlying causes? In one of his essays the historian Eric Hobsbawm asks why poor people who 'do not usually find ways of expressing their discontents effectively or at all, mainly because a stable social order keeps them docile', at times rebel.[40] He concludes that such rebellions occur 'during periodic dislocations of the social order'.[41] This seems to be the case of the rebellions mentioned here.

The 30 years prior to the emergence of the seventeenth-century rebellions in England have been described 'as economically among the most terrible in English history'.[42] Apart from the chaos caused by the civil war, the plight of the poor was aggravated by poor harvests, high food prices, low wages, heavy taxes and economic mismanagement. These were the conditions that led to Hill's 'period of glorious flux and intellectual excitement' when 'literally anything seemed possible'.[43] Instead of moving swiftly at the end of the civil war into a period of stability in which the gentry and merchants, who had supported the victorious Parliamentary cause during the revolution, were able to reconstruct the institutions of society as they wished, England experienced a period of great uncertainty. 'Only gradually was control re-established during the Protectorate of Oliver Cromwell, leading to a restoration of the rule of the gentry, and then of King and bishops in 1660.'[44]

In the early nineteenth century, too, England went through a period of serious dislocation of the social order, with the countryside and the towns experiencing extremely painful change. The removal of common land from the rural poor reached a new and brutal stage: 'the social violence of enclosure consisted precisely in the drastic, total imposition upon the village of capitalist property definitions. ... Enclosure, indeed, was the culmination of a long secular process by which men's customary relations to the agrarian means of production were undermined. ... The loss of the commons entailed, for the poor, a radical sense of displacement.'[45] In the towns there was the widespread disruption caused by industrialisation.

In the US, Populism arose at a time of unprecedented pauperisation of family farms in the South. Such exploitation was possible because of the devastation caused by the Civil War and the collapse of the economic structure in the South, following the defeat of the Confederacy. Forced into debt peonage, farmers paid 100 per cent – even 200 per cent – interest on their loans. Many families saw their incomes fall by half. As has been shown in chapter 9, the MST, too, arose at a time of profound and far-reaching social dislocation, as thousands of rural workers and small farmers lost their livelihoods to mechanisation and the expansion of large-scale, export-led agriculture.

There is another important element that needs to be added to the equation. During the periods under discussion, both England and the United States were powerful sovereign states. England was emerging as the world's first industrial power, at the heart of a huge colonial empire, and the United States was consolidating its recently acquired economic and political independence. In both countries the agrarian movements arose in response to social dislocations caused by national economic upheaval. In Brazil the upheaval of the 1970s and 1980s was mostly caused by external factors because, since its discovery by the Portuguese in 1500, Brazil has never ceased to be a dependent country whose history has been largely determined by the needs of its colonial and post-colonial masters. This dependency has fashioned the history of land struggle into which the MST taps and it will profoundly affect the course of the MST's development in the future.

The Brazilian Case

While the working class gradually organised and conquered rights in England, Brazil remained until the end of the 1880s a slave-owning society, ruled by a monarchy and geared to the export of goods to Europe. In 1500 the Portuguese Crown had claimed the land that became Brazil, an area larger than Western Europe. The king divided it up into 12 giant provinces, called *capitanias*, and within these he had distributed great tracts of land, known as *sesmarias*, as gifts to loyal subjects, favourites and relatives. Although the land continued to belong to the Crown, the recipients were able to exploit these areas for their own wealth. The teeming indigenous nations that inhabited Brazil before the Portuguese arrived were enslaved, dispossessed and almost exterminated.

Over a period of 350 years, several million slaves were transported from all over Africa to work in Brazil's sugar fields, goldmines and coffee plantations. Dispatched to Europe, the goods created huge fortunes – but the wealth enriched European merchants and a handful of plantation owners, not the labourers. Some of the slaves dropped dead from overwork, some simply endured, others took part in uprisings and rebellions, and yet others escaped, setting up free territories, or *quilombos,* in the hills or forest. Most of the escaped slaves were hunted down and their *quilombos* destroyed, but one community in Pernambuco – the Republic of Palmares – lasted from 1630 to 1695. Up to 30,000 people lived in dozens of villages covering an area of 44,000 square km. They farmed, hunted and fished and 'for a few years solidarity, equality and cooperation replaced the degradation and exploitation of the plantation'.[46] For the slave-owners Palmares was too dangerous an example to be allowed to survive, but it took several punitive expeditions before it was finally overrun and the slaves killed or recaptured. The expeditionary force decapitated Zumbi, the charismatic leader of Palmares, and displayed his head on a pole as a warning to the population. Today he is one of the MST's heroes.

All over the world slavery was a vicious institution, with slaves living short and brutal lives, but in Brazil it had another insidious and highly pernicious impact on society, which is still being felt today. Because the Portuguese explorers were usually single men, they routinely abused female slaves, and the *mestizo* children that resulted from these unions fitted into neither group. With no clear racial division between 'blacks' and 'whites', Brazil became a socially fragmented society in which the slaves became ashamed of their colour and every *mestizo* vied to be whiter than his fellow. Instead of developing a collective awareness of their ethnicity, blacks and *mestizos* tried to ingratiate themselves with their owners, setting a pattern of social behaviour in which advancement comes from individual favours rather than collective rights.[47] Slavery was abolished in 1888, long after every other country. Today the Brazilian constitution enshrines the principle that all Brazilians, irrespective of colour, economic status and gender, have equal rights, but in practice discrimination still exists and the culture of the *jeitinho* (by which people solve their problems by wheedling favours from those in power rather than insisting on their rights) still thrives.

When the British Navy blockaded Brazilian ports in 1850 to stop the slave traffic it was abundantly clear that the writing was on the wall for the slave system. So it is no coincidence that in that same year Brazil's Emperor, Pedro II, passed the country's first land law. By then it was obvious that, once they were free, slaves would prefer to open up their own plots in Brazil's huge hinterland rather than continue to work for coffee- and sugar-plantation owners for a pittance. To prevent this the new law determined that land could be obtained only by purchase, not by occupation, effectively barring access to the land to all but the wealthy.[48] It was the opposite of the policy adopted in the United States, where the Homestead Act of 1862 actively encouraged the settlement of the 'free lands' in the west, now cleared of the indigenous populations who originally lived there. 'Homeseekers! A Farm for $3 per Acre! Every Farmer, Every Farmer's Son, Every Clerk, Every Mechanic, Every Labouring Man Can Secure a Home!' went the advertisements distributed to European emigrants even before they landed in New York.[49] As the sociologist José de Souza Martins has written, Brazil went from being a land where men were enslaved but the land was free to a land where men were free but land was not.[50] The law, in effect, set in stone the very unequal division of land established by the sesmarias.

There were rebellions: the most famous was Canudos. It began in 1893, when Antônio Conselheiro, a popular itinerant preacher who railed against taxes, the new republican government and the elites, called on his followers to set up their own community in a remote corner in the far north of the state of Bahia. Among the thousands who flocked to join him, some were homeless and penniless ex-slaves but many more were impoverished farm workers. Local landowners found themselves without labour. The straggling village of Canudos grew to a town of 20,000 inhabitants, which traded and even exported goatskins to Europe. There were schools, churches and 'visitors reported in wonder there are neither rich nor poor, the land belongs to all, there is no hunger or misery, no money, no police or thieves, no locks on doors, no brothels, no alcohol, everyone is happy in a big brotherhood'.[51]

In his book on Canudos, sociologist Clovis Moura says that local landowners came to loath Canudos for the example it was setting to the rural poor: 'A communitarian, alternative self-sufficient economy developed which was very superior, in both its social relations and in the distribution of its production, to the latifúndios (the large estates), based on the exploitation of the peasants, in the rest of the region. From that came the hate and the fear of the landowners and the authorities to the growth of Canudos and to the name of its leader, Antônio Conselheiro. For the latifúndio Canudos was a challenging and dangerous example.'[52] To justify their decision to destroy this thriving alternative society, the authorities had to criminalise Antônio Conselheiro and paint Canudos as a hotbed of fanatics bent on re-establishing the monarchy, abolished in 1889. Such was the resistance of the people that it took four military expeditions – the Brazilian army's biggest ever peacetime campaign – with the loss of thousands of men, before Canudos was finally overrun and destroyed in 1897. The surviving men were executed, and the women and children were distributed among the soldiers as booty.

Canudos could have served as an example of how to bring progress to the countryside through the creation of self-sufficient communities, but such a model demanded land distribution, which was anathema to the landed elites. According to Moura, 'the victory over Canudos represented the victory of the most archaic forces of Brazilian society, which claimed to be the representatives of progress and modernity'.[53] The ruling elite, he said, had managed to have itself defined as 'progressive', merely because it employed a higher level of technology on its farms, while Canudos, which actually provided the people with a better quality of life – something which surely should lie at the heart of the definition of progress – was regarded as 'backward' for using more basic farming methods.

This ability of the reactionary rural elites to present themselves as 'modern' has been a constant in Brazilian history. As Souza Martins has said: 'Brazil's oligarchs have always presented a modern face as a façade behind which they hide the economic backwardness of the *latifúndio* and its social and labour relations.'[54] This paradox is evident today. The Cardoso government attacks the MST for being 'archaic' and for adhering to an 'out-dated' socialist ideology, refusing to recognise the social advances in its camps and settlements, while it allows sugar-mills such as Petribu (*see* chapter 4), to describe themselves as 'modern' because they have a sophisticated logo and up-to-date machinery in their mills, even though they use violent, barbaric methods to combat the MST, methods that would be regarded as 'archaic' by any decent society.

Canudos was not an isolated case. There has been a series of revolts in Brazilian history, most of which are recorded in MST publications today. Not all the rebels were fighting for a more egalitarian society but, almost without exception, the revolts were fuelled by the smouldering discontent of the dispossessed rural population. In January 1835, even while slavery was still in force, a large group of Indians, Africans, *mestizos*, slaves and poor whites (who took their name from the *cabanas*, or shacks, they lived in) took over the city of Belém in the Amazon basin. They were demanding better living conditions, lower taxes and greater freedom. The central government had to send in heavy reinforcements before the *Cabanagem* rebellion was quashed. Thousands were massacred. In the same month, a group of Muslim Africans, brought over to Brazil as slaves, who had managed to preserve much of their Arabic culture, staged a revolt in the state of Bahia. The *Malês* revolt, as it became known, was ferociously repressed by government troops, and many rebels preferred to drown themselves in the sea rather than be taken captive.

The next large-scale popular revolt occurred in the southern state of Santa Catarina. The state government had granted a private English railway company ownership over a 100-kilometre band of land on either side of the railway line it was building, ignoring the fact that peasant families already occupied much of the area. A messianic leader led the families in revolt and the conflict – which became known as the war of Contestado – lasted from 1912 to 1916. Again, the authorities treated the rebels as an archaic pro-monarchy, anti-republican movement, when they were really fighting for their survival. Though the peasant army pulled off several surprise victories, it was eventually defeated with heavy loss of life. Some ten years later, rebel military officers led by Captain Luís Carlos Prestes staged their own revolt. In April 1925, a decade before Mao Zedong began his epic journey, about 1,500 officers and civilian supporters began a long march through the Brazilian interior. Their aim was to spark off a Communist revolution by enlisting the support of the rural poor. In two years the group, known as the Prestes' Column, marched thousands of miles, clashing dozens of times with government troops. They were never defeated, but neither did they overthrow the government, because they failed to rouse the poor to insurrection. Finally, undefeated but unsuccessful, the column sought refuge in Bolivia in February 1927.

One of the most important attempts to improve conditions for rural workers was made by the *Ligas Camponesas*, or Peasant Leagues, which spread throughout the northeast in the mid-1950s. They began inauspiciously when a group of tenant farmers on the Galileia sugarcane plantation near Recife in Pernambuco asked permission from the landowner to set up a funeral cooperative. Shortly afterwards, the world price of sugar rose and the landowner, eager to plant more sugarcane, tried to repossess the *sítios*, the individual plots of land used by the families to grow vegetables. The tenant farmers obtained the support of a lawyer, Francisco Julião, and fought back, using the administrative structure of the funeral cooperative to organise their resistance. Almost by chance the cooperative became a powerful instrument for mobilising the workers. Even though the landowners labelled them communists and the police and judges called them in to explain themselves, the tenant farmers gained popular support. About 3,000 peasants marched to Recife to lobby the Legislative Assembly in support of a bill to expropriate the Galileia estate. Their show of strength was successful and the estate was expropriated. Inspired by this success, rural families set up scores of Leagues throughout the region.

To avoid problems, the peasants called the new bodies civil associations, not trade unions, and referred to their local branches as *delegacias*, the word used for police stations. It was all part of a strategy for overcoming the peasants' tremendous fear of the authorities.[55] The Leagues were a legalistic rather than a revolutionary movement, although some of their leaders went to Cuba in 1959 and 1960 to look at the radical land reform being introduced by Castro. The ultimate aim of the Leagues was not to create an alternative model of society, or to become a parallel power, but to reform society so that there was a proper space in it for rural workers and their organisations. They wanted the authorities to respect the law, which guaranteed peasants far greater rights than they were allowed in practice by the landowners. But as landowners resisted change, the movement gained a new momentum: the peasants prepared to mobilise to gain the land they believed to be rightfully theirs. They adopted the slogan 'Land Reform – By Law or By Force' (*Reforma Agrária – Na Lei Ou No Cambão*[56]). In the countryside they united smallholders, tenant farmers, cane-cutters – all those who struggled to make a living in a society dominated by the landowners. Photographs of the time show bands of hardy men on horseback, rifles slung across their backs, wearing the leather clothes of the *sertanejo* (inhabitant of the drylands), which protected them from the thorns and spikes of the *caatinga* bush. In the cities they gained the support of trade unions, students, lawyers, and some of the press. In 1961 the delegations from the Leagues made a big impact at the First National Congress of Peasants and Agricultural Workers, held in Rio de Janeiro; they were not only the poorest but also the most radical delegation, demanding land in front of President João Goulart, who attended the Congress.

By then, the Cuban Revolution had frightened the US into setting up the Alliance for Progress with Latin American governments in an attempt to pre-empt further revolutions. The Charter, signed at Punta del Este in 1961, called for 'the effective transformation of unjust structures and systems of land tenure and use'.[57] The writer Paul Harrison commented: 'Many governments, afraid to lose economic and military aid, complied on paper with the Charter requirements. There was a boom in land reform legislation and land reform institutes mushroomed in every capital. But – except in a few countries such as Peru, pre-Pinochet Chile, pre-Banzer Bolivia – the reality fell far short of the promise. Land reform remained a slogan, or a cunning stratagem to quieten down the rebellious peasants while giving as few concessions as humanly possible.'[58]

In Brazil, too, the authorities tried to limit land reform to symbolic gestures, but by then the rebellious peasants were too organised to be bought off in this way. The fame of the Leagues was spreading throughout the country, raising awareness about land reform. The widening influence of the militant peasants, whom many conservatives were calling 'communist agitators', spurred the Catholic Church into organising its own peasant leagues. These Church-backed leagues tried in conciliatory fashion to negotiate with landowners but their actions were ineffective: unlike the Peasant Leagues, they could not back up their demands with the threat of strike action and were therefore regarded with little respect by the landowners. In June 1963, when a unionisation campaign was launched to provide support for the beleaguered Goulart government, which was belatedly embracing radical agrarian reform, many Peasant Leagues turned themselves into unions. As many as 2,000 new trade unions were created in six months. In November 1963 some 200,000 cane-cutters went on strike, with the support of the Leagues, to force the authorities to extend to them the benefits of labour legislation already enjoyed by urban workers, such as a minimum wage and a maximum working week.

But by then Brazil was heading for crisis. Strikes and mass demonstrations in the cities organised by workers in support of social reforms, including land reform, had created fear and panic among the elites. In 1964 Brazil's conservative forces, aided by the US, which feared a communist takeover of Latin America's largest nation, plotted against the government, and on 1 April 1964 the military deposed President Goulart. On the eve of the coup, Francisco Julião claimed that the 300,000 rural workers in the Leagues would take on the armed forces, but in the event there was little resistance. Thousands of peasants were arrested and many were tortured. Leaders were hunted down and killed. The Leagues were banned and broken up. 'It was as though the peasant sector in Brazil stopped existing as a dynamic social agent', wrote Clovis Moura. 'The peace of the graveyard was established.'[59]

The many revolts and rebellions in Brazilian history have had surprisingly little impact on the country's system of land tenure. The rural oligarchy has always been powerful enough to block agrarian reform, and attempts to reduce the political power of the landowners have foundered on their continuing influence over large sectors of the rural electorate, whether by corruption, intimidation or control of the mass media. The consequences for Brazil are highly significant. The sociologist Souza Martins believes that the land question lies at the heart of the many problems that Brazil has encountered in turning itself into a modern, democratic country.

> A certain poverty of perspective has sustained the view, even among sociologists, that the land question is only of interest to rural workers and no one else. A residual problem of the past, they say, that will be resolved with the inevitable progress and urban development. ... [But] in reality the agrarian question engulfs us all, whether we know it or not, whether we want it or not. Land ownership explains the resilience of Brazil's out-dated political system. Landowners have allied themselves with modern capitalism, thus injecting the old political system with a renewed force that has enabled it to block the creation of civil society and to prevent its members from becoming true citizens.[60]

Today the metamorphosis of the old, unproductive rural oligarchy has gained pace under pressure from a modernising government that wishes to make Brazilian agriculture more competitive in the globalised economy. A small group within the oligarchy is being absorbed into the new agribusiness elite, while another larger faction is clinging on to its privileges with the viciousness of desperation. This opens up new opportunities – and new risks – for social movements, particularly the MST. After violent confrontations, the MST is winning land in areas such as the sugar plantations in the northeast, where some of the weakened oligarchs, now bankrupt, are finally being dislodged. This is the upside. On the downside, the MST is also facing the unrelenting opposition of powerful new export-oriented farming groups, which are the Brazilian face of the multinational corporations that increasingly dominate world farming. These groups, which enjoy the full support of the Brazilian government, are implacably opposed to the MST not because it represents an economic threat but because it is shouting for all to hear that there is another way forward. It is challenging the authorities' mantra that Brazil has no option but to integrate itself into the globalised world under the existing rules of the game.

Popular movements and the history of nations

Rebel peasant movements have long exercised a fascination over left-wing historians, but have they really had any influence on the shaping of nations? The situation has clearly varied from country to country. The Diggers in seventeenth-century England and the London Corresponding Society in the late eighteenth century rose and disappeared, leaving little apparent trace. Yet this is evidently not the full story. Along with more powerful organisations set up by industrial workers, these movements fed into the formation of the British labour movement and to the eventual conquest of full franchise, labour rights and the welfare state. Though these themes lie beyond the scope of this book, it is clear that at some stage a 'critical mass' of workers was accumulated, making inevitable real concessions from the ruling classes. Beatrice Webb wrote in 1915: 'the power of the (labour) Movement lies in the massive obstinacy of the rank-and-file, every day more representative of the working class. Whenever this massive feeling can be directed for or against some particular measure, it becomes almost irresistible. Our English governing class would not dare overtly to defy it.'[61] There are echoes of this, too, in the Brazilian experience. After the MST March on Brasília in April 1997, the government clearly feared that it was gaining the impetus described by Beatrice Webb and becoming 'irresistible'; it was at that point that the government turned on the MST, using all the force of its sophisticated propaganda machine, far more effective than the resources available to the British government in 1915.

Historians believe that peasant movements have played a pivotal role in the history of some countries. Eric Hobsbawm argues that the importance of peasant movements has frequently been underestimated by historians who, 'being mainly educated and townsmen, have until recently simply not made sufficient effort to understand people who are unlike themselves'.[62] The acquisition of political consciousness by peasant populations made the twentieth century 'the most revolutionary in history'[63] and lay at the heart of the big revolutionary upheavals such as the Mexican Revolution from 1910–19, the Russian Revolution in 1917, the Spanish Revolution in 1936, the Chinese Revolution in 1949 and the Cuban Revolution in 1958. In essence, Hobsbawm argues that these revolutions stemmed from the upheavals that the arrival of capitalism in the countryside caused to the life of the peasantry.

In his book on peasant rebellion in Latin America, Gerrit Huizer argues in similar fashion that peasant mobilisation lay behind the revolutions in Mexico, Bolivia and other Latin American countries. Yet, he says, peasants were reluctant revolutionaries, forced into taking a radical stance by the intransigence of the landowners. 'The resistance to change of the landed elite, and its influence on the national governments, directly or indirectly, provoked the drastic, even violent, forms which the peasants' actions have taken, often with guidance or leadership from urban groups.'[64] As a result, 'the peasant movement became ... a revolutionary factor in society as a whole, in spite of the originally limited demands and moderate actions'.[65] The landowners rejected the peasants' demands, which were often modest, not because they were reluctant to make specific concessions, but because they were frightened that, once they started to allow changes in the established order, all their privileges would be threatened. Huizer cites the Mexican revolution, led by Emiliano Zapata, which began in 1910 when the indigenous communities organised a movement with the sole aim of recovering their communal lands, which had been seized by landowners and turned into sugar plantations, and were fiercely repressed. Similarly in Bolivia it was the brutality with which the landowners put down peasant protests that led a previously non-violent movement to develop into a popular revolutionary force. Under the leadership of Victor Paz Estenssoro, this movement took power in 1952 and introduced land reform.

Although peasant rebellions have taken place at different times in Latin America, Huizer believes that the successful ones have usually shared several characteristics. They have had strong or charismatic local leaders, like Zapata, for this has made it easier for peasants to withdraw from, or even oppose, the traditional system of patronage exercised by local landowners. They have made their demands in clear and radical language, using simple, strong slogans like 'Land and Freedom' or 'Land or Death'. And the organisations have covered a regional – rather than just a local – area, because in this way people have been able to lose their sense of isolation and enjoy the feeling of power that comes from belonging to a larger movement. 'Going to a meeting or marching by the hundreds through the streets of an important city to represent their interests and show themselves as a unified body ... help overcome the effects of having lived for centuries in the "culture of repression".'[66] The MST has all these characteristics, although it has attempted to develop a culture of strong leadership rather than relying exclusively on a single dominating figure.

Yet clearly the ability of the MST to spark off revolutionary change does not just depend on the movement's own organisational characteristics; far more important are the conditions within which the MST is operating. Several authors, including Souza Martins and Hobsbawm, have argued that at the beginning of the twenty-first century the peasantry has become a spent political force that is largely irrelevant. The whole world, including Brazil, has become predominantly urbanised. Millions have migrated to the cities, losing their rural roots. The peasantry, they say, is dead (or at least moribund) and worn-out forces do not lead revolutions. In Hobsbawm's list of countries that experienced revolutionary upheavals, the peasantry was at the time the largest population group in the country and its dissatisfactions mattered. Today, Hobsbawm suggests, the peasantry has become marginal.

Following a similar train of thought, Souza Martins argues forcibly that Brazil has lost the historical moment for classic agrarian reform. 'Radical agrarian reform can only happen when it is required to resolve an historical impasse for the development of capitalism', he said.

> This is no longer the case in Brazil. Globalisation is a fact of life. Today the world market provides an outlet for Brazil's cash crops, cultivated by the big farmers, and new farming techniques mean that a handful of efficient commercial farmers can provide food for the cities. There is no longer a pressing economic need for agrarian reform. So today the only possible form of agrarian reform is the market-oriented type being undertaken by the government, which allows family farms to fit into market niches left by the big capitalist farms. Whether we like it or not, that is the situation today and the MST is doing a disservice to the cause of agrarian reform by its radical opposition to the only possible form of agrarian reform.

These are all powerful arguments, but not sufficient in our view to cast the MST into the dustbin of history. First of all, no one is seriously suggesting that the MST – or any other rural workers' movement – will be able by itself to ignite revolutionary change. The movement's hope is to create an alliance of 'excluded Brazilians', rural and urban, who favour radical change. There are today 50 million Brazilians living in extreme poverty, with a monthly income of less than US$100, which means that they cannot afford to buy the minimum food – 2,280 calories per day – required for survival.[67] About 45 per cent of those living in extreme poverty are children under 15. Today it is not uncommon to find Brazilian children suffering from kwashiorkor, an illness caused by protein deficiency which leads to the swelling of the belly. The weekly news magazine *Veja*, not renowned for its progressive views, commented in early 2002: 'We don't yet know who will be the next president but we know what the biggest challenge of the next government will be: to reduce the number of Brazilians living in Africa-like poverty. It would be just as well for the candidates to learn by heart the word *kwashiorkor* and to understand the tough meaning it has for millions of Brazilians.'[68]

What perhaps is most shocking is that the hunger in Brazil, as President Cardoso has pointed out, is the result not of underdevelopment but of social injustice. Brazil has doubled its output of grain over the last 30 years, but the food is not reaching the poor because they don't have the money to buy it. As *Veja* pointed out, Brazil has a similar per capita income to Mexico, Bulgaria, Chile and Costa Rica, yet each of these countries has far, far fewer people living in extreme poverty. The closest is Costa Rica, which has proportionately less than half the number of extremely poor people. Brazil's level of poverty puts its on a par with Botswana, the Dominican Republic and Mauritania, whose per capita income is less than half of Brazil's. The underlying problem is clearly the way in which income is distributed, for Brazil regularly appears on the list published by the World Bank of countries with the highest income concentration. As analysts have regularly pointed out, income concentration is linked to – and exacerbated by – land concentration. Though it did not go as far as to recommend agrarian reform for Brazil, *Veja* pointed out that Hong Kong, Singapore, Taiwan and South Korea had all faced similar problems in the past, which they had resolved 'through massive investments in education, health and agrarian reform'.[69]

While Souza Martins may be right in asserting that radical agrarian reform is possible only if it resolves a 'historical impasse', he seems wrong to assume that this impasse can occur only in a narrowly defined process of national economic development. Today Brazil faces such a serious social crisis that the discontent, crime and hopelessness it generates can also be seen as an impasse to the country's full economic and social development. Celso Furtado, one of the country's best-known economic historians, believes this to be the case. Speaking in his flat in Rio de Janeiro, the 83-year-old economist said that there was only one way forward if Brazil was to go on developing as a country. 'Agrarian reform has to come sooner or later, for it is the only solution for our very serious problems. Brazil is in a very privileged position. We have more land available than any other country. We have millions of people who want to work on the land – and in many countries that isn't the case. And there is a huge market for the food that the families could produce. Millions of Brazilians are going hungry. All the elements are there. All that's lacking, it seems, is political will. It's an enormous paradox.'

The second reason why the MST may play a larger role than its roots in the country's rural population would seem to justify is, paradoxically, globalisation. The MST is no longer a lone voice. The growing control that a tiny group of huge agro-industrial corporations has over the whole global food and farming industry is leading the world towards social and ecological crisis. Millions of people are being deprived of their livelihoods, and natural resources are being devastated at an alarming rate. The world is heading for a historic social and ecological impasse that goes far beyond the narrow limits of the national economic impasse described by Martins.

There are already signs that the world is beginning to react. After decades in which neo-liberalism and market economics went unchallenged, some farmers and consumers throughout the world are beginning to reject industrial-scale farming, with its fall-out of polluted rivers, contaminated land and pesticide poisoning, of BSE, E-coli and foot-and-mouth disease, and are campaigning for a return to small-scale, non-chemical, organic farming. The MST is well placed to join such a global revolution. As some *sem-terra* themselves are realising, their future is not as economically unviable peasant communities living in a time warp but as modern, sustainable, green communities.

Of course, this shift to sustainable agriculture on a global scale may never happen. The numbers involved in the revolt are still small. It is possible – perhaps even probable – that, through biotechnology, the giant corporations will devise a temporary 'technical fix' for the farming crisis, similar to the 'green revolution', and will use this breathing space to tighten their control over global agriculture. The popular movements that oppose them will be destroyed or so tightly contained within tiny market niches that they will offer no threat. For a brief period after the attacks in the US in September 2001 it seemed that the anti-globalisation movement had been forced on to the defensive, accused as it was in some quarters of sharing a common cause with terrorists. Yet within weeks saner voices were supporting what environmentalists had claimed from the outset: that terrorism, organised by profoundly disaffected groups in the developing world, underlined the need for far-reaching global reforms that would integrate the dispossessed and the disempowered into the world community.

If it is to play a role in the international response to the global crisis, the MST must change, adapting its programme – and its rhetoric – to the current moment. Hobsbawm studied a peasant movement that successfully completed such a transformation: peasant leagues in Sicily.[70] These leagues arose in the late nineteenth century as a revolt against the introduction of capitalism into the rural zone, the consequences of which had been aggravated by the world recession in the 1880s. The movement was primitive and millenarian in that it preached a new religion, the 'true religion of Christ', and predicted the imminent arrival of a new world, without poverty, cold or hunger. Devotees, many of whom were women, carried crosses and holy images. This archaic movement survived by transforming itself: 'the original millenarian enthusiasm metamorphosed into something more lasting: permanent and organised fidelity to a modern social-revolutionary movement'.[71] More specifically, this region of Sicily became a Communist stronghold in the mid-twentieth century and has remained so ever since. Hobsbawm concluded: 'When it is integrated to a modern movement, millenarianism is not only able to become politically efficient, but to do so without losing the shining faith in a new world and the generosity of spirit that have characterized it.'[72]

Perhaps the most important lesson that can be drawn from the Sicilian case is that movements must be prepared to reinvent themselves if they wish to survive in changed historical circumstances. The activists transformed an out-dated movement that had lost political relevance into a modern one, which supported what was at that time a vibrant revolutionary ideology. And they acquired this new face without losing their essential millenarian characteristics. The French political scientist Michael Lowy believes that this lesson is highly relevant to contemporary peasant movements in Latin America. 'It appears to me that Professor Hobsbawm has opened a fascinating line of enquiry, not only for historians, but for sociologists, political anthropologists and analysts of current affairs. I will quote only two examples from my research area: the Zapatistas in Mexico and the MST in Brazil. Both are peasant movements of protest (and resistance) against capitalist modernisation, both possess millenarian components that make them comparable with the movements studied by the English historian, and both are fundamentally modern in their programmes, their demands, their practice and their forms of organisation.'[73]

Circumstances in Brazil in the early twenty-first century are very different from those in Sicily in the mid-twentieth century. Communist ideology, as defined by the former Soviet Union, belongs to the past, part of the old clothes that the MST needs to shed. It must rid itself of outdated rigid communist dogma without losing its profound commitment to social – and even socialist – change. Indeed, the metamorphosis described by Hobsbawm is well under way: the MST's former admiration of Cuban communism, including the collectivisation of agriculture, is giving way to a determination to build an ecologically friendly and technologically advanced form of peasant farming based around the community. This chimes well with other initiatives undertaken by diverse anti-globalisation movements around the world.

Conclusion

It is not through resignation but through rebellion that we affirm ourselves as human beings.

Paulo Freire[1]

In this book we have tried as much as possible to let the words of the men and women of the MST speak for themselves. Most of the *sem-terra* began life at the lowest end of the social scale, desperately poor people on the margin of society, with little chance of building a better life. Through the MST they have found not only land but education and knowledge, self confidence and hope. They have been transformed from the landless, the unwanted, the excluded, surplus to requirements, into citizens with a role to play. The MST has empowered them, turning them into the subjects of their own history. The term *sem-terra* has itself been 'empowered' and today, as well as meaning a landless peasant, it has also become a symbol of dissent, opposition, confrontation. In a country where so many movements have been co-opted and absorbed by the dominant political system, the *sem-terra* have obstinately refused to compromise.

This defiance has even turned them into a sort of *alter ego* for the progressive middle classes who hanker after the barricades, but not at the risk of losing their comfortable lives. In the words of the late Milton Santos, one of Brazil's most prestigious academics, 'the *sem-terra* speak for us. They represent us. We can't protest because we're afraid of losing our jobs, too frightened to stand up for our ideals. We restrict ourselves to personal projects. And, when the MST protests, we feel happy, all of us.'[2] Journalist José Arbex agrees, saying 'the MST shows us a way forward. It has recreated public space. It has built a movement around political discussion, collective values, feelings of compassion and faith in the future.'[3]

The MST has also created a physical space in Brazilian society where hundreds of thousands of families can live decent, independent lives instead of having to submit themselves to the degradation and poverty of the shanty-towns and slums of the cities. The settlements are places where it is possible to experiment and to try alternative methods of agriculture, education and healthcare, where profit is not the only measure of success, where it is also important to try and build a happy, dynamic community and to protect the environment. They are a space for developing citizenship and for constructing a viable alternative to the government's economic model.

The MST's refusal to compromise, which gives it a kind of ideological purity, has hit such a raw nerve in the Cardoso government that it has been far more ferocious in its repression of the MST than of other social movements. When thousands of lorry drivers brought Brazil to a standstill with a lightning strike in May 2000, the government negotiated. When indigenous groups occupied public buildings and took hostage staff of the federal Indian agency, FUNAI, the authorities talked and conceded some of their demands. But when the MST organised a 'day of action' throughout Brazil in May 2000, the police were called out in force.

What the government finds intolerable is the scope of the MST's ambitions. While the lorry drivers and the indigenous groups are defending their own particular interests, the MST wants a far-reaching transformation of society. The MST believes that, because of the control that the old political elites still hold over Congress, the state assemblies, the media and the judiciary, it cannot achieve this change through electoral politics and has opted instead for direct action. For the Cardoso government this is an illegitimate form of protest, and therefore the MST is branded as a 'dangerous' and 'anti-democratic' ideological foe. The movement's capacity for organising the poorest of the poor and turning them into citizens is not seen as an asset to the country but as an unwelcome intrusion into the government's own area of social policy-making. The MST is seen as *um caso de polícia* – a law and order problem – rather than as a highly representative movement that has a right to participate in decision-making. It is a reaction towards mass movements that, in the flurry of anti-terrorist laws that followed the attacks in the US on 11 September 2001, has unfortunately become increasingly common in the western world.

But the threat to the MST comes not only from hostile forces outside; it also comes from within, from the needs and demands of a younger generation, many of whom have not been through the privations of occupations and life in a camp and who see instead the glamorous images of city life projected every night in TV soaps. Through these soaps, which rural people follow as much as anyone else, young people see a modern world of consumerism, apparently much more attractive than the hard working life of the settlement. The challenge for the movement is to maintain its principles and aims, while encouraging the settlers to construct a new culture more in tune with the needs and the dreams of young people in the twenty-first century.

Another problem that the MST faces is its relative isolation inside Brazil. The independence and refusal to compromise that have helped it to expand and have won it admiration also mean that the movement can at times be intolerant and inflexible, making it a difficult bedfellow for other organisations. Both the Catholic Church's CPT, which played such a key role in the creation of the MST, and the

Workers' Party (PT), Brazil's leading left-wing party, which is now running several local governments with popular participation, have encountered problems. Because the MST is mistrustful of electoral politics, it has at times failed to support the PT in key elections. Some PT leaders, too, it seems, avoid close contact with the MST, afraid that its radical rhetoric might alienate voters. Yet closer relations could clearly benefit both sides: the MST is learning through experience that support from the authorities, as has been the case in Rio Grande do Sul where the PT won the state governorship for the first time in 1998, brings considerable benefits; and the PT, too, which has lost some of its earlier dynamism, profits from the injection of MST idealism and vigour.

In similar fashion, the MST has tended to write off the Brazilian press as 'bourgeois' and 'corrupt'. Although there is some truth in this charge, it is also mis-leadingly simplistic. Just as MST has benefited over the years from sympathetic individuals within INCRA, even when the top officials have been openly hostile to the movement, so the MST could turn to far better advantage the handful of well-placed journalists who argue that Brazil must urgently defuse its social crisis by taking thousands of families back to the land and believe that the MST has an important role to play. Because of the MST's intransigent refusal to court the press, there is an astonishing degree of ignorance among Brazilians in general about the MST. The occupations, conflicts, evictions and protests get ample press coverage, but there are few reports on its educational achievements and its ecological farming.

With so much uncertainty at home and abroad, it is difficult to predict the future of the MST. Historians in the future may treat the MST as the last gasp of a dying peasant culture, a bizarre and anachronistic remnant of a class of farmers that in much of the rest of the world became extinct in the twentieth century. They may look back at the *sem-terra*, as Christopher Hill did at England's seventeenth-century rebels, and see landless peasants who attempted a 'revolution that never happened'.[4] But another outcome is also possible. Brazilians are increasingly aware that unless something can be done to reduce the huge gap between rich and poor and to lift millions out of abject poverty, the country will remain a giant trying to struggle to its feet. By itself, the MST can achieve relatively little. But if new social forces emerge that are determined to turn Brazil into a just and humane society, then the MST will be a powerful ally. It may be that the *sem-terra* are precursors, moving chaotically and uncertainly towards a tomorrow's world of greater sustainability and greater equality, a world in which globalisation does not mean rapacious exploitation for the benefit of the few, but fair trade and first-world standards of health and education for the hitherto underprivileged majority.

Notes

PART ONE

Chapter 1

1 Eric Hobsbawm, *Age of Extremes – The Short Twentieth Century*, Michael Joseph, London, 1994, p. 585.

2 João Pedro Stédile and Bernardo Mançano Fernandes, *Brava Gente – A Trajetória do MST e a Luta pela Terra no Brasil*, Editora Perseu Abramo, São Paulo, 1999, p. 15.

3 See José Graziano da Silva, *A Modernização Dolorosa*, Rio de Janeiro, Zahar Editora, 1982.

4 José de Souza Martins, 'Reforma Agrária – O Impossível Diálogo sobre a História Possível', in *Tempo Social*, Revista de Sociologia da USP, February 2000, p. 105.

5 Quoted in José de Souza Martins, *O Poder do Atraso – Ensaios de Sociologia da História Lenta*, Editora Hucitec, São Paulo, 1999, p. 78.

6 Souza Martins, *O Poder do Atraso*, p. 82.

7 Estudos da CNBB (13), *Pastoral da Terra 2 – Posse e Conflitos*, Edições Paulinas, São Paulo, 1977, p. 156

8 Souza Martins, *O Poder do Atraso*, p. 83.

9 Souza Martins, 'Reforma Agrária' p. 106.

10 Telmo Marcon, *Acampamento Natalino – História da Luta Pela Reforma Agrária*, 1997, Universidade de Passo Fundo, p. 52.

11 Ibid., p. 53.

12 Quoted in Roseli Salete Caldart, *Pedagogia do Movimento Sem Terra*, Editora Vozes, Petropolis, 2000, p. 81.

13 Marcon, *Acampamento*, p. 59.

14 Quoted in Caldart, *Pedagogia*, p. 190.

15 Caldart, *Pedagogia*, p. 190.

16 Marcon, *Acampamento Natalino*, p. 147.

17 Sue Branford & Oriel Glock, *The Last Frontier – Fighting over Land in the Amazon*, Zed Books, London and New Jersey, 1985.

18 Stédile and Fernandes, *Brava Gente*, p. 65.

19 Ibid., p. 20.

20 Ibid., p. 49.

21 Ibid., p. 32.

22 Ibid., p. 50.

23 Ibid., p. 47.

Chapter 2

1 Dom Pedro Casaldáliga, *Nova Ronda Alta*, poem written for MST, July 1982.
2 José de Souza Martins, *O Poder do Atraso – Ensaios de Sociologia da História Lenta*, Editora Hucitec, São Paulo, 1999, p. 89.
3 João Pedro Stédile and Bernardo Mançano Fernandes, *Brava Gente: a Trajetória do MST e a Luta pela Terra no Brasil*, Editôra Fundação Perseu Abramo, São Paulo, 1999, p. 51.
4 Ibid., p. 52.
5 Comissão Pastoral da Terra, *Assassinatos no Campo: Crime e Impunidade 1964–85*, Goiânia, 1985.
6 Ranulfo Peloso, *A Força que Anima os Militantes*, internal MST publication, 1994.
7 João Pedro Stédile (ed.), *A Reforma Agrária e a Luta do MST*, Editora Vozes, Petrópolis, 1997, p. 61.
8 Stédile and Fernandes, *Brava Gente*, p. 67.
9 Souza Martins, *O Poder do Atraso*, p. 1.
10 Fernando Henrique Cardoso, *A Democracia Necessária*, Papirus, Campinas, 1985, p. 35
11 Zero Hora, 30 October 1985
12 Quoted in Roseli Salete Caldart, *Pedagogia do Movimento Sem Terra*, Editora Vozes, Petrópolis, 2000, p. 82.
13 Quoted in Movimento dos Trabalhadores Rurais Sem Terra, Coleção Fazendo História no. 3, *A História de Uma Luta de Todos*, p. 11.
14 Stédile and Fernandes, *Brava Gente*, p. 67.

Chapter 3

1 Lawrence Goodwin, *A Short History of the Agrarian Revolt in America*, Oxford University Press, 1978.
2 Bernardo Mançano Fernandes, 'Contribuição ao Estudo do Campesinato Brasileiro – Formação e Territorialização do Movimento dos Trabalhadores Rurais Sem Terra – MST, 1979–1999', Ph.D. thesis, Faculdade de Filosofia, Letras e Ciências Humanas, University of São Paulo, 1999, p. 107.
3 Fernandes, 'Contribuição', p. 167.
4 João Pedro Stédile and Bernardo Mançano Fernandes, *Brava Gente: a Trajetória do MST e a Luta pela Terra no Brasil*, Fundação Perseu Abramo, São Paulo, 1999, p. 67.
5 José de Souza Martins, 'Reforma Agrária: O Impossível Diálogo sobre a História Possível', in *Tempo Social*, Revista de Sociologias da USP, February 2000, p. 107.
6 See Bernardo Mançano Fernandes, *MST – Movimento dos Trabalhadores Rurais Sem-Terra, Formação e Territorialização em São Paulo*, Editora Hucitec, São Paulo, 1999, pp. 85–129.
7 Fernandes, *MST*, p. 98.
8 Stédile and Fernandes, *Brava Gente*, p. 68.
9 Ibid., p. 68.
10 Carlos Azevedo, 'Pontal: Do Grande Grito aos Sem-Terra', in *Caros Amigos*, May 1997.
11 P. Monbeig, *Pioneiros e Fazendeiros de São Paulo*, São Paulo, Hucitec, 1984, p. ??
12 José Ferrari Leite, *A Ocupação do Pontal de Paranapanema*, Editora Hucitec, São Paulo, 1998, p. 174.
13 Fernandes, *MST*, p. 172.
14 *A Folha de S. Paulo*, 10 April 1995.
15 Fernandes, 'Contribuição', p. 85.

PART TWO

Chapter 4

1 George Orwell, *Homage to Catalonia*, Penguin Books, Harmondsworth, 1966, p 102.
2 Roseli Salete Caldart, *Pedagogia do Movimento Sem Terra*, Editora Vozes, Petrópolis, 2000, p. 109.

3 Ibid., p. 110.
4 Pedro Tierra, 'A Política como Dimensão da Cultura', unpublished article, 1995.
5 Caldart, *Pedagogia*, p. 110.
6 Christopher Hill, *The World Turned Upside Down*, Penguin Books, Harmondsworth, 1975, p. 385.
7 Frantz Fanon, *The Wretched of the Earth*, Penguin Books, Harmondsworth, 1963, p. 74.
8 Caldart, *Pedagogia*, p. 209.
9 Ibid., p. 217.
10 Ibid., p. 216.
11 Quoted in ibid., p. 172.
12 João Pedro Stédile and Bernardo Mançano Fernandes, *Brava Gente: a Trajetória do MST e a Luta pela Terra no Brasil*, Fundação Perseu Abramo, São Paulo, 1999, p. 74.

Chapter 5

1 Bernardo Mançano Fernandes, 'Contribuição ao Estudo do Campesinato Brasileiro – Formação e Territorialização do Movimento dos Trabalhadores Rurais Sem Terra – MST, 1979–1999', Ph.D. thesis, Faculdade de Filosofia, Letras e Ciências Humanas, University of São Paulo, 1999, p. 271.
2 CONCRAB, *Sistema Cooperativista dos Assentados*, Caderno de Cooperação Agrícola, no. 5, p. 28.
3 Ibid., p. 29.
4 Ibid., p. 29.
5 Ibid., p. 30.
6 Ibid., p. 32.
7 CONCRAB, *A Evolução da Concepção de Cooperação Agrícola do MST (1989 a 1999)*, Caderno de Cooperação Agrícola, no. 8, p. 8.
8 CONCRAB, *Sistema Cooperativista*, p. 34.
9 CONCRAB, *A Evolução*, p. 9.
10 Ibid., p. 6.
11 CONCRAB, *Sistema Cooperativista*, p. 34.
12 CONCRAB, *Nossa Política para os Assentamentos*, March 2000.
13 Josefa Salete Barbosa Cavalcanti (ed.), *Globalização, Trabalho, Meio Ambiente*, Editora Universitária UFPE, Recife, 1999, p. 132.
14 Ibid., p. 139.
15 Ibid., p. 149.
16 Ibid., p. 157.
17 Ibid., p. 156.
18 Quoted in Roseli Salete Caldart, *Pedagogia do Movimento Sem Terra*, Editora Vozes, Petr?polis 2000, p. 226.

Chapter 6

1 E.P. Thompson, *The Making of the English Working Class*, Pelican, Harmondsworth, revised edition, 1968, p. 165.
2 Paulo Freire, *Educação como prática de liberdade*, Paz e Terra, São Paulo, 1989, p. 104.
3 Roseli Salete Caldart, *Pedagogia do Movimento Sem Terra*, Editora Vozes, Petrópolis, 2000, p. ??.
4 Quoted in ibid., p. 139.
5 *Escola Itinerante em Acampamentos do MST*, Coordenação Nacional do Setor de Educação, 1998, p. 23.
6 Ibid., p. 24.
7 *IstoE*, 17 June 1998.
8 James Petras, 'Os Camponeses: Uma Nova Força Revolucionária na América Latina', in João Pedro Stédile, *A Reforma Agrária e a Luta do MST*, Editora Vozes, Petrópolis, 1997, p. 273.

9 See *Folha de S. Paulo*, 17 December 2000.
10 José de Souza Martins, *O Poder do Atraso – Ensaios de Sociologia da História Lenta*, Editora Hucitec, São Paulo, 1999, p. 156.
11 Roseli Salete Caldart, *Pedagogia do Movimento Sem Terra*, Editora Vozes, Petrópolis, 2000, p. 215

PART THREE

Chapter 7

1 This account of the early years of the MST in Para is taken from Bernardo Mançano Fernandes, 'Contribuição ao Estudo do Campesinato Brasileiro – Formação e Territorialização do Movimento dos Trabalhadores Rurais Sem Terra – MST, 1979–1999', Ph.D. thesis, Faculdade de Filosofia, Letras e Ciências Humanas, University of São Paulo, 1999.
2 In an interview with the magazine, *Caros Amigos*, in a special issue on the Eldorado de Carajás massacre, November 1999, p. 29.
3 Francisco Graziano, *Qual Reforma Agrária?*, Geração Editorial, São Paulo, 1996, p. 23.
4 Ibid., p. 23.
5 Ibid., p. 24.
6 Ibid., p. 26.
7 *Caros Amigos*, p. 13.
8 Ibid., p. 13.
9 Amnesty International, *Brazil: Corumbiara and Eldorado de Carajás: Rural Violence, Police Brutality and Impunity*, January 1998, p. 19.
10 Ibid.
11 *Caros Amigos*, p. 8.
12 Amnesty International, *Brazil: Corumbiara and Eldorado de Carajás*, p. 21.
13 Ibid., p. 20.
14 Ibid., p. 24.
15 *Veja*, 24 April 1996, p. 39.
16 *Caros Amigos*, p. 9.
17 Ibid., p. 30.
18 Ibid., p. 29.
19 *Folha de S. Paulo*, 16 August 2001.

Chapter 8

1 Bernardo Mançano Fernandes, 'Contribuição ao Estudo do Campesinato Brasileiro – Formação e Territorialização do Movimento dos Trabalhadores Rurais Sem Terra – MST, 1979–1999', Ph.D. thesis, Faculdade de Filosofia, Letras e Ciências Humanas, University of São Paulo, 1999, p. 54.
2 Sebastião Salgado, *Terra – Struggle of the Landless*, Phaidon, London, 1997, p. 143.
3 *Caros Amigos*, June 1999, p. 17.
4 On 22 November 2001, Darci Frigo was presented with the Robert F. Kennedy award, one of the most prestigious human rights awards in the world. He dedicated it to Lúcia Mainha, Teixeirinha's widow. With tears in his eyes, he said that he had been at Lúcia's side when her husband was murdered.
5 *Folha de S. Paulo*, 7 May 1999.
6 *O Diário do Norte do Paraná*, 11 November 1999, and *Diário do Noroeste*, 11 November 1999.
7 *Folha do Paraná*, 28 November 1999.

Chapter 9

1 Brian Halweil, 'Where Have All the Farmers Gone?', *World Watch*, Vol. 13, No. 5 (Sept–Oct 2000), p. 21.
2 Quoted in Armando Sartori, Lia Imanishi Rodrigues, Raimundo Rodrigues Pereira and Roberto Davis, *Agricultura e Modernidade: A Crise Brasileira Vista do Campo* (Porto Alegre: Edição dos Autores, 1998), p. 38.
3 Censo Agropecuário 1995–1996, IBGE, Rio de Janeiro, 1998, p. 44.
4 Censo Agropecuário 1995–1996, IBGE, Rio de Janeiro, 1998, p. 42.
5 Hugo Biehl and Renato Zandonadi, 'Implicações Socio-Econômicas do Abandono da Cultura do Algodão no Brasil', *Revista de Política Agrícola*, no. 3, July–September 1998.
6 *Jornal do Brasil*, 15 October 2000.
7 *Financial Times*, 22 February 2001.
8 Gerson Teixeira, *Um Perfil da Agricultura e da Reforma Agrária no Brasil entre 1995 e 1999*, Brasília, May 2000, p. 7.
9 Halweil, 'Where Have All the Farmers Gone?', p. 14.
10 John Wilkinson (ed.) with Pierina German Castelli, 'The Internationalization of Brazil's Seed Industry – Biotechnology, patents and biodiversity', unpublished English translation of *A Transnacionalização da Indústria de Sementes no Brasil – Biotecnologias, patentes e biodiversidade*, ActionAid Brasil, Rio de Janeiro, 2000, p. 47.
11 Ibid., p. 50.
12 Ibid., p. 59.
13 *Zero Hora*, 9 July 1999.
14 Wilkinson and Castelli, *The Internationalization of Brazil's Seed Industry*, p. 65.
15 BIOTHAL, GRAIN, MASIPAG and PAN Indonesia, 'Whose Agenda: The Corporate Takeover of Corn in SE Asia', press release, Genetic Resources Action International (GRAIN), September 1999.
16 Ibid.
17 Halweil, 'Where Have All the Farmers Gone?', p. 19.
18 Christian Aid/Deser, *Hooked on Tobacco – Report on British American Tobacco Subsidiary, Souza Cruz*, Christian Aid, London, February 2002.
19 Figures from FAO/USDA, 25 January 2000.
20 *Agroanalysis*, January 2000.
21 Halweil, 'Where Have All the Farmers Gone?', p. 25.
22 *Jornal do Comércio*, 18 August 2000.
23 *The Ecologist*, May 2000, p. 46.
24 Halweil, 'Where Have All the Farmers Gone?', p. 15.
25 *O Estado de S. Paulo*, 25 September 2000.
26 Ibid.
27 Quoted by Halweil, 'Where Have All the Farmers Gone?', p. 22.

Chapter 10

1 José de Souza Martins, *O Poder do Atraso – Ensaios de Sociologia da Hist?ria Lenta*, Editora Hucitec, Sao Paulo, 1999, p. 13.
2 Constituição da República Federativa do Brasil, 1988, Horizonte Editora, Brasília, Chapter III, Article 184.
3 *Folha de S. Paulo*, 27 September 1999, carried a headline story in which it claimed that a landowner in the state of Pará had paid R$22,500 (US$12,500) to 1,500 landless families (not members of the MST) to occupy his estate.
4 Ministério de Desenvolvimento Agrário, *Versão Preliminar – Divulgação Proibida, Agricultura Familiar, Reforma Agrária e Desenvolvimento Local para um Novo Mundo Rural: Política, Estratégias,*

Programas, Instrumentos e Institucionalidade, Brasília, November 1998.

5 Under the old scheme, the families were supposed to be given land titles and to start paying for their plots of land once INCRA had supplied the settlement with all the necessary infrastructure and the families were deemed to be economically unviable. Given the ongoing crisis in family farming, this rarely happened.

6 Quoted in Edelcio Vigna and Gerson Teixeira, *Banco da Terra*, INESC, Brasília, November 1999.

7 Quoted in *Veja*, 3 June 1998.

8 See Sérgio Sauer, *Reforma Agrária e Geração de Emprego e Renda no Meio Rural*, ABET, São Paulo, 1998, p. 74.

9 Boletím do Deser, June 1999, special edition, *Banco da Terra: Análise Econômica e Exemplos de Financiamento*.

10 Stephan Schwartzman, *The World Bank and Land Reform in Brazil*, Serviço Brasileiro de Justiça e Paz (SEJUP), April 2000, p. 8.

11 See letter by Osvaldo Russo, who at the time of the evaluation was a member of NEAD, in *Correio da Cidadania*, 30 October 2000.

12 Quoted in Schwartzman, *The World Bank*, p. 11.

13 Ibid., p. 13.

14 Vigna and Teixeira, *Banco Da Terra*.

15 Gerson Texeira, *Um Perfil da Agricultura e da Reforma Agrária no Brasil entre 1995 e 1999*, Partido dos Trabalhadores – PT, Liderança da Bancada na Câmara Federal, Brasília, May 2000, p. 45.

16 Quoted in *Informes Brasil*, no. 67, February 2002.

17 Quoted in article by Antonio Barros de Castrom, in *Folha de S. Paulo*, 1 December 1999.

18 Ministério da Política Fundiária e do Desenvolvimento Agrário, *O Livro Branco da Grilagem de Terras no Brasil*, no date, p. 7.

Chapter 11

1 *El País*, 10 December 1993.

2 Eric Hobsbawm, *Age of Extremes – The Short Twentieth Century 1914–1991*, Michael Joseph, London 1994, p. 289.

3 Francisco Graziano, *Qual Reforma Agrária? – Terra, Pobreza e Cicadania*, Geração de Comunicação Integrada Comercial Ltda, São Paulo, 1996, p. 12.

4 Ibid., p. 13.

5 Ministério Público, Procuradoria da Justiça, Denúncia, p. 20, quoted in Amnesty International, *Brazil: Corumbiara and Eldorado de Carajás: Rural Violence, Police Brutality and Impunity*, London, January 1998, p. 28.

6 Câmara de Deputados, Coordenação de Publicações, *Relat?rio da Comissão Externa Destinada a Averiguar a Acquisação de Madeiras, Serrarias e Extensas Porções de Terras Brasileiras por Grupos Asiáticos*, Brasília, p. 18.

7 In statement by Amnesty International, 19 August 1997.

8 Clovis Moura, *Sociologia Política da Guerra Camponesa de Canudos*, Editora Expressão Popular, São Paulo, 2000, p. 134

9 *Veja* 3 June 1998.

10 *Folha de S. Paulo*, 1 August 1997.

11 *Caros Amigos*, June 2000.

12 *Folha de S. Paulo*, 20 October 1998.

13 Amnesty International, *Brazil – Human Rights Defenders: Protecting Human Rights for Everyone*, April 1998, p.17.

14 Ibid., p. 12.

15 See George Meszaros, 'Taking the Land into Their Hands: The Landless Workers' Movement and the Brazilian State', *Journal of Law and Society*, vol. 27, no. 4, December 2000, Blackwell, Oxford.

16 Amnesty International, *Brazil – Human Rights Defenders*, p. 14.

17 *Veja*, 3 June 1998.
18 *O Estado de S. Paulo*, 24 March 2000.
19 *Folha de S. Paulo*, 3 May 2000.
20 *Folha de S. Paulo*, 4 May 2000.
21 *Folha de S. Paulo*, 7 May 2000.
22 *Folha de S. Paulo*, 6 May 2000.
23 *Folha de S. Paulo*, 3 May 2000.
24 *Diário de Pernambuco*, 20 August 2000.
25 *O Estado de S. Paulo*, 15 October 2000.
26 *Jornal do Brasil*, 19 September 2000.
27 *Folha de S. Paulo*, 15 May 2000.
28 João Mellão Neto, 'A Honrável Sociedade dos Sem Terra', *O Estado de S. Paulo*, 20 October 2000.
29 *Veja*, 10 May 2000.
30 *Veja*, 15 November 2000.
31 *O Estado de S. Paulo*, 16 May 2000.
32 *Zero Hora*, 27 October 2000.
33 *Folha de S. Paulo*, 6 February 2001.
34 Letter circulated on the Internet.
35 *IstoE*, 23 November 2001.

PART FOUR

Chapter 12

1 Quoted in the *Guardian*, 17 January 2001.
2 *Carta Capital*, year 11, no. 41, 5 February 1997.
3 Like hundreds of other agronomists, Claudemir Mocellin lost his job when the government abruptly closed *Lumiar* in May 2000.
4 Personal report.
5 Ademar Bogo, 'Novo Ascenso na Organização da Produção', internal MST document, April 1999.

Chapter 13

1 Francisco Julião, *Cambão – the Yoke*, Penguin, Harmondsworth, 1972, p. 55.
2 CONCRAB, *Nossa Política para os Assentamentos*, internal document, no date.
3 Ademar Bogo, *Lições da Luta da Terra*, Memorial das Letras, Salvador, 1999, p. 47.
4 Interview in *Caros Amigos*, November 1997.
5 Dulcinéia Pavan, 'As Marias Sem-Terras – Trajetória e Experiências de Vida de Mulheres Assentadas em Promissão–SP – 1985–1996', Pontífica Universidade Cat?lica de Sao Paulo–SP, MA dissertation, p. 161.
6 Ibid., p.162.
7 Quoted in Andrea Paula dos Santos, Suzana Lopes Salgado Ribeiro and José Carlos Sebe Bom Meihy, *Vozes da Marcha pela Terra*, Edições Loyola, São Paulo, 1998, p. 164.
8 *Jornal Sem Terra*, MST newspaper, May 2000.
9 Roseli Salete Caldart, *Pedagogia do Movimento Sem Terra*, Editora Vozes, Petrópolis, 2000, p. 50.
10 Marina Amaral, *Caros Amigos*, September 1998, p. 30.
11 Eric Hobsbawm, *Worlds of Labour – Further Studies in the History of Labour*, Weidenfeld and Nicolson, London, 1984, pp. 199–212.
12 Bernardo Mançano Fernandes, *MST – Movimento dos Trabalhadores Rurais Sem-Terra, Formação e Territorialização em São Paulo*, Editora Hucitec, São Paulo, 1999, p. 125.

13 Quoted in ibid., p. 117.
14 Quoted in ibid., p. 143.
15 Ibid., p. 148.
16 *Caros Amigos*, September 1998, p. 31.
17 *Caros Amigos*, special issue on the Eldorado de Carajás massacre, November 1999, p. 29.
18 João Pedro Stédile and Bernardo Mançano Fernandes, *Brava Gente – A Trajetória do MST e a Luta pela Terra no Brasil*, Editora Perseu Abramo, São Paulo, 1999, p. 82.
19 João Pedro Stédile (ed.), *A Reforma Agrária e a Luta do MST*, Editora Vozes, Petrópolis, 1997, p. 60.
20 José de Souza Martins, 'Os Dilemas de Interpretação da Luta pela Terra', unpublished paper, February 2001.
21 Ibid.
22 Pavan, 'As Marias Sem-Terras', p. 46.
23 Ibid.
24 Video testimony, Tambke Films, Rio de Janeiro, 1997. Quoted in Pavan, 'As Marias Sem-Terras', p. 19.
25 Pavan, 'As Marias Sem-Terras', p. 96.

Chapter 14

1 E.P. Thompson, *The Making of the English Working Class*, Penguin, Harmondsworth, 1968, p. 886.
2 Christopher Hill, *The World Turned Upside Down*, Penguin Books, Harmondsworth, 1975, p. 110.
3 Ibid., p. 108.
4 Ibid., p. 110.
5 Ibid., p. 110.
6 Ibid., p. 129.
7 Ibid., p. 131.
8 Ibid., p. 131.
9 Ibid., p. 131.
10 Ibid., p. 13.
11 Ibid., p. 133.
12 Ibid., p. 341.
13 Ibid., p. 341.
14 Ibid., p. 342.
15 E.P. Thompson, *The Making of the English Working Class*, Penguin, Harmondsworth, 1968, p. 25.
16 Ibid., p. 61.
17 Ibid., p. 24.
18 Ibid., p. 26, citing the words of Edmund Burke.
19 Ibid., p. 245.
20 Ibid., p. 253; Thompson's emphasis.
21 Ibid., p. 239.
22 Ibid., p. 237.
23 Ibid., p. 243.
24 Ibid., p. 242.
25 Ibid., p. 604; Thompson's emphasis.
26 Ibid., p.748.
27 Cited in ibid., p.748.
28 Lawrence Goodwyn, *Democratic Promise, The Populist Moment in America*, Oxford University Press, New York, 1976, p. 31.
29 Ibid., p. 33.
30 Quoted in ibid., p. 92.
31 Ibid., p. 92.

32 Ibid., p. 131.
33 Ibid., p. 134.
34 Ibid., p. 125.
35 Ibid., p. 88.
36 Ibid., p. 311.
37 Ibid., p. 537.
38 Ibid., p.541; emphasis in original.
39 Thompson, The Making, p. 12.
40 Eric Hobsbawm, 'Should Poor People Organise?', in *Worlds of Labour*, Weidenfeld and Nicolson, London 1984, p. 289.
41 Ibid., p.289.
42 In Joan Thirsk (ed.),*The Agrarian History of England and Wales*, IV, (1500–1640), Cambridge University Press, Cambridge, 1967, pp. 620–1.
43 Hill, *The World Turned Upside Down*, p. 14.
44 Ibid., p.15.
45 Thompson, *The Making*, pp. 238–9.
46 Jan Rocha, *Brazil in Focus*, Latin America Bureau, London, 1997, p. 8.
47 David Treece (ed.), *Long Night of Waiting – The Struggle for Human Rights in Brazil*, Brazil Network, London, 1998, p. 8.
48 Clovis Moura, *Sociologia Política da Guerra Camponesa de Canudos*, Editora Expressão Popular, São Paulo, 2000, p. 54.
49 Dee Brown, *The American West, A Touchstone Book*, Simon & Schuster, New York, 1994, p. 140.
50 José de Souza Martins, O Poder do Atraso – Ensaios de Sociologia da Historia Lenta, Editora Hucitec, São Paulo, 1999, p. 76.
51 Quoted in Rocha, *Brazil in Focus*, p. 12.
52 Moura, *Sociologia Política*, p. 40.
53 Ibid., p. 47.
54 Souza Martins, O *Poder do Atraso*, p. 147.
55 Gerrit Huizer, *Peasant Rebellion in Latin America: the origins, forms of expression, and potential of Latin American peasant unrest*, Pelican Latin American Library, Harmondsworth, 1973, p. 88.
56 'Cambão' means, literally, a 'yoke' placed on an ox, so the Leagues were campaigning to have the yoke of land reform placed on the estate owners.
57 Paul Harrison, *Inside the Third World*, Pelican, Harmondsworth, 1979, p. 117.
58 Ibid.
59 Moura, *Sociologia Política*, p. 122.
60 Souza Martins, O *Poder do Atraso*, p. 13.
61 Cited in Eric Hobsbawm, 'The Making of the Working Class 1870–1914', in *Worlds of Labour*.
62 Eric Hobsbawm, *Primitive Rebels*, Manchester University Press, Manchester, 1959, p. 2.
63 Ibid., p. 3.
64 Huizer, *Peasant Rebellion*, p. 131.
65 Ibid., p. 141.
66 Ibid., p. 127.
67 Fundação Getúlio Vargas, *Mapa dos Ativos – Combate Sustentável à Pobreza*, Rio de Janeiro, December 2001.
68 *Veja*, 25 January 2002.
69 Ibid.
70 Hobsbawm, *Primitive Rebels*, pp. 93–107.
71 Ibid., p. 105.
72 Ibid., p. 107.
73 *Folha de S. Paulo*, 2 April 2001.

Conclusion

1 Paulo Freire, *Pedagogia da Autonomia*, Rio de Janeiro, Paz e Terra, 1997, p. 87.
2 *O Estado de S. Paulo*, 19 January 1997.
3 *Caros Amigos*, October 1998.
4 Christopher Hill, *The World Turned Upside Down*, Penguin, Harmondsworth, 1973, p. 17.

Index

Mattos, Paulo Venâncio, 44, 47, 245
Mauro, Gilmar, 253
Mazioli, Itelvina Maria, 251, 259-61
media: anti-MST campaign, 42, 205-8;
   consumer propaganda, 257; journalists, 17;
   MST use, 163; MST-hostile, 67;
   occupations coverage, 84; press freedom,
   161
Medici, Emílio Garastazzu, 5
Melo, Marluce, 44
Mendes, Chico, 54
Mesbla department store, 46
messianic movements, 70
Mexico, currency crisis, 172
mística, 20, 30, 34, 65, 72, 83, 86, 117, 245,
   250-1, 261
militantes, 31, 44-5, 47, 56, 74, 93, 96, 99, 121,
   123, 132, 223, 242-3, 245, 251-2, 254-5
military coup 1964, 4, 12
military police, 138-9, 141, 145-6, 149, 151-4,
   159, 162-3, 168, 170, 197-8, 203-4, 228,
   249; impunity, 131
military regime, 5-6, 15, 25-6; collapse, 31;
   economic model, 28
mining companies, 50
MIRAD, land reform agency, 32, 91
mobile phones, MST use, 81
Mocellin, Claudemir, 218-19, 237
Monbeig, P., 55
monoculture, 172
Monsanto, 177, 234; Monsoy subsidiary, 176
Moraes, Antônio Ermírio de, 82
Moraes, Marcus Vinicius Pratini de, 75
Morais, José Roberto, 121-2
Morato, Inês, 214-15
Morro do Diablo ecological reserve, 213-14
Moura, Clovis, 200, 274-5, 278
Moura, Daví Alves de, 13, 15
Movimento dos Trabalhadores rurais Sem Terra
   (MST): activists training, 120-3;
   agricultural schools, 244; Amazon record,
   226; attrition tactics, 59; autonomy, 51;
   camps, 80, 88, 167, 241, 243; Cascaval
   meeting, 21-6; collective production, 92-3,
   95; collectivisation, 216; cooperatives, 207,
   220-4; 'counter-culture', 245; courses, 24;
   'cutting the wire' 65-6, 70-2, 99; divisions,
   38; eco-attitudes, 213, 219; economic
   strategies lack, 107; education, 64, 109-19,
   124-5, 246; evictions, 228; expansion, 48;
   farming methods shift, 226-7; First
   Congress; 49-50, 53, 154; future role, 281,
   282-4; gender, 23, 87, 116, 258, 262;

government attack on, 195, 199, 204-6,
   208, 286; image, 74; independence, 27, 40;
   initial decisions, 28; lawyers, 97, 158;
   leadership, 106; Liberdade settlement, 45;
   local sensibilities, 43; March on Brasília,
   279; marketing cooperatives, 212; 'mass
   resistence strategy', 84; media relations,
   287; methodology, 63, 67; mistakes, 44, 47,
   94; naming, 24; national health programme,
   235-6; occupations, 32, 34, 42, 44, 75-6,
   193; organic farming, 235-7; organization,
   30; public building occupations, 49, 115,
   203; publicity, 163; recruitment, 69;
   repression of, 131-3, 142, 144, 146, 149-50,
   152-9, 166, 201-2, 268; self-reliance, 31;
   settlements, 90-1, 151, 255; sexuality, 257;
   short cuts, 56; slogans, 54, 83, 87; structure,
   85, 121, 251-4; sustainable farming, 238;
   symbols, 248-9; 'territorialisation', 60; TV
   coverage, 68, 96; 'war economy' strategy,
   92; women, 110-11, 259-61; youth, 256-7
Movimento Justiça e Terra, 150
multinational corporations, 127, 171, 174-5,
   178, 238, 255, 278; seed oligopoly, 176
Muniz, Orlando, 207, 208
music, 29
mutirão, 90

Nankani, Gobind T., 190
Nascimento, Maurício Henrique de, 76
Nascimento, Maria Joaquina de (Nazhina), 99-
   101
National Commission of Settlers, 91
National Education Collective (MST), 116
National Farmers Alliance and Cooperative
   Movement, 270
National Forum on Land Reform, 188-90
National Plan for Agrarian Reform (PNRA),
   32
National Programme of Land Reform
   Education (PRONERA), 119
National Security Law, 204-5
Navarro, Zander, 40, 55-6, 121, 124, 238, 251
Neri, Jorge, 123, 245-6
Neves, Major Valdir Cumpetti, 153, 168
Neves, Tancredo, 26-7, 32
Nonoaí: eviction, 7, 10-11; refugees, 13
Novo Mundo Rural, 186-7
Nucleus of Agrarian Reform and Rural
   Development Studies (NEAD), 189
Nunes, Adelina Ventura, 149, 155, 157–9, 161,
   164, 169
Nunes, Rosalí, 247, 259

If you enjoyed *Cutting the Wire*, these books on Brazil will provide you with excellent background on this huge and fascinating country.

The Brazil Reader: History, Culture, Politics

Robert M. Levine and John J. Crocetti (eds)

An unparalleled introduction to Brazil, through extracts of essays, history, poetry, literature and contemporary comment. Capturing the scope of Brazil's rich diversity and distinctiveness as no other book has done – with over a hundred entries from a wealth of perspectives – *The Brazil Reader* offers a fascinating guide to Brazilian life, culture, and history.

'What gives *The Brazil Reader* its special cachet is freshness, sensitivity and empathy in its diversity of perspectives on Brazil, from the top down, from the bottom up, and from somewhere in the middle.'
Stanley J. Stein, Princeton University

£16.99
528 pages
ISBN 1 899365 39 7

Brazil in Focus

Jan Rocha

The most comprehensive introduction to Brazil, *Brazil in Focus* gives you 'the story the guidebooks don't tell you' with argumentative, authoritative discussions of politics, history, ethnicity and the environment, as well as tips on where to go and what to see.

£7.99
100 pages
ISBN 1 899365 00 1